Financial Capability and Asset Holding in Later Life

Financial Capability and Asset Holding in Later Life

A Life Course Perspective

EDITED BY

Nancy Morrow-Howell

Margaret S. Sherraden

OXFORD
UNIVERSITY PRESS

OXFORD
UNIVERSITY PRESS

Oxford University Press is a department of the University of Oxford.
It furthers the University's objective of excellence in research,
scholarship, and education by publishing worldwide.

Oxford   New York
Auckland   Cape Town   Dar es Salaam   Hong Kong   Karachi
Kuala Lumpur   Madrid   Melbourne   Mexico City   Nairobi
New Delhi   Shanghai   Taipei   Toronto

With offices in
Argentina   Austria   Brazil   Chile   Czech Republic   France   Greece
Guatemala   Hungary   Italy   Japan   Poland   Portugal   Singapore
South Korea   Switzerland   Thailand   Turkey   Ukraine   Vietnam

Oxford is a registered trademark of Oxford University Press
in the UK and certain other countries.

Published in the United States of America by
Oxford University Press
198 Madison Avenue, New York, NY 10016

Library of Congress Cataloging-in-Publication Data.
Financial capability and asset holding in later life : a life course perspective / edited by
Nancy Morrow-Howell and Margaret S. Sherraden.
pages cm
ISBN 978-0-19-937430-4 (hardback)
1. Older people—Economic conditions.   2. Older people—Finance, Personal.   3. Retirement
income.   4. Financial security.   I. Sherraden, Margaret S.   II. Morrow-Howell, Nancy, 1952-
HQ1061.F526 2015
332.024′01—dc23
2014028321

9 8 7 6 5 4 3 2 1
Printed in the United States of America
on acid-free paper

CONTENTS

Illustrations   vii
Acknowledgments   ix
Contributors   xi
Abbreviations   xv
Introduction: *Financial Capability in Later Life:*
A Life Course Perspective   xvii
MARGARET S. SHERRADEN AND NANCY MORROW-HOWELL

PART ONE   ■   **Financial Capability in Later Life: Theory**
               and Evidence of Life Course Impacts

1   The Economic and Financial Status of Older Americans:
    Trends and Prospects   3
    WILLIAM R. EMMONS AND BRYAN J. NOETH

2   "All That Glitters Is Not Gold": Social Mobility, Health,
    and Mental Health among African Americans   27
    DARRELL L. HUDSON

PART TWO   ■   **Financial Capability in Later Life: Vulnerable**
               Populations

3   Assets and Older African Americans   49
    TRINA R. WILLIAMS SHANKS AND WILHELMINA A. LEIGH

4   Economic Security of Older Hispanics: The Role of Social
    Security and Employer-Sponsored Plans   69
    JACQUELINE L. ANGEL AND STIPICA MUDRAZIJA

5   Enhancing the Financial Capability of Native American Elders   87
    AMANDA BARUSCH, MOLLY TOVAR, AND TRACY GOLDEN

6   Older Immigrants: Economic Security, Asset Ownership,
    Financial Access, and Public Policy   104
    YUNJU NAM

7   The Interactions of Disability, Aging, Assets, and
    Financial Instability   120
    MICHELLE PUTNAM

PART THREE   ■   Policies and Innovations

8   Asset Development among Older Adults: A Capability Approach   139
    JIN HUANG AND JENNIFER C. GREENFIELD

9   Long-Term Care in the United States: Who Pays?   161
    JENNIFER C. GREENFIELD

10 Workplace Policies and Practices: Opportunities for
    and Barriers to Accumulating Assets in Midlife and Later   175
    ERNEST GONZALES

11 Age-Friendly Banking: Policy, Products, and Services
    for Financial Capability   195
    SEHAR N. SIDDIQI, ROBERT O. ZDENEK, AND
    EDWARD J. GORMAN III

    Conclusion: *Financial Capability in Later Life:
    Summary and Applications*   218
    NANCY MORROW-HOWELL, MICHAEL SHERRADEN, AND
    MARGARET S. SHERRADEN
    Index   233

∎ ILLUSTRATIONS

▨ FIGURES

1.1 Mean Family Net Worth by Age Group (First Quarter 2013 Estimated) 7
1.2 Family Median Net Worth by Age of Family Head 8
1.3 Median Family Income by Age of Family Head 10
1.4 Effect of Family Head's Birth Year on Family Income Relative
     to Being Born in the Period 1938–1942 17
1.5 Effect of Family Head's Birth Year on Family Wealth Relative
     to Being Born in the Period 1938–1942 21
1.6 Estimated Number of Children under 1 Year Old 22
4.1 Sources and Relative Size of Retirement Income for Older Individuals
     by Race and Mexican Origin 71
4.2 Poverty Rates for Older Adult Households by Race
     and Hispanic Ethnicity 73
4.3 Retirement Plans of Older Adult Households by Race, Mexican Origin,
     and Nativity 77
5.1 Unbanked Households by Race and Ethnicity 93
8.1 Asset Development for Older Adults: A Life-Cycle
     Capability Approach 142
9.1 Dynamic Relationships between Sources of LTC Delivery
     and Funding 170

▨ TABLES

1.1 Median Inflation-Adjusted Family Income by Age Group 9
1.2 Median Inflation-Adjusted Net Worth by Age Group 10
1.3 Inflation-Adjusted Family Income by Age Group at the Twentieth
     Percentile of the Distribution 12
1.4 Inflation-Adjusted Net Worth by Age Group at the Twentieth
     Percentile of the Distribution 13
1.5 Pooled Regression of Logarithm of Family Income on Demographic,
     Idiosyncratic, Birth-Year Cohort, and Time Variables 16
1.6 Pooled Regression of Transformed Net Worth on Demographic,
     Idiosyncratic, Birth-Year Cohort, and Time Variables 20
3.1 Asset Holding among Household Heads Older than Age 55 Years 52
4.1 Employment Characteristics of Employed Population by Race and
     Mexican Origin 76

7.1 Prevalence of Disability by Category of Disability Identified in 2011 ACS (Percentages) 121

7.2 Prevalence of Disability by Selected Characteristics Identified in 2011 ACS (Percentages) 122

8.1 Asset-Based Programs and Older Adults 147

8.2 Programs Related to Older Adults and Asset-Based Approaches 154

10.1 Lifetime Pension Access and Type of Pension among Individuals Aged 55–61 Years in 1994 and 2004, by Selected Characteristics (in Percentages) 177

■ ACKNOWLEDGMENTS

We are indebted to the talented and dedicated scholars who contributed chapters. Each brings a different perspective to the question of the financial well-being of older adults, but together they draw attention to the plight of financially vulnerable older adults and what we might do as a society to build financial capability in older age.

This book is based on the work presented at the 2012 conference, Financial Capability across the Life Course: Focus on Vulnerable Populations, held at Washington University in St. Louis. Organized by the Center for Social Development, the Harvey A. Friedman Center for Aging, and the Kathryn M. Buder Center for American Indian Studies, and supported by the Atlantic Philanthropies and Wells Fargo Advisors, the meeting brought together scholars and practitioners in the fields of aging and financial capability for a productive discussion. Comments by two speakers, Bárbara Robles of the Board of Governors of the Federal Reserve and Tyson Brown of Vanderbilt University, provided a backdrop for the meetings. Dr. Robles reviewed policies and programs that seek to build financial security in later life, with a special focus on taxes. Dr. Brown examined the intersection of racial and gender disparities in wealth over time and the impact on older adults.

Others brought program and policy perspectives. Mae Watson Grote, founder of the Financial Clinic in New York City, discussed how her organization helps low-income households maximize their financial resources. Ben Mangan of EARN in San Francisco, another pioneer in reaching financially vulnerable children and families, discussed EARN's efforts to focus on social mobility early in life through Child Development Accounts to help children attend college and reach their full potential. At the policy level, Ramsey Alwin and Barb Stucki of the National Council on Aging discussed policies that help low-income and vulnerable older adults forge a path to economic security. Emily Allen of AARP discussed initiatives to create financial products for unbanked and underbanked older adults. Michelle Washko discussed the newly formed Administration for Community Living, which is investing in economic security for older adults and individuals with disabilities. In the months following the conference, Robert Zdenek and his colleagues at the National Community Reinvestment Coalition wrote a policy paper on "age-friendly banking" and revised the work for this book.

We are grateful to the Lee Foundation in Singapore for funding of the Next Age Institute, which has helped to support editing, publication, and selected distribution of this volume.

We are deeply grateful to Chris Leiker at the Center for Social Development, whose sharp eye and skillful editing made this a much improved book. He worked with each author to bring out the best in each chapter. Thanks also go to Dana Bliss and Brianna Marron at Oxford University Press for their unwavering support, guidance, and logistical assistance. We also thank colleagues who read parts of the book and generously offered suggestions: Margaret Clancy, Lissa Johnson, and Tiffany Heineman.

Nancy and Margaret dedicate this book to today's older adults, especially those who are struggling financially. We hope this book will contribute to discussions that will build financial capability among those adults and among future generations.

NMH
MSS
June 2014

■ CONTRIBUTORS

Nancy Morrow-Howell, MSW, PhD, is the Bettie Bofinger Brown Distinguished Professor of Social Policy at Washington University. She also is the director of the university's Harvey A. Friedman Center for Aging. Her research focuses on the productive and civic engagement of older adults. She is editor of the book *Productive Aging*, published by Johns Hopkins University Press. Her research has contributed to an increased understanding of programs, policies, and institutional arrangements that maximize the productive engagement of older adults while promoting positive outcomes for the individuals themselves. As director of the university's Center for Aging, she promotes gerontological research and education across disciplines, schools, and departments. In 2014, she was elected to serve as president of the Gerontological Society of America.

Margaret S. Sherraden, MA, PhD, is professor of social work at the University of Missouri–St. Louis and research professor at Washington University in St. Louis. Recent books include *Financial Capability and Asset Development: Research, Education, Policy, and Practice*, edited with Julie Birkenmaier and Jami Curley (Oxford University Press, 2013); *Striving to Save: Creating Policies for Financial Security of Low-Income Families*, with Amanda Moore McBride (University of Michigan Press, 2010); and *Kitchen Capitalism: Microenterprise in Low-Income Households*, with Cynthia K. Sanders and Michael Sherraden (State University of New York Press, 2004). Currently, she is developing a financial capability and asset-building curriculum for social workers.

Jacqueline L. Angel is professor of sociology and public affairs, and an affiliate of the Population Research Center, at the University of Texas at Austin. Her research encompasses the areas of sociology of aging and diversity, demography of Hispanics, and aspects of health and retirement security.

Amanda Barusch, MSW, PhD, holds appointments at the University of Utah and the University of Otago, New Zealand. She is the author of a major text, *Foundations of Social Policy*, and has published extensively on issues related to older adults. Her chapter on Native American elders appeared in Oxford University Press's 2006 *Handbook of Social Work in Aging*.

William R. Emmons, PhD, is an economist with the Center for Household Financial Stability at the Federal Reserve Bank of St. Louis and adjunct professor of finance in the Olin Business School at Washington University in St. Louis. He conducts research on household balance sheets, financial markets, and financial regulation.

Tracy Golden, PhD, is an assistant professor in the Behavioral Science Department at Utah Valley University.

Ernest Gonzales, PhD, MSSW, is an assistant professor in the School of Social Work at Boston University. His fields of special interest include productive aging (employment, volunteering, caregiving, and education in later life), discrimination, and vulnerable populations (women, people of color, and older adults).

Edward J. Gorman III, JD, is chief community development officer with the National Community Reinvestment Coalition (NCRC). He has also served NCRC as chief membership and workforce officer (2010–2013), conceiving and helping develop the term "Age-Friendly Banking," and as a board member (1999–2010). Mr. Gorman has also practiced labor law (JD, CUA) and spent 20 years leading organizations in the fields of workforce and economic development.

Jennifer C. Greenfield, MSW, PhD, is an assistant professor in the Graduate School of Social Work at the University of Denver. Her areas of interest include long-term care policy, health policy, gerontological social work, and the relationship between health and wealth across the life course.

Jin Huang, PhD, is an assistant professor in the School of Social Work, College for Public Health and Social Justice, at Saint Louis University. His fields of special interest include material hardship, financial capability, and asset building among disadvantaged populations.

Darrell L. Hudson, PhD, MPH, is an assistant professor in the Brown School of Social Work at Washington University in St. Louis. His primary research interests center on exploring the social epidemiology of depression among African Americans. His research focuses on two critical determinants of health and health disparities: race/ethnicity and socioeconomic position.

Wilhelmina A. Leigh, PhD, was, at the time the chapter was prepared, a senior research associate with the Joint Center for Political and Economic Studies. During her career, she has analyzed a variety of issues related to retirement security and asset building (or wealth creation) within communities of color.

Stipica Mudrazija, PhD, is a postdoctoral scholar at the Edward R. Roybal Institute on Aging, University of Southern California. His research focuses on the economics of aging and comparative social policy, especially the relationship between public and private intergenerational transfers and pension and health care systems sustainability in aging societies.

Yunju Nam, PhD, is an associate professor in the School of Work at the University at Buffalo, State University of New York. Her research interests include social policy, economic equality, and long-term economic security. She is particularly interested in asset-building policies and programs for vulnerable populations, including low-income families and older immigrants.

Bryan J. Noeth, MA, MS, is a policy analyst with the Center for Household Financial Stability at the Federal Reserve Bank of St. Louis. He has master's degrees in economics and finance and conducts research on household balance sheets.

Michelle Putnam, PhD, is an associate professor in the School of Social Work at Simmons College. Her scholarship focuses on aging with disability and the intersection of aging and disability public policies and service delivery systems.

Trina R. Williams Shanks, PhD, is an associate professor in the School of Social Work at the University of Michigan. Her fields of interest include asset-building policy and practice across the life cycle; the impact of poverty and wealth on child development outcomes; and community and economic development, especially in urban areas.

Michael Sherraden, PhD, is the George Warren Brown Distinguished University Professor at the George Warren Brown School of Social Work and the founder and director of the Center for Social Development at Washington University in St. Louis. He is a prolific scholar known for testing social innovations and impacts on public policy.

Sehar N. Siddiqi, JD, is a graduate of Ohio State University and the University of Michigan Law School. She currently works and resides in Arlington, VA.

Molly Tovar, EdD, MAT, is the director of the Kathryn M. Buder Center for American Indian Studies and Professor of Practice at the Brown School of Social Work at Washington University in St. Louis. She is coauthor of *A Cup of Cappuccino for the Entrepreneur's Spirit: American Indian Women Entrepreneurs' Edition.*

Robert O. Zdenek, DPA, is the director of National Neighbors Silver at the National Community Reinvestment Coalition. His work focuses on economic security strategies for older adults. With over 30 years of leadership and management experience at national, state, and local levels, Dr. Zdenek has published over 20 articles. He is a part-time graduate faculty member at New School University.

ABBREVIATIONS

ACA	Patient Protection and Affordable Care Act of 2010
ACS	American Community Survey
CDA	Child Development Account
CLASS Act	Community Living Assistance Services and Supports Act
EC	Experience Corps
FCAB	Financial Capability and Asset Building
HCBS	Home- and community-based services
IHS	Inverse hyperbolic sine
LTC	Long-term care
LTCI	Long-term care insurance
LTSS	Long-term services and supports
NCRC	National Community Reinvestment Coalition
SEED OK	SEED for Oklahoma Kids
SEP	Socioeconomic position
SSDI	Social Security Disability Insurance
SSI	Supplement Security Income

■ INTRODUCTION

Financial Capability in Later Life: A Life Course Perspective

■ MARGARET S. SHERRADEN AND
NANCY MORROW-HOWELL

The recent economic crisis has thrown a spotlight on the financial troubles of ordinary Americans, including older adults. Many have lost financial ground during the crisis and now face threats to their retirement security. The chapters in this book take up the financial capability, well-being, and security of financially vulnerable older adults.

Several themes guide these explorations. First, we think of older age as a life stage of affluence, and this is true for many but not all (El Nasser 2012). Although large social welfare programs such as Social Security provide a financial foundation, some older adults face significant financial hardships. Those groups are the focus of this book.

The second theme is that financial capability in later life is the outcome of financial experiences accumulated through a lifetime. Financial well-being in later life is shaped by a series of actions over many years. For instance, the decision to save early for retirement has serious implications for an older adult's resources in retirement. Financial well-being in older age is also shaped by the historical times and contexts in which people grow up.

However, financial vulnerability is *created* earlier in life, though it may not be *revealed* until old age (Emmons and Noeth, Chapter 1 in this book). The recent economic crisis, for example, worsened the financial outlook for many: people thrown out of work; older adults who lost large shares of their retirement savings; and younger workers who were unable to find a job, especially one with retirement benefits (Emmons and Noeth, Chapter 1 in this book). Twenty percent of workers in their 50s do not expect to retire (Campbell et al. 2013).

The third theme is that there are ways to improve the position of financially vulnerable older adults. Compared with adults in their 20s and 30s, older adults have less time to recover from losses of wealth (USGAO [U.S. Government Accountability Office] 2011) but can take measures that will make a difference in well-being. Using the concept of financial capability, this book explores ways to enhance older adults' financial well-being, stability, and security by improving access to quality financial products and services, consumer protection, opportunities for income generation and wealth preservation, and financial information and guidance. We turn to these themes in the following sections.

■ **FINANCIAL VULNERABILITY IN LATER LIFE**

Financial vulnerability is a multidimensional concept that implies suscepti- bility to financial insecurity as well as "exposure to risk, shocks, and stress" (Chambers 1989, 1). One study finds that 29% of households with an adult aged 65 years or older were at "economic risk" as the recent economic crisis commenced, yet over three-quarters (78%) were financially vulnerable and lacked "sufficient economic security to sustain household members through their lives" (Meschede, Shapiro, and Wheary 2009, 1, 11). The study takes into account asset fragility, including the projected fragility of Social Security and asset income, as well as other sources of financial fragility (e.g., housing, health, and other living costs). Additional research confirms that financial vulnerability has grown among older adults over the past 10 years (Campbell et al. 2013). Minorities and women are especially likely to be financially vul- nerable (USGAO 2011; Weiss 2009; Wider Opportunities for Women 2012). In the following sections, we examine the patterns of income, employment, sav- ings, and debt that contribute to these assessments of financial vulnerability.

Income and Employment

Scholars estimate that many older adults will experience a significant income deficit; in other words, their current standard of living will differ significantly from the standard permitted by available retirement savings, pension income, and Social Security benefits (Munnell, Webb, and Golub-Sass 2009). Although older adults are less likely to be poor than are the young, 9% of older adults live below the poverty line and about 6% are nearly poor (Administration on Aging 2011). If the poverty line were calculated to include nondiscretionary spending, such as that on medication and health care costs, 16% of Americans over the age of 65 years would be considered poor (DeNavas-Walt, Proctor, and Smith 2011). During the economic recession, poverty rates increased for adults aged 55 to 64 years but declined for adults aged 65 years or older (USGAO 2011). This suggests that the baby boomer cohort entering old age may be more financially vulnerable than their parents' generation.

Social Security is a key source of income in old age (Waid, Koenig, and Caldera 2012). Although the program was created as a supplement to other resources, many older adults rely on it for household income. In 2008, the program's ben- efits provided nearly two-thirds (65%) of the average income in households with someone aged 65 years or older (USGAO 2011). Among the poorest quintile of older adults, 83% of the average annual income came from Social Security (USGAO 2011). Medicare and Medicaid also provide important income support, although they rarely cover all health expenses (USGAO 2011). Notably, families paid an estimated 19% of long-term care costs in 2009 (Kaiser Commission on Medicaid and the Uninsured 2012). The average cost of nursing home care ($88,000 per year in 2010) suggests that older adults and their families shoulder a significant financial burden (Ujvari 2012).

Increasingly, older adults with inadequate retirement income seek paid employment to make ends meet. During the Great Recession, declining investment income drove them into the workforce, but many have been unable to secure work, especially at a living wage (Rix 2011). Among workers who were aged 55 to 85 years and lost jobs in the 3 prior years, more were unemployed (37%) in 2010 than in 2008 (21%; USGAO 2011). The median duration of unemployment among older workers also grew from 8 weeks in 2007 to 29 weeks in 2010 (USGAO 2011). In June 2011, 17.8% of unemployed adults aged 55 years or older were out of work for at least 99 weeks. In contrast, only 8.1% of working adults under age 35 years had such an unemployment spell (USGAO 2011). These data are consistent with findings that employers are less likely to hire older workers than otherwise identical younger workers (Johnson 2012). Even if older adults find a job after being unemployed, they tend to earn much less than they did in their previous employment (Johnson and Mommaerts 2011).

Savings and Debt

Overall, older adults have greater wealth than do younger counterparts. Even in the recent financial crisis, as older adults' retirement accounts declined, their loss in wealth was smaller than that of younger adults (Boshara and Emmons 2013). Over 40% of adults nearing retirement (aged 50–64 years) believe that they will be worse off in retirement than their parents (Rix 2011).

A large segment of older adults lacks sufficient savings to provide financial stability in older age. For example, one study finds that over half (54%) of people over 65 years of age lack financial assets to cover median projected expenses (Meschede et al. 2009, 12).[1] In 2013, 60% of working adults aged 55 years or older reported that, if the value of their primary residence were excluded, they would have less than $100,000 in retirement savings (Employee Benefit Research Institute 2013). One-third of older adults in a recent national survey said that they could not come up with $2,000 in emergency funds to cover an unexpected need in 30 days (FINRA Investor Education Foundation 2013). Moreover, retirement savings is significantly lower for women and minorities than for white men. The disparity is due in part to differential access to employer-based retirement plans, but other factors also play roles (Advisory Committee on Employee Welfare and Pension Benefit Plans 2010).

Lack of savings is rooted in a shift in recent decades from employer-based defined-benefit retirement plans to defined-contribution plans. The proportion of workers participating in defined-benefit plans (pensions) decreased from 32%

in 1992 to 21% in 2005, whereas participation in defined-contribution plans (such as 401[k]s) increased from 35% to 42% during the same period (Federal Interagency Forum on Aging-Related Statistics 2012). Early withdrawals further contribute to low levels of retirement savings; despite the penalties they incur for doing so, many withdraw from their individual retirement savings prior to retiring (FINRA Investor Education Foundation 2013).

On the debt side of the balance sheet, the picture is also mixed. Older adults have less debt than younger adults do, but the proportion of older adults with debt grew from 30% to 43% between 1998 and 2010 (Karamcheva 2013). Although fewer older adults carry monthly credit card balances than do younger adults, significant numbers of older people carry such debt, including debt from costly medical care (Campbell et al. 2013; FINRA Investor Education Foundation 2013). Angelyque Campbell and colleagues (2013) document that 48% of people aged 40 to 94 years carry a balance and only half of those pay it off on a monthly basis. A recent study finds that many adults between the ages of 50 and 64 turn to their retirement savings and home equity for funds to make credit card payments (Traub 2013, 9). Similarly, older adults have far less student loan debt than do younger generations, but such debt is more prevalent in older age than it has been in the past; households with heads over 40 years of age now owe one-third of all student debt but owed only one-fifth of the total 10 years ago (Campbell et al. 2013).

Housing equity is an important asset in many older adult households, but recent research shows that growing numbers of older adults have mortgage debt. Six in 10 people in their 60s have mortgage debt; a third of those adults refinanced a mortgage between 2010 and 2013. Not surprisingly, adults over age 65 years are more likely to be "cost burdened" by housing than are younger adults; that is, they spend more than 30% of their income on housing (Lipman, Lubell, and Salomon 2012, 8). Another study examines the impact of the economic crisis on older adults by investigating changes in the value of homes owned by adults who are aged 50 years or over and worked for pay in the 3 prior years. It finds that nearly a third of respondents (31.5%) saw a substantial decline in the value of their house (Rix 2011). One-quarter reported exhausting their savings, and a fifth fell into greater debt during the economic slowdown between 2007 and 2010 (Rix 2011). Over the same period, only 2% of households used reverse mortgages, which are a tool for helping older adults retain affordable housing (Campbell et al. 2013).

Financial Services Inclusion

Overall, older adults benefit from rates of financial inclusion that are higher than those among younger adults. For instance, people over 60 years of age are more likely to own a checking or savings account (Campbell et al. 2013). Rates of online banking and bill paying are increasing among older adults, but use of new financial service technologies, such as mobile banking, remains very low (2%; Campbell et al. 2013; Zickuhr and Madden 2012).

Older people with low income and older minorities are less likely than other groups of older adults to use mainstream financial services. They are more likely to turn to potentially hazardous financial products and services (Board of Governors of the Federal Reserve 2013).[2] Recent studies estimate that one in five older adults uses alternative financial-service providers, such as check-cashing outlets, car-title and payday lenders, pawnshops, and rent-to-own stores (Campbell et al. 2013; FINRA Investor Education Foundation 2013).

Financial Literacy and Financial Guidance

Older adults generally have good knowledge about household finances and confidence in their ability to manage their financial lives (Campbell et al. 2013). Nearly all older adults (97%) express high confidence in their financial management ability (Investor Protection Trust 2010).

Unfortunately, such confidence is not necessarily well founded. Many adults lack plans for managing their financial affairs in old age (Mandell 2013). One study finds that only 50% of older adults have arranged for someone to help them with financial decisions, and less than 50% have arranged for a written power of attorney (Campbell et al. 2013). Older adults tend to draw on Social Security too early, forfeiting higher monthly checks (Shu and Payne 2013). Moreover, 18% of older adults who report needing financial guidance say that they cannot find assistance (Campbell et al. 2013). Cognitive decline can also lead to serious problems in financial decision making (Agarwal et al. 2009).

Financial literacy and guidance are particularly important in old age because of the threat of financial abuse. Although previous research has underestimated the cost of such abuse, a recent study places the total cost to older adults at $2.9 billion, finding that victimization is high among women, adults in their 80s, the frail, and people who live alone (MetLife Mature Market Institute 2011). Older adults are exploited by family, friends, strangers, and businesses, as well as through efforts to defraud Medicare and Medicaid (MetLife Mature Market Institute 2011). Many factors contribute to financial abuse of older adults. Among them are cognitive decline and disability, low financial literacy, the complexity of financial services, the lack of social support, and the absence of sound guidance.

In sum, older adults are better off than their younger counterparts across most measures of financial well-being, but many enter old age in shaky financial condition. Especially among minorities, the poor, and women, factors such as low income, lack of savings and assets, lack of access to quality financial services, and low financial literacy contribute to financial vulnerability in old age. In thinking about how to address such vulnerability, we explore conceptual approaches to building financial capability across the life course and across generations, especially among the most financially vulnerable.

■ LIFE CYCLE AND LIFE COURSE PERSPECTIVES ON BUILDING FINANCIAL CAPABILITY

In keeping with a life course perspective, we see the development of financial capability as a cumulative process rather than a series of discrete stages (Erikson 1959; Glaser and Strauss 1965). People gain knowledge about finances and financial management skills, and they use increasingly complex financial products and services over their lifetimes.

Although details and order of events vary, it is possible to chronicle a typical financial life cycle trajectory. For example, as children grow, they develop an increasingly complex understanding of economics (Berti and Bombi 1988; Strauss 1952). Very young children learn money basics (e.g., coinage) and how to spend funds (Strauss 1952). They soon learn how to earn money from informal work, how to borrow money from friends, how to save money in a piggy bank, and how to donate money. Adolescents begin earning income from employment, learn how to manage a transaction account, and save money in a formal savings account. Young adults continue to build on knowledge and skills. In particular, formal employment requires additional knowledge, new skills, and access to many financial products and services. They learn how to handle finances between paychecks: managing a financial transaction account, financing a car or higher education, buying auto insurance, and learning about consumer rights and responsibilities. They learn about renting an apartment, tenant rights and responsibilities, financial planning, keeping financial records, and paying bills and taxes.

As individuals progress into adulthood, their developmental tasks have increasingly important implications for financial capability. Although little research focuses on these implications, we can chart key milestones. Family formation and having children open new doors to financial functioning. Parents communicate about household financial management and attend to the financial well-being of children and aging parents. They make decisions about joint financial accounts (and beneficiaries), plan for the costs of raising children, buy health insurance and life insurance, and save.

In older age, people prepare for an extended period of diminished earnings and increased health expenditures. Postretirement employment and volunteering require planning as well as an understanding of tax liabilities and of Social Security benefits. Older adults, especially women, frequently serve as long-term caregivers for a spouse or another older relative; financial protections should be in place to protect the cared for and the caregiver. In addition, older age is often affected by health problems, with negative implications for financial functioning (Marson and Sabatino 2012). As people age, they are increasingly motivated to be generative: they wish to make a positive impact on younger generations (McAdams 2001) and to leave something of value to children or grandchildren.

The concept of the life course adds sociological and historical dimensions to the idea of the life cycle. As Glen Elder and colleagues write, "The life course provides a framework for studying phenomena at the nexus of social pathways, developmental trajectories, and social change" (Elder, Johnson, and Crosnoe 2003, 10). The concept imparts this by linking "structural conditions influencing individuals' reaction to personal resources that can be mobilized to cope with events" (Rohall et al. 2005, 166). In this way, the life course perspective provides important human, social, cultural, political, and economic dimensions to the concept of financial capability.

According to Elder (1994, 1998; see also Elder and Giele 2009), four factors affect the life course: timing of lives, historical time and place, human agency, and linked lives. Each factor has implications for financial well-being in later life. The first, *timing*, suggests that the point at which events occur or when an individual experiences advantages or disadvantages may have persistent effects. For example, the experience of severe economic disadvantage in early childhood often has life-long implications (Duncan et al. 2012). Each transition from one stage of life (e.g., marriage, entry into the labor force, and exit from it) affects the next stage, and the effect differs with timing in the life course. Elder and colleagues (2003) explain, for example, that a stint in the army is less disruptive when a person is young than when he or she has a family and is well down a career path. Similarly, a chronic disease will have a different impact on the lives of people in their 60s than it would in the lives of people in their 80s.

The point in life at which a person learns about finances and begins to use financial products has important implications for his or her long-term financial capability. For example, the point in people's lives at which they enroll in an employer-matched savings account has enormous implications for the level of retirement savings. Retirement savings accumulated over a lifetime, especially savings augmented with an employer match, will far exceed the retirement savings of someone who benefits from such an account only later in life.

The second factor, *historical time and place*, also shapes people's life trajectories. People born in different times and places grow older in different ways, encountering opportunities and constraints related to specific socioeconomic, cultural, historical, and geographical conditions. Elder and colleagues express this succinctly: "When times change, lives change" (2003, 14). Periods of war, economic recession, technological shift, cultural transformation, and other large-scale change affect age cohorts in different ways (Fogel and Costa 1997; Mayer 2003).

Changing times profoundly affect people's financial capability as well as their ability to build secure financial lives and futures. In the recent economic crisis, for example, different age cohorts experienced different sets of consequences. High unemployment has delayed the entry of young people into the labor market, with serious implications for their lifetime earnings and retirement security. On average, the crisis claimed 5% of the future (at age 70) income of adults aged 55 to 59 years (Butrica, Johnson, and Smith 2011). The crisis increased the likelihood that those entering old age will delay retirement and the probability that already retired adults will seek paid employment (Rampel 2012).

However, humans are not passive in the face of history and circumstance. The third factor, *human agency*, recognizes that individuals are active: they plan, make choices, make mistakes, solve problems, learn, resist, and procrastinate (Bandura 2001). Moreover, education and the emergence of opportunities can facilitate individual action (Becker 1994).

In the financial sphere, human agency influences financial well-being throughout life. A new parent who opens a college savings account for his or her child at birth improves the educational resources and opportunities available to the child. Although adults enter their later years with a lifetime of experience and wisdom in making financial decisions, cognitive and physical decline may attenuate the ability of some to act in their own best financial interest (Lusardi 2012; Mandell 2013).

The fourth factor in the life course perspective, *linked lives*, focuses on the ways in which people are socially embedded and on how socialization and control by others affect individuals' actions and decisions (Elder and Giele 2009). Families and social networks exert the most influence (Stack 1974; Vinovskis 2005). Such influences have varied implications for financial capability and financial decisions. For instance, a woman may withdraw from paid work to care for a sick spouse or an older relative. An individual's retirement savings can also affect that person's spouse and their children.

As our discussion of these four factors suggests, the life course perspective underscores the reality that individual choices, though important, are shaped by and interact with other factors: the timing of events in people's lifetimes, the historical times and the place where they live, and the circumstances and actions of the people who surround them. The situation of older adults differs from that of the young in that older adults have less time and limited means to reverse disadvantage, poor choices, and other setbacks.

The concept of the life course informs current policies and programs. Notably, the concept of the life cycle is a foundational part of Social Security. However, the idea of the life course and recognition of the role of historical time and place are also central features of the program in that it is recession-proof. Although the recent recession resulted in the loss of personal retirement savings, Social Security benefits were unaffected.

However, policies and programs often fail to address life course principles. For example, policies do not assist older adults who face breathtakingly high long-term care costs, and they do not protect older adults, especially those with cognition problems, from high-fee home repair loans.

■ IMPROVING FINANCIAL CAPABILITY IN OLDER AGE

People need both financial knowledge and financial inclusion to build financially secure and hopeful lives. If individuals have both, they are financially capable. We define *financial capability* as both an individual idea and a structural one; it combines people's *ability to act* in their best financial interest with their *opportunity to act* (Johnson and Sherraden 2007). Ability and opportunity contribute to financial capability in ways that may lead to improved financial well-being and life chances (Sherraden 2013).

As we have seen, financial knowledge and financial inclusion are challenges for many older adults. The chapters that follow tackle key financial issues faced by vulnerable populations in later life. They also explore the implications of these issues for efforts to build financial capability across the life cycle and with a life course perspective.

■ BOOK CONTENTS

Setting the Stage

In Chapter 1, William R. Emmons and Bryan J. Noeth set the stage by examining trends in the economic and financial status of older Americans. Using life cycle and life course perspectives, their analyses illustrate how the birth cohort affects the financial well-being of different segments of society. With data from the Federal Reserve's Survey of Consumer Finances, they explore how the Great Recession reduced the income and wealth of many families. The young, some middle-aged families, adults with less than a college education, and members of historically disadvantaged minority groups (especially African Americans and Hispanics) were hit particularly hard. Further illustrating the importance of the life course perspective, they find evidence that wealth trajectories over the life course have been more favorable for age cohorts born before the baby boom than for cohorts born since the middle of the twentieth century. Darrell L. Hudson (Chapter 2) provides a segue to the book's second part, on vulnerable populations. He points out that African Americans face stressors that may undermine some of the health benefits often associated with improved socioeconomic position. Hudson offers an understanding of how race, mental health, and financial capabilities across the life course interrelate. He also explores the benefits, costs, and policy implications of upward socioeconomic mobility among African Americans.

Financially Vulnerable Groups

Chapters in the second part focus on the vulnerability of specific population groups.

Chapter 3, by Trina R. Williams Shanks and Wilhelmina A. Leigh, discusses assets held by older African American households. They find that older African Americans are less likely than other older adults to have adequate assets and wealth for retirement. Drawing on data from the Panel Study of Income Dynamics, they find that the median net worth of older non-Hispanic whites is nearly seven times that of older African Americans, and the difference nearly triples if home equity is excluded from the estimate. They conclude with policy recommendations that focus on ways to expand access to asset development opportunities for youth and working-age adults.

In Chapter 4, Jacqueline L. Angel and Stipica Mudrazija focus on the economic stability of older Hispanics in the years close to and after retirement. Hispanics represent a fast-growing segment of the nation's minority population, and they are relatively disadvantaged in the labor force. A high proportion of them lacks savings in retirement plans, and the lack of such resources is especially prevalent in Mexican-origin families. These observations suggest that older Hispanics face high financial vulnerability. Angel and Mudrazija highlight the potential of public pension programs to improve the financial security of this population.

In Chapter 5, Amanda Barusch, Molly Tovar, and Tracy Golden address the serious financial circumstances of Native American elders. They also identify model programs that build on cultural assets, traditions of authority, and rights to family assistance in Native communities. They caution that recent trends, such as out-migration of young adults from reservation lands, threaten these cultural assets. Economic development measures that generate jobs and infrastructure can serve as a counterweight, reinforcing cultural assets and contributing to the financial well-being of tribal elders.

Yunju Nam turns in Chapter 6 to relatively understudied groups of immigrant older adults, finding that they are more likely than other older adults to live in poverty. Due to labor market disadvantages, immigrant older adults are less likely to receive Social Security and private retirement benefits. Vulnerability is particularly high among immigrants as a whole, noncitizens, recent immigrants, older immigrants, and immigrants from non-European countries. Nam recommends the creation of culturally sensitive products and services for these adults. She also endorses alternative forms of identification to reduce confusion among immigrants and financial institutions.

In Chapter 7, Michelle Putnam addresses the question of disability in old age, considering its implications for wealth and financial stability. Although adults may enter old age with a disability or experience one in later life, the ensuing problems are similar: they encounter difficulty in obtaining and retaining employment, paying for and accessing health care, and negotiating social welfare programs and systems. Putnam underscores the importance of designing and testing policies and interventions that reduce financial hardship among older adults who live with disabilities.

Financial Capability Policies and Innovations in Older Adulthood

In Chapter 8, Jin Huang and Jennifer C. Greenfield examine ways in which asset policies can address the challenge of maintaining economic stability across the life cycle. In proposing a conceptual framework of asset development for older adults, they incorporate capability and life course perspectives.

They examine program data on asset-building programs through the lens of the new framework and find that rates of program participation are low among older adults, who are less likely than other adults to take up programs that distribute benefits through the tax system. Furthermore, they find that an asset-based approach to financial capability in old age is relatively underused and is a promising direction for future policy making.

Turning to health in older age (Chapter 9), Jennifer C. Greenfield examines the financial implications of long-term care on caregivers. Current policies aimed at reducing public expenditures on long-term care may inadvertently jeopardize families' financial capability, including the capability of caregivers. Longitudinal analysis suggests that the income of many caregivers, especially that of caregivers in vulnerable groups, is lower over time than the income of counterparts who are not caregivers, and this difference translates into a wealth disparity. Thus, Greenfield asserts that long-term care should be reframed as an economic issue with relevance across the life cycle. The retirement planning process should include caregiver assessments and supports, asset protection that prevents family impoverishment, and financial education on the costs of long-term care.

In Chapter 10, Ernest Gonzales describes the changing landscape that fosters longer working lives. A contributing factor is low wealth in old age, especially among women, people of color, adults with low education, and individuals with poor health. These groups have such wealth levels because they did not benefit from employment-based retirement savings plans. Gonzalez analyzes the implications of workplace policies and practices for economic security in later life. He concludes with policy and program ideas that may facilitate longer working lives and the accrual of wealth in later life.

In Chapter 11, Sehar N. Siddiqi, Robert O. Zdenek, and Edward J. Gorman III propose a set of age-friendly banking principles that address key financial risks in old age. Those risks currently undermine economic security in retirement. Siddiqi and colleagues address the shortcomings of old retirement savings models that are no longer effective for many. The age-friendly banking principles they propose are intended to help older adults obtain critical income supports, financial education, financial counseling, protection from fraud and abuse, and assistance with aging in place. The authors also endorse customized financial products and services that would build capacity, reduce vulnerability in old age, and contribute to community well-being.

In the conclusion, Nancy Morrow-Howell, Michael Sherraden, and Margaret S. Sherraden summarize major themes related to financial insecurity in later life, especially insecurity among the most vulnerable of older populations. They call for innovation in programs, policies, and research that focus on developing financial capability across the life cycle and across generations:

- Provide culturally appropriate financial education, planning, and guidance throughout life, as well as strategies that enable proactive financial decision making by the poor and vulnerable in an increasingly complex financial landscape.

- Test new ideas for "age-friendly" banking that increase accessibility of financial products and services.
- Ensure that asset-building policies are broadly inclusive.
- Advance health and long-term care policies that promote financial security in later life.
- Encourage researchers, program developers, and policymakers to take a strong life course approach aimed at ensuring financial security in late life.
- Include older adults and the social aging process more directly.

Richard Titmuss, a giant in social welfare scholarship, warned more than half a century ago that "two nations in old age" were emerging (1958, 166; see also Meyer and Bridgen 2008). Although he was writing about a different time, Titmuss's statement was prescient. Many people do fine in old age—in fact, better than much of the rest of the population—but others spend their older years in financial difficulty. This book contributes to our understanding of the financial well-being and security of vulnerable older adults and explores constructive pathways to improve their financial capability.

■ NOTES

1. The authors define financial assets as projections of financial net worth plus Social Security and pension incomes (Meschede et al. 2009).

2. For a definition of alternative financial services, see Bradley and colleagues (2009).

■ REFERENCES

Administration on Aging. 2011. *A Profile of Older Americans: 2012*. Report. Washington, DC: U.S. Department of Health and Human Services, Administration on Aging. http://www.aoa.gov/Aging_Statistics/Profile/2012/docs/2012profile.pdf.

Advisory Committee on Employee Welfare and Pension Benefit Plans. 2010. *Disparities for Women and Minorities in Retirement Savings*. Report. Washington, DC: U.S. Department of Labor, Employee Benefits Security Administration. http://www.dol.gov/ebsa/publications/2010ACreport3.html.

Agarwal, Sumit, John C. Driscoll, Xavier Gabaix, and David Laibson. 2009. "The Age of Reason: Financial Decisions over the Life Cycle and Implications for Regulation." *Brookings Papers on Economic Activity* Fall: 51–117. http://www.brookings.edu/~/media/Projects/BPEA/Fall%202009/2009b_bpea_agarwal.PDF.

Bandura, Albert. 2001. "Social Cognitive Theory: An Agentic Perspective." *Annual Review of Psychology* 52: 1–26.

Becker, Gary S. 1994. *Human Capital: A Theoretical and Empirical Analysis, with Special Reference to Education*, 3rd ed. Chicago: University of Chicago Press.

Berti, Anna Emilia, and Anna Silvia Bombi. 1988. *The Child's Construction of Economics*. Translated by Gerard Duveen. Cambridge: Cambridge University Press.

Board of Governors of the Federal Reserve. 2013. *Insights into the Financial Experiences of Older Adults: A Forum Briefing Paper.* Washington, DC: Board of Governors of the Federal Reserve System. http://www.federalreserve.gov/newsevents/conferences/older-adults-forum-paper-20130717.pdf.

Boshara, Ray, and William R. Emmons. 2013. *After the Fall: Rebuilding Family Balance Sheets, Rebuilding the Economy.* Annual Report 2012. St. Louis, MO: Federal Reserve Bank of St. Louis. http://www.stlouisfed.org/publications/ar/2012/pdfs/ar12_complete.pdf.

Bradley, Christine, Susan Burhouse, Heather Gratton, and Rae-Ann Miller. 2009. "Alternative Financial Services: A Primer." *FDIC Quarterly* 3 (1): 39–47. http://www.fdic.gov/bank/analytical/quarterly/2009_vol3_1/AltFinServicesprimer.html.

Butrica, Barbara A., Richard W. Johnson, and Karen E. Smith. 2011. *How Will the Great Recession Affect Future Retirement Income?* Older Americans' Economic Security Report 30, May. Washington, DC: Urban Institute, Program on Retirement Policy. http://www.urban.org/UploadedPDF/412339-Future-Retirement-Incomes.pdf.

Campbell, Angelyque, Alejandra Lopez-Fernandini, Daniel Gorin, Barbara Lipman, and Brian Tabit. 2013. *Insights into the Financial Experiences of Older Adults: A Forum Briefing Paper.* Report, July. Washington, DC: Board of Governors of the Federal Reserve System. http://www.federalreserve.gov/newsevents/conferences/older-adults-forum-paper-20130717.pdf.

Chambers, Robert. 1989. "Editorial Introduction: Vulnerability, Coping and Policy." *IDS Bulletin* 20 (2): 1–7. doi: 10.1111/j.1759-5436.1989.mp20002001.x.

DeNavas-Walt, Carmen, Bernadette D. Proctor, and Jessica C. Smith. 2011. *Income, Poverty, and Health Insurance Coverage in the United States: 2010.* Current Population Reports: Consumer Income, P60–239, September. Washington, DC: U.S. Census Bureau. http://www.census.gov/prod/2011pubs/p60-239.pdf.

Duncan, Greg J., Katherine Magnuson, Ariel Kalil, and Kathleen Ziol-Guest. 2012. "The Importance of Early Childhood Poverty." *Social Indicators Research* 108 (1): 87–98. doi: 10.1007/s11205-011-9867-9.

Elder, Glen, H., Jr. 1994. "Time, Human Agency, and Social Change: Perspectives on the Life Course." *Social Psychology Quarterly* 57 (1): 4–15. doi: 10.2307/2786971.

Elder, Glen, H., Jr. 1998. "The Life Course as Developmental Theory." *Child Development* 69 (1): 1–12. doi: 10.2307/1132065.

Elder, Glen H., Jr., and Janet Z. Giele. 2009. "Life Course Studies: An Evolving Field." In *The Craft of Life Course Research*, edited by Glen H. Elder Jr. and Janet Z. Giele, 1–24. New York: Guilford.

Elder, Glen H., Jr., Monica Kirkpatrick Johnson, and Robert Crosnoe. 2003. "The Emergence and Development of Life Course Theory." In *Handbook of the Life Course*, edited by Jeylan T. Mortimer and Michael J. Shanahan, 3–19. New York: Kluwer Academic/Plenum.

El Nasser, Haya. 2012. "Poll: Life's Just Good for Most Older Americans." *USA Today*, August 8. http://www.usatoday.com/news/nation/story/2012-08-07/aging-americans-attitudes-retirement/56860194/1.

Erikson, Erik H. 1959. *Identity and the Life Cycle.* New York: International Universities Press.

Federal Interagency Forum on Aging-Related Statistics. 2012. *Older Americans 2012: Key Indicators of Well-Being.* Report, June. Washington, DC: U.S. Government

Printing Office. http://www.agingstats.gov/agingstatsdotnet/Main_Site/Data/2012 _Documents/Docs/EntireChartbook.pdf.

FINRA Investor Education Foundation. 2013. *Financial Capability in the United States: Report of Findings from the 2012 National Financial Capability Study*. Report, May. Washington, DC: FINRA Investor Education Foundation. http://www.usfinancialcapability.org/downloads/NFCS_2012_Report_Natl_Findings.pdf.

Fogel, Robert W., and Dora L. Costa. 1997. "A Theory of Technophysio Evolution, with Some Implications for Forecasting Population, Health Care Costs, and Pension Costs." *Demography* 34 (1): 49–66. doi: 10.2307/2061659.

Glaser, Barney G., and Anselm L. Strauss. 1965. *Awareness of Dying*. Piscataway, NJ: Aldine.

Investor Protection Trust. 2010. *Elder Investment Fraud and Financial Exploitation: A Survey Conducted for Investor Protection Trust*. Report. Washington, DC: Investor Protection Trust. http://www.investorprotection.org/downloads/EIFFE_Survey_Report.pdf.

Johnson, Richard W. 2012. *Older Workers, Retirement, and the Great Recession*. Great Recession Brief, October. New York: Russell Sage Foundation and the Stanford Center on Poverty and Inequality. https://www.stanford.edu/group/recessiontrends /cgi-bin/web/sites/all/themes/barron/pdf/Retirement_fact_sheet.pdf.

Johnson, Richard W., and Corina Mommaerts. 2011. *Age Differences in Job Loss, Job Search, and Reemployment*. Retirement Policy Discussion Paper 11-01, January. Washington, DC: Urban Institute. http://www.urban.org/uploadedpdf /412284-Age-Differences.pdf.

Johnson, Elizabeth, and Margaret S. Sherraden. 2007. "From Financial Literacy to Financial Capability among Youth." *Journal of Sociology and Social Welfare* 34 (3): 119–145.

Kaiser Commission on Medicaid and the Uninsured. 2012. *Medicaid and Long-Term Care Services and Supports*. Medicaid Facts, June. Washington, DC: Kaiser Commission. http://kaiserfamilyfoundation.files.wordpress.com/2013/01/2186-09.pdf.

Karamcheva, Nadia. 2013. *Is Household Debt Growing for Older Americans?* Older Americans' Economic Security Report 33, January. Washington, DC: Urban Institute, Program on Retirement Policy. http://www.urban.org/UploadedPDF/412742-Is -Household-Debt-Growing-for-Older-Americans.pdf.

Lipman, Barbara, Jeffrey Lubell, and Emily Salomon. 2012. *Housing an Aging Population: Are We Prepared?* Report. Washington DC: Center for Housing Policy. http://www.nhc.org/media/files/AgingReport2012.pdf.

Lusardi, Annamaria. 2012. "Financial Literacy and Financial Decision-Making in Older Adults." *Generations* 36 (2): 25–32.

Mandell, Lewis. 2013. *What to Do When I Get Stupid: A Radically Safe Approach to a Difficult Financial Era*. Bainbridge Island, WA: Point White Publishing.

Marson, Daniel C., and Charles P. Sabatino. 2012. "Financial Capacity in an Aging Society." *Generations* 36 (2): 6–11.

Mayer, Karl Ulrich. 2003. "The Sociology of the Life Course and Lifespan Psychology: Diverging or Converging Pathways?" In *Understanding Human Development: Dialogues with Lifespan Psychology*, edited by Ursula M. Staudinger and Ulman Lindenberger, 463–481. Dordrecht, the Netherlands: Kluwer Academic.

McAdams, Dan P. 2001. "Generativity in Midlife." In *Handbook of Midlife Development*, edited by Margie E. Lachman, 395–443. New York: Wiley & Sons.

Meschede, Tatjana, Thomas M. Shapiro, and Jennifer Wheary. 2009. *Living Longer on Less: The New Economic (In)Security of Seniors.* By a Thread Report 4. Waltham, MA: Institute on Assets and Social Policy and Dēmos. http://www.demos.org /publication/living-longer-less-new-economic-insecurity-seniors.

MetLife Mature Market Institute. 2011. *The MetLife Study of Elder Financial Abuse: Crimes of Occasion, Desperation, and Predation against America's Elders.* Report. New York: MetLife Mature Market Institute. https://www.metlife.com/assets/cao /mmi/publications/studies/2011/mmi-elder-financial-abuse.pdf.

Meyer, Traute, and Paul Bridgen. 2008. "Class, Gender and Chance: The Social Division of Welfare and Occupational Pensions in the United Kingdom." *Ageing and Society* 28 (3): 353–381. doi: 10.1017/S0144686X07006873.

Munnell, Alicia H., Anthony Webb, and Francesca Golub-Sass. 2009. *The National Retirement Risk Index: After the Crash.* Issue in Brief 9-22, October. Chestnut Hill, MA: Center for Retirement Research at Boston College. http://crr.bc.edu/wp-content /uploads/2009/10/IB_9-22.pdf.

Rampel, Catherine. 2012. "Big Income Losses for Those Near Retirement." *Economix* (blog), *New York Times*, August 23. http://economix.blogs.nytimes.com/2012/08/23 /big-income-losses-for-those-near-retirement.

Rix, Sara E. 2011. *Recovering from the Great Recession: Long Struggle ahead for Older Americans.* Insight on the Issues 50, May. Washington, DC: AARP Public Policy Institute. http://assets.aarp.org/rgcenter/ppi/econ-sec/insight50_recovering.pdf.

Rohall, David E., V. Lee Hamilton, David R. Segal, and Jessica Y. Y. Kwong. 2005. "Job-Search Strategies in Time and Place: A Study of Post-Service Employment among Former Russian Army Officers." In *Historical Influences on Lives and Aging*, edited by K. Warner Schaie and Glen H. Elder Jr., 166–189. New York: Springer.

Sherraden, Margaret S. 2013. "Building Blocks of Financial Capability." In *Financial Capability and Asset Development: Research, Education, Policy, and Practice*, edited by Julie Birkenmaier, Margaret S. Sherraden, and Jami Curley, 3–43. New York: Oxford University Press.

Shu, Suzanne B., and John W. Payne. 2013. "Life Expectation Judgments, Fairness, and Loss Aversion in the Psychology of Social Security Claiming Decisions." Paper presented at the 15th Annual Joint Meeting of the Retirement Research Consortium, Washington, DC, August 1–2. http://www.mrrc.isr.umich.edu/transmit/rrc2013 /summaries/1B_ShuPayneSummary.pdf.

Stack, Carol B. 1974. *All Our Kin: Strategies for Survival in a Black Community.* New York: Harper.

Strauss, Anselm L. 1952. "The Development and Transformation of Monetary Meanings in the Child." *American Sociological Review* 17 (3): 275–286. doi: 10.2307/2088073.

Titmuss, Richard M. 1958. *Essays on "The Welfare State."* London: Unwin.

Traub, Amy. 2013. *In the Red: Older Americans and Credit Card Debt.* Middle Class Security Project Report. Washington, DC: AARP Public Policy Institute and Dēmos. http:// www.aarp.org/content/dam/aarp/research/public_policy_institute/security/2013 /older-americans-and-credit-card-debt-AARP-ppi-sec.pdf.

Ujvari, Kathleen. 2012. *Long-Term Care Insurance: 2012 Update.* Fact Sheet 261, June. Washington, DC: AARP Public Policy Institute. http://www.aarp.org/content /dam/aarp/research/public_policy_institute/ltc/2012/ltc-insurance-2012-update -AARP-ppi-ltc.pdf.

USGAO [U.S. Government Accountability Office]. 2011. *Income Security: Older Adults and the 2007–2009 Recession*. Report GAO-12-76 to the chairman, Subcommittee on Primary Health and Aging, Committee on Health, Education, Labor and Pensions, U.S. Senate, October. Washington, DC: USGAO. http://www.gao.gov/new.items /d1276.pdf.

Vinovskis, Maris A. 2005. "Historical Changes and the American Life Course." In *HistoricalInfluencesonLivesandAging,*editedbyK.WarnerSchaieandGlenH.ElderJr., 1–20. New York: Springer

Waid, Mikki, Gary Koenig, and Selena Caldera. 2012. *Social Security: A Key Retirement Income Source for Older Minorities*. Fact Sheet 262, November. Washington, DC: AARP Pubic Policy Institute. http://www.aarp.org/content/dam/aarp/research /public_policy_institute/econ_sec/2012/ss-key-retirement-income-source-older-minorities-AARP-ppi-econ-sec.pdf.

Weiss, Liz. 2009. "Unmarried Women Hit Hard by Poverty." Women's Rights News Alert, September 10, Center for American Progress, Washington, DC. http://www.americanprogress.org/issues/women/news/2009/09/10/6683 /unmarried-women-hit-hard-by-poverty.

Wider Opportunities for Women. 2012. *Doing Without: Economic Insecurity and Older Americans; No. 2: Gender*. Brief, March. Washington, DC: Wider Opportunities for Women. http://www.wowonline.org/documents/OlderAmericansGenderbrief FINAL.pdf.

Zickuhr, Kathryn, and Mary Madden. 2012. *Older Adults and Internet Use: For the First Time, Half of Adults Ages 65 and Older Are Online*. Internet and American Life Project Report, June 6. Washington, DC: Pew Research Center. http://www.pewinternet .org/~/media//Files/Reports/2012/PIP_Older_adults_and_internet_use.pdf.

PART ONE
Financial Capability in Later Life
Theory and Evidence of Life Course Impacts

1 The Economic and Financial Status of Older Americans

Trends and Prospects

■ WILLIAM R. EMMONS AND
BRYAN J. NOETH

The global financial crisis and ensuing Great Recession reduced the income and wealth of most families. Continuing a long-term trend, however, older Americans generally fared better than their younger counterparts on both dimensions. This chapter provides an economic and financial profile of older Americans in the period from 1989 through 2010. The profile is based on data from the Federal Reserve's triennial Survey of Consumer Finances.[1] Using data from the Federal Reserve's quarterly Financial Accounts of the United States, we extend one measure of wealth through early 2013; our findings suggest that outcomes for older Americans continue to be favorable compared to those for adults under age 62 years.[2]

We distinguish between two groups of older families: *younger-old families*, which are headed by someone aged 62–69 years, and *older-old families*, which are headed by someone aged 70 years or older. We compare these older families to each other, to young families (headed by someone under 40 years), and to middle-aged families (headed by someone aged 40–61 years). We highlight the important dimensions of educational attainment and race or ethnicity, as these are powerful predictors of income and wealth throughout the life course. We pinpoint some of the factors that may be responsible for the relatively favorable outcomes enjoyed by many but not all older adults. These factors include their sources of income and the structure of their balance sheets—that is, their assets and liabilities. We also track the median income and median wealth of all cohorts born between 1893 and 1992, observing them as many as eight times at 3-year intervals between 1989 and 2010. We find strong evidence that if many other important contributing factors are held constant, birth year matters for both the median income and median wealth of a cohort.

■ INCOME AND WEALTH THROUGH TIME AND ACROSS THE LIFE COURSE

Among all families and across all age groups, real (inflation-adjusted) average household income and real average household net worth declined significantly during the financial crisis and ensuing Great Recession of 2007–2009 (see Emmons and Noeth [2013d] for further discussion). The wealth decline was especially note-worthy, exceeding both in dollar amount and in percentage terms any previous downturn during the past six decades. Real median family income and real median household net worth similarly turned sharply down during the crisis.

A natural question follows: what exactly comprises income and wealth in the measures being discussed? Describing income and wealth in the Survey of Consumer Finances, Jacob Krimmel and colleagues (2013) provide estimates of the economic magnitudes of items excluded from income and wealth. Fringe and in-kind benefits (e.g., from Medicare, Medicaid, and food stamps) are excluded from income; the present value of future distributions from defined-benefit pensions and Social Security is excluded from wealth. Another important category of intangible wealth not included in balance sheets is so-called human capital (here representing expected earnings from future work). Important categories of excluded liabilities include reasonably certain future expenditures on housing and living expenses, estimates of medical expenses, necessary replacement of long-lived assets such as automobiles, future taxes payable, and a host of other items.

■ RESEARCH ON WEALTH ACCUMULATION ACROSS THE LIFE COURSE AND THROUGH ECONOMIC CYCLES

It is not obvious whether young, middle-aged, or older families are likely to fare best during various economic and financial cycles. A recession that involves significant job and income losses will hurt young and middle-aged families more than it will hurt older families, because larger parts of the incomes of young and middle-aged families are exposed to job loss. However, large declines in asset prices, including declines in prices for stocks and housing, would hurt middle-aged and older families more because they have more accumulated assets. In addition, balance sheet leverage (i.e., debt used to finance family assets) typically is greatest among young families, so asset-price declines are multiplied into proportionately larger declines in net worth, hurting young families. Which effect will dominate is an empirical question.

Asset prices tend to be procyclical. That is, they rise and fall in concert with the economy. Thus, stagnant or falling asset prices are likely to accompany a downturn in the economy, and it is not obvious which channel—income, wealth, or leverage—will be most important in a given situation or for a given family. Another consideration adds to the complexity of the situation: the original impacts of recessions and asset-price declines could be muted or entirely reversed by the time we observe families' incomes and wealth.

A recent attempt has been made to sort out the life cycle wealth effects of such a severe downturn as the Great Recession. Research concludes that older families are likely to fare worse than young ones, because the proportional decline in asset prices during the recent downturn was greater than the decline in wage income (Glover et al. 2011). Older families suffered wealth and income losses from depressed asset prices and interest rates, but young families lost relatively little wealth or interest income because they had little wealth at risk. In principle, the young should have benefited by being able to purchase assets at relatively low prices from older families, which needed to continue selling stocks to finance their retirements and, in some cases, sold houses in order to move to living arrangements more appropriate for older adults. To some extent, these life-stage-driven asset sales would continue even though stock prices and house prices had fallen. In effect, Andrew Glover and associates (2011) conclude that older families cannot wait forever to sell their assets after a severe asset-price decline, which harms them and benefits young families.

Yet, as we discuss below, almost all of the data that have become available since the downturn suggest that older families have fared better than young ones both during the recent period of economic and financial weakness as well as during longer periods of greater economic and financial strength. We suggest that the basic intuition in the analysis by Glover and colleagues (2011) is correct as far as it describes economic and financial downturns but that it misses an equally important point about household economic and financial resilience during the ensuing recoveries. A key differentiating factor between young and older families is the overall strength and resilience of young families' income sources and balance sheets.[3] Sharp declines in asset prices affected older families more severely, but many of these families had diversified assets, low or no debt, sufficient liquid assets, and adequate net worth before the crisis. Such families were able to ride out what turned out to be a temporary downturn. Stock prices rose sharply even before the overall economy began its recovery, and although housing markets took longer, they have also bounced back.

Even before the financial crisis and Great Recession, researchers noted that older adults fared relatively well in economic and financial terms in recent years. William Gale and Karen Pence (2006), for example, find that almost all of the increase in household wealth between 1989 and 2001 accrued to older families, which Gale and Pence define as those aged 55 years or older.[4] They attribute most of the wealth accumulation by older families to the changing nature of the families themselves; over time, there have been increases in the likelihood that these families are married, in good health, and headed by someone with a college education. However, their explanations do not exclude the possibility that there is something unusual about older families today; in other words, there may be cohort effects as well as changing demographic characteristics. Indeed, John Sabelhaus (2006, 223), commenting on the Gale and Pence paper, conjectures that a cohort effect may be present: "But in addition to demographic variables that the authors focus on for explaining wealth, some unexplained cohort effects show up in the earnings data. For example, the data show that baby-boomer males have had (holding education constant) lower relative earnings than their fathers." Below we describe new evidence based on Survey of Consumer Finances data that extend through 2010. Those data confirm a positive birth-year cohort effect on earnings and wealth accumulation among families headed by someone who was born in the late 1930s or 1940s (i.e., is currently in their 60s or 70s).

David Love, Michael Palumbo, and Paul Smith (2009) provide a theoretical explanation for why older families may have experienced relatively favorable wealth outcomes over recent decades. They (along with many others) conjecture about the primary reasons that the typical older family spends down its assets more slowly than the rate at which its remaining life expectancy is declining: (1) uncertain longevity, (2) unknown medical expenses, and (3) a bequest motive. They confirm their model's predictions with data from the Health and Retirement Study for the period from 1998 to 2006. The basic mechanism appears to be that many older families simply are more highly motivated to save than are younger families—that is, older families' precautionary-saving and bequest motives are more immediate and salient than are distant saving goals among younger families. It is possible that although young and middle-aged families encountered relatively more economic and financial turbulence in recent years, older families' comparatively calmer circumstances allowed their stronger saving motivation to operate unencumbered. In line with the conclusions of Gale and Pence (2006), Love and colleagues (2009) find that strong returns on financial assets and housing contributed to but were not decisive in the more favorable wealth trajectories for older families. As we show below, the results from Love and associates are also consistent with positive cohort effects on both income and wealth accumulation for families headed by someone born in the two decades or so prior to the baby boom generation.

Homeownership experiences in recent years highlight the important interaction between life cycle financial decision making and the historical period in which a family lives. We show elsewhere that young homeowners were hit particularly hard by the recent housing-centered financial and economic crisis (Emmons and Noeth 2013a). That is, simply by virtue of being at a stage in life that made them particularly vulnerable to a severe crash in the housing market, many young families suffered very large wealth losses. Many older families, by way of contrast, were at a stage in which housing played a secondary role on the asset side of their balance sheets. Older families typically also owed much less debt than did young and middle-aged families, so the leverage-induced loss of wealth was much less severe for older families.

Jesse Bricker and associates (2012) examine data from the latest wave of the Survey of Consumer Finances (conducted in 2010). Released in mid-2013, the data show that, among six mutually exclusive and exhaustive age groups, only the two oldest groups—including families headed by someone aged 65–74 years and those headed by someone aged 75 years or older—had higher median inflation-adjusted incomes in 2010 than in 2007. Although every age group in the population had lower inflation-adjusted net worth in 2010 than in 2007, the declines in the medians for the two oldest age groups were, by a clear margin, the smallest.

■ DISTRIBUTIONS OF FAMILY INCOME AND WEALTH ACROSS THE LIFE COURSE

Because we need to know the entire distribution of a particular statistic to calculate a median (fiftieth percentile) or any other percentile, we cannot go beyond 2010 for those measures. The next wave of data from the Survey of Consumer Finances was collected in 2013, and results will be available in 2015. However, we can estimate the mean net worth of disaggregated groups by tracking aggregate financial asset and liability categories as well as demographic developments such as household growth and population change by age group. With such data, we estimate how those overall changes affected subgroups by estimating group-specific balance sheets.[5]

Mean Wealth by Age Group

Due to the limited size of the sample and our desire to gauge broad trends accurately, our estimates of mean net worth consider only one older age group, which consists of all families headed by someone aged 62 years or older. Figure 1.1 shows the mean net worth of three age groups at 3-year intervals

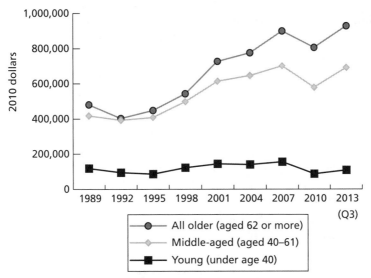

Figure 1.1 Mean Family Net Worth by Age Group (First Quarter 2013 Estimated).
Sources: Federal Reserve Board, Bureau of Labor Statistics. Estimates for the first quarter of 2013 are based on data from the following sources and our own assumptions: Federal Reserve Board, Survey of Consumer Finances; Federal Reserve Board, Financial Accounts of the United States (formerly the Flow of Funds Accounts); Federal Reserve Bank of New York, Equifax Consumer-Credit Panel; Bureau of the Census, Current Housing Reports; Bureau of the Census, Current Population Survey; Bureau of Labor Statistics, Consumer Price Index, Research Series.

between 1989 and 2013. The figure uses our balance sheet estimates for the first quarter of 2013. The mean net worth of older families exceeds that of middle-aged and young families in every year. The strong upward trajectories of average net worth for middle-aged and especially older families stand in stark contrast to the long-term stagnation of average wealth among young families. Between 1989 and 2013, the ratio of middle-aged and older families' average wealth to the average wealth of a young family grew from about four times to between six and nine times, respectively.

The average decline in wealth between 2007 and 2010 was much greater for young families: it was down about 44%, compared to average losses of about 17% and 10%, respectively, for middle-aged and older families. However, the estimated 2010–2013 recovery has been comparable across age groups: there was an average gain of almost 10% for young families and gains of about 9% for both middle-aged and older families.

The severe recent downturn in mean wealth amplified a longer-term trend, seen for at least two decades, toward dispersion of wealth according to age (Figure 1.2). Although we estimate that the average wealth of a young family was about 19% lower in 2013 than it was in 1989, we find that, after adjusting for inflation, the comparable figures for middle-aged and older families are 51% and 82% higher, respectively. In other words, the ratio of average wealth of middle-aged families to that of younger families increased from 3.5 to 6.6 between 1989 and

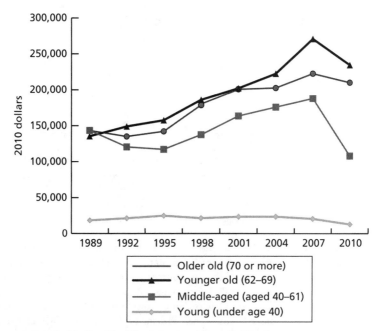

Figure 1.2 Family Median Net Worth by Age of Family Head.
Sources: Federal Reserve Board, Bureau of Labor Statistics.

2013. During the same period, the ratio of the average wealth of an older family to that of a young family increased from 4.1 to 9.2.

Income and Wealth Trends at the Median (Fiftieth Percentile) of Their Distributions

Trends in median family income and wealth have been similar to those evident in mean measures. The median pretax income among all families surveyed by the Federal Reserve in 2010 ($45,743) was about 7.7% lower than the corresponding 2007 median ($49,561; both expressed in terms of 2010 purchasing power). But as shown in Table 1.1, the median family income among younger-old families (family head aged 62–69 years) was about 12.3% *higher* in 2010 than it was in 2007. The median income among older-old families (family head aged 70 years or older) was about 15.6% higher in 2010 than it was 3 years earlier. The median incomes among young (under 40 years) and middle-aged (ages 40–61 years) families, by way of contrast, were each about 12% lower in 2010.

The contrast is even starker over a 21-year period (chosen to reflect the maximum span of survey data available; Figure 1.3). Although the median family incomes among both young and middle-aged families were slightly lower in 2010 (in inflation-adjusted terms) than in 1989, the median incomes among both the younger-old and the older-old were substantially higher: 60.5% and 27.9%, respectively.

Table 1.2 shows that the same basic age-related patterns are also evident for inflation-adjusted net worth. The median wealth of all families was about 39.2% lower in 2010 ($77,000) than in 2007 ($126,539). Among families headed by adults in the younger-old and the older-old categories, wealth was a bit lower in 2010 than in 2007 (about 13.8% and 5.8%, respectively). However, these declines were significantly less than those suffered by the median young and middle-aged families: about 37.6% and 42.9%, respectively.

Comparing each age group's median net worth in 2010 with its level in 1989, we find that the younger-old and older-old wealth levels were respectively 74.0%

TABLE 1.1. *Median Inflation-Adjusted Family Income by Age Group*

Age of family head	Median family income ($)[a]			Difference in respective medians (%)	
	1989	2007	2010	1989–2010	2007–2010
All ages	43,985	49,561	45,743	4.0	−7.7
Young (under age 40)	42,226	45,251	39,644	−6.1	−12.4
Middle-aged (ages 40–61)	58,061	64,644	56,924	−2.0	−11.9
Younger-old (ages 62–69)	31,669	45,251	50,825	60.5	12.3
Older-old (ages 70 and older)	24,632	27,258	31,512	27.9	15.6

Source: Federal Reserve Board, Survey of Consumer Finances.
[a]Figures in 2010 dollars, deflated by the Consumer Price Index Research Series Using Current Methods.

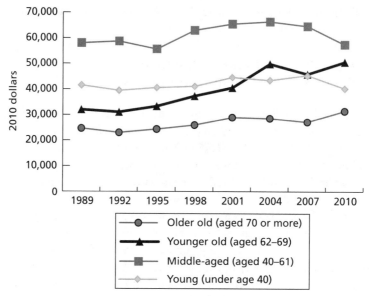

Figure 1.3 Median Family Income by Age of Family Head.
Sources: Federal Reserve Board, Bureau of Labor Statistics.

and 47.7% *higher* in the latter year. Among young and middle-aged families, the median levels of net worth were, respectively, 30.5% and 24.1% *lower* in 2010 than in 1989. In terms of the absolute levels of wealth, the median younger-old family and the median older-old family each had slightly less wealth in 1989 than that of the median middle-aged family. By 2010, the median wealth of both older age groups was more than twice as large as the median wealth of a middle-aged family and close to 20 times as large as the median wealth of a young family.

The striking divergence between the economic and financial fortunes of the median family in different age groups probably is due to several factors. Perhaps

TABLE 1.2. *Median Inflation-Adjusted Net Worth by Age Group*

Age of family head	Median family net worth ($)[a]			Difference in respective medians (%)	
	1989	2007	2010	1989–2010	2007–2010
All ages	79,374	126,539	77,000	−3.0	−39.2
Young (under age 40)	18,553	20,671	12,900	−30.5	−37.6
Middle-aged (ages 40–61)	142,353	189,148	108,00	−24.1	−42.9
Younger-old (ages 62–69)	134,493	271,507	234,000	74.0	−13.8
Older-old (70 and older)	141,678	222,108	209,290	47.7	−5.8

Source: Federal Reserve Board, Survey of Consumer Finances.
[a]Figures in 2010 dollars, deflated by the Consumer Price Index Research Series Using Current Methods.

most important during the recent financial crisis and recession are employment, access to income, and access to health insurance: older families generally had lower exposure to job loss, more stable sources of income, and uninterrupted access to health insurance. The median share of income derived from wages or business or farm returns in 2007 was 55% among younger-old families and only 24% among older-old families. The share was 94% among young families and 86% among middle-aged ones.

Older families' balance sheets also were less concentrated in housing and showed lower levels of debt.[6] Among all older homeowners (aged 62 years or more), housing accounted for 35% of total assets.[7] Middle-aged homeowners (representing 75% of all middle-aged families) held 40% of their assets in housing, but younger homeowner families (accounting for 48% of younger families) had 59% of their assets in housing. Meanwhile, older families owed very little debt, so the loss-amplifying effect of leverage was much smaller among them than among middle-aged and younger families. In 2007, for example, 91% of younger homeowner families and 82% of middle-aged homeowner families had mortgage debt, but only 57% of younger-old homeowner families and 26% of older-old homeowner families had such debt. Moreover, the rebound in financial markets from their low point in 2009 has bolstered the wealth of many older families. On average, these families hold higher levels of stocks and bonds in their portfolios than do younger families.[8]

In sum, the typical older family fared much better in terms of both income and wealth than did the typical young or middle-aged family over both a short-term horizon and a long-term one. The recent experience therefore accentuates long-term trends of stronger income and wealth growth among older families than among young and middle-aged families.

Income and Wealth Trends at the Twentieth Percentile of Their Distributions

To better understand the changing distributions of income and wealth across families in various age groups, we investigate trends over time in family income and family wealth measured at the twentieth percentile of each distribution.[9] To provide additional clarity, we break the sample into two groups according to the race or ethnicity of the family head.

We caution the reader to remember throughout this discussion that comparisons at the twentieth, fiftieth (median), or any other percentile refer to changes over time in particular points in statistical distributions, not to changes in the situations of individual families. A better way to characterize changes over time, in our view, is to construct quasipanels of households (see discussion below). This involves following groups of families identified by demographic characteristics (including age, educational attainment, and race or ethnicity); we use medians and means to describe the statistical characteristics of those groups over time.

TABLE 1.3. *Inflation-Adjusted Family Income by Age Group at the Twentieth Percentile of the Distribution*

Age of family head	Family income ($)[a]			Difference in values (%)	
	1989	2007	2010	1989–2010	2007–2010
All families					
All ages	17,594	21,548	20,330	15.6	−5.7
Whites and Asians					
All ages	21,113	23,703	23,380	10.7	−1.4
Young (under age 40)	21,113	26,935	21,143	.1	−21.5
Middle-aged (ages 40–61)	36,596	32,322	29,275	−20.0	−9.4
Younger-old (ages 62–69)	17,594	23,487	24,599	39.8	4.7
Older-old (ages 70 and older)	14,075	15,084	17,281	22.8	14.6
African Americans and Hispanics of any race					
All ages	8,797	15,084	15,248	73.3	1.1
Young (under age 40)	10,556	15,084	15,248	44.4	1.1
Middle-aged (ages 40–61)	9,149	19,178	18,297	100.0	−4.6
Younger-old (ages 62–69)	7,038	15,946	16,264	131.1	2.0
Older-old (age 70 and older)	7,038	8,425	11,995	70.4	42.4

Source: Federal Reserve Board, Survey of Consumer Finances.
[a]Figures in 2010 dollars, deflated by the Consumer Price Index Research Series Using Current Methods.

Another approach is to track birth-year cohorts over time (see the cohort analysis below). Nonetheless, changes in points within the income and wealth distributions are of some interest in and of themselves given the widespread discussion of issues related to growing income and wealth inequality within the entire population.

Table 1.3 displays family income measured at the twentieth percentile of the distribution of all families and the twentieth percentile of income for families grouped by race or ethnicity in each of the four age ranges we consider. Among white or Asian families that rank at the twentieth percentile in a given year, the strongest increases in family income over both short and long horizons accrued to older families, although the older-old family at the twentieth percentile of the income distribution remained the poorest among the four age groups considered here. Among African American or Hispanic families that rank at the twentieth percentile in a given year, the two older age groups (younger-old, older-old) again experienced relatively strong increases over both short and long horizons.

In an analogous way, Table 1.4 shows net worth at the twentieth percentile of its distribution. Families are again grouped on the demographic dimensions of race or ethnicity and age. Although almost all low-wealth groups lost wealth between 2007 and 2010, the smallest percentage losses among whites and Asians were among older families. Over the 1989–2010 horizon, the two older groups of whites and Asians experienced significant increases whereas the young and middle-aged groups suffered enormous losses. Among African American and Hispanic families at the twentieth percentile in all age groups, wealth was

TABLE 1.4. *Inflation-Adjusted Net Worth by Age Group at the Twentieth Percentile of the Distribution*

Age of family head	Family net worth ($)[a]			Difference in values (%)	
	1989	2007	2010	1989–2010	2007–2010
All families					
All ages	3,711	7,680	4,300	15.9	−44.0
Whites and Asians					
All ages	13,325	16,491	8,800	−34.0	−46.6
Young (under age 40)	1,741	2,079	−570	−132.7	−127.4
Middle-aged (ages 40–61)	47,459	40,711	18,376	−61.3	−54.9
Younger-old (ages 62–69)	43,516	71,684	54,004	24.1	−24.7
Older-old (age 70 and older)	43,381	69,673	60,848	40.3	−12.7
African Americans and Hispanics of any race					
All ages	—	221	—	NM	−100.0
Young (under age 40)	−128	—	−236	NM	NM
Middle-aged (ages 40–61)	—	1,619	890	NM	−45.0
Younger-old (ages 62–69)	—	5,810	6,972	NM	20.0
Older-old (age 70 and older)	877	3,357	830	−5.4	−75.3

Source: Federal Reserve Board, Survey of Consumer Finances.
Note: NM indicates that the difference is not meaningful.
[a]Figures in 2010 dollars, deflated by the Consumer Price Index Research Series.

extremely low in all years. The only encouraging development was a 20% increase between 2007 and 2010 in the wealth of poor African American and Hispanic families headed by someone aged 62–69 years.

Qualitatively, the patterns observed among relatively low-income and low-wealth families (Tables 1.3 and 1.4) are very similar to those identified at the medians of the overall income and wealth distributions.[10] In particular, income peaks in middle age; net worth peaks in the younger-old age group; income growth and net worth changes between 2007 and 2010 generally were more favorable for the older groups than for the middle-aged and young groups. Long-run changes in family income and net worth (1989–2010) were strongest among the older groups, especially the younger-old. Furthermore, cumulative income and wealth changes between 1989 and 2010 were positive and significant for almost all older groups, but cumulative changes were essentially zero or negative more often than not among the young and middle-aged groups. In sum, the income and wealth trends during both the recent downturn and over a longer horizon generally favored older age groups, even when the twentieth percentiles of their respective distributions are considered.

■ TRENDS IN MEDIAN FAMILY INCOME AND WEALTH GROUPED BY AGE, RACE OR ETHNICITY, AND EDUCATIONAL ATTAINMENT

Age and race or ethnicity of the family head are powerful predictors of income and wealth. Educational attainment is another important and relatively stable determinant. Attainment is stable in the sense that, once determined early in life, a person's educational attainment rarely if ever changes subsequently; it is also stable in the sense that higher levels of educational attainment are consistently associated over time with higher levels of income and wealth.

As we mentioned above, a previous study used age, educational attainment, and race or ethnicity of the family head to create a set of mutually exclusive groups of families in a quasipanel framework (Emmons and Noeth 2013d). This enabled us to explore the economic and financial diversity of the population over time. We classified each family in each survey year according to its age (young, middle-aged, younger-old, or older-old), educational attainment (less than high school, high school graduate, 2-year college graduate, or 4-year college graduate), and race or ethnicity (white or Asian vs. African American or Hispanic). This resulted in 24 unique groups. Unsurprisingly, we found great differences in the levels of income and wealth across disaggregated groups of families. We also found considerable differences in how the financial crisis and recession affected the families.

Across the entire population, real median family income declined substantially between 2007 and 2010: 7.7% (Table 1.1). Yet, almost half of the demographically defined groups identified in Emmons and Noeth (2013d)—11 of 24—experienced an increase in median incomes between 2007 and 2010, despite the overall decline. Over the longer 1989–2010 span, the median family income increased by 4.0%. Nonetheless, almost half of the groups—10 of 24—experienced a decline during this period. Thus, it is important to isolate key demographic determinants of income trends.

Across the groups with different education levels, races, and ethnicities, the likelihood of a decline in median income was just about equal over both short-term (2007–2010) and long-term (1989–2010) periods. What stands out is that the older groups, regardless of education, race, or ethnicity, were much less likely to experience declines in median incomes than were young and middle-aged groups. In particular, 10 of the 12 young or middle-aged groups had lower median incomes in 2010 than in 2007, but only three of 12 older groups had declines.[11] Over the longer period, seven of 12 young or middle-aged groups experienced declines but only three of 12 older groups experienced them.

Across the entire population and among most families sorted by the single dimensions of age, education, and race, median and mean net worth also declined between 2007 and 2010. In documenting trends in median family net worth across their 24 groups, we found that age, like median family income, is the dominant factor associated with increased dispersion of wealth over time (Emmons and Noeth 2013d).

■ COHORT ANALYSIS

To this point, we have focused on the economic and financial conditions of families in fixed age groups—the young, middle-aged, younger-old, and older-old—and discussed patterns observed across eight waves of the Survey of Consumer Finances. The fixed age group (or life cycle) framework highlights effects that operate on all or most families in a certain age range, whenever they reach it. The underlying assumption is that the stage of life itself is more important than a family's experiences before it reached that age.

Cohort analysis is an alternative analytical framework. Through it, we can consider the possibility that certain groups of families born at one point in time may experience a life cycle stage differently than other groups born in different years. By following through time various cohorts of families defined by their (i.e., the family head's) year of birth, we may be able to identify unique aspects of their life courses that are not strictly life cycle regularities.

Regression analysis helps us sort out and quantify cohort and other factors. We first look for birth-year cohort effects in family income. If they exist, such effects could help explain patterns in wealth accumulation. Table 1.5 contains estimation results from a regression of family income on demographic, idiosyncratic, birth-year-cohort, and time variables. We have over 35,000 observations across the eight survey waves, and the fit of the pooled regression model is good. The R^2 is 46%, and estimated levels of statistical significance are high for many coefficients.

We regress the logarithm of family income in a given year on a cubic function of age to control for life cycle effects; on standardized (i.e., demeaned by demographic profile) measures of marital status, family size, saving behavior, and health status to isolate idiosyncratic factors potentially important for wealth accumulation; on education and race or ethnicity indicators to capture the effects of human capital and potential legacies of discrimination, respectively; on year dummies to capture time effects during the year of observation; and, of primary interest, on a large set of birth-year cohort indicator variables.

We construct 5-year cohorts, beginning with families born between 1893 and 1897. We refer to this as the 1895 cohort. We compare each successive 5-year cohort (through 1990) to the 1940 cohort. The indicator for that cohort is omitted because it is near the middle of the sample of birth years. We also omit it because it turns out to be a good example of families that were born at a particular time and encountered an unusually favorable cohort effect.

Estimates of the coefficients on demographic and idiosyncratic variables are reported in Table 1.5. In general, the estimates are highly significant with the expected signs. Family income rises with the age of the family head, but it grows at a decreasing rate. Idiosyncratic factors reliably associated with family income increases include being married, having more children than average, saving money regularly, and enjoying above-average health. Higher levels of educational attainment are very strongly predictive of higher income, as is being white. If all other factors are held constant, being African American predicts lower income and there is no reliably estimated distinction between the family incomes of Hispanics of any race and the incomes of Asians (the excluded category).

TABLE 1.5. *Pooled Regression of Logarithm of Family Income on Demographic, Idiosyncratic, Birth-Year Cohort, and Time Variables*

Variable	Beta	T-Statistic
Intercept	7.432***	25.12
Age in years	.170***	13.17
Age squared	−.002***	−8.61
Age cubed	.000***	4.64
Standardized marital status	.458***	67.16
Standardized number of children	.060***	8.97
Standardized saving indicator	.198***	28.64
Standardized health status	.491***	30.19
High school dropout indicator	−1.419***	−60.71
High school graduate or GED indicator	−1.037***	−62.65
Some college indicator	−.697***	−35.96
College graduate (omitted)		
White indicator	.282***	8.27
African American or black indicator	−.165***	−4.18
Hispanic of any race indicator	−.043	−1.02
Asian or other (omitted)		
Birth year 1893–1897 indicator	−.131	−.20
Birth year 1898–1902 indicator	.022	.08
Birth year 1903–1907 indicator	−.080	−.41
Birth year 1908–1912 indicator	−.329**	−2.13
Birth year 1913–1917 indicator	−.219*	−1.72
Birth year 1918–1922 indicator	−.189*	−1.85
Birth year 1923–1927 indicator	−.136*	−1.73
Birth year 1928–1932 indicator	−.098*	−1.66
Birth year 1933–1937 indicator	−.016	−.39
Birth year 1938–1942 (omitted)		
Birth year 1943–1947 indicator	−.027	−.70
Birth year 1948–1952 indicator	−.185***	−3.39
Birth year 1953–1957 indicator	−.162**	−2.18
Birth year 1958–1962 indicator	−.195**	−2.04
Birth year 1963–1967 indicator	−.226*	−1.92
Birth year 1968–1972 indicator	−.271*	−1.94
Birth year 1973–1977 indicator	−.192	−1.18
Birth year 1978–1982 indicator	−.179	−.97
Birth year 1983–1987 indicator	−.214	−1.02
Birth year 1988–1992 indicator	−.224	−.91
Year 1989 (omitted)		
Year 1992 indicator	−.034	−1.05
Year 1995 indicator	−.027	−.67
Year 1998 indicator	.019	.39
Year 2001 indicator	.148**	2.42
Year 2004 indicator	.177**	2.42
Year 2007 indicator	.266***	3.10
Year 2010 indicator	−.091	−.92
R^2 of first regression	.46	
Observations	35,245	

Note: GED = general equivalency diploma. The dependent variable is the logarithm of the inflation-adjusted family income in year t, excluding all nonpositive observations. Sample years are 1989, 1992, 1995, 1998, 2001, 2004, 2007, and 2010. Coefficients are expressed as decimal fractions; for example, the value −.195 for birth year 1958–1962 indicator means negative 19.5%.
*$p < .10$; **$p < .05$; ***$p < .01$.

Time dummies for the 1989–2010 sample dates generally are not significant, although income was statistically significantly higher in 2007 than in 1989. Estimates from models that hold all else constant indicate that inflation-adjusted family income was significantly lower in 2010 than in 1989. This reflects the very severe recent recession.

Figure 1.4 shows the marginal effect of birth cohort on a family's inflation-adjusted income.[12] If, after controlling for a host of other factors, there were no birth-year cohort effects determining family income, all of the parameter estimates would be statistically indistinguishable from zero. Coefficient estimates that are statistically significantly different from zero at the 10% level are shown as solid bars; those that are not statistically sufficient are open.

The birth-year cohort variables show that, if other factors are taken into account, families born in the 5 years centered in 1940 (the reference group) do not differ to a statistically significant degree from those born during the 1895, 1900, or 1905 cohorts. It may be that there are cohort effects but that the small number of sample members born before 1908 leads to imprecise estimates; or there may be no such effects. Survivorship bias may also be important, because those born before 1908 and still alive at the time of the surveys may not be representative of the entire original cohort to which they belong. In particular, they may be relatively better off in terms of health, education, lifetime earnings, and wealth.

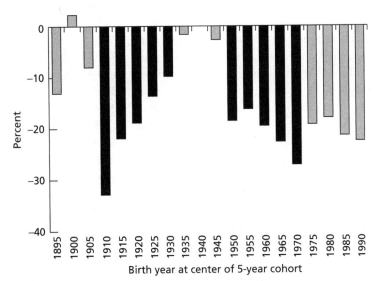

Figure 1.4 Effect of Family Head's Birth Year on Family Income Relative to Being Born in the Period 1938–1942.
Source: Federal Reserve Board.
Note: Coefficients represent the estimated difference (percentage) in income between a family in a 5-year birth-year cohort centered around the given year and the cohort of families with heads born in the 5-year cohort centered around 1940. Solid bars are statistically different from zero at the 10% confidence level.

The cohorts with family heads born between 1910 and 1930, however, have statistically significantly lower incomes than those of families with heads born in the 1940 cohort. The differences persist even after analysis controls for a number of demographic, idiosyncratic, and time effects. The estimated magnitudes of difference—increasing monotonically from a 33% lower level among the 1910 cohort to a 10% lower level among the 1930 cohort—are consistent with a generally rising level of family income across successive birth-year cohorts: levels of income rose with overall standards of living. This alone might help explain higher wealth among later-born generations. We investigate this possibility below.

In terms of family income (see Table 1.5), families headed by someone born in the 1935, 1940, or 1945 cohort (i.e., between 1933 and 1947) are statistically indistinguishable from each other. However, an analysis with controls for many important factors suggests that, beginning with the 1950 cohort (i.e., families headed by someone born between 1948 and 1952), successive cohorts through 1970 (born between 1968 and 1972) had statistically significantly *lower* incomes than those of the 1940 cohort, and the estimated magnitudes are economically significant: between 16% and 27% lower than that for the 1940 cohort. Moreover, all 5-year cohorts that began in 1975 or later had estimated income shortfalls of about 20%; however, these effects were not measured precisely. The fading of a negative cohort effect after 1970 may be due to a true diminution of the effect, or it may be due to relatively small sample sizes and high variability among younger families' incomes.

The cohort effects in family income are striking (Table 1.5). Beginning with the 1910 cohort, incomes rose strongly and consistently. The estimates show that this continued through about the 1935 cohort, and the result persists even after the analysis holds constant a number of key income determinants such as age, education, race, or ethnicity, as well as idiosyncratic factors such as family structure, saving behavior, and health status. Incomes are similar among the 1935, 1940, and 1945 cohorts but drop abruptly beginning with the 1950 cohort. There is strong evidence that income in all cohorts between 1950 and 1970 (i.e., heads born between 1948 and 1972; approximately the baby boom era) fell short by 16–27% of the 1940 cohort's income. There is suggestive evidence that the shortfall has continued through at least the 1990 cohort, but more data and time are needed before we can know for sure.

Given the evidence that there are important cohort effects in family income (Table 1.5 and Figure 1.4)—income strongly increases for successive cohorts between 1910 and 1930, little changed between the 1935 and 1945 cohorts, and income fell significantly lower for the cohorts between 1950 and at least 1970—it would not be surprising to find similar effects in family wealth. After all, unusually high incomes for the 1935, 1940, and 1945 cohorts might have supported higher saving rates than those observed among earlier- and later-born cohorts.

Emmons and Noeth (2013d) report the results of two model specifications that provide strong evidence of cohort effects that lifted the wealth of families born in the 1930s and 1940s above the wealth of families born before or after. Those specifications hold constant many factors that determine wealth. A logarithmic specification corresponds closely to the model of income reported in Table 1.5 but requires us to drop all observations that include zero or negative values of net worth. In other words, the specification requires that we drop about 8.5% of all family-year observations. These families are more likely to be young or middle-aged than younger-old or older-old, so eliminating them may reduce our ability to measure wealth accumulation accurately among baby boomers and generation Xers.

An alternative transformation of net worth—the inverse hyperbolic sine (IHS) function—allows us to include zero or negative wealth observations while retaining an interpretation of results that is similar to the interpretation of results in the log model.[13] The model estimated with the IHS transformation of net worth includes 3,013 more observations than the log model and captures information contained in the observations of families with zero or negative reported net worth.

We applied the Halvorsen–Palmquist transformation to coefficient estimates of indicator variables and report the results in Table 1.6, which presents estimates for a set of independent variables that is identical to the set used in the log of income specification (Table 1.5). Figure 1.5 illustrates our estimates of the birth-year cohort's marginal effects on a family's wealth. The analysis holds demographic, idiosyncratic, and time effects constant. The solid bars in the figure represent effects that are statistically significant at the 10% level, and the open bars represent effects that are not significant.

The IHS model in Table 1.5 improves the model's overall fit relative to the log specification, raising the R^2 slightly (Emmons and Noeth 2013d). More importantly, it provides much stronger evidence for significant birth-year cohort effects in wealth accumulation than the log specification did.

If anything, we now find even stronger birth-year cohort effects on family wealth than on income during the first third of the twentieth century. If all else is held constant, the wealth of families in the 1905, 1910, and 1915 cohorts is estimated to be 43–46% lower than that of families in the 1940 cohort. The largest cohort effect on income—observed in the 1910 cohort—was only –33% (see Table 1.5). We find that cohorts from 1910 through 1935 enjoy successively lower shortfalls in wealth, although even the 1935 cohort has about 10% lower wealth than does the 1940 cohort. Recall that we found no statistical difference between the 1935 and 1940 cohorts in the income regression.

We cannot distinguish between the wealth of the 1940 and 1945 cohorts, as was true of income for those cohorts. Moreover, the IHS wealth specification also fails to distinguish the 1940 cohort from the 1950, 1955, and 1960 cohorts. The latter three cohorts are found to have statistically significantly lower income than

TABLE 1.6. *Pooled Regression of Transformed Net Worth on Demographic, Idiosyncratic, Birth-Year Cohort, and Time Variables*

Variable	Beta	T-Statistic
Intercept	9,211.16**	2.17
Standardized square root income (by demographic)	10,302.76***	96.52
Age in years	209.93	1.13
Age squared	19.55***	5.78
Age cubed	(.18)***	−8.69
Standardized marital status	3,835.15***	38.84
Standardized number of children	828.88***	8.75
Standardized saving indicator	2,937.74***	29.02
Standardized health status	5,972.67***	26.39
High school dropout indicator	−.901***	−70.02
High school graduate or GED indicator	−.791***	−65.22
Some college indicator	−.736***	−49.23
College graduate (omitted)		
White indicator	.313***	5.72
African American or black indicator	−.585***	−15.83
Hispanic of any race indicator	−.494***	−11.38
Asian or other (omitted)		
Birth year 1893–1897 indicator	.032	.03
Birth year 1898–1902 indicator	−.097	−.25
Birth year 1903–1907 indicator	−.451**	−2.15
Birth year 1908–1912 indicator	−.463***	−2.86
Birth year 1913–1917 indicator	−.428***	−3.14
Birth year 1918–1922 indicator	−.327***	−2.75
Birth year 1923–1927 indicator	−.295***	−3.15
Birth year 1928–1932 indicator	−.198***	−2.66
Birth year 1933–1937 indicator	−.098*	−1.77
Birth year 1938–1942 (omitted)		
Birth year 1943–1947 indicator	.004	.07
Birth year 1948–1952 indicator	−.103	−1.41
Birth year 1953–1957 indicator	−.123	−1.25
Birth year 1958–1962 indicator	−.175	−1.43
Birth year 1963–1967 indicator	−.282**	−2.01
Birth year 1968–1972 indicator	−.428***	−2.83
Birth year 1973–1977 indicator	−.408**	−2.29
Birth year 1978–1982 indicator	−.395*	−1.92
Birth year 1983–1987 indicator	−.263	−1.02
Birth year 1988–1992 indicator	.953*	1.93
Year 1989 (omitted)		
Year 1992 indicator	−.017	−.38
Year 1995 indicator	.024	.41
Year 1998 indicator	.009	.13
Year 2001 indicator	.176*	1.86
Year 2004 indicator	.140	1.25
Year 2007 indicator	.282**	2.03
Year 2010 indicator	−.392***	−3.56
R^2 of first regression	.642	
Observations	35,514	
Scaling parameter, theta	.0001	

Note: GED = general equivalency diploma. The dependent variable is the inflation-adjusted net worth after application of the inverse hyperbolic-sine transformation: ASINH (Net Worth × Theta)/Theta, where Theta = .0001. Estimates shown for coefficients for indicator variables are expressed after application of the Halvorsen–Palmquist transformation (100 × [exp(theta × beta) − 1]). The interpretation of coefficients for indicator variables is analogous to the log specification; for example, the value −.175 for the birth-year 1958–1962 indicator means negative 17.5%.
*$p < .10$; **$p < .05$; ***$p < .01$.

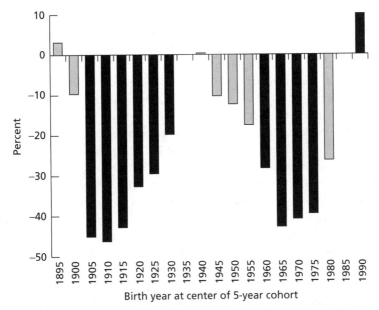

Figure 1.5 Effect of Family Head's Birth Year on Family Wealth Relative to Being Born in the Period 1938–1942.

Source: Federal Reserve Board.

Note: Coefficients represent the estimated difference (percentage) in wealth between a family in a 5-year birth-year cohort centered around the given year and the cohort of families with heads born in the 5-year cohort centered around 1940. The coefficients are transformed as suggested by Halvorsen and Palmquist (1980). Solid bars are statistically different from zero at the 10% level.

that of the 1940 cohort. Nonetheless, if all else is held constant, the 1950, 1955, and 1960 cohorts are estimated (albeit imprecisely) to have between 10% and 18% lower wealth.

The IHS specification looks much more like the income results for baby boomers and generation Xers. The estimated wealth shortfall for families in the 1970, 1975, and 1980 cohorts is about 40%—roughly twice the estimated income shortfall. The very large and significant positive wealth effect for the 1990 cohort is striking, but must be taken with a grain of salt, because these individuals and families are few in number and were observed only at very young ages in the most recent surveys.

Our regression results strongly support the hypothesis that levels of income and wealth rose during the first several decades of the twentieth century, but the increases came to an end at some time around mid-century. The analysis that produced these results holds constant demographic characteristics such as health status and educational attainment. One possible explanation is that the arrival of the baby boomers somehow disrupted the rise of living standards in ways that affected given demographic characteristics. Another possibility is that the ends of the Great Depression and World War II were associated with social, political, and economic changes that favored generations born before the baby boomers. We speculate only on underlying causes here and leave deeper investigations for future research.

An obvious place to start is with relative cohort sizes. The idea is that relatively small cohorts may have attracted scarcity premiums in labor, housing, and financial markets whereas relatively large cohorts paid crowding penalties in those markets.[14] Figure 1.6 displays the number of babies (under 1 year old) in the United States between 1896 and 2015 (numbers for latter years are derived from U.S. Census Bureau projections). The striking 20% decline in the number of infants between 1925 and 1937 likely reflects the massive disruption of the Great Depression as well as the slowdown in the population's natural growth rate after earlier high immigration rates declined. The infant population began to rise again in the late 1930s, but it was not until 1945 that the size of this population reached the level of 20 years earlier. Thus, these very small birth-year cohorts may have been favored later in life in a variety of ways, including relatively higher earnings, lower house prices, and stronger growth in financial-asset prices. Sociologist Elwood Carlson (2008) called the generation born between 1929 and 1945 "the lucky few" precisely because it was the first American generation to be smaller in number than those that came before. Carlson argued that African Americans and women born in those years also enjoyed historically unprecedented opportunities throughout their adult lives. Members of previous generations missed such opportunities, and they had less of an impact on later-born cohorts.

The infant population recovered during the baby boom that began in the 1940s. Peaking in the early 1960s, the infant population doubled in little more

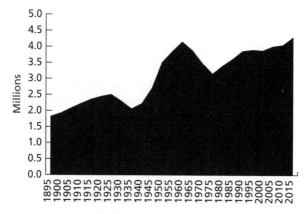

Figure 1.6 Estimated Number of Children Under 1 Year Old.
Source: Census Bureau and authors' own estimates.

than two decades. Given trends in births both before and after, the baby boom now appears to have been an historical aberration rather than a return to an old trend or transition to a new one. Indeed, the so-called baby bust that commenced in the early 1960s appears to have taken the infant population back toward its new long-term trend. Hence, it is plausible that baby boomers may have suffered from crowding in labor, housing, and financial markets (Easterlin 1987). This may have resulted in unfavorable developments in income and wealth accumulation.

Another possible set of explanations of the apparent end of rising levels of income and wealth for a given set of demographic factors relates to changes in economic growth and social policies. Post–World War II economic growth was very rapid, and the value of housing and financial assets increased strongly. Rather than attracting any special advantages related to their absolute numbers, people born in the first half of the twentieth century simply may have been in the right place at the right time. A related channel of causation is the postwar expansion of the safety net, especially for retired people. The steadily increasing generosity of Social Security, the creation of Medicare in the 1960s, and 40 years later, the significant expansion of Medicare in the prescription drug benefit greatly increased the resources directed to adults reaching retirement age in the 1990s and 2000s.

Will the favorable income and wealth trends observed among today's older adults resume at some point? We cannot know for sure, but it appears unlikely to us that baby boomers—who are just now entering retirement in large numbers—will accrue the same incomes and wealth that pre–baby boomers received for given demographic characteristics. First, the baby boomers already have significantly lower demographically adjusted incomes and wealth, as we document above. There is little time to make up these shortfalls and little reason to believe that social policies will change to assist these adults. Second, reductions in redistribution toward older adults appear to be more likely than increases to make up any putative shortfall.

As for cohorts born after the baby boomers, our evidence points to very little change from the trends experienced by the boomers. That is, we would not expect a significant increase in the level of income or wealth for a given set of demographic characteristics. Only the passage of time and the accumulation of more data will allow us to be more confident about our predictions.

■ CONCLUSIONS

During the recent financial crisis and recession, and over a two-decade span reaching back to 1989, the income and wealth of the typical older adult generally have held up better than those of young and middle-aged families. The same is true of families at the respective twentieth percentiles of the distributions of income and wealth when those families are grouped by race or ethnicity and age. One important factor appears to be that, both recently and in previous downturns, older families are less susceptible to economic and financial turbulence. Older families rely more heavily on stable sources of income such as Social Security and pension wealth. In addition, their balance sheets are less risky because of greater asset diversification, less leverage, and more liquid-asset holdings. These factors underlie the greater resilience of older adults.

Another important factor underlying the favorable income and wealth trends observed currently among adults in older age ranges appears to be significantly increasing birth-year cohort effects for people born in the first half of the twentieth century. This means that, among families that were born in that period and shared a given set of demographic characteristics, such as educational attainment and health status, income and wealth were higher the later the family head was born. After about 1950, however, families actually received lower incomes and accumulated less wealth for a given set of demographic characteristics. For reasons we do not fully understand, there is little evidence that this deterioration has ended, let alone reversed itself.

■ NOTES

The views expressed here are those of the authors alone and do not necessarily represent those of the Federal Reserve Bank of St. Louis or the Federal Reserve System.

1. See Bricker et al. (2012) and Emmons and Noeth (2012) for detailed discussions of the Survey of Consumer Finances and recent income and wealth trends revealed by the survey.

2. The Financial Accounts of the United States were formerly known as the Flow of Funds Accounts.

3. Boshara and Emmons (2013) document important age-related differences in balance-sheet composition.

4. As we describe below, we find essentially the same outcome for the 2001–2010 period. That is, older families' wealth gains accounted for essentially all of the net increase in overall wealth in the nation.

5. See Krimmel et al. (2013) for results from a similar exercise using a somewhat different approach.

6. Emmons and Noeth (2013a, 2013b) and Boshara and Emmons (2013) document significant age-related differences in typical family balance sheets.

7. About 85% of younger-old families in the survey were homeowners in 2007, as were 80% of surveyed older-old families.

8. Emmons and Noeth (2013c) estimate that by late 2012, older families recovered much of the wealth lost during the financial crisis. Because young families have portfolios with very different structures, they did not recover the losses.

9. Emmons and Noeth (2013d) also investigate income and wealth at the eightieth percentiles of their distributions.

10. A notable exception is the wealth of poor African American and Hispanic families. In almost every year and in most age groups, their wealth was extremely low.

11. The 12 older groups include six younger-old and six older-old groups.

12. The analysis holds constant all of the variables described above. The figure plots coefficients reported in Table 1.3.

13. See Pence (2006) and Gale and Pence (2006) for extensive discussion and application of the IHS transformation to balance sheet data.

14. Easterlin (1987) documents the influence of cohort size on economic and social outcomes, with particular emphasis on the baby boom generation.

■ **REFERENCES**

Boshara, Ray, and William R. Emmons. 2013. *After the Fall: Rebuilding Family Balance Sheets, Rebuilding the Economy*. Annual Report 2012, May. St. Louis, MO: Federal Reserve Bank of St. Louis. https://www.stlouisfed.org/publications/ar/2012/pages/ar12_2a.cfm.

Bricker, Jesse, Arthur B. Kennickell, Kevin B. Moore, and John Sabelhaus. 2012. "Changes in U.S. Family Finances from 2007 to 2010: Evidence from the Survey of Consumer Finances." *Federal Reserve Bulletin* 98, no. 2 (June 11). http://www.federalreserve.gov/pubs/bulletin/2012/pdf/scf12.pdf.

Carlson, Elwood. 2008. *The Lucky Few: Between the Greatest Generation and the Baby Boom*. New York: Springer.

Easterlin, Richard A. 1987. *Birth and Fortune: The Impact of Numbers on Personal Welfare*, 2nd ed. Chicago: University of Chicago Press.

Emmons, William R., and Bryan J. Noeth. 2012. "Household Financial Stability: Who Suffered the Most from the Crisis?" *Regional Economist* (Federal Reserve Bank of St. Louis), 20, no. 3 (July): 11–17. http://www.stlouisfed.org/publications/pub_assets/pdf/re/2012/c/financial_stability.pdf.

Emmons, William R., and Bryan J. Noeth. 2013a. "Why Did Young Families Lose So Much Wealth during the Crisis? The Role of Homeownership." *Federal Reserve Bank of St. Louis Review* 95 (1): 1–26. http://research.stlouisfed.org/publications/review/13/01/Emmons.pdf.

Emmons, William R., and Bryan J. Noeth. 2013b. "Economic Vulnerability and Financial Fragility." *Federal Reserve Bank of St. Louis Review* 95 (5): 361–388. http://research.stlouisfed.org/publications/review/13/09/Emmons.pdf.

Emmons, William R., and Bryan J. Noeth. 2013c. *The Nation's Wealth Recovery since 2009 Conceals Vastly Different Balance-Sheet Realities among America's Families*. In the Balance 3. St. Louis, MO: Federal Reserve Bank of St. Louis. http://www.stlouisfed.org/publications/pub_assets/pdf/itb/2013/In-the-Balance-issue-3.pdf.

Emmons, William R., and Bryan J. Noeth. 2013d. "The Economic and Financial Status of Older Americans: Trends and Prospects." Center for Household Financial Stability Working Paper, September. St. Louis, MO: Federal Reserve Bank of St. Louis. http://www.stlouisfed.org/household-financial-stability/assets/Emmons-Noeth-Economic-and-Financial-Status-of-Older-Americans-4-Sept-2013.pdf.

Gale, William G., and Karen M. Pence. 2006. "Are Successive Generations Getting Wealthier, and If So, Why? Evidence from the 1990s." *Brookings Papers on Economic Activity* 2006 (1): 155–234.

Glover, Andrew, Jonathan Heathcote, Dirk Krueger, and José-Víctor Ríos-Rull. 2011. "Intergenerational Redistribution in the Great Recession." Working Paper 684, March. Minneapolis, MN: Federal Reserve Bank of Minneapolis. http://www.minneapolisfed.org/research/wp/wp684.pdf.

Halvorsen, Robert, and Raymond Palmquist. 1980. "The Interpretation of Dummy Variables in Semilogarithmic Equations." *American Economic Review* 70 (3): 474–475. http://www.jstor.org/stable/1805237.

Krimmel, Jacob, Kevin B. Moore, John Sabelhaus, and Paul Smith. 2013. "The Current State of U.S. Household Balance Sheets." *Federal Reserve Bank of St. Louis Review* 95 (5): 337–359. http://research.stlouisfed.org/publications/review/13/09/Krimmel.pdf.

Love, David A., Michael G. Palumbo, and Paul A. Smith. 2009. "The Trajectory of Wealth in Retirement." *Journal of Public Economics* 93 (1–2): 191–208. doi: 10.1016/j.jpubeco.2008.09.003.

Pence, Karen M. 2006. "The Role of Wealth Transformations: An Application to Estimating the Effect of Tax Incentives on Saving." *Contributions to Economic Analysis and Policy* 5 (1): article 20. doi: 10.2202/1538-0645.1430.

Sabelhaus, John. 2006. "Comment on Gale and Pence." *Brookings Papers on Economic Activity* 2006 (1): 220–225.

2 "All That Glitters Is Not Gold"

Social Mobility, Health, and Mental Health among African Americans

■ DARRELL L. HUDSON

Findings from countless research studies have documented the breadth, depth, and prevalence of racial disparities in a variety of socioeconomic, health, and mental health outcomes. Despite findings that tie socioeconomic inequality to these outcomes, there is little understanding of how the outcomes are influenced by socioeconomic mobility. This chapter seeks to expand our understanding of upward socioeconomic mobility among African Americans. After discussing causes of upward mobility and factors that impede it, I consider the benefits, costs, and implications of upward socioeconomic transitions among African Americans.

Health is associated with socioeconomic position (SEP) throughout the life course.[1] Having asthma, mental disorders, and other health problems early in life elevates the risk of low educational attainment (Cohen et al. 2010; Johnson and Schoeni 2011; Tse et al. 2012; Turner and Lloyd 2004). Low educational attainment is in turn strongly associated with low earnings, which are associated with an increased likelihood of experiencing health problems (Breslau et al. 2008; Kawakami et al. 2012). Wealth disparities between African Americans and whites are large, pervasive, and widely documented (Oliver and Shapiro 1995; Shapiro 2004), yet few studies have thoroughly investigated the effects of wealth on health among African Americans. Additionally, chronic exposure to stress, particularly during early life, negatively affects health (Jackson, Knight, and Rafferty 2010; Lynch, Kaplan, and Shema 1997; Mezuk et al. 2010). Thus, although education and income are negatively associated with poor health, high-SEP African Americans may still face lingering effects from health problems experienced early in life (Colen et al. 2006; Hardaway and McLoyd 2009; Pearson 2008). Due to the pronounced lack of wealth within the African American community, most individuals who achieve upward social mobility do so through extensive investments in human capital (Kochhar, Fry, and Taylor 2011; Oliver and Shapiro 1995).

Social mobility has been described as "movement which places an adult person into a social world that significantly differs from the one into which she or he was socialized during childhood" (Sellers 2001, 117). Sherrill Sellers (2001, 122) notes that "mobility takes place over time (as well as space) and involves trajectories such as downward [movement] relative to one's parents." African Americans may pay mental health costs of upward social mobility (Cole and Omari 2003), and stressors such as racial discrimination may diminish their returns on human capital investments, truncating their financial capabilities (Hudson, Bullard, et al. 2012). It is clear that race, mental health, and life course financial capabilities are all tightly woven together. The goal of this chapter is to gain a better understanding of how these factors are interrelated.

■ RACE AND SEP

Black–white health disparities are well documented in the literature, and health studies indicate that, compared to whites, African Americans are at greater risk for myriad, chronic, debilitating, physical-health conditions. So too, rates of premature mortality associated with these conditions and infant mortality rates are higher among African Americans (Adler and Stewart 2010; Braveman and Barclay 2009; Geronimus 1996; Geronimus et al. 1996). Reducing socioeconomic inequities between African Americans and whites is identified as a key factor in reducing health disparities (Phelan, Link, and Tehranifar 2010). However, even in studies that adjust statistically for socio-economic resources, black–white health disparities do not disappear (Pollack et al. 2007; Williams 1999). Thus, understanding of the relationship between SEP and mental health outcomes remains elusive (Gavin et al. 2010; Hudson, Neighbors, et al. 2012).

The average net worth is estimated to be $113,149 for white families and $5,677 for African American families (Kochhar et al. 2011). In other words, African American families possess only 10 cents of wealth for every dollar of it held by white families (Kochhar et al. 2011). Popular assumptions attribute wealth disparities to differences in saving behaviors, conspicuous consumption, and labor compensation (Gordon Nembhard 2006; Keister and Moller 2000; Shapiro 2004), yet these myths have been thoroughly debunked (Conley 1999; Oliver and Shapiro 1995; Shapiro 2004).

There are significant racial disparities in labor compensation, but income inequalities alone do not account for the wealth disparities. Income fluctuates over time and does not always provide an accurate picture of future or past earnings (Keister and Moller 2000; Landry 1987). Research that fails to account for wealth may miss important information about financial capability over the life course (Braveman et al. 2001; Pollack et al. 2007). Even if the levels of education, income, and occupational status among African Americans equal those among whites, wealth plays a large role in determining individuals' financial capabilities. It influences important life chances like the types of homes individuals can purchase and the quality and quantity of education they can attain (Conley 1999; Gordon Nembhard 2006; Oliver and Shapiro 1995; Shapiro 2004).

The systematic exclusion of African Americans from New Deal era govern-ment policies has significantly contributed to racial disparities in wealth and to the high levels of persistent racial residential segregation found throughout the United States. The New Deal was one of the most significant sociopolitical events of the twentieth century, and this exclusion shaped the socioeconomic resources of generations of African Americans (Conley 1999; Katznelson 2005; Shapiro 2004).[2] For example, African American veterans were systematically denied equal access to the GI Bill, which provided free postsecondary educa-tion for veterans of the armed forces (Katznelson 2005). Ira Katznelson (2005) illustrates how African Americans in the southern states were allowed to use benefits from the GI Bill primarily to attend vocational schools and not 4-year colleges. In addition, the Social Security Act of 1935 excluded agricultural and domestic workers from the Social Security program.[3] At the time, most African Americans fell into those labor categories. Another New Deal era policy provided low-interest home loans. Prior to the New Deal era, home buyers had to save a much larger proportion of the total home cost. However, low-interest, federally backed housing loans instituted during the New Deal greatly expanded the pro-portion of Americans that could buy homes, since it reduced the down payment to about 20% of the final price (Conley 1999). Mortgage companies used redlin-ing practices to systematically deny the loan applications of African Americans (Conley 1999).[4] American families derive most of their wealth from the value of their home (Conley 1999; Gordon Nembhard 1999; Shapiro 2004), and home equity accounts for about 60% of the average family's total wealth (Shapiro 2004). These differences in home equity have intergenerational implications that affect African American wealth holdings.

In turn, home values are profoundly connected to racial residential segrega-tion. The lack of wealth and lack of access to credit among African Americans limit the financial resources available to buy desirable, high-value homes in neigh-borhoods with health-promoting resources (Charles, Dinwiddie, and Massey 2004; Williams and Collins 2001). Moreover, studies indicate that even African Americans who can afford homes in integrated neighborhoods have encountered residential steering and have been offered subprime mortgages (Farley and Frey 1994; Frey and Farley 1996; Ondrich, Ross, and Yinger 2003; Yinger 1986, 1995).[5]

Persistent levels of racial residential segregation contribute to the perpetu-ation of black–white wealth and health disparities, and wealth plays a critical, determining role in most African Americans' social context (Woldoff 2008). Often due to declining tax bases in predominately African American communi-ties, the schools attended by African Americans largely serve poor students and are not equal in resources or quality to predominantly white schools (Williams and Collins 2001; Williams and Williams-Morris 2000). Thus, white and African American students with the same amount of schooling and equivalent degrees will often differ in educational preparation and marketable skills because of underlying differences in education and inequalities among schools (Williams

2003; Williams and Collins 2001). Additionally, a student's school can provide or limit access to networks and opportunities, influencing the quality and quantity of resources available throughout the life course.

■ HEALTH ACROSS THE LIFE COURSE

Using a life course lens is critical to understanding the link between financial capabilities and health. There is evidence that the origins of adult health begin to emerge in the intrauterine environment, and early socioeconomic conditions play pivotal roles in development as well as in adult health (Barker 1997; Hertzman and Power 2003). David Barker and colleagues demonstrate that the intrauterine environment profoundly affects adults' risk of diabetes (Barker 2003), hypertension (Barker et al. 1989), and cardiovascular disease (Barker 1997, 1999). Birthweight is positively associated with heart rate and blood pressure (Barker et al. 1989). If the proportion of childhood spent in sickness is greater among African Americans than among other groups, do African Americans have equal opportunities to accumulate wealth for later life and for intergenerational transmission?

The relationship between poverty and exposure to stress is widely documented (Hertzman and Boyce 2010; Meyer, Schwartz, and Frost 2008). Also, the deleterious health sequelae from chronic exposure (e.g., dysregulation of the hypothalamic–pituitary–adrenal cortical axis and chronic inflammation) are inextricably linked to mental health (Jackson et al. 2010; Kemeny and Schedlowski 2007; Mezuk et al. 2010). Racial and ethnic disparities in health outcomes have led Arline Geronimus and colleagues to offer the weathering hypothesis, which suggests that African Americans experience early health deterioration due to the cumulative effects of chronic exposure to social or economic adversity and political marginalization (Geronimus et al. 2006). Because the prevalence of poverty is disproportionately greater among African Americans than among whites, African Americans may experience accelerated aging throughout the life course (Geronimus et al. 1996; Mezuk et al. 2010).

Vis-à-vis the SEP of their families, individuals enter the world at different SEP starting points, and socioeconomic resources are accumulated over their entire lives. However, most studies do not examine the effects of parental SEP or consider whether SEP accumulated across the life course could affect health. Despite a dearth of literature in this area, previous studies indicate that childhood SEP affects adult mental and physical health (Gilman et al. 2002; Kawachi, Adler, and Dow 2010). Moreover, socioeconomic disadvantage over the life course is negatively associated with mental health (Stansfeld et al. 2011; Walsemann, Geronimus, and Gee 2008).

A number of studies indicate that understanding of the relationship between SEP and depression lies in measuring childhood SEP and fluctuations in SEP over the life course. For instance, research finds that low childhood SEP is predictive of adult depression (Gilman et al. 2002; Kessler and Magee 1993; Sadowski et al. 1999). John Lynch and colleagues (1997) find that chronically low-income respondents are more likely to meet the criteria for clinical depression than are counterparts who have never experienced poverty. So too, Stephen Gilman and colleagues (2002) find that the risk for major depression among participants from lower SEP backgrounds is nearly double that of participants from the highest SEP background. Lisa Strohschein (2005) finds that income trajectories are related to depression and antisocial behavior among African Americans: low household income is positively associated with levels of depression and antisocial behavior. She notes that improvements in household income over the course of the study are associated with declines in the incidence of childhood depression but have no effect on antisocial behavior.

Craig Pollack and associates (2007) systematically review health studies published between 1990 and 2006, concluding that wealth is positively associated with health and that accounting for wealth in measures of SEP reduces observed racial and ethnic disparities in health. However, they note that studies examining the relationship between wealth and mental health produce inconclusive results and ambiguous findings. Carles Muntaner and colleagues (1998) analyze data from a nationally representative sample of Americans and control for a number of characteristics (race, ethnicity, age, sex, and other SEP measures), finding that wealth is negatively related to mood disorders, including depression. Conversely, in a study of Americans and Germans over age 60 years, Olaf von dem Knesebeck and associates (2003) find that assets and homeownership are associated with depression only among respondents aged 75 years and older. Joan Kahn and Elena Fazio (2005) examine data from the 2001 Aging, Stress, and Health Study, finding no relationship between net worth and depressive symptoms among a sample of whites and African Americans from the Washington, DC, metropolitan area.

Even fewer studies have examined the relationship between wealth and mental health among African Americans. Joan Ostrove, Pamela Feldman, and Nancy Adler (1999) find that SEP, measured by income, education, and wealth, is negatively associated with depressive symptoms among African American respondents. Analyzing data derived from the Americans' Changing Lives survey and the National Comorbidity Study, Eunice Rodriguez and colleagues (1999) find that greater levels of wealth are associated with lower levels of depression among white respondents but not among African American ones. Darrell Hudson, Harold Neighbors, and colleagues (2012), using data from the National Survey of American Life, find that levels of income and unemployment are significant predictors of depression among African American men, but they observe no relationship between wealth and depression in this nationally representative sample of African Americans.

Information is lacking on the relationship between the trajectory of SEP over the life course and depression among African Americans. The life course studies mentioned above use regional or national data sets that include African American respondents. However, that research does not focus on the unique role that life course SEP plays for African Americans, and some data sets do not include enough African American respondents to permit analyses. Overall, very few studies explore the relationship between life course SEP and mental health, and not enough studies evaluate the impact of life course SEP upon the mental health of African Americans.

Given that many African Americans begin their lives in poverty (Corcoran and Chaudry 1997; Hardaway and McLoyd 2009; Macartney 2011), it is important to understand how these childhood exposures affect the mental health of African Americans. But it is also important to understand how the process of upward social mobility affects the development of mental health problems among African Americans.

■ SOCIAL MOBILITY AMONG AFRICAN AMERICANS

Researchers have investigated whether the process of upward mobility could be deleterious to the mental and physical health of African Americans (Cole and Omari 2003; Colen 2005, 2011; Forman 2003). The consideration that benefits derived from SEP vary by race poses a fundamental challenge to the deeply embedded American notion that working hard and playing by the rules will result in an improved life position, including improved health.

For African Americans, there are clear advantages to embarking on the path of upward social mobility. Studies demonstrate a sense of achievement and personal satisfaction among respondents who find success in a society in which the odds are steeply stacked against them (Neckerman, Carter, and Lee 1999). However, African Americans of high SEP may encounter unique psychosocial stressors in the process of upward mobility. In addition to their effects on health, these "costs of upward mobility" have a negative impact on financial capabilities (Cole and Omari 2003, 786).

Unequal Returns on Human Capital Investments

For African Americans, upward mobility may impose costs through diminished returns on human capital investments. It is widely posited that health disparities are largely due to differences in socioeconomic resources. For instance, Melissa Farmer and Kenneth Ferraro (2005) outline the minority poverty theory, which suggests that absolute differences in the SEP of African Americans are thought to explain black–white health disparities (Farmer and

Ferraro 2005). There is substantial evidence that health differences narrow as levels of socioeconomic resources grow, but these health differences do not entirely disappear. Absolute material differences in SEP are not the only explanation for black–white health disparities. Additionally, expectations are often mismatched to efforts; that is, individuals have unreasonable expectations concerning the possible returns for their efforts and human capital investments. This perspective is called the "diminishing returns hypothesis" (Farmer and Ferraro 2005, 192). Thus, African Americans who have experienced diminishing returns on human capital investments could also experience poorer health, particularly mental health, than whites do.

Expectations of African Americans are often unfulfilled because their investments in education do not provide gains in income parallel to those enjoyed by whites (Williams 2003). At every level of education, African Americans generally tend to earn lower levels of income than do whites (Oliver and Shapiro 1995; Shapiro 2004; Williams 2003). David Williams (2003) contends that differences in returns on human capital investment may be a unique source of stress and alienation for African Americans. Additionally, disparities in wage composition affect the financial resources available to African Americans (Forman 2003; Watkins-Hayes, Patterson, and Armour 2011). Researchers document the struggles of African Americans with the gap between their lifestyle expectations and the positions they occupy (Dressler, Bindon, and Neggers 1998; Sellers and Neighbors 1999, 2008). As such, African Americans who improve their life chances through education and subsequent increases in income and occupational prestige may develop expectations for a certain standard of living—expectations that are higher than those of counterparts with less education and fewer occupational accomplishments. However, if the expectations are not realized, the resulting inconsistency may increase levels of distress. "Lifestyle incongruence," a theory developed by William Dressler (1991, 61), posits that the discrepancy between a person's lifestyle and economic status, or the "status incongruence," can lead to conflict and stress, which may also be associated with mental disorders such as depression. Williams (1999) states that African Americans tend to receive poorer quality educations than whites do and to work in more hazardous jobs. Compared with white counterparts who possess equivalent levels of education and work experience, African Americans are paid lower salaries and experience less wealth. They have less purchasing power at equivalent income levels (Williams 1999).

Sociologists have written about the process of upward mobility among African Americans. Alford Young (1999) chronicles the stories of four young African American men who came from humble beginnings but found their way into highly competitive graduate and professional programs. They described the personal, familial, and community-level factors that allowed them to overcome incredible odds and achieve educational and professional success. Notably, several of Young's respondents stated that, as they ascended the socioeconomic hierarchy, they recognized structural barriers that prevent African Americans from attaining success similar to that of whites. Concordantly, Jennifer Hochschild (1995) finds that poor African Americans believe in the American dream more than do rich African Americans, because African Americans with high SEP recognize that, despite their greater levels of education, higher incomes, and more prestigious occupations, they are unable to overcome the enormous gap between their assets and those accumulated by white counterparts with similar characteristics.

Respondents in some studies of upwardly mobile African Americans express feelings of anger, hurt, disappointment, and even rage as they struggle against glass ceilings or compare their success with that of white peers and coworkers (Feagin and McKinney 2003). Therefore, African Americans with high income, advanced education, prestigious jobs, and wealth may be at risk for mental disorders that arise as a result of stress associated with diminishing returns on their human capital investments.

Strained Social Support Networks

Pressure on African Americans' social support networks can be another key cost of upward social mobility. Research emphasizes the importance of social support in coping with psychosocial stressors: it can ameliorate the imbalance between perceived demands and perceived resources, increasing resources to meet perceived demands or altering the consequences of failure to meet them (Jacobson 1986). However, little is known about the structure and density of social support networks among high-SEP African Americans.

Some studies suggest that proximity to social support networks could be particularly important for upwardly mobile African Americans. Elizabeth Cole and Safiya Omari (2003) argue that guilt and grief accompany the economic privilege, security, and well-being obtained by African Americans through gains in SEP. Colleen Heflin and Mary Pattillo (2002) find that middle-class African Americans are highly likely to have low-income siblings and to incorporate the socioeconomic status of their extended families into their own conceptions of class standing. Through interviews with a sample of 200 working-class and middle-class African American and white women, Elizabeth Higginbotham and Lynn Weber (1992) investigate the levels of responsibility and obligation these women feel toward members of their social networks. They asked women, "Generally, do you feel you owe a lot for the help given to you by your family and relatives?" (430). The authors report that many white women were perplexed by the question but that most African American women responded affirmatively, indicating that they maintain strong links to their social support networks. Due to variations in the SEP of many African American social networks, African Americans with greater socioeconomic resources may be called upon to provide financial assistance and informal support to poorer friends and family (Brayboy Jackson and Stewart 2003; Cattell 2001; Prelow, Mosher, and Bowman 2006).

These additional responsibilities may psychologically and financially overwhelm African Americans with greater SEP. Some researchers have documented feelings of guilt and grief with respect to the friends and family members left behind in poverty (Heflin and Pattillo 2002; Higginbotham and Weber 1992). These feelings may be manifest internally or as discord with friends and family from different SEP levels.

Other scholars observe that middle-class and poor African Americans live in close proximity; their research suggests that African Americans with greater socioeconomic resources are asked to provide social capital to poorer members of their social support networks (Pattillo 2007). Pattillo (2007, 3) argues that middle-class African Americans often play the role of "middlemen and middlewomen," since they possess the kind of cultural and social capital that working-class and poor African Americans lack. Such capital is needed, she notes, to advocate for safe neighborhoods and good schools, to help others find decent jobs, and to navigate higher education systems. As such, middle-class African Americans act as "brokers" (2007, 3) between white economic and political power and the needs of a predominantly African American neighborhood.

Despite these findings, some evidence suggests that many high-SEP African Americans do not live in close proximity to potentially salubrious social support networks. Annette Lareau (2003) reports that middle-class African Americans have less frequent contact with members of their extended families and live farther away from those families than do African Americans with fewer socioeconomic resources. Finding that African American children born into homes with a resident grandmother have more favorable birth outcomes than do those from homes without a grandmother present, Cynthia Colen and colleagues (2006) conclude that social mobility may reduce the likelihood that African American women rely on their mothers for support during a pregnancy or for assistance with child-rearing responsibilities. These findings suggest that, if high-SEP African Americans lack adequate access to social support networks capable of helping them navigate stressful situations, the resulting lack of support may contribute to the development of mental disorders such as depression.

Additionally, the social support networks accessible to African Americans may provide less informative and material support than do the networks accessible to other groups. This could help affect African Americans' financial capabilities. Future research should investigate where upwardly mobile African Americans reside and the kinds of social support accessible to them.

Racial Discrimination, Stress, and SEP

Research suggests that racial discrimination is a unique, socially patterned type of stress exposure and that discrimination plays an important role in the mental health of African Americans. Ronald Kessler, Kristin Mickelson, and Williams (1999) rank the stress of experiencing racial discrimination alongside other stressful life events such as job loss, divorce, and the death of a loved one. Perceived racial discrimination is associated with impaired psychological well-being, decreased self-esteem, and increased risk of depression (Karlsen and Nazroo 2002; Williams, Takeuchi, and Adair 1992; Williams et al. 1997). Sellers and associates (2006) find a negative relationship between racial discrimination and self-rated mental health but observe no relationship between discrimination and self-rated physical health. They conclude that racial discrimination may be more deleterious to mental health than to physical health. Noting the prevalence of exposure to racial discrimination among African Americans, Williams (2003, 725) argues that "perceptions of discrimination" are stressors capable of adversely affecting their physical and mental health.

Some researchers have begun to investigate the intersection between racial discrimination and SEP (Gee 2008; Kessler et al. 1999; Williams, Neighbors, and Jackson 2008). Several studies focus on middle-class African Americans and suggest that they contend with numerous stressors related to racial discrimination. This discrimination can take experiential (e.g., unequal returns on human capital investments and racialized glass ceilings) and structural forms (e.g., residential segregation); it can be overt and latent (Cole and Omari 2003; Forman 2003; Hochschild 1995; Williams 2003). African Americans of higher SEP are more likely to work and live in integrated settings, and research concludes that SEP is positively correlated with exposure to racial discrimination (Brayboy Jackson and Stewart 2003; Forman 2003).

Considering the body of evidence demonstrating the significant association between racial discrimination and depression, it seems possible that racial discrimination could attenuate the positive effects of increases in SEP among African Americans. Yet, studies do not typically account for the effects of racial discrimination on SEP or on health (Bratter and Gorman 2011; Williams et al. 1997). Using data from the National Survey of American Life, which included a nationally representative sample of African American adults, Hudson, Kai Bullard, and colleagues (2012) show that racial discrimination negatively affects the association between SEP and depression among African American men. The findings for African American men largely support the study's a priori hypothesis that SEP and racial discrimination interact in SEP's positive relationship with odds of depression.

Hudson and colleagues (2013) investigate whether life course SEP is associated with depressive symptoms and self-rated health. In particular, they consider whether these associations differ by the race of the participant. Finding that the cumulative effects of life course SEP protect both African American and white respondents against depressive symptoms, they note that the association is stronger for blacks than for whites but find no evidence that racial discrimination moderates cumulative SEP's association with depressive symptoms. Analyses indicate that experiences of racial discrimination and cumulative SEP do not interact to significantly influence levels of depressive symptoms for blacks or whites.

■ CONCLUSIONS

The goal of this chapter is to describe the relationships among race, mental health, and the financial capabilities of African Americans. It focuses particularly on the mental health costs of upward mobility (Cole and Omari 2003), noting that such costs could undermine African Americans' efforts to accumulate socioeconomic resources. African Americans' efforts to improve their financial capabilities are limited in part by a dearth of wealth within the African American community (Shapiro 2004). Redlining and other discriminatory practices initially excluded African Americans from wealth-generating mechanisms such as federally backed, low-interest home loans. Most Americans derive the majority of their wealth from the value of their home (Oliver and Shapiro 1995), but widespread residential segregation in the United States is likely to ensure that the wealth gap persists between African Americans and whites. Furthermore, segregation truncates African Americans' access to health-producing resources and to such vehicles for upward social mobility as quality education and job-training programs (Williams and Collins 2001). The lack of wealth among African Americans means that, in many cases, their grip on middle-class status is tenuous: it is subject to shifts in economic policy and is vulnerable to economic recessions (Conley 1999; Hardaway and McLoyd 2009; Landry 1987; Oliver 2008; Pattillo-McCoy 1999; Shapiro 2004). These factors have an incredibly constraining effect on the financial capabilities of African Americans.

This chapter does not discuss several subjects that warrant the attention of future research. Financial literacy, an important component of financial capability, is one such area. The social networks accessible to African Americans could truncate their financial literacy. Additionally, as illustrated above, there is little wealth among African Americans, even among those who have high incomes and high levels of education. Thus, African Americans may not have the resources or ability to invest much of their income into wealth-generating mechanisms. Health-related studies that account for the effects of wealth do not yield consistent findings. One potential reason for this could be the measure used to capture wealth, as respondents in health studies are often reluctant to disclose personal financial information (Groves et al. 2004). Moreover, wealth is somewhat difficult to estimate (Pollack et al. 2007; Shapiro 2004), and wealth's effects on health may be underestimated. Another aspect of this work is that the effects of racial discrimination are negative for both African Americans and whites. Furthermore, there is growing evidence that economic inequality threatens overall population health at every socioeconomic level (Wilkinson and Pickett 2006). The health and best interests of all groups are served by reducing economic disparities.

I close by noting that psychosocial factors can also threaten the mental health of African Americans, particularly those who possess substantial income, education, and occupational prestige (Cole and Omari 2003). African Americans with high levels of socioeconomic resources often experience diminished returns on their human capital investments. Their compensation and career trajectories compare unfavorably with those of whites who have similar qualifications. Studies indicate that socioeconomic benefits can produce positive health outcomes, but the effects are undermined by exposure to racial segregation (Hudson, Bullard, et al. 2012; see also Hudson et al. 2013).

■ NOTES

1. *Socioeconomic position* is defined as social and economic factors that influence what position (or positions) individuals and groups hold within the structure of society (Lynch and Kaplan 2000). John Lynch and George Kaplan argue that SEP should be conceptualized beyond the individual level to incorporate structural-level aspects into thinking about individuals' position in society as well as their subsequent social and environmental exposures, social environment, and behaviors. Muntaner and colleagues (2004) describe SEP as a term that encompasses both social class (referring to social relations of ownership and control over productive assets) and socioeconomic status.

2. Coined by President Franklin D. Roosevelt, the term *New Deal* refers to a set of policies initially adopted by the U.S. government between 1933 and 1938. During the administrations of Franklin Roosevelt and Harry Truman, the United States adopted progressive policies such as Social Security, protective labor laws, and the GI Bill (Katznelson 2005). See also Servicemen's Readjustment Act of 1944 (GI Bill), Pub. L. 78-346, 58 Stat. 284.

3. Social Security Act of 1935, Pub. L. No. 74-271, 49 Stat. 620 (codified as amended at 42 U.S.C. §§ 1301–1397mm [2011]).

4. *Redlining* refers to a practice in which banks refused to provide loans and other financial services in certain residential areas of cities, and these often were areas populated by blacks (Conley 1999; Farley and Frey 1994). Banks color-coded maps of entire cities, and red was the color assigned to the areas in which banks would not offer home loans (Conley 1999; Massey and Denton 1993).

5. *Residential steering* is a practice whereby real estate agents consider the potential buyer's race in deciding which homes and neighborhoods are shown. For example, an agent might steer an African American client toward a predominantly African American neighborhood or away from a predominantly white one. Research suggests that steering is likely to be strongly influenced by the racial attitudes and beliefs held by real estate agents (Ondrich et al. 2003).

■ REFERENCES

Adler, Nancy E., and Judith Stewart. 2010. "Health Disparities across the Lifespan: Meaning, Methods, and Mechanisms." *Annals of the New York Academy of Sciences* 1186: 5–23. doi: 10.1111/j.1749-6632.2009.05337.x.

Barker, David J. P. 1997. "Intrauterine Programming of Coronary Heart Disease and Stroke." *Acta Paediatrica* 86 (S423): 178–182. doi: 10.1111/j.1651-2227.1997.tb18408.x.

Barker, David J. P. 1999. "The Fetal Origins of Type 2 Diabetes Mellitus." *Annals of Internal Medicine* 130, no. 4 (Part 1): 322–324. doi: 10.7326/0003-4819-130-4-199902160-00019.

Barker, David J. P. 2003. "The Developmental Origins of Adult Disease." *European Journal of Epidemiology* 18: 733–736. doi: 10.1023/A:1025388901248.

Barker, David J. P., C. Osmond, J. Golding, D. Kuh, and M. E. Wadsworth. 1989. "Growth in Utero, Blood Pressure in Childhood and Adult Life, and Mortality from Cardiovascular Disease." *British Medical Journal* 298 (6673): 564–567. doi: 10.1136/bmj.298.6673.564.

Bratter, Jenifer L., and Bridget K. Gorman. 2011. "Does Multiracial Matter? A Study of Racial Disparities in Self-Rated Health." *Demography* 48 (1): 127–152. doi: 10.1007/s13524-010-0005-0.

Braveman, Paula, and Colleen Barclay. 2009. "Health Disparities Beginning in Childhood: A Life-Course Perspective." *Pediatrics* 124 (Suppl. 3): S163–S175. doi: 10.1542/peds.2009-1100D.

Braveman, Paula, Catherine Cubbin, Kristen Marchi, Susan Egerter, and Gilberto Chavez. 2001. "Measuring Socioeconomic Status/Position in Studies of Racial/Ethnic Disparities: Maternal and Infant Health." *Public Health Reports* 116 (5): 449–463. doi: 10.1016/S0033-3549(04)50073-0.

Brayboy Jackson, Pamela, and Quincy Thomas Stewart. 2003. "A Research Agenda for the Black Middle Class: Work Stress, Survival Strategies, and Mental Health." *Journal of Health and Social Behavior* 44 (3): 442–455. doi: 10.2307/1519789.

Breslau, Joshua, Michael Lane, Nancy Sampson, and Ronald C. Kessler. 2008. "Mental Disorders and Subsequent Educational Attainment in a US National Sample." *Journal of Psychiatric Research* 42 (9): 708–716. doi: 10.1016/j.jpsychires.2008.01.016.

Cattell, Vicky. 2001. "Poor People, Poor Places, and Poor Health: The Mediating Role of Social Networks and Social Capital." *Social Science and Medicine* 52 (10): 1501–1516. doi: 10.1016/S0277-9536(00)00259-8.

Charles, Camille Z., Gniesha Dinwiddie, and Douglas S. Massey. 2004. "The Continuing Consequences of Segregation: Family Stress and College Academic Performance." *Social Science Quarterly* 85 (5): 1353–1373. doi: 10.1111/j.0038-4941.2004.00280.x.

Cohen, Sheldon, Denise Janicki-Deverts, Edith Chen, and Karen A. Matthews. 2010. "Childhood Socioeconomic Status and Adult Health." *Annals of the New York Academy of Sciences* 1186: 37–55. doi: 10.1111/j.1749-6632.2009.05334.x.

Cole, Elizabeth R., and Safiya R. Omari. 2003. "Race, Class and the Dilemmas of Upward Mobility for African Americans." *Journal of Social Issues* 59 (4): 785–802. doi: 10.1046/j.0022-4537.2003.00090.x.

Colen, Cynthia G. 2005. "Socioeconomic Mobility and Reproductive Outcomes among African American and White Women in the United States." PhD dissertation, University of Michigan, Ann Arbor.

Colen, Cynthia G. 2011. "Addressing Racial Disparities in Health Using Life Course: Toward a Constructive Criticism." *Du Bois Review: Social Science Research on Race* 8 (1): 79–94. doi: 10.1017/S1742058X11000075.

Colen, Cynthia G., Arline T. Geronimus, John Bound, and Sherman A. James. 2006. "Maternal Upward Socioeconomic Mobility and Black-White Disparities in Infant Birthweight." *American Journal of Public Health* 96 (11): 2032–2039. doi: 10.2105/AJPH.2005.076547.

Conley, Dalton. 1999. *Being Black, Living in the Red: Race, Wealth, and Social Policy in America*. Berkeley: University of California Press.

Corcoran, Mary E., and Ajay Chaudry. 1997. "The Dynamics of Childhood Poverty." *Future of Children* 7 (2): 40–54. doi: 10.2307/1602386.

Dressler, William W. 1991. "Social Support, Lifestyle Incongruity, and Arterial Blood Pressure in a Southern Black Community." *Psychosomatic Medicine* 53 (6): 608–620. doi: 10.1097/00006842-199111000-00003.

Dressler, William W., James R. Bindon, and Yasmin H. Neggers. 1998. "Culture, Socioeconomic Status, and Coronary Heart Disease Risk Factors in an African American Community." *Journal of Behavioral Medicine* 21 (6): 527–544. doi: 10.1023/A:1018744612079.

Farley, Reynolds, and William H. Frey. 1994. "Changes in the Segregation of Whites from Blacks during the 1980s: Small Steps toward a More Integrated Society." *American Sociological Review* 59 (1): 23–45. doi: 10.2307/2096131.

Farmer, Melissa M., and Kenneth F. Ferraro. 2005. "Are Racial Disparities in Health Conditional on Socioeconomic Status?" *Social Science and Medicine* 60 (1): 191–204. doi: 10.1016/j.socscimed.2004.04.026.

Feagin, Joe R., and Karyn D. McKinney. 2003. *The Many Costs of Racism.* Lanham, MD: Rowman & Littlefield.

Forman, Tyrone A. 2003. "The Social Psychological Costs of Racial Segmentation in the Workplace: A Study of African Americans' Well-Being." *Journal of Health and Social Behavior* 44 (3): 332–352. doi: 10.2307/1519783.

Frey, William H., and Reynolds Farley. 1996. "Latino, Asian, and Black Segregation in U.S. Metropolitan Areas: Are Multiethnic Metros Different?" *Demography* 33 (1): 35–50. doi: 10.2307/2061712.

Gavin, Amelia R., Emily Walton, David H. Chae, Margarita Alegria, James S. Jackson, and David Takeuchi. 2010. "The Associations between Socio-Economic Status and Major Depressive Disorder among Blacks, Latinos, Asians and Non-Hispanic Whites: Findings from the Collaborative Psychiatric Epidemiology Studies." *Psychological Medicine* 40 (1): 51–61. doi: 10.1017/S0033291709006023.

Gee, Gilbert C. 2008. "A Multilevel Analysis of the Relationship between Institutional and Individual Racial Discrimination and Health Status." *American Journal of Public Health* 98 (Suppl. 1): S48–S56. doi: 10.2105/AJPH.98.Supplement_1.S48.

Geronimus, Arline T. 1996. "Black/White Differences in the Relationship of Maternal Age to Birthweight: A Population-Based Test of the Weathering Hypothesis." *Social Science and Medicine* 42 (4): 589–597. doi: 10.1016/0277-9536(95)00159-X.

Geronimus, Arline T., John Bound, Timothy A. Waidmann, Marianne M. Hillemeier, and Patricia B. Burns. 1996. "Excess Mortality among Blacks and Whites in the United States." *New England Journal of Medicine* 335 (21): 1552–1558. doi: 10.1056/NEJM199611213352102.

Geronimus, Arline T., Margaret Hicken, Danya Keene, and John Bound. 2006. "'Weathering' and Age Patterns of Allostatic Load Scores among Blacks and Whites in the United States." *American Journal of Public Health* 96 (5): 826–833. doi: 10.2105/AJPH.2004.060749.

Gilman, Stephen E., Ichiro Kawachi, Garrett M. Fitzmaurice, and Stephen L. Buka. 2002. "Socioeconomic Status in Childhood and the Lifetime Risk of Major Depression." *International Journal of Epidemiology* 31 (2): 359–367. doi: 10.1093/ije/31.2.359.

Gordon Nembhard, Jessica. 1999. "Community Economic Development: Alternative Visions for the 21st Century." In *Readings in Black Political Economy*, edited by John Whitehead and Cobie Kwasi Harris, 295–304. Dubuque, IA: Kendall/Hunt.

Gordon Nembhard, Jessica. 2006. "Trends and Trappings, Research and Policy Implications: An Unorthodox Policy Guide." In *Wealth Accumulation and Communities of Color in the United States: Current Issues*, edited by Jessica Gordon Nembhard and Ngina Chiteji, 326–342. Ann Arbor: University of Michigan Press.

Groves, Robert M., Floyd J. Fowler Jr., Mick P. Couper, James M. Lepkowski, Eleanor Singer, and Roger Tourangeau. 2004. *Survey Methodology*. Hoboken, NJ: Wiley & Sons.

Hardaway, Cecily R., and Vonnie C. McLoyd. 2009. "Escaping Poverty and Securing Middle Class Status: How Race and Socioeconomic Status Shape Mobility Prospects for African Americans during the Transition to Adulthood." *Journal of Youth and Adolescence* 38 (2): 242–256. doi: 10.1007/s10964-008-9354-z.

Heflin, Colleen M., and Mary Pattillo. 2002. "Kin Effects on Black-White Account and Home Ownership." *Sociological Inquiry* 72 (2): 220–239. doi: 10.1111/1475-682X.00014.

Hertzman, Clyde, and Tom Boyce. 2010. "How Experience Gets under the Skin to Create Gradients in Developmental Health." *Annual Review of Public Health* 31: 329–347. doi: 10.1146/annurev.publhealth.012809.103538.

Hertzman, Clyde, and Chris Power. 2003. "Health and Human Development: Understandings from Life-Course Research." *Developmental Neuropsychology* 24 (2–3): 719–744. doi: 10.1080/87565641.2003.9651917.

Higginbotham, Elizabeth, and Lynn Weber. 1992. "Moving up with Kin and Community: Upward Social Mobility for Black and White Women." *Gender and Society* 6 (3): 416–440. doi: 10.1177/089124392006003005.

Hochschild, Jennifer L. 1995. *Facing up to the American Dream: Race, Class, and the Soul of the Nation*. Princeton, NJ: Princeton University Press.

Hudson, Darrell L., Kai M. Bullard, Harold W. Neighbors, Arline T. Geronimus, Juan Yang, and James S. Jackson. 2012. "Are Benefits Conferred with Greater Socioeconomic Position Undermined by Racial Discrimination among African American Men?" *Journal of Men's Health* 9 (2): 127–136. doi: 10.1016/j.jomh.2012.03.006.

Hudson, Darrell L., Harold W. Neighbors, Arline T. Geronimus, and James S. Jackson. 2012. "The Relationship between Socioeconomic Position and Depression among a US Nationally Representative Sample of African Americans." *Social Psychiatry and Psychiatric Epidemiology* 47 (3): 373–381. doi: 10.1007/s00127-011-0348-x.

Hudson, Darrell L., Eli Puterman, Kirsten Bibbins-Domingo, Karen A. Matthews, and Nancy E. Adler. 2013. "Race, Life Course Socioeconomic Position, Racial Discrimination, Depressive Symptoms and Self-Rated Health." *Social Science and Medicine* 97: 7–14. doi: 10.1016/j.socscimed.2013.07.031.

Jackson, James S., Katherine M. Knight, and Jane A. Rafferty. 2010. "Race and Unhealthy Behaviors: Chronic Stress, the HPA Axis, and Physical and Mental Health Disparities over the Life Course." *American Journal of Public Health* 100 (5): 933–939. doi: 10.2105/ajph.2008.143446.

Jacobson, David E. 1986. "Types and Timing of Social Support." *Journal of Health and Social Behavior* 27: 250–264. doi: 10.2307/2136745.

Johnson, Rucker C., and Robert F. Schoeni. 2011. "Early-Life Origins of Adult Disease: National Longitudinal Population-Based Study of the United States." *American Journal of Public Health* 101 (12): 2317–2324. doi: 10.2105/AJPH.2011.300252.

Kahn, Joan R., and Elena M. Fazio. 2005. "Economic Status over the Life Course and Racial Disparities in Health." In "Health Inequalities across the Life Course," edited by Steven H. Zarit and Leonard I. Pearlin, special issue, *Journals of Gerontology: Social Sciences* 60B (Special issue 2): S76–S84. doi: 10.1093/geronb/60.Special_Issue_2.

Karlsen, Saffron, and James Y. Nazroo. 2002. "Relation between Racial Discrimination, Social Class, and Health among Ethnic Minority Groups." *American Journal of Public Health* 92 (4): 624–631. doi: 10.2105/AJPH.92.4.624.

Katznelson, Ira. 2005. *When Affirmative Action Was White: An Untold History of Racial Inequality in Twentieth-Century America.* New York: Norton.

Kawachi, Ichiro, Nancy E. Adler, and William H. Dow. 2010. "Money, Schooling, and Health: Mechanisms and Causal Evidence." *Annals of the New York Academy of Sciences* 1186: 56–68. doi: 10.1111/j.1749-6632.2009.05340.x.

Kawakami, Norito, Emad Abdulrazaq Abdulghani, Jordi Alonso, Evelyn J. Bromet, Ronny Bruffaerts, José Miguel Caldas-de-Almeida, Wai Tat Chiu, et al. 2012. "Early-Life Mental Disorders and Adult Household Income in the World Mental Health Surveys." *Biological Psychiatry* 72 (3): 228–237. doi: 10.1016/j.biopsych.2012.03.009.

Keister, Lisa A., and Stephanie Moller. 2000. "Wealth Inequality in the United States." *Annual Review of Sociology* 26: 63–81. doi: 10.1146/annurev.soc.26.1.63.

Kemeny, Margaret E., and Manfred Schedlowski. 2007. "Understanding the Interaction between Psychosocial Stress and Immune-Related Diseases: A Stepwise Progression." *Brain, Behavior, and Immunity* 21 (8): 1009–1018. doi: 10.1016/j.bbi.2007.07.010.

Kessler, Ronald C., and William J. Magee. 1993. "Childhood Adversities and Adult Depression: Basic Patterns of Association in a US National Survey." *Psychological Medicine* 23 (3): 679–690. doi: 10.1017/S0033291700025460.

Kessler, Ronald C., Kristin D. Mickelson, and David R. Williams. 1999. "The Prevalence, Distribution, and Mental Health Correlates of Perceived Discrimination in the United States." *Journal of Health and Social Behavior* 40 (3): 208–230. doi: 10.2307/2676349.

Kochhar, Rakesh, Richard Fry, and Paul Taylor. 2011. *Wealth Gaps Rise to Record Highs between Whites, Blacks Hispanics.* Pew Social and Demographic Trends Report Executive Summary. Washington, DC: Pew Research Center. http://pewsocialtrends .org/2011/07/26/wealth-gaps-rise-to-record-highs-between-whites-blacks-hispanics/.

Landry, Bart. 1987. *The New Black Middle Class.* Berkeley: University of California Press.

Lareau, Annette. 2003. *Unequal Childhoods: Class, Race, and Family Life.* Berkeley: University of California Press.

Lynch, John W., and George A. Kaplan. 2000. "Socioeconomic Position." In *Social Epidemiology,* edited by Lisa F. Berkman and Ichiro Kawachi, 13–35. New York: Oxford University Press.

Lynch, John W., George A. Kaplan, and Sarah J. Shema. 1997. "Cumulative Impact of Sustained Economic Hardship on Physical, Cognitive, Psychological, and Social Functioning." *New England Journal of Medicine* 337 (26): 1889–1895. doi: 10.1056 /NEJM199712253372606.

Macartney, Suzanne. 2011. *Child Poverty in the United States 2009 and 2010: Selected Race Groups and Hispanic Origin.* American Community Survey Briefs ACSBR/10-05, November. Washington, DC: U.S. Census Bureau. https://www.census.gov /prod/2011pubs/acsbr10-05.pdf.

Massey, Douglas S., and Nancy A. Denton. 1993. *American Apartheid: Segregation and the Making of the Underclass.* Cambridge, MA: Harvard University Press.

Meyer, Ilan H., Sharon Schwartz, and David M. Frost. 2008. "Social Patterning of Stress and Coping: Does Disadvantaged Social Statuses Confer More Stress and Fewer Coping Resources?" *Social Science and Medicine* 67 (3): 368–379. doi: 10.1016/j .socscimed.2008.03.012.

Mezuk, Briana, Jane A. Rafferty, Kiarri N. Kershaw, Darrell Hudson, Cleopatra M. Abdou, Hedwig Lee, William W. Eaton, and James S. Jackson. 2010. "Reconsidering the Role of Social Disadvantage in Physical and Mental Health: Stressful Life Events, Health Behaviors, Race, and Depression." *American Journal of Epidemiology* 172 (11): 1238–1249. doi: 10.1093/aje/kwq283.

Muntaner, Carles, William W. Eaton, Chamberlain C. Diala, Ronald C. Kessler, and Paul D. Sorlie. 1998. "Social Class, Assets, Organizational Control and the Prevalence of Common Groups of Psychiatric Disorders." *Social Science and Medicine* 47 (12): 2043–2053. doi: 10.1016/S0277-9536(98)00309-8.

Muntaner, Carles, William W. Eaton, Richard Miech, and Patricia O'Campo. 2004. "Socioeconomic Position and Major Mental Disorders." *Epidemiologic Reviews* 26 (1): 53–62. doi: 10.1093/epirev/mxh001.

Neckerman, Kathryn M., Prudence Carter, and Jennifer Lee. 1999. "Segmented Assimilation and Minority Cultures of Mobility." *Ethnic and Racial Studies* 22 (6): 945–965. doi: 10.1080/014198799329198.

Oliver, Melvin L. 2008. "Sub-Prime as a Black Catastrophe." *American Prospect*, September 20. http://www.prospect.org/cs/articles?article=sub_prime_as_a_black _catastrophe.

Oliver, Melvin L., and Thomas M. Shapiro. 1995. *Black Wealth, White Wealth: A New Perspective on Racial Inequality*. New York: Routledge.

Ondrich, Jan, Stephen Ross, and John Yinger. 2003. "Now You See It, Now You Don't: Why Do Real Estate Agents Withhold Available Houses from Black Customers?" *Review of Economics and Statistics* 85 (4): 854–873. doi: 10.1162/003465303772815772.

Ostrove, Joan M., Pamela Feldman, and Nancy E. Adler. 1999. "Relations among Socioeconomic Status Indicators and Health for African-Americans and Whites." *Journal of Health Psychology* 4 (4): 451–463. doi: 10.1177/135910539900400401.

Pattillo, Mary E. 2007. *Black on the Block: The Politics of Race and Class in the City*. Chicago: University of Chicago Press.

Pattillo-McCoy, Mary E. 1999. *Black Picket Fences: Privilege and Peril among the Black Middle Class*. Chicago: University of Chicago Press.

Pearson, Jay A. 2008. "Can't Buy Me Whiteness: New Lessons from the Titanic on Race, Ethnicity, and Health." *Du Bois Review: Social Science Research on Race* 5 (1): 27–47. doi: 10.1017/S1742058X0808003X.

Phelan, Jo C., Bruce G. Link, and Parisa Tehranifar. 2010. "Social Conditions as Fundamental Causes of Health Inequalities: Theory, Evidence, and Policy Implications." *Journal of Health and Social Behavior* 51 (Suppl.) S28–S40. doi: 10.1177/0022146510383498.

Pollack, Craig Evan, Sekai Chideya, Catherine Cubbin, Brie Williams, Mercedes Dekker, and Paula Braveman. 2007. "Should Health Studies Measure Wealth? A Systematic Review." *American Journal of Preventive Medicine* 33 (3): 250–264. doi: 10.1016/j.amepre.2007.04.033.

Prelow, Hazel M., Catherine E. Mosher, and Marvella A. Bowman. 2006. "Perceived Racial Discrimination, Social Support, and Psychological Adjustment among

African American College Students." *Journal of Black Psychology* 32 (4): 442–454. doi: 10.1177/0095798406292677.

Rodriguez, Eunice, Josephine A. Allen, Edward A. Frongillo Jr., and Pinky Chandra. 1999. "Unemployment, Depression, and Health: A Look at the African-American Community." *Journal of Epidemiology and Community Health* 53 (6): 335–342. doi: 10.1136/jech.53.6.335.

Sadowski, H., B. Ugarte, I. Kolvin, C. Kaplan, and J. Barnes. 1999. "Early Life Family Disadvantages and Major Depression in Adulthood." *British Journal of Psychiatry* 174 (2): 112–120. doi: 10.1192/bjp.174.2.112.

Sellers, Sherrill L. 2001. "Social Mobility and Psychological Distress: Differences among Black American Men and Women." *African American Research Perspectives* 7: 117–147.

Sellers, Sherrill L., Vence Bonham, Harold W. Neighbors, and James W. Amell. 2006. "Effects of Racial Discrimination and Health Behaviors on Mental and Physical Health of Middle-Class African American Men." *Health Education and Behavior* 36 (1): 31–44. doi: 10.1177/1090198106293526.

Sellers, Sherrill L., and Harold W. Neighbors. 1999. "Goal-Striving Stress, Social Economic Status, and the Mental Health of Black Americans." *Annals of the New York Academy of Sciences* 896: 469–473. doi: 10.1111/j.1749-6632.1999.tb08172.x.

Sellers, Sherrill L., and Harold W. Neighbors. 2008. "Effects of Goal-Striving Stress on the Mental Health of Black Americans." *Journal of Health and Social Behavior* 46 (1): 92–103. doi: 10.1177/002214650804900107.

Shapiro, Thomas M. 2004. *The Hidden Cost of Being African American: How Wealth Perpetuates Inequality*. New York: Oxford University Press.

Stansfeld, Stephen A., Charlotte Clark, Bryan Rodgers, Tanya Caldwell, and Chris Power. 2011. "Repeated Exposure to Socioeconomic Disadvantage and Health Selection as Life Course Pathways to Mid-Life Depressive and Anxiety Disorders." *Social Psychiatry and Psychiatric Epidemiology* 46 (7): 549–558. doi: 10.1007/s00127-010-0221-3.

Strohschein, Lisa. 2005. "Household Income Histories and Child Mental Health Trajectories." *Journal of Health and Social Behavior* 46 (4): 359–375. doi: 10.1177/0022 14650504600404.

Tse, Alison C., Janet W. Rich-Edwards, Karestan Koenen, and Rosalind J. Wright. 2012. "Cumulative Stress and Maternal Prenatal Corticotropin-Releasing Hormone in an Urban U.S. Cohort." *Psychoneuroendocrinology* 37 (7): 970–979. doi: 10.1016/j .psyneuen.2011.11.004.

Turner, R. Jay, and Donald A. Lloyd. 2004. "Stress Burden and the Lifetime Incidence of Psychiatric Disorder in Young Adults: Racial and Ethnic Contrasts." *Archives of General Psychiatry* 61 (5): 481–488. doi: 10.1001/archpsyc.61.5.481.

Von dem Knesebeck, Olaf, Günther Lüschen, William C. Cockerham, and Johannes Siegrist. 2003. "Socioeconomic Status and Health among the Aged in the United States and Germany: A Comparative Cross-Sectional Study." *Social Science and Medicine* 57 (9): 1643–1652. doi: 10.1016/S0277-9536(03)00020-0.

Walsemann, Katrina M., Arline T. Geronimus, and Gilbert C. Gee. 2008. "Accumulating Disadvantage over the Life Course: Evidence from a Longitudinal Study Investigating the Relationship between Educational Advantage in Youth and Health in Middle Age." *Research on Aging* 30 (2): 169–199. doi: 10.1177/0164027507311149.

Watkins-Hayes, Celeste, Courtney J. Patterson, and Amanda R. Armour. 2011. "Precious: Black Women, Neighborhood HIV/AIDS Risk, and Institutional

Buffers." *Du Bois Review: Social Science Research on Race* 8 (1): 229–240. doi: 10.1017 /S1742058X1100021X.

Wilkinson, Richard G., and Kate E. Pickett. 2006. "Income Inequality and Population Health: A Review and Explanation of the Evidence." *Social Science and Medicine* 62 (7): 1768–1784. doi: 10.1016/j.socscimed.2005.08.036.

Williams, David R. 1999. "Race, Socioeconomic Status, and Health: The Added Effects of Racism and Discrimination." *Annals of the New York Academy of Sciences* 896: 173– 188. doi: 10.1111/j.1749-6632.1999.tb08114.x.

Williams, David R. 2003. "The Health of Men: Structured Inequalities and Opportunities." *American Journal of Public Health* 93 (5): 724–731. doi: 10.2105 /AJPH.93.5.724.

Williams, David R., and Chiquita Collins. 2001. "Racial Residential Segregation: A Fundamental Cause of Racial Disparities in Health." *Public Health Reports* 116 (5): 404–416.

Williams, David R., Harold W. Neighbors, and James S. Jackson. 2008. "Racial/Ethnic Discrimination and Health: Findings from Community Studies." *American Journal of Public Health* 98 (Suppl. 1): S29–S37. doi: 10.2105/AJPH.98.Supplement_1.S29.

Williams, David R., David T. Takeuchi, and Russell K. Adair. 1992. "Socioeconomic Status and Psychiatric Disorder among Blacks and Whites." *Social Forces* 71 (1): 179– 194. doi: 10.2307/2579972.

Williams, David R., and Ruth Williams-Morris. 2000. "Racism and Mental Health: The African American Experience." *Ethnicity and Health* 5 (3–4): 243–268. doi: 10.1080/713667453.

Williams, David R., Yan Yu, James S. Jackson, and Norman B. Anderson. 1997. "Racial Differences in Physical and Mental Health: Socio-Economic Status, Stress and Discrimination." *Journal of Health Psychology* 2 (3): 335–351. doi: 10.1177/13591053 9700200305.

Woldoff, Rachael A. 2008. "Wealth, Human Capital and Family across Racial/Ethnic Groups: Integrating Models of Wealth and Locational Attainment." *Urban Studies* 45 (3): 527–551. doi: 10.1177/0042098007087334.

Yinger, John. 1986. "Measuring Racial Discrimination with Fair Housing Audits: Caught in the Act." *American Economic Review* 76 (5): 881–893. http://www.jstor.org /stable/1816458.

Yinger, John. 1995. *Closed Doors, Opportunities Lost: The Continuing Costs of Housing Discrimination.* New York: Russell Sage.

Young, Alford A., Jr. 1999. "Navigating Race: Getting Ahead in the Lives of 'Rags to Riches' Young Black Men." In *The Cultural Territories of Race: Black and White Boundaries,* edited by Michèle Lamont, 30–62. Chicago: University of Chicago Press.

PART TWO

Financial Capability in Later Life

Vulnerable Populations

3 Assets and Older African Americans

■ TRINA R. WILLIAMS SHANKS AND
WILHELMINA A. LEIGH

Although African Americans and white Americans aged 20 years or older are equally likely to participate in the labor force (i.e., to be employed or actively seeking employment), the two groups differ in the incomes earned and assets accumulated from this participation. African Americans are more likely than whites to work at low-wage jobs and to experience spells of unemployment. They consequently have less disposable income, lower lifetime earnings, and less income derived from assets (e.g., interest, dividends, rents, royalties, estates, or trusts). They are also more likely to have poverty-level income (DeNavas-Walt, Proctor, and Smith 2011).

By the time adults reach preretirement age (50 years or older), these disparities in labor force experiences and outcomes may have persisted for 30 or more years. Thus, compared to their white counterparts, preretirement African Americans have less money in employer-sponsored pensions and other employer-sponsored retirement plans, less money paid into the Social Security system, lower rates of homeownership, and less personal savings. Such preretirement disparities set the stage for limited financial security during later years.

This chapter examines a range of indicators that collectively provide a summary of the income and asset positions of African Americans throughout the life course. It ends with a discussion of the policy implications of the disparities identified and with suggestions for improving financial capability among older African Americans.

■ DATA AND FINDINGS

Employment, Income, Poverty, and Lifetime Earnings

Employment

For most, asset building begins with disposable income, and this is generally income from employment. Although labor-force participation rates were comparable for whites (67%) and African Americans (66%) in the population aged 20 years or older in 2010, whites in some age subgroups were more likely to be employed than were their African American counterparts (U.S. Bureau of Labor Statistics 2011). The labor-force participation rate among whites aged 25 to 54 years (83%) exceeded that among African Americans in this age group

(79%). Labor-force participation rates also were higher for whites aged 55 to 64 years (66% vs. 56% for African Americans) and for whites aged 65 years or older (18% vs. 15% for African Americans).

Employment-to-population ratios corroborate the evidence that labor-force engagement is greater among whites than among African Americans. An examination of such engagement among adults who were aged 55 to 64 years in 2010 indicates that 62% of whites were employed but that only 50% of African Americans were (U.S. Bureau of Labor Statistics 2011). Although employment-to-population ratios are generally smaller among persons aged 65 years or older than among younger persons, the 2010 ratio for these older whites (16.5%) exceeded that for their African American counterparts (13.8%). These findings suggest that African Americans aged 55 years or older who need income to cover living expenses during their later years are less likely than similarly situated whites to get this income from employment.

Income

Older African Americans have less disposable income than do older whites. In 2010, the percentage of African American householders aged 65 years or older with an annual income of less than $15,000 (31%) was nearly double that of their white counterparts (16%). In addition, the median household income among African Americans aged 65 years or older ($20,000–$24,999) was notably less than that among whites in the same age group ($35,000–$39,999).[1]

African American aged units 65 years or older are notably less likely than their white counterparts to report income derived from assets.[2] And African Americans with asset income report lower values. On average, income from assets accounts for 2% of income among African American aged units 65 years or older and is received by about 8% of these units. Such income accounts for 8% of the income among white aged units 65 years or older and is received by 13% of these units. The median value of asset income received by African American aged units was only $400 per year in 2010. That is less than a third of the asset income reported by comparable white aged units ($1,300; Social Security Administration 2012).

Poverty

The pattern of racial disparities revealed in labor-force participation rates and employment-to-population ratios is mirrored in poverty rates: African Americans are more likely than whites to be poor. Among 18- to 64-year-old African Americans, 23.3% reported income below the poverty level in 2010, but only 9.9% of non-Hispanic whites reported the same (DeNavas-Walt et al.

2011). Although the poverty rate is lower among adults aged 65 years or older than among persons aged 18 to 64 years, the racial disparity is also evident among the older group. Nearly 7% of these older non-Hispanic whites reported income less than the poverty level. In contrast, 18% of their African American counterparts reported the same.

Lifetime Earnings

As with employment and annual income, lifetime earnings are less for African Americans than for whites. Median lifetime earnings for all workers are $1.7 million, which is just under $42,000 per year ($20 per hour; Carnevale, Rose, and Cheah 2011). An analysis by Amon Emeka (2007) finds that average total lifetime earnings are $1,977,200 for non-Hispanic white men but just $1,132,967 for non-Hispanic African American men. Non-Hispanic white women have average total lifetime earnings of $1,043,207 and are more likely than non-Hispanic African American women to be free from the need to work (i.e., the household includes another earner with sufficient income to provide an acceptable quality of life). Non-Hispanic African American women have average total lifetime earnings of $859,034. They are only a third as likely as white counterparts to be free from the need to work (10.3% vs. 29.9%).

Educational attainment plays a major role in the amount of lifetime earnings. Earnings differences by education level are relatively small at the beginning of an individual's career (ages 25–29 years) but grow during an individual's working life. Anthony Carnevale and colleagues (2011) find that the earnings of all workers aged 40 to 44 years are considerably higher than those of workers aged 25 to 29 years, and these differences are not dependent on educational attainment. However, they observe an earnings increase over time, and the size of the increase is positively associated with educational attainment. Lifetime earnings are 13% to 16% lower for African Americans than for whites, but there are three prominent exceptions: the earnings of African Americans with less than a high school diploma are 18% lower than those of whites with the same attainment, the earnings of African Americans with bachelor's degrees are 20% less than those of whites who hold such degrees, and the earnings of African Americans with professional degrees are 23% lower than those of whites with such degrees. Emeka (2007) also examines the lifetime earnings differential (which she calls the "white advantage," 23), finding that the total difference drops by $456,320 among African American men if they receive the same return as their white counterparts on education and benefits related to other characteristics. If African American and white women receive the same return on their educational investments and the same benefits associated with demographic characteristics, this difference would drop by $95,152.

Assets

Table 3.1 presents estimates on the assets and wealth of African American household heads older than age 55 years. Data for these estimates come from the 2009 Panel Study of Income Dynamics.[3] The most commonly held real asset, an owned home, is reported by 61.6% of this population. Homeownership is reported almost as frequently as having money in the bank (62.3%). Markedly fewer African American respondents have assets in categories other than the home and transaction accounts. Approximately 10.1% report other real estate holdings, 9.4% report that they have an annuity or IRA, and 13.4% report holding other assets. Around 4% of African American household heads own a farm or business, and about the same proportion owns stock. Approximately 45% of this sample has some debt, which could become burdensome in retirement. These figures translate into a median net worth of $37,100 if home equity is included and $5,000 if it is not.

The results are quite different for non-Hispanic whites over age 55 years. Compared to their African American counterparts, those older whites are more likely to own a home, farm, business, other real estate, stocks, other assets, and annuity or IRA, but the values of these assets are much higher. As shown in Table 3.1, median home equity is twice as high for older white homeowners as for

TABLE 3.1. *Asset Holding among Household Heads Older than Age 55 Years*

Asset	% with asset	25th percentile ($)	Median ($)	75th percentile ($)
	African Americans (n = 636)			
Own home or has equity	61.6	30,000	60,000	100,300
Farm or business	4.1	0	9,500	55,000
Money in savings or checking	62.3	500	2,000	8,000
Debt (not home or car)	44.8	2,000	6,100	20,000
Other real estate	10.1	15,000	55,000	150,000
Stocks	3.9	40,000	60,000	220,000
Other assets	13.7	5,000	15,000	50,000
Annuity or IRA	9.4	13,500	28,000	88,250
Wealth with home equity	100	1,000	37,100	102,375
Wealth without home equity	100	0	5,000	30,000
	Non-Hispanic whites (n = 1,691)			
Own home or has equity	81.4	70,000	137,000	233,900
Farm or business	16.7	3,500	100,000	444,000
Money in savings or checking	90.1	3,000	12,000	50,000
Debt (not home or car)	39.3	2,000	6,000	15,000
Other real estate	25.4	45,000	100,000	300,000
Stocks	33.8	15,000	65,000	200,000
Other assets	24.9	8,000	20,000	57,500
Annuity or IRA	46.2	25,000	69,500	183,500
Wealth with home equity	100	72,046	250,000	582,000
Wealth without home equity	100	16,000	110,000	355,000

Source: Tabulation by authors using data from the 2009 Panel Study of Income Dynamics.
Note: IRA = individual retirement account.

African American ones ($137,000 vs. $60,000). The median value of older whites' farm and business assets is 10 times that held by African Americans ($100,000 vs. $9,500). The value of other real estate held by older whites is almost twice that held by older African Americans ($100,000 vs. $55,000). The value of annuities and IRAs held by these white household heads is also more than double that of their African American counterparts, and the whites have six times the amount of money in the bank. Thus, the overall net worth of these white respondents is many times that of the African American household heads. If home equity is included, the net worth of these white respondents is nearly seven times that of the sampled African Americans ($250,000 vs. $37,100). If home equity is excluded, the older whites have 20 times the financial net worth of their African American counterparts ($110,000 vs. $5,000). As previously mentioned, home equity is the most common form of wealth in the United States, and it is reported by high proportions of respondents in both groups. However, the proportion (81.4%) is considerably greater among white household heads, and this suggests that white Americans are more likely to have access to this resource for retirement needs.

Sources of Retirement Income

The metaphorical three-legged stool of retirement income is supported by employer-sponsored retirement plans, Social Security benefits, and personal savings. Because of differences in access to retirement plans and their benefits, and because some African Americans have limited ability to accrue personal savings, the three-legged stool does not provide adequate income to keep many African American older adults out of poverty.

Employer Pensions and Retirement Plans

Among workers aged 25 to 59 years, access to employer-sponsored pensions and retirement plans varies markedly by race. These differences foreshadow the racial gap in financial security among retirees. Across all racial groups, nearly three of every five workers aged 25 to 59 years (in 2009) reported that they were offered an employer-sponsored pension. About half reported that they participated in the plans offered to them (Butrica and Johnson 2010). Thus, 84% of workers offered plans participated in them. These percentages were smaller among younger workers and larger among older ones. Among workers aged 25 to 29 years, 73% were both offered and participated in plans. The same is true of 89% of workers aged 55 to 59 years.

Looking at the workers aged 55 to 59 years by race, we find that non-Hispanic whites are more likely than non-Hispanic African Americans to be offered retirement plans: 68% of whites but only 62.8% of African Americans (Butrica and Johnson 2010). Also, the uptake on employer-sponsored retirement plans is greater among non-Hispanic whites (61% vs. 54%). Consequently, the percentage of older white workers offered and participating in employer-sponsored retirement plans (90%) is greater than the corresponding percentage of their non-Hispanic African American counterparts (87%).

Trends in the receipt of employer-sponsored pensions and annuities among adults aged 65 years or older reflect the racial disparities noted among the working age population. One of every five (20.3%) African American aged units 65 years or older reports receiving income from private pensions or annuities, but 28% of corresponding white aged units report this (Social Security Administration 2012). In addition, 11% of these same African American units receive a public pension, but 16% of their white counterparts receive one. However, the value of employer-sponsored pensions received by African American aged units 65 years or older is greater than that of pensions received by white units in the same age group ($14,148 vs. $12,380; Social Security Administration 2012). This counterintuitive finding may reflect differences in the distribution of earnings among African Americans and whites who receive pensions.

Social Security

The Social Security system guarantees that workers in covered occupations (and their dependents) will receive benefits in the event of disability, death, or retirement (Social Security Administration 2013). These benefits are paid for by FICA (Federal Insurance Contributions Act) taxes levied on workers in covered occupations and by their employers (on behalf of these workers).[4] Most Africans Americans and whites aged 65 years or older receive Social Security benefits: 79% of African Americans and 86% of whites in 2010. For both racial groups, the proportion receiving benefits increases after age 70 years. Benefits are received by 89% of whites between the ages of 70 and 74 years and by 82% of African Americans in that age group. These percentages increase as adults age: 92% of whites aged 80 years or older and 87% of their African American counterparts (Social Security Administration 2012).

Social Security is a particularly essential support for older adult households living in poverty. In both racial groups, most poor households with at least one member aged 65 years or older receive Social Security benefits, and the proportions are similar for the two groups: in 2010, the Social Security Administration paid benefits to about 70% of poor older adults in multiperson households and to 75% of those living alone (Social Security Administration 2011). In addition, these benefits constitute three-fourths or more of the income received by more than two-thirds of poor African American and white older adults living alone (Social Security Administration 2011).

Thus, Social Security benefits function as a true income safety net for many older adults, but the modest benefits guarantee that recipients are likely to live in poverty if the payments are a major source of their income. Average annual Social Security retiree benefits from 2009 suggest that

African American retiree households fall below the poverty threshold if Social Security benefits are their only source of income: the federal poverty threshold for householders aged 65 years or over is $12,982, African American retiree households received an average Social Security benefit of $12,415.20 annually, and their white counterparts received $14,280 (Social Security Administration 2011).[5]

Personal Savings

On average, African American workers save less for retirement than do workers of all races combined. As indicated in Table 3.1, 46% of non-Hispanic whites have retirement savings in an annuity or IRA, but only 9% of non-Hispanic African Americans have savings in such a vehicle (the overall values also are lower). Furthermore, in 2007, nearly half of all workers reported that they have saved less than $25,000 for their retirement, but 70% of African American workers reported this (Helman, VanDerhei, and Copeland 2007). A racial disparity is observed at the other end of the savings scale as well: 14% of all workers reported having saved $250,000 or more for retirement, but only 4% of African American workers reported this.

■ POLICY IMPLICATIONS

The most successful way to acquire assets is to save throughout one's lifetime. Starting to save during childhood and early working years can increase the number and value of assets acquired. In particular, each of the three legs of the retirement income stool becomes sturdier the longer contributions are made to it. Historically, the employer-sponsored pension plan was the strongest leg of the stool, with Social Security and personal savings providing additional income as needed. Over time, however, changes to the employer-sponsored retirement system and the inability of many workers to save for retirement have shifted the support available for this stool. Social Security is the primary leg (if not the only one) on their retirement income stool.

Each leg of the stool could be strengthened to benefit older adults, especially African Americans and those with low income. For example, child savings accounts (in the form of college savings plans) are available in the 50 states and Washington, DC, but no such account is available early in life to encourage saving toward retirement needs. As we have noted, Social Security benefits are not adequate to cover the living expenses of retirees who have no other source of income (Social Security Administration 2011). Finally, the normative type of employer-sponsored savings plan has changed in recent decades as employers have chosen to shift the financial responsibility and risk for amassing retirement savings, transferring such obligations from themselves to their employees (U.S. Bureau of Labor Statistics 2009).

This section explores policy issues and offers recommendations to address challenges that impede older African Americans from acquiring the assets needed for this period in their lives. It covers two broad areas: policies that change the type and value of assets available to individuals in retirement and policies that focus on youth and working-age adults in an attempt to expand access to assets prior to retirement. We begin by summarizing the nine major recommendations:

- Change the legislation and regulations that govern defined-benefit (DB) retirement plans to make them more attractive to employers and thereby more widely available to employees.
- Increase monthly Social Security retirement payments to lifetime low-wage earners.
- Decrease the disadvantage embedded in the Social Security benefit formula for beneficiaries who never marry.
- Modify the formula used to calculate Social Security benefits payable to the widowed spouses of lifetime low-wage workers.
- Provide job and career training or retraining to enable low-wage workers to increase their lifetime earnings.
- To better meet the needs of workers aged 55 years or older, enhance job flexibility and the types of benefits provided.
- Create a universal Child Development Account model that allows children to build assets for the future.
- Update and streamline current incentives in the tax code so that low- and moderate-income households have the opportunity to prepare and save for key life events.
- Expand the availability of accounts dedicated for retirement so that everyone, regardless of employment, has the opportunity to receive matched savings for use in later life.

Employer-Sponsored Retirement Plans

In recent years, the landscape of employer-sponsored retirement plans has shifted from an environment dominated by pensions (i.e., DB plans) to one in which workers are more likely to have defined-contribution (DC) plans. A DB plan guarantees a participant a specified monthly benefit at retirement. Often the benefit is calculated using a formula based on factors such as the participant's salary, age, and length of employment with an employer. With a DC plan, the employee and employer contribute to the employee's retirement account, and these contributions are subsequently invested to increase the account's yield. Thus, the amount in the account is determined by the contributions to it, investment gains, investment losses, and investment or administrative fees paid. Examples of DC plans include 401(k) plans, 403(b) plans, employee stock-ownership plans, and profit-sharing plans (Internal Revenue Service 2014).

Since 1980, the share of private-sector employees who participate in DB plans has declined dramatically, and the share participating in DC plans has increased. Between 1980 and 2008, the proportion of private-sector workers participating solely in DB pension plans dropped from 38% to 20%. Simultaneously, the share of these workers who participated solely in DC plans increased from 8% to 31% (Butrica et al. 2009). These plans have become increasingly available to workers in both the private and public sectors: as of March 2010, 59% of private-sector workers had access to a 401(k) plan, and 41% participated in such a plan. At the same time, 29% of state and local government workers had access to such a plan, and 17% participated (U.S. Bureau of Labor Statistics 2010).

Why does the type of employer-sponsored retirement plan matter, especially for African American seniors? To maximize asset holdings at retirement, an employee with access to a DC plan would need to enroll in the plan, make regular contributions, and refrain from diminishing the value of plan contributions (via loans or hardship withdrawals) over his or her working life (Ariel Education Initiative and Aon Hewitt 2012). Employees would also have to invest wisely. This is a tall order for many workers and especially for African American workers who have persistently high unemployment rates and lower-than-average incomes.

A key difference between DB and DC plans is that the DB plans protect workers from themselves. In particular, DB plans protect workers from the idiosyncratic, temptation, market, and longevity risks that they face if enrolled in DC plans (Ghilarducci 2006).

Idiosyncratic risk is the risk that workers will make unwise or unlucky investment decisions. This is avoided with DB plans because they are managed professionally and plan managers cannot place more than 10% of holdings in any one asset. The structure and magnitude of assets in employer-sponsored DB plans allow enrollees to pay wholesale (rather than retail) investment costs, limiting the amount of each dollar that is diverted from retirement savings to cover account fees. Temptation risk in DC plans is tied to provisions that allow preretirement expenditures via loans and withdrawals. These plans also face market risk: stock market trends may leave DC participants with too few assets for a financially secure retirement. In contrast, the large pool of assets held in DB plans smooths market risk for individual workers. Finally, DB plans avoid longevity risk (the risk of outliving one's savings) because they offer monthly lifetime benefit payments that self-annuitize.[6] These plans provide monthly benefits from the beginning of retirement through the end of life.

Thus, DB plans would be especially beneficial to older African Americans: compared with older whites, they are less likely to maximize saving outcomes from DC plans. This is so because African Americans are less likely to participate in a DC plan if one is accessible and are more likely to take loans and hardship withdrawals, especially during periods such as the Great Recession (Ariel Education Initiative and Aon Hewitt 2012).

Given the relative benefits, why do DB plans constitute a declining proportion of employer-sponsored retirement options? One reason is that the shift from DB to DC plans can reduce the costs employers face in providing retirement benefits to employees (U.S. Bureau of Labor Statistics 2009). Another is that federal laws and regulations give DC plans an advantage (Butrica et al. 2009; Gebhardtsbauer 2004). Employees favor DC plan provisions that enable them to defer tax payments on contributions and allow their employers to match employee contributions. In addition, the Pension Protection Act of 2006 strengthened DB plan reporting, disclosure, and funding rules (Pub. L. 109-280, 120 Stat. 780 [2006]). Such changes support employers and employees' growing preferences for DC plans. Modifying these factors could enhance the likelihood that employers will offer DB plans or hybrid arrangements that combine the features of DB and DC plans (Butrica et al. 2009; Gebhardtsbauer 2004).

Social Security System

Social Security retirement benefits help to decrease income insecurity for many older African Americans and are the sole source of retirement income for others. However, the program rules and structure of Social Security impose disadvantages on some older African Americans. Examples of these features can be found in Social Security's provisions for individuals who have earned low wages throughout the working years and for those who never married. Compared with whites, African Americans are more likely to belong to both groups.[7] As the family structure of the U.S. population evolves, policymakers should consider restructuring the system to better meet the needs of persons who have low lifetime earnings and those who never marry (Rockeymoore and Lui 2011).

Low-Income Lifetime Earners

Although Social Security uses a progressive formula to calculate benefits, returning more to lower-earning workers, individuals who have earned low incomes throughout their working years receive small monthly benefit payments because these payments are based on FICA taxes paid into the Social Security system, and those tax obligations are calculated as a fixed percentage of earnings up to a capped amount (Social Security Administration 2013). In the 1970s, policymakers adopted a special minimum benefit to address this problem by ensuring that low-wage workers with at least 30 years of covered employment would receive a certain minimum benefit if their regularly calculated payment was less than this amount (Social Security Administration 2014). Because Social Security does not index the special minimum benefit to keep pace with wage growth, the benefit is phasing out over time (Olsen and Hoffmeyer 2001/2002). A strategy is needed to ensure that Social Security benefits provide retirees with a minimum level of financial assistance and that this level remains above the federal poverty threshold over time.

Marital Status

Because adults who never marry are ineligible for the spousal and survivor benefits that Social Security provides, they may be more financially insecure during retirement than are their married and widowed counterparts. This is particularly the case for older African Americans (Kreider and Ellis 2011), whose average lifetime earnings and those of their spouses are lower than the average lifetime earnings of white counterparts. Social Security rules governing the benefits received by widowed spouses are likely to impose a disadvantage on African American beneficiaries, since survivor benefits are calculated as a fraction (usually between 50% and 67%) of a couple's benefits (Entmacher 2009). Policymakers would help surviving spouses by increasing benefits for surviving spouses to 75% of that received by the two spouses. Such a change would help decrease poverty among low-income Social Security beneficiaries. This new benefit could be targeted to low-income couples by capping it at the benefit level for the lifelong average earner ($1,484 for a person retiring at age 66 years in 2009; Reno and Lavery 2009).

Employment Enhancements

Labor-force participation rates and employment-to-population ratios suggest that African Americans aged 55 years or older are disadvantaged relative to their white and younger African American counterparts. Intermittent and low-wage employment limits lifetime earnings and, thus, the assets available to older African Americans in retirement. However, several innovations could play important roles in strengthening the economic positions that workers will face in retirement.

Job and Career Training and Retraining

Training and retraining offer ways to address these labor market disparities and the associated lifetime earnings for African Americans. Mentoring and retraining programs could help workers aged 55 years or older move from physically demanding jobs into positions that are less so, enabling them to continue working (Urban Institute 2011). Training in the use of technology may be especially helpful. However, the livelihood of older African Americans also depends on their ability to find and secure these suitable jobs. Both the labor market and older African Americans would benefit from increased interest in and employment of seasoned workers.

Since the late 1970s, government training funds have declined nearly 70% (Holzer and Martinson 2008; Urban Institute 2011). The limited funding available for workforce development and training programs is an impediment to expanding job access via training or retraining. For example, the federal Senior Community Service Employment Program provides training and subsidized employment to low-income adults aged 55 years or older, but the program has funding to serve only 1% of eligible adults (U.S. Department of Labor 2010).

Enhanced Job Flexibility

Increasing flexibility in the workplace (e.g., via shortened hours or teleworking) also could benefit workers aged 55 years or older. For example, these workers and others who serve as caregivers for family members would benefit from expansion of the Family and Medical Leave Act (26 U.S.C. § 2601 [2012]) to cover additional segments of the workforce and to provide paid (instead of unpaid) leave during the 12-week period allowed annually by the law. Currently, the act covers only workers who are employed in firms with 50 or more employees, worked for their employer at least 12 months, and have worked for at least 1,250 hours that year (Urban Institute 2011). California is the only state with a comprehensive, paid, family and medical leave insurance program.[8]

Child Development Accounts

Socioeconomic status has a well-documented influence on child outcomes (McLoyd 1998; Williams Shanks et al. 2010). Low-income, low-wealth families struggle to provide resources for their children and often cannot afford to assist them with the costs of college, a home mortgage, or other important investments that could help them get a good start in life. Thus, compared with other children, those from low-income, low-wealth backgrounds grow up with less economic security and are not as likely to be prepared for retirement.

Child Development Accounts are one suggestion for breaking the link between low household socioeconomic status and poor child outcomes. Although 529 college savings plans are offered in all 50 states, only a small proportion of low-income families participate: these 529 accounts are held by 17% of households with children and income of $35,000 or less but by more than half of households with children and income of $100,000 or more (Sallie Mae and Gallup 2009). Interestingly, 95% of African American families expect their children to go to college, and 62% of African American parents with children under age 18 have actually saved something toward that goal. Yet only 28% of African American parents surveyed are actually likely to meet their college savings target (Sallie Mae and Gallup 2009). Thus, many African American parents need support in helping children reach long-term economic and personal development goals.

Although several commentators have recommended a universal Child Development Account policy that features a developmentally appropriate infrastructure as well as incentives (Friedline 2012; Goldberg 2005), this approach is not a part of federal policy in the United States. Yet, there have been important legislative proposals. For example, the Americans Saving for Personal Investment, Retirement, and Education Act (the ASPIRE Act) has been proposed in Congress several times with bipartisan support.[9] Maine's Harold Alfond College Challenge offers $500 to every newborn who is enrolled in that state's 529 college plan before reaching 1 year of age (Clancy and Lassar 2010). The City of San Francisco has launched a Kindergarten to College program that offers an account with an initial $50 deposit to all children attending kindergarten in public schools (Phillips and Stuhldreher 2011). Many similar Child Development Account programs are being discussed or have been proposed around the country.

Several other countries have implemented child account policies (Loke and Sherraden 2008). The two most prominent examples are the United Kingdom and Singapore. The United Kingdom's Child Trust Fund was a very ambitious program that provided a certificate for at least £250 to the parents of every baby born in the country and offered additional funds to the parents of low-income children. Parents used these certificates to open an account on their child's behalf, and savings in the accounts grow tax free until the child reaches age 18 years. At that point, the government lifts all restrictions on usage. When the program launched in 2005, three million Child Trust Funds were opened. By 2007, about 25% of these accounts held additional contributions beyond the initial government deposit (Bennett et al. 2008). Unfortunately, political developments in 2010 and subsequent budget cuts led to an amendment of the original legislation and to abolition of the universal program. Children with existing accounts can retain them, but infants born after January 2, 2011, are no longer eligible for guaranteed enrollment with the initial £250 deposit.

Singapore has several types of child accounts. One can be used for preschool and other education- or health-related expenses from birth to age 6 years (Loke and Sherraden 2008). The government has also created the Post-Secondary Education Account to cover the approved education-related expenses of children aged 7 to 20 years. Unused balances from the accounts for young children (birth to age 6 years) roll over into these children's Post-Secondary Education Accounts, and account beneficiaries can, in turn, roll unused balances from them into their Central Provident Fund account, the vehicle provided by Singapore's retirement system. Thus, Singapore has established a lifelong system of accounts to help its citizens build assets and meet personal and financial goals (Loke and Cramer 2009).

The ideal way to assist African Americans would be to implement a set of policies that facilitate asset building throughout the life course. A substantive, well-funded Child Development Account policy could provide a good start, however. Such accounts would have to be inclusive and reach every child in a specified area. If implemented well, the accounts could initiate the habit of saving and perhaps inspire young people to seek other savings products as they enter young adulthood. As in Singapore, children could transition from a child account to an adult fund, taking any leftover money with them. The next section introduces several forms that an adult account might take.

Asset-Building Opportunities for Low- and Moderate-Income Households

In 2009, nearly $400 billion in federal funding went to help families buy homes, start businesses, put their children through college, and retire comfortably (Woo, Rademacher, and Meier 2010). Yet, most of these asset-building expenditures go to high-income earners. The top fifth of income taxpayers receive 84% of the asset-building subsidies and benefits, but the bottom 60% of taxpayers receive only 4% of these asset-building benefits (Woo et al. 2010). Similar estimates from the New America Foundation examine the proposed federal budget for 2013, indicating that direct spending programs and policies embedded in the tax code together would account for $548 billion in prosavings and asset-building resources (Cramer, Black, and King 2012). And again, most of these proposals would benefit the highest income earners.

There are several reasons why low- to moderate-income families get a smaller share of these funds. Some have very little tax liability and are not eligible for a refund. Others do not hold or do not itemize the assets that receive the most tax breaks (e.g., do not pay interest on a home mortgage, own a personal business, or hold specific, tax-favored retirement funds). It is paradoxical that federal benefits are so dramatically skewed to benefit the well-off when assisting those who are economically less secure could potentially have a greater economic impact. This exacerbates existing inequities and often leaves older African Americans with few options for supplementing the assets available in retirement.

Many things can be done to shift this balance. The Aspen Institute has made the case for "new accounts and new money" (Mensah 2012, 2). This vision calls for policies, products, and practices that provide low-income people with access to the financial system in ways that are safe and fair. It also proposes modifying the tax code to benefit the millions who are currently left out when it comes to building assets (potentially the bottom 60% of households). Specific proposals have been advanced to accomplish this vision, and examples include the Freedom Savings Credit (Mensah et al. 2012), AutoIRAs, Universal 401(k)s, the Savings for Working Families Act (H.R. 2964, 113th Cong. [2013]), AutoSave, expansion and improvement of the current saver's credit, and a saver's bonus at tax time (for discussion of these and more examples, see Cramer et al. 2010). Most scholars, advocates, and policymakers working in this area are less concerned about finding an ideal approach than about using tax reform negotiations to carve out much larger benefits and incentives to support asset building among low- and moderate-income families.

Expansion of Dedicated Retirement Accounts

Currently, structured retirement savings programs are tied primarily to employers and workplace benefits. Unfortunately, even those who have access to 401(k) plans and other voluntary savings programs typically do not save sufficient amounts to achieve financial security in retirement (Ghilarducci 2012). On average, the bottom 75% of earners nearing retirement age have saved just over $26,000 (Saad-Lessler and Ghilarducci 2012). Finding ways to help African Americans save for retirement during their working years would help strengthen this important leg of their retirement-income stool. Some have proposed the creation of Retirement Investment Account Plans to provide a clearinghouse for workplace contributions (Cramer et al. 2010). Others note the high fees in managed mutual fund plans and suggest that a low-fee government index option could be a cost-saving alternative (Cramer et al. 2010; Ghilarducci 2012). President Obama (2014) even proposed a plan to create government-backed retirement accounts in his 2014 State of the Union address—he called them MyRA accounts.

■ CONCLUSIONS

This chapter provides a detailed analysis of the assets of older African Americans and discusses policies that might improve their economic security. As can be seen in the data presented here, older African Americans are in a tenuous position. They need additional supports when young as well as ways to increase and preserve assets available to them during retirement. Policies could achieve these objectives; they have precedents in other countries. In the United States, however, implementing innovative policies and programs typically occurs in piecemeal fashion or as part of large-scale political compromises. Such policymaking often fails to focus on how low-income African Americans (or any other subpopulation) might fare. Economic security for older African Americans can be achieved if we can summon the political will to make it a priority.

■ NOTES

1. American FactFinder (data from the U.S. Census Bureau's American Community Survey); accessed May 11, 2014, http://factfinder2.census.gov/faces/nav/jsf/pages/index .xhtml. Data by age group are provided for income ranges only.

2. Per the Social Security Administration (2012), aged units 65 years or older are married couples living together (at least one member of the couple is aged 65 years or older)

or nonmarried persons in the same age group. Income derived from assets is defined as interest, dividends, rent or royalties, and estates or trusts.

3. These data are taken only from heads of household. Thus, these estimates do not reflect persons aged 55 years or over who live with relatives.

4. Federal Insurance Contributions Act, I.R.C. § 3101 (2012).

5. Social Security data on the racial composition of retirement beneficiaries are not available for 2010. Averages are available on the race of beneficiaries in the three programs (disability, survivor, and retirement) combined and are provided here for comparison with the 2009 data. The average annual Social Security benefit received by African Americans in 2010 was $11,367. That is less than the $13,105 average benefit received by whites (Social Security Administration 2011). Similarly, the 2010 median Social Security benefit received by African American aged units 65 years or older ($12,612) was less than that received by corresponding white beneficiary units ($16,157; Social Security Administration 2012).

6. In other words, benefit payments come from assets and regular income. Therefore, participants are not required to work with or pay fees to an insurance company in order to initiate payments.

7. In 2009, the percentage of never-married African American women exceeded that of non-Hispanic white women in each age group (25–29, 30–34, 35–39, 40–44, 45–49, 50–54, and 55 or older; Kreider and Ellis 2011).

8. The California family and medical leave insurance program has been described as follows: "Funded solely by employee contributions, the program pays workers up to 60% of their wages when they take leave to care for newborns, newly adopted children, newly placed foster children, or seriously ill family members or domestic partners. Workers can receive up to 6 weeks of paid leave per year" (*Are the Explosive Costs of Elder Care Hurting Family Finances and Business Competition? Hearing Before the Joint Economic Comm.*, 110th Cong. 29, 33 [May 16, 2007] [statement of Richard W. Johnson]). See also Urban Institute (2011).

9. See, e.g., H.R. 3740, 110th Cong. (2007); H.R. 4682, 111th Cong. (2010).

■ **REFERENCES**

Ariel Education Initiative and Aon Hewitt. 2012. *401(k) Plans in Living Color: A Study of 401(k) Savings Disparities across Racial and Ethnic Groups.* Report. Chicago: Ariel Education Initiative. http://www.arielinvestments.com/images/stories/PDF/ariel-aonhewitt-2012.pdf.

Bennett, Jim, Elena Chávez Quezada, Kayte Lawton, and Pamela Perun. 2008. *The U.K. Child Trust Fund: A Successful Launch.* Report. London: Institute for Public Policy Research and Aspen Institute. https://www.aspeninstitute.org/sites/default/files/content/docs/pubs/UK_Paper_Text.pdf.

Butrica, Barbara A., Howard M. Iams, Karen E. Smith, and Eric J. Toder. 2009. "The Disappearing Defined Benefit Pension and Its Potential Impact on the Retirement Incomes of Baby Boomers." *Social Security Bulletin* 69 (3): 1–27. http://www.ssa.gov/policy/docs/ssb/v69n3/v69n3p1.pdf.

Butrica, Barbara A., and Richard W. Johnson. 2010. "Racial, Ethnic, and Gender Differentials in Employer-Sponsored Pensions." Statement before the ERISA Advisory Council, June 30. Washington, DC: Urban Institute. http://www.urban.org/UploadedPDF/901357-racial-ethnic-gender-differentials.pdf.

Carnevale, Anthony P., Stephen J. Rose, and Ban Cheah. 2011. *The College Payoff: Education, Occupations, and Lifetime Earnings*. Report, August 5. Washington, DC: Georgetown University Center on Education and the Workforce. http://cew.georgetown.edu /collegepayoff.

Clancy, Margaret, and Terry Lassar. 2010. *College Savings Plan Accounts at Birth: Maine's Statewide Program*. CSD Policy Brief 10-16, May. St. Louis, MO: Washington University, Center for Social Development. http://csd.wustl.edu/Publications /Documents/PB10-16.pdf.

Cramer, Reid, Rachel Black, and Justin King. 2012. *The Assets Report 2012: An Assessment of the Federal "Asset-Building" Budget*. Asset Building Program Report, April. Washington, DC: New America Foundation. http://assets.newamerica.net/sites /newamerica.net/files/policydocs/AssetsReport2012.pdf.

Cramer, Reid, Alejandra Lopez-Fernandina, Lindsay Guge, Justin King, and Jamie Zimmerman. 2010. *The Assets Agenda 2011: Policy Options to Promote Savings and Asset Development*. Asset Building Program Report, September. Washington, DC: New America Foundation. http://assets.newamerica.net/sites/newamerica.net /files/policydocs/Assets_Agenda_2011.pdf.

DeNavas-Walt, Carmen, Bernadette D. Proctor, and Jessica C. Smith. 2011. *Income, Poverty, and Health Insurance Coverage in the United States: 2010*. Current Population Reports: Consumer Income, P60-239. Washington, DC: U.S. Census Bureau. http://www. census.gov/prod/2011pubs/p60-239.pdf.

Emeka, Amon. 2007. "Race and Lifetime Earnings: Assessing the Cumulative Costs of Minority Status Using Cross-Sectional Data." Paper presented at the biannual meetings of the ISA Research Committee on Social Stratification and Mobility, Quebec, August 14–17. http://www.mcgill.ca/iris/files/Panel6.1Emeka.pdf.

Entmacher, Joan. 2009. "Strengthening Social Security Benefits for Widow(er)s: The 75 Percent Combined Worker Benefit Alternative." In *Strengthening Social Security for Vulnerable Groups*, 23–26. Washington, DC: National Academy of Social Insurance. http://www.nasi.org/sites/default/files/research/Strengthening_Social_Security _for_Vulnerable_Groups.pdf.

Friedline, Terri. 2012. *The Case for Extending Financial Inclusion to Children: The Role of Parents' Financial Resources and Implications for Policy Innovations*. Asset Building Program Report, May. Washington, DC: New America Foundation. http://assets.newamerica.net/sites/newamerica.net/files/policydocs /CaseforFin InclusionFriedlineMay12.pdf.

Gebhardtsbauer, Ron. 2004. "What Are the Trade-Offs? Defined Benefit vs. Defined Contribution Systems." Paper presented at AARP/CEPS Forum, A Balancing Act: Achieving Adequacy and Sustainability in Retirement Income Reform, Brussels, March 4. http://www.actuary.org/pdf/pension/tradeoffs_030404.pdf.

Ghilarducci, Teresa. 2006. *Future Retirement Income Security Needs Defined Benefit Pensions*. Report, March. Washington, DC: Center for American Progress. http://americanprogress.org/issues/economy/news/2006/05/19/1971 /future-retirement-income-security-needs-defined-benefit-pensions/.

Ghilarducci, Teresa. 2012. "Our Ridiculous Approach to Retirement." *New York Times*, July 21. http://www.nytimes.com/2012/07/22/opinion/sunday/our-ridiculous -approach-to-retirement.html?_r=0.

Goldberg, Fred. 2005. "The Universal Piggy Bank: Designing and Implementing a System of Savings Accounts for Children." In *Inclusion in the American Dream*, edited by Michael Sherraden, 302–322. New York: Oxford University Press.

Helman, Ruth, Jack VanDerhei, and Craig Copeland. 2007. *Minority Workers Remain Confident about Retirement, Despite Lagging Preparations and False Expectations.* Issue Brief 306, June. Washington, DC: Employee Benefit Research Institute. http://www .ebri.org/pdf/briefspdf/EBRI_IB_06-20079.pdf.

Holzer, Harry J., and Karin Martinson. 2008. *Helping Poor Working Parents Get Ahead: Federal Funds for New State Strategies and Systems.* New Safety Net Report 4, July. Washington, DC: Urban Institute. http://www.urban.org/UploadedPDF /411722_working_parents.pdf.

Internal Revenue Service. 2014. "Definitions." Last modified January 24. http://www.irs .gov/Retirement-Plans/Plan-Participant,-Employee/Definitions.

Kreider, Rose M., and Renee Ellis. 2011. *Number, Timing, and Duration of Marriages and Divorces: 2009.* Current Population Reports, P70-125. Washington, DC: U.S. Census Bureau. http://www.census.gov/prod/2011pubs/p70-125.pdf.

Loke, Vernon, and Reid Cramer. 2009. "Singapore's Central Provident Fund: A National Policy of Life-Long Asset Accounts." Working Paper, April. Washington, DC: New America Foundation. http://www.newamerica.net/files/0409singapore_report_and _ appendix.pdf.

Loke, Vernon, and Michael Sherraden. 2008. *Building Assets from Birth: A Global Comparison of Child Development Account Policies.* CSD Working Paper 08-03. St. Louis, MO: Washington University, Center for Social Development. http://csd .wustl.edu/Publications/Documents/WP08-03.pdf.

McLoyd, Vonnie C. 1998. "Socioeconomic Disadvantage and Child Development." *American Psychologist* 53 (2): 185–204. doi: 10.1037/0003-066X.53.2.185.

Mensah, Lisa. 2012. *Building Financial Security in America: A 2020–2030 Vision.* Initiative on Financial Security Brief, March. Washington, DC: Aspen Institute. http://asset-funders.org/documents/AFN_AssetPrimer_FINAL.pdf.

Mensah, Lisa, Raymond O'Mara III, Colby Farber, and Robert Weinberger. 2012. *The Freedom Savings Credit: A Practical Step to Build Americans' Household Balance Sheets.* Initiative on Financial Security Issue Brief, February. Washington, DC: Aspen Institute. http://www.aspeninstitute.org/sites/default/files/content/docs /pubs/Freedom SavingsCredit_0.pdf.

Obama, Barack H. 2014. *Address before a Joint Session of the Congress on the State of the Union.* Daily Compilation of Presidential Documents DCPD-201400050, January 28. Washington, DC: National Archives and Records Administration, Office of the Federal Register. http://www.gpo.gov/fdsys/pkg/DCPD-201400050/pdf/DCPD-201400050.pdf.

Olsen, Kelly A., and Don Hoffmeyer. 2001/2002. "Social Security's Special Minimum Benefit." *Social Security Bulletin* 64 (2): 1–15. http://www.ssa.gov/policy/docs/ssb /v64n2/v64n2p1.pdf.

Phillips, Leigh, and Anne Stuhldreher. 2011. *Kindergarten to College (K2C): A First-in-the-Nation Initiative to Set All Kindergartners on the Path to College.* Asset Building Program Report, September. Washington, DC: New America Foundation. http://assets.newamerica.net/sites/newamerica.net/files/policydocs /K2CFinal9_26_2011_0.pdf.

Reno, Virginia P., and Joni Lavery. 2009. *Fixing Social Security: Adequate Benefits, Adequate Financing.* Report, October. Washington, DC: National Academy of Social Insurance. http://www.nasi.org/sites/default/files/research/Fixing_Social_Security.pdf.

Rockeymoore, Maya M., and Meizhu Lui. 2011. *Plan for a New Future: The Impact of Social Security Reform on People of Color.* Report, October. Washington, DC: Commission to Modernize Social Security. http://modernizesocialsecurity.files.wordpress .com/2013/04/new_future_social_security_10_24_11.pdf.

Saad-Lessler, Joelle, and Teresa Ghilarducci. 2012. *Near Retiree's Defined Contribution Retirement Account Balances: Analysis of the 2008 Survey of Income and Program Participation (SIPP), Wave 7.* Retirement Income Security Project Fact Sheet, July. New York: New School, Schwartz Center for Economic Policy Analysis. http://www .economicpolicyresearch.org/images/docs/SCEPA_blog/guaranteeing_retirement _income/Fact_Sheet_Retirement_Balances_july_2012_revised_FINAL.pdf.

Sallie Mae and Gallup. 2009. *How America Saves for College: Sallie Mae's National Study of Parents with Children under the Age of 18.* Report, September. Reston, VA: Sallie Mae. http://news.salliemae.com/sites/salliemae.newshq.businesswire.com/files/doc _library/file/GCR2123HowAmericaSavesforCollege2009Report.pdf.

Social Security Administration, Office of Retirement and Disability Policy, Office of Research, Evaluation, and Statistics. 2011. *Annual Statistical Supplement to the Social Security Bulletin, 2010.* SSA Publication 13-11700, February. Washington, DC: Social Security Administration. https://www.socialsecurity.gov/policy/docs/statcomps /supplement/2010/supplement10.pdf.

Social Security Administration, Office of Retirement and Disability Policy, Office of Research, Evaluation, and Statistics. 2012. *Income of the Population 55 or Older, 2010.* SSA Publication 13-11871. Washington, DC: Social Security Administration. https://www .socialsecurity.gov/policy/docs/statcomps/income_pop55/2010/incpop10.pdf.

Social Security Administration, Office of Retirement and Disability Policy, Office of Research, Evaluation, and Statistics. 2013. *Fast Facts and Figures about Social Security, 2013.* SSA Publication 13-11785. Washington, DC: Social Security Administration. http://www.ssa.gov/policy/docs/chartbooks/fast_facts/2013/fast_facts13.pdf.

Social Security Administration, Office of Retirement Policy. 2014. "Special Minimum Benefit." Program Explainer, May. http://www.ssa.gov/retirementpolicy/program /special-minimum.html.

Urban Institute. 2011. *50+ African American Workers: A Status Report, Implications, and Recommendations.* Report, February. Washington, DC: AARP Research and Strategic Analysis. http://assets.aarp.org/rgcenter/econ/aa-workers-11.pdf.

U.S. Bureau of Labor Statistics. 2009. "Defined-Contribution Plans More Common Than Defined-Benefit Plans." *Program Perspectives* 1, no. 3 (March). http://www.bls.gov /opub/perspectives/issue3.pdf.

U.S. Bureau of Labor Statistics. 2010. "BLS Examines Popular 401(k) Retirement Plans." *Program Perspectives* 2, no. 6 (November). http://www.bls.gov/opub/perspectives /program_perspectives_vol2_issue6.pdf.

U.S. Bureau of Labor Statistics. 2011. *Labor Force Characteristics by Race and Ethnicity, 2010.* Report 1032. Washington, DC: U.S. Department of Labor. http://www.bls.gov /cps/cpsrace2010.pdf.

U.S. Department of Labor. 2010. "About SCSEP." Accessed May 20. http://assets.aarp.org /rgcenter/econ/aa-workers-11.pdf.

Williams Shanks, Trina R., Youngmi Kim, Vernon Loke, and Mesmin Destin. 2010. "Assets and Child Well-Being in Developed Countries." *Children and Youth Services Review* 32 (11): 1488–1496. doi: 10.1016/j.childyouth.2010.03.011.

Woo, Beadsie, Ida Rademacher, and Jillien Meier. 2010. *Upside Down: The $400 Billion Federal Asset-Building Budget.* Report. Washington, DC: CFED. http://cfed.org/assets/pdfs/UpsideDown_final.pdf.

4 Economic Security of Older Hispanics

The Role of Social Security and Employer-Sponsored Plans

■ JACQUELINE L. ANGEL AND
STIPICA MUDRAZIJA

As the U.S. population grows older and more diverse, understanding the impact of policies and programs on the financial security of older Americans becomes increasingly important.[1] The expansion of welfare programs throughout the twentieth century changed the economic situation of older adults in major ways. Since 1959, when the U.S. government established an official poverty line, the percentage of older adults in poverty has dropped by over two-thirds: from 35% to 9% (U.S. Census Bureau 2008). The rate is far lower than that among families with small children (Isaacs 2009), and older adults no longer depend to the extent they did in the past on financial support from their grown children.

Policymakers originally envisioned the Social Security program as one of three equally important sources of retirement security (employer-based retirement plans and private savings are the others), but more than eight decades after the program's inception, millions of older adults depend on Social Security to survive (Diamond and Orszag 2004; Quadagno 1988). Without it, over one-third of older Americans would live in poverty. Among households that are in the bottom 60% of the income distribution and are headed by an older adult, Social Security benefits make up at least two-thirds of household income (Social Security Administration 2013). They are the only source of income for one in five older Americans (Social Security Administration 2013).

Although Social Security has improved the well-being of adults in retirement, it has not benefited everyone equally (Butrica, Iams, and Smith 2003/2004). Women and racial and ethnic minorities remain highly vulnerable to financial insecurity. In particular, the economic situation of older Hispanics has improved little relative to that of older non-Hispanic whites, and a large proportion of older Hispanics faces serious financial hardship in retirement (Angel and Angel 2009).

In this study, we examine financial well-being among Hispanics in the years close to and after retirement. We compare the basic economic situations of Hispanics, non-Hispanic whites, and non-Hispanic blacks. Through this comparison, we seek to document large differences in economic well-being: differences in lifetime asset accumulation as well as differences that result from their reliance on disparate types of income and differences that stem from the profound and lingering impact of the recession.

However, Hispanics are not a monolithic group. Cultural differences distinguish those with roots in the Caribbean, those who emigrated from Mexico, and those who have lived in the American Southwest, which was once part of Mexico. Many Cuban-origin Americans are political refugees, Mexican-origin Americans are generally economic immigrants, and Puerto Ricans are citizens with all of the associated rights and privileges. Thus, Hispanic subgroups differ by nation of origin, immigration status, culture, and geography. This chapter focuses on Mexican-origin Americans, the largest Hispanic subpopulation, which comprises about 50% of the older Hispanic population (Yoo 2001).

We draw upon data from multiple sources to uncover relevant patterns as well as the reasons for low incomes and wealth among older Hispanics and Mexican-origin adults. We conclude by discussing the politics of reform and the policy options for overcoming the major barriers that prevent Hispanics from obtaining adequate income and wealth to sustain them in their later years.

■ HISPANICS IN THE UNITED STATES

Although younger than the non-Hispanic population, the Hispanic population in the United States is aging swiftly (U.S. Census Bureau 2008). The U.S. Census Bureau (2008) projects that older Hispanics will outnumber older black Americans by one million in 2030, and the number of older Hispanics will increase from three million to almost 17 million in the next 40 years.

Despite such growth, older Hispanics differ from the majority of older Americans. For example, Hispanic educational attainment is low. This leads to labor force disadvantage and impedes economic inclusion. Similar scenarios will confront the next generation of Hispanics, limiting economic resources available for their later years (Duncan, Hotz, and Trejo 2006) and adversely affecting their health outcomes (Villa et al. 2012). The situation is particularly grim for Hispanic youth who are first-generation immigrants (U.S. Census Bureau 2011). Effects from these factors accumulate over the life course, undermine economic vitality, and have important implications for social policy. As the life expectancy of older Hispanics grows, it is critical to gauge the extent to which they can afford to age. That assessment lies at the core of this chapter.

■ HISPANICS AND RETIREMENT SECURITY

In the United States, work is central to economic success and to retirement security. Compared to European populations, that in the United States relies less on the government to fulfill the basic requirements of a dignified life (Quadagno 1994). In the United States, the adequacy of retirement income is usually tied to one's place in the labor market. The size of a worker's monthly Social Security benefit is tied to the contributions he or she made during the working years: contributions rise as earnings grow, though contributions are capped at a specified level. Although most retired workers receive Social Security and Medicare, a private retirement plan (often provided by employers) and supplementary Medigap health insurance are necessary for health and financial security (Schulz and Binstock 2006). This system of employment-based benefits reflects basic American values related to self-sufficiency, but those who are disadvantaged in the labor market are also disadvantaged in terms of retirement security and health insurance coverage. Although one's place in the labor force clearly reflects individual factors, such as ambition and initiative, it also reflects historical and structural factors that determine the availability of opportunities.

Retirement Income and Old-Age Poverty

Racial and ethnic differences in the availability of labor market opportunities have long-term consequences for the size and composition of income in retirement, as suggested in Figure 4.1. Differences in the relative slices

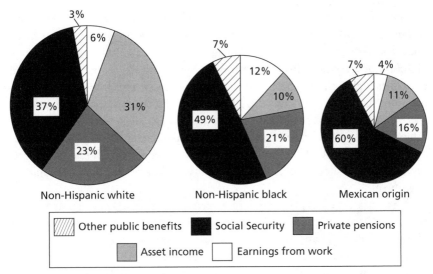

Figure 4.1 Sources and Relative Size of Retirement Income for Older Individuals by Race and Mexican Origin.
Source: Health and Retirement Study data, wave 2010.
Note: The average retirement income in 2010 was $17,000 for Mexican-origin individuals, $22,500 for non-Hispanic blacks, and about $35,000 for non-Hispanic whites.

of the pie correspond to racial and ethnic differences in the average annual retirement income in 2010 for older adults. That average is about $35,000 for non-Hispanic whites, $22,500 for non-Hispanic blacks, and slightly over $17,000 for Mexican-origin individuals. In addition, the structure of retirement income is more favorable for non-Hispanic whites, who benefit from the combination of Social Security benefits, private pensions, and asset income. In contrast, minorities, and particularly Mexican-origin individuals, largely rely on Social Security for their retirement income: 60% of the average annual retirement income of older Mexican-origin Americans comes from Social Security, but asset income and private pension benefits provide only 27%. This pattern is reversed for non-Hispanic whites: 37% of their annual retirement income comes from Social Security, and 54% comes from asset income and private pension benefits. Yet, in absolute terms, non-Hispanic whites receive more money from Social Security than do minorities. The average annual benefit for non-Hispanic whites is about $13,400, which is almost $1,700 higher than that for non-Hispanic blacks and $3,000 higher than that for Mexican-origin individuals.

Social Security guarantees older adults a minimal income, but several factors undermine the adequacy of retirement income for older Hispanics in households living near or below the poverty line. Among them are the level of benefits (determined in part by the earnings upon which they paid taxes), the number of years they paid into the system, and the size of out-of-pocket expenses such as medical costs (Aaron 2011).

As shown in Figure 4.2, poverty is a common experience among minorities. About one-third of older Hispanic households and one-fourth of older black ones reported income below the official poverty line in 2010. Throughout most of 2000s, poverty rates for older minority households were between four and five times higher than those for older non-Hispanic whites. Moreover, poverty has worsened since 2007, and the 2010 rate among older Hispanic households was over six times the poverty rate among older non-Hispanic whites. Growing differences in poverty rates between older Hispanic and non-Hispanic households may suggest that the social safety net has been less effective in protecting older Hispanics from falling into poverty during the recent economic downturn.

What may partly explain the larger increase in poverty rates for Hispanics than non-Hispanics is the fact that nonpoor Hispanics on average have the lowest incomes of all racial and ethnic groups; low income can heighten vulnerability to adverse economic circumstances and increase the odds of falling into poverty. Data from the 2010 wave of the Health and Retirement Study, a nationally representative study of older Americans, indicate that the average income of older Mexican-origin households was only 2.1 times higher than the national poverty threshold. With average incomes at 2.4 and 2.8 times the poverty threshold, other older Hispanic households and older non-Hispanic black households fared

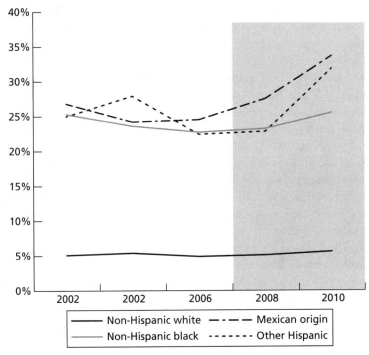

Figure 4.2 Poverty Rates for Older Adult Households by Race and Hispanic Ethnicity.
Source: Health and Retirement Study data, waves 2002–2010.

slightly better, but the average income of older non-Hispanic white households was 4.6 times higher than the poverty threshold.

Wealth Accumulation

Accumulated wealth is another important source of distinction between non-Hispanic whites and minorities, Hispanics in particular, that can help explain why minorities are more vulnerable to economic downturns. Health and Retirement Study data indicate that most of the wealth held by non-Hispanic white households comes from nonhousing assets but that wealth held by minorities is highly concentrated in a single asset class: their primary residence. The average total wealth of older non-Hispanic white households was around $640,000 in 2010, and nonhousing assets account for approximately $460,000 of those holdings. In contrast, the average total value of assets was about $200,000 among older non-Hispanic blacks and $180,000 among older Mexican-origin households. Approximately half that value can be attributed to housing equity. The recent economic crisis had especially severe and protracted effects in the real estate market; the total wealth of minorities has suffered disproportionately. Hispanics were hit particularly hard during the housing crisis because they are geographically concentrated in regions that bore the worst of its effects. Consequently, the proportion of Hispanic households that owed more than the value of their home in 2011 (28%) was twice as high as that of similarly situated households in the general population (Taylor et al. 2012).

Health and Retirement Study data from 2010 also suggest that the income and asset levels of female-headed minority households are even lower than those of minority couples. Single, female-headed, minority households have only about half of the assets—housing and nonhousing—of minority households headed by couples or single males (approximately $98,000 for non-Hispanic black and $89,000 for Mexican-origin households headed by single females). Moreover, two-thirds of the total wealth of minority households headed by a single female is in housing equity. This fact comes as no surprise. Across racial and ethnic groups and throughout the life course, income is far lower among single women than among married couples or single men, and single women are less able to invest in assets. The situation is particularly precarious for older, female-headed minority households. They have very limited resources for the later years of life and, consequently, face an elevated risk that public support will be the only resource available to them.

Although most of the wealth held by minorities and women comes from the value of their primary residence, homeownership rates are noticeably lower for minorities than for non-Hispanic whites and, across all racial and ethnic groups, lower for women than for men (Health and Retirement Study 2010). Because of limited work histories and employment in jobs without pensions, many women receive minimal Social Security and survivors benefits and face a high risk of poverty (Altman 2009). Low income is associated with low asset accumulation, and few of these single older women have substantial assets (Angel, Prickett, and Angel 2014).

To summarize, the typical middle-class non-Hispanic white family has substantial equity in a home by the time the family's main breadwinner retires. However, the family also has at least some income from a private pension; in addition, many have income from stocks, bonds, and rental property. Among households headed by non-Hispanic blacks and Hispanics, and especially among female-headed households in those groups, the average home equity is low. There is almost no income from private pensions, stocks, bonds, or rent. Altogether, analysis of the Health and Retirement Study data reveals that race, Hispanic ethnicity, and gender form three dimensions of disadvantage in the distributions of household income and assets. We next turn to an examination of retirement planning.

■ EMPLOYMENT STATUS AND RETIREMENT INCOME

Because the system of support for older adults is so complex, it is necessary to know how the system works in order to understand why it places Hispanics at a disadvantage. For most older adults, work-related retirement plans are the primary source of retirement income. Almost by definition, a good job is one that offers such a plan, a decent salary, and health insurance. Private employer-based plans represent a major source of income for middle-class older adults. Such plans can make the difference between a minimally adequate income and one that allows a person the freedom to enjoy his or her retirement.

As we have discussed, a lifetime of labor force disadvantage and the inability to build a nest egg during the working years increase the risk that Hispanics will rely solely on public programs. Individuals who spend their lives in low-wage service-sector jobs are unable to save for retirement, and the jobs in which they work rarely offer health or retirement benefits (Crystal and Shea 2003). The U.S. labor force is highly stratified, and the best jobs, including professional and managerial positions, are disproportionately held by non-Hispanic white males (Angel, Angel, and Montez 2009). As shown in Table 4.1, the Mexican-origin population is concentrated in specific occupational sectors; salaries are low and benefits are rare. The population is underrepresented in lucrative management, professional, and related occupations. Moreover, underrepresentation in the public sector affects access to pensions, health insurance, and other benefits associated with government jobs.

Low retirement plan coverage also stems from other factors unique to the Mexican-origin population. Compared with non-Hispanic workers, Mexican-origin workers are more likely to be employed in small firms, and vulnerability to economic downturns is greater among employees of such firms than among employees of larger firms. Some evidence suggests that employment in small firms may be associated with a lack of retirement benefits, employment insecurity, and frequency of layoffs. However, the reasons for these associations are quite complicated. Many other factors adversely influence income and benefit coverage for Mexican-origin workers.

Immigration history, citizenship status, language proficiency, and education also play roles in older Mexican-origin adults' access to retirement benefits, interacting with structural factors to block opportunities for upward mobility. For example, the timing (in the life course) of immigration influences individual income and wealth trajectories. Some immigrants are economically integrated within one or two generations, yet others remain trapped in low-paying occupations and fail to move into the middle class even after generations (U.S. Census Bureau 2011). Data suggest that fluency in English and level of education are both associated with declines over time in occupational differences among immigrants, non-Hispanic whites, and native-born Hispanics (Bean, Berg, and Van Hook 1996). Unfortunately, most Mexican immigrants have relatively little education and many are only marginally fluent in English (Tienda and Mitchell 2006a, 2006b). Individual characteristics probably interact with occupational structure to affect the long-term mobility chances (and, thus, retirement prospects) of Hispanic men and women.

TABLE 4.1. *Employment Characteristics of Employed Population by Race and Mexican Origin*[a]

Characteristic	Non-Hispanic white	Non-Hispanic black	Mexican origin
Total employment (in thousands)	114,690	15,051	12,698
Men (%)	54.0	46.2	61.8
Employment hours			
Full-time	80.1	82.0	80.6
Employment sector			
Private	78.5	76.9	84.1
Public	14.2	19.3	9.9
Self-employed	7.3	3.8	6.0
Union membership[b]	11.6	13.5	9.7
Occupation			
Management, professional, and related occupations	38.3	29.2	16.2
Management, business, and financial operations occupations	16.1	10.5	7.0
Professional and related occupations	22.2	18.7	9.3
Service occupations	16.6	25.4	26.1
Health care support occupations	2.0	5.5	2.0
Protective service occupations	2.2	3.7	1.8
Food preparation and serving-related occupations	5.3	6.5	9.2
Building and grounds cleaning and maintenance occupations	3.9	5.0	9.9
Personal care and service occupations	3.3	4.7	3.3
Sales and office occupations	23.6	24.9	20.2
Sales and related occupations	11.1	10.0	8.7
Office and administrative support occupations	12.5	14.9	11.6
Natural resources, construction, and maintenance occupations	10.1	5.6	18.9
Farming, fishing, and forestry occupations	0.8	0.3	3.1
Construction and extraction occupations	5.6	2.8	12.1
Installation, maintenance, and repair occupations	3.7	2.6	3.8
Production, transportation, and material moving occupations	11.4	14.9	18.5
Production occupations	5.7	5.9	9.8
Transportation and material moving occupations	5.7	9.0	8.7

Source: Bureau of Labor Statistics (2012a, 2012b, 2012c).
[a]Mexican-origin individuals may be of any race.
[b]Union membership is based on the number of employed workers, not on the total employment. Union membership refers to all Hispanics and not Mexican-origin individuals only.

Regardless of the mechanisms that give rise to the vulnerability of this population, low socioeconomic status persists for a large proportion of Mexican-origin families even after generations in the United States. The dramatic earnings disadvantages among Hispanics, and among members of the Mexican-origin population in particular, have clear implications for all aspects of health and welfare in later life. However, the situation is particularly serious when it comes to participation in employer-based retirement plans.

Employer-based pension coverage has increased greatly since World War II, and many middle-class Americans count on their employer-provided plans for retirement security (Esping-Andersen 2002). Such plans are an important supplement to Social Security and personal savings for many retired Americans (Quadagno and Street 2006). Private pensions can make the difference between just getting by and having enough money for necessities such as medical care and other services. However, such pensions are rarely the primary source of income among older adults. It is not uncommon for poor older adults to have some savings, but these are hardly sufficient to generate substantial interest and are quickly depleted.

Hispanics are disadvantaged by the close link between the availability of a private pension and employment history: they are less likely than are non-Hispanic whites to have spent their working years in jobs that provide any retirement benefits and are at greater risk of having inadequate income in retirement (Fry et al. 2005). Ethnic disparities in the financial resources of older adults can be attributed largely to the lack of private retirement plan and pension coverage. As shown in Figure 4.3, 72% of older non-Hispanic white households owned retirement accounts in 2010, but this was so for only 39% of older non-Hispanic black households and for less than 37% of older Mexican-origin households with a U.S.-born household head. Access is worst among older households headed by Mexican-born adults: less than 15% are covered by any type of private retirement plan. This means that many older Mexican-origin American households depend on a combination of resources from the social safety net (to which they have less access than do other groups), continued work (if health allows), family, and friends (who often are equally disadvantaged).

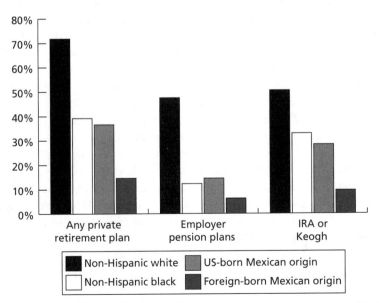

Figure 4.3 Retirement Plans of Older Adult Households by Race, Mexican Origin, and Nativity. *Source*: Health and Retirement Study data, wave 2010.

Social Security is the sole source of income for more Hispanics than for non-Hispanic whites, and the amounts received by Hispanics leave many very close to poverty. As we discuss elsewhere in this chapter, even Hispanics with access to Social Security and Medicare are at serious risk of falling into poverty. The maximum monthly Social Security benefit for an individual in 2012 was $2,512, and most received much less (Social Security Administration 2013). At the beginning of 2012, the average monthly benefit was only $1,230.40 (Social Security Administration 2013). Furthermore, Hispanics reach the age of retirement with far fewer accumulated assets than do non-Hispanic whites.

Supplemental Security Income provides a minimal safety net for the aged, blind, and disabled. However, the benefit levels are set below the poverty threshold and elevate few above the poverty line (Schulz and Binstock 2006). Many Hispanics who qualify for Supplemental Security Income do not participate because they find the means-tested nature of the program stigmatizing (Davies 2001/2002).

The nature of public assistance programs and associated perceptions of stigma stem in part from federal legislative efforts. Prior to 1996, federal assistance covered many of the needs of older adults. In that year, the average annual income of older immigrants was $5,958 (roughly $497 per month), and most of it came from Supplemental Security Income (Social Security Administration 2013). However, the Personal Responsibility and Work Opportunity Reconciliation Act of 1996 (commonly known as "welfare reform") restricted funding for federal assistance to older noncitizen residents (Esping-Andersen 2002; Pub. L. 104-193, 110 Stat. 2105 [1996]). It codifies the belief that legal noncitizens should be denied welfare and that, rather than relying on public funds, they should be supported by their families, sponsors, or private organizations.[2] Older Mexican-origin immigrants, especially those who came to the United States in middle or late adulthood, face particular financial problems and may reach the age of retirement before contributing sufficiently to the Social Security system or to a private retirement account (Angel et al. 1999). For many older Mexican-origin adults born outside of the United States, the family represents the only refuge from financial vulnerability (Angel 2003).

Among groups of older Hispanics, the risk of poverty is highest for older legal residents; they are much more likely to live in poverty than are their citizen counterparts (Angel and Angel 1999), and they typically retire on less than two-thirds of what older Hispanic citizens receive: $950 and $1,438 per month, respectively (Social Security Administration 2013). These figures highlight the role of the U.S. social safety net in the retirement income of Hispanic U.S. citizens: support from the safety net comprises a large share of the retirement income for them and especially for the Mexican-origin population.

Health Insurance

Medical advances are extending the lives of many Americans, but the sources of coverage differ by race and ethnicity. Most non-Hispanic whites have some form of private insurance in addition to Medicare. Minorities overwhelmingly rely on the publicly provided health insurance plans (Health and Retirement Study 2010). Of all racial and ethnic groups, the foreign-born Mexican-origin population is in the worst position by far: Mexican-origin adults are very unlikely to have private health coverage, few qualify for Medicare, and about one-third rely on Medicaid. About 10% of older foreign-born, Mexican-origin adults lack health insurance because citizenship and durational residency requirements prevent them from qualifying for Medicaid.

A brief examination of the preretirement population, which does not yet qualify for Medicare, illustrates possible outcomes of proposals that would limit access to health insurance coverage and to Medicare in particular. Health and Retirement Study data suggest that a substantial portion of adults in preretirement (aged 51–61 years) lacks health insurance coverage: 10% of non-Hispanic whites, 20% of non-Hispanic blacks, 33% of Mexican-origin adults in the United States, and nearly half of Mexican-origin adults born abroad. Such proposals would likely result in a precipitous rise in the number of uninsured older adults. The employment-based health insurance system is the primary driver of health care insecurity in the United States. As we note above, disadvantage in the labor market is generally equivalent to disadvantage in health insurance coverage. Throughout the life course, Mexican-origin individuals and families have lower rates of health insurance coverage than do non-Hispanic whites and other minorities (Angel and Angel 2006). It is not unreasonable to assume that, in the absence of Medicare, this lack of insurance coverage would spill over into adults' later years.

Implications of Income and Asset Inadequacy in Late Life

We have shown that the Mexican-origin population is the largest and most economically disadvantaged segment of Hispanics in the United States. Individuals without a private pension face far more serious economic difficulties in retirement than do those with a private pension. A disproportionate share of Hispanics, and Hispanic women in particular, lacks such pensions. Because jobs that offer retirement plans are also those in which workers pay high Social Security taxes, adults who have employer-provided retirement plans tend to receive higher Social Security benefits than do retirees who lack private pensions (Angel and Angel 2009).

The prevailing welfare philosophy, which also informed the development of the Social Security program, centers on three tenets: one should provide for oneself, those who cannot should be helped, and such assistance should only be enough to get by. A system derived from this philosophy almost guarantees the stratification of older adults along racial and ethnic lines. Individuals who never participated in the Social Security program and those who immigrated to the United States in middle or late adulthood face particular problems. Moreover, the overrepresentation of Hispanics in low-wage service-sector jobs has serious implications for their social and economic well-being and for the opportunities accessible to future generations. Low-wage work may prevent millions of Hispanic Americans from falling into abject poverty, but it does not provide many of the benefits that have come to define minimal citizenship rights in most of the developed world. Employment and migration histories, regional concentration, occupational ghettoization in the low-wage service sector, an insufficient supply of economic resources, and high demand for such resources all combine to limit the capital on which Hispanics can draw for education, business opportunities, and other ventures.

The recent financial crisis and economic downturn exacerbated already negative trends (Gustman, Steinmeier, and Tabatabai 2011). One of the strongest indicators of harm to the Hispanic community in the United States is an estimate of food insecurity levels: 38% of all Hispanics (and 53% of foreign-born nonresident Hispanics, many of whom are undocumented immigrants) reported that economic pressures forced them to cut back on the size of meals or skip meals altogether during 2010 (Taylor et al. 2012). Over 15 years ago, approximately one-third of nonpoor Hispanics expressed fear that they would experience poverty in their later years, but one-fifth of nonpoor, non-Hispanics (non-Hispanic whites and blacks) expressed the same fear (Angel and Angel 1999). This chapter and recent trends in income inadequacy suggest that these fears have come true for many older Hispanics.

Although the adversities facing Hispanics in the United States are, on average, greater than those faced by other racial and ethnic groups, intragroup differences among Hispanics are substantial. Therefore, researchers and policymakers should be aware that focusing solely on race and ethnicity can mask important sources of inequality (e.g., gender, level of education, nativity status, and citizenship status). For example, findings in this chapter show the disproportionate levels of disadvantage among the foreign-born Mexican-origin population. Furthermore, Zachary Gassoumis and colleagues (2009) emphasize the importance of citizenship status: foreign-born citizens fare much better than noncitizens do across various socioeconomic measures important for financial security in late life.

Unfortunately, large differences in economic well-being among older adults will likely persist in the future, and these differences will be associated with gender, race, Hispanic ethnicity, and immigration status. The future of public pensions, including Social Security, will profoundly affect the financial security of older adults. Scholarship should endeavor to understand how education and labor force disadvantages affect the financial security of older Hispanics, particularly Mexican-origin Americans. More research is needed.

■ PROGRAM AND POLICY RECOMMENDATIONS

It is possible that the U.S. Congress will cut retirement benefits as a part of entitlement reform. Projections indicate that the Social Security Trust Fund will be unable to pay promised benefits in full by 2033 (Angel and Angel 2009). Benefit cuts would be particularly harmful to minority and immigrant workers who do not share the education, income, health advantages, and retirement plan access enjoyed by their non-Hispanic white peers (Aaron 2011; DeNavas-Walt, Proctor, and Smith 2011). Our discussion suggests that, in the absence of private retirement income, these retirees will face a higher risk of economic insecurity at a time when program benefits will likely decrease.

Three main factors increase the odds that the Mexican-origin population will receive retirement benefits other than Social Security: core industry employment, high educational levels, and young age at immigration (Angel and Angel 2009; Van de Water and Sherman 2010). Given the low levels of education, high dropout rates, and labor force disadvantage among Hispanics (Angel and Angel 2009), efforts to promote education would likely improve their long-term financial security in a future characterized by fiscal austerity. A comprehensive approach to education is required to promote upward mobility and employment opportunity. Such an approach would begin in early childhood education and extend through high school to vocational training and beyond. Furthermore, some initiatives suggest that providing educational opportunities for children and parents can increase parental involvement in children's learning and improve children's academic outcomes (Hispanic/Latino Quality of Life Initiative Committee 2013). Higher education has a particularly potent role in successful later-life economic outcomes (Angel and Angel 2009).

Although most Americans nearing retirement age report that they have no savings in employer-based individual retirement plans or that they have only meager savings in such plans, the situation for Hispanics is especially grim. They are disproportionately likely to have saved too little (Orszag and Rodriguez 2005). Financial sophistication is particularly important for adults with limited resources but rare among those with low levels of education. When asked about their knowledge of investing and saving for retirement, 43% of Latinos say that they know "nothing" about it, yet the same is reported by 12% of the general population (National Council of La Raza 2004, 2). As research shows, defined-contribution retirement plans require much more informed involvement than do defined-benefit plans (Papke, Walker, and Dworsky 2008). At present, little research examines the use of other financial instruments (e.g., reverse mortgages) by minority elders, but they may not have the financial sophistication to make informed choices about the products that make sense for them.

There are several ways to address the problem of inadequate assets and to facilitate saving. Default options on 401(k)s could be changed to increase contributions, and automatic individual retirement accounts could simplify the process of saving part of an income tax refund. Policymakers could reduce regressivity in policies that subsidize saving (e.g., regressivity in policies that provide incentives to encourage saving for retirement) so that public support is more evenly distributed across the population. Peter Orszag and Eric Rodriguez (2005, 11) also offer recommendations: "Broader adoption of automatic enrollment and the other key pieces of the automatic 401(k) could be encouraged by reforming an exception to the rules governing nondiscrimination in 401(k) plans. Many firms are attracted to automatic enrollment because they care for their employees and want them to have a secure retirement, but others may be motivated more by the associated financial incentives, which stem in large part from the 401(k) nondiscrimination standards. Policymakers could change the rules to allow the matching safe harbor only for plans that feature automatic enrollment and the other key parts of the automatic 401(k)." Finally, financial counseling and financial education could improve the financial capability of Hispanics.

To facilitate saving for retirement among the working poor, policymakers could consider extending eligibility for the Earned Income Tax Credit program to a broader portion of the population. It is also possible to increase the savings of the working poor by funding nonprofit tax preparation services that piggyback on other well-established community services (child care and health services) and institutions (affordable-housing and microlending organizations; Robles 2013).

■ CONCLUSIONS

We have drawn a complex picture of the future. The post–World War II economic boom propelled Japan, Europe, and the United States to historically unprecedented levels of wealth, but that boom has slowed. Populations in developed and developing countries are aging rapidly. Keynesian economic policies may be reaching political limits. Although rapid aging poses a significant fiscal challenge for the whole U.S. population, minorities and foreign-born individuals are among the most vulnerable to the effects of this development. Across many developed countries, including the United States, inequality is increasing. There is uncertainty about whether nations will ensure equity in distribution of resources and how they might do so. There also remains uncertainty about whether the elderly will be guaranteed a dignified existence. However, it is certain that there will be active political debates, and their outcomes will be vitally important to the financial well-being of older Hispanics. Research on factors that promote successful aging is therefore essential for informed policymaking. It will also play a critical role in identifying ways to protect the vulnerable while achieving long-term fiscal solvency for the nation as a whole.

■ NOTES

1. As do other chapters, we use *older* (e.g., in older adults and older Americans) to refer to adults aged 65 years or older.

2. Section 400(2)(A), 110 Stat. 2260 (codified at 8 U.S.C. § 1601(2)(A)(2012)).

■ REFERENCES

Aaron, Kat. 2011. "New Data Show Fewer Children, More Seniors in Poverty." America: What Went Wrong Project, November 7. American University School of Communication, Investigative Reporting Workshop. http://americawhatwentwrong.org/story/new-measurements-american-poverty/.

Altman, Nancy. 2009. "A Silver Lining to the Economic Crisis: The Case for Improving Social Security and Medicare." *Generations* 33 (3): 63–68.

Angel, Jacqueline L. 2003. "Devolution and the Social Welfare of Elderly Immigrants: Who Will Bear the Burden?" *Public Administration Review* 63 (1): 79–89. doi: 10.1111/1540-6210.00266.

Angel, Jacqueline L., and Ronald J. Angel. 1999. *Who Will Care for Us? Aging and Long-Term Care in Multicultural America*. New York: New York University Press.

Angel, Jacqueline L., and Ronald J. Angel. 2006. "Minority Group Status and Healthful Aging: Social Structure Still Matters." *American Journal of Public Health* 96 (7): 1152–1159. doi: 10.2105/AJPH.2006.085530.

Angel, Jacqueline L., and Ronald J. Angel. 2009. *Hispanic Families at Risk: The New Economy, Work, and the Welfare State*. New York: Springer.

Angel, Ronald J., Jacqueline L. Angel, Geum-Yong Lee, and Kyriakos S. Markides. 1999. "Age at Migration and Family Dependency among Older Mexican Immigrants: Recent Evidence from the Mexican American EPESE." *Gerontologist* 39 (1): 59–65. doi: 10.1093/geront/39.1.59.

Angel, Ronald J., Jacqueline L. Angel, and Jennifer Karas Montez. 2009. "The Work/Health Insurance Nexus: A Weak Link for Mexican-Origin Men." *Social Science Quarterly* 90 (5): 1112–1133. doi: 10.1111/j.1540-6237.2009.00649.x.

Angel, Jacqueline L., Kate Prickett, and Ronald J. Angel. 2014. "Sources of Retirement Security for Black, non-Hispanic White, and Mexican-Origin Women: The Changing Roles of Marriage and Work." *Journal of Women, Politics and Policy* 35 (3): 222–241. doi: 10.1080/1554477X.2014.921541.

Bean, Frank D., Ruth R. Berg, and Jennifer V. W. Van Hook. 1996. "Socioeconomic and Cultural Incorporation and Marital Disruption among Mexican Americans." *Social Forces* 75 (2): 593–617. doi: 10.1093/sf/75.2.593.

Bureau of Labor Statistics. 2012a. "Employed Hispanic or Latino Workers by Sex, Occupation, Class of Worker, Full- or Part-Time Status, and Detailed Ethnic Group." Labor Force Statistics from the Current Population Survey, Table 13. Last modified March 1. http://www.bls.gov/cps/aa2011/cpsaat13.htm.

Bureau of Labor Statistics. 2012b. "Employed Persons by Sex, Occupation, Class of Worker, Full- or Part-Time Status, and Race." Labor Force Statistics from the Current Population Survey, Table 12. Last modified March 1. http://www.bls.gov/cps/aa2011/cpsaat12.htm.

Bureau of Labor Statistics. 2012c. "Union Affiliation of Employed Wage and Salary Workers by Selected Characteristics." Labor Force Statistics from the Current Population Survey, Table 40. Last modified March 1. http://www.bls.gov/cps/aa2011/cpsaat40.htm.

Butrica, Barbara A., Howard M. Iams, and Karen E. Smith. 2003/2004. "The Changing Impact of Social Security on Retirement Income in the United States." *Social Security Bulletin* 65 (3): 2–13.

Crystal, Stephen, and Dennis Shea. 2003. *Focus on Economic Outcomes in Later Life: Public Policy, Health, and Cumulative Advantage*. Annual Review of Gerontology and Geriatrics, Vol. 22. New York: Springer.

Davies, Paul S. 2001/2002. "SSI Eligibility and Participation among the Oldest Old: Evidence from the AHEAD." *Social Security Bulletin* 64 (3): 38–63. http://www.ssa.gov/policy/docs/ssb/v64n3/v64n3p38.html.

DeNavas-Walt, Carmen, Bernadette D. Proctor, and Jessica C. Smith. 2011. *Income, Poverty, and Health Insurance Coverage in the United States: 2010*. Current Population Reports: Consumer Income, P60-239, September. Washington, DC: U.S. Census Bureau. http://www.census.gov/prod/2011pubs/p60-239.pdf.

Diamond, Peter A., and Peter R. Orszag. 2004. *Saving Social Security: A Balanced Approach*. Washington, DC: Brookings Institution.

Duncan, Brian, V. Joseph Hotz, and Stephen J. Trejo. 2006. "Hispanics in the U.S. Labor Market." In *Hispanics and the Future of America*, edited by Marta Tienda and Faith Mitchell, 228–290. Washington, DC: National Academies Press.

Esping-Andersen, Gøsta. 2002. *Why We Need a New Welfare State*. New York: Oxford University Press.

Fry, Richard, Rakesh Kochhar, Jeffrey Passel, and Roberto Suro. 2005. *Hispanics and the Social Security Debate*. Report, March 16. Washington, DC: Pew Hispanic Center. http://www.pewhispanic.org/files/reports/43.pdf.

Gassoumis, Zachary D., Kathleen H. Wilber, Lindsey A. Baker, and Fernando M. Torres-Gil. 2009. "Who Are the Latino Baby Boomers? Demographic and Economic Characteristics of a Hidden Population." *Journal of Aging and Social Policy* 22 (1): 53–68. doi: 10.1080/08959420903408452.

Gustman, Alan L., Thomas L. Steinmeier, and Nahid Tabatabai. 2011. "How Did the Recession of 2007–2009 Affect the Wealth and Retirement of the Near Retirement Age Population in the Health and Retirement Study?" Working Paper 17547, October. Cambridge, MA: National Bureau of Economic Research. http://www.nber.org/papers/w17547.

Health and Retirement Study database (data from waves 2002–10). http://hrsonline.isr.umich.edu.

Hispanic/Latino Quality of Life Initiative Committee. 2013. *Ciudad de Austin Hispano-Latino Iniciativa para la Calidad de Vida*. Austin, TX: City of Austin. http://austintexas.gov/sites/default/files/files/City_Manager/HispanicReport-ver_6-0901_13.pdf.

Isaacs, Julia B. 2009. *Spending on Children and the Elderly*. Issue Brief, November. Washington, DC: Brookings Institution, Center on Children and Families. http://www.brookings.edu/research/reports/2009/11/05-spending-children-isaacs.

National Council of La Raza. 2004. *Financial Education in Latino Communities: An Analysis of Programs, Products, and Results/Effects*. Issue Brief, December 9. Washington, DC: National Council of La Raza. http://www.nclr.org/images/uploads/publications/28618_file_FinancialEdRpt04_FNL.pdf.

Orszag, Peter R., and Eric Rodriguez. 2005. *Retirement Security for Latinos: Bolstering Coverage, Savings and Adequacy.* Retirement Security Project Report 2005-7, July. Washington, DC: National Council of La Raza, Retirement Security Project. http://www.nclr.org/index.php/publications/retirement_security _for_latinos_bolstering_coverage_savings_and_adequacy/.

Papke, Leslie E., Lina Walker, and Michael Dworsky. 2008. *Retirement Security for Women: Progress to Date and Policies for Tomorrow.* Retirement Security Project Report 2008-1, February. Washington, DC: Brookings Institution, Retirement Security Project. http://www.brookings.edu/~/media/projects/retirementsecurity /03_retirement_women.pdf.

Quadagno, Jill S. 1988. *The Transformation of Old Age Security: Class and Politics in the American Welfare State.* Chicago: University of Chicago Press.

Quadagno, Jill S. 1994. *The Color of Welfare: How Racism Undermined the War on Poverty.* New York: Oxford University Press.

Quadagno, Jill, and Debra Street. 2006. "Recent Trends in U.S. Social Welfare Policy: Minor Retrenchment or Major Transformation?" *Research on Aging* 28 (3): 303–316. doi: 10.1177/0164027505285921.

Robles, Bárbara J. 2013. "Financial and Asset-Building Capabilities of Southwest Border Working Families: An Action Research Approach to Culturally Responsive Economic Resiliency Behaviors." In *Financial Capability and Asset Development: Research, Education, Policy, and Practice,* edited by Julie Birkenmaier, Margaret S. Sherraden, and Jami Curley, 228–248. New York: Oxford University Press.

Schulz, James H., and Robert H. Binstock. 2006. *Aging Nation: The Economics and Politics of Growing Older in America.* Westport, CT: Praeger.

Social Security Administration. 2013. "Maximum Retirement Benefit." Last modified May 2. http://ssa-custhelp.ssa.gov/app/answers/detail/a_id/5/~/maximum -retirement-benefit.

Taylor, Paul, Mark Hugo Lopez, Gabriel Velasco, and Seth Motel. 2012. *Hispanics Say They Have the Worst of a Bad Economy.* Report, January 26. Washington, DC: Pew Research Center. http://www.pewhispanic.org/files/2012/01/NSL-2011 -economy-report_3_22_FINAL_REVISED.pdf.

Tienda, Marta, and Faith Mitchell, eds. 2006a. *Hispanics and the Future of America.* Washington, DC: National Academies Press.

Tienda, Marta, and Faith Mitchell, eds. 2006b. *Multiple Origins, Uncertain Destinies: Hispanics and the American Future.* Washington, DC: National Academies Press.

U.S. Census Bureau, Population Division. 2008. "Projections of the Population by Sex, Race, and Hispanic Origin for the United States: 2010 to 2050." 2008 National Population Projections, Table 4 (NP2008-T4), August 14. Washington, DC: U.S. Census Bureau. http://www.census.gov/population/projections/data/national/2008 /summarytables.html.

U.S. Census Bureau, Population Division. 2011. "Poverty Status of People, by Age, Race, and Hispanic Origin: 1959 to 2010." Historical Poverty Tables, Table 3. U.S. Census Bureau. http://www.census.gov/hhes/www/poverty/data/historical /people.html.

Van de Water, Paul N., and Arloc Sherman. 2010. *Social Security Keeps 20 Million Americans Out of Poverty: A State-by-State Analysis.* Report, August 11. Washington, DC: Center on Budget and Policy Priorities. http://www.cbpp.org/files/8-11-10socsec.pdf.

Villa, Valentine M., Stephen P. Wallace, Sofya Bagdasaryan, and Maria P. Aranda. 2012. "Hispanic Baby Boomers: Health Inequities Likely to Persist in Old Age." *Gerontologist* 52 (2): 166–176. doi: 10.1093/geront/gns002.

Yoo, Grace J. 2001. "Constructing Deservingness: Federal Welfare Reform, Supplemental Security Income, and Elderly Immigrants." *Journal of Aging and Social Policy* 13 (4):17–34. doi: 10.1300/J031v13n04_02.

5 Enhancing the Financial Capability of Native American Elders

■ AMANDA BARUSCH, MOLLY TOVAR, AND TRACY GOLDEN

Consistent with the general aging of the U.S. population, the number of American Indian and Alaska Natives aged 65 years or older is projected to increase by three and a half times between 2010 and 2050. Specifically, estimates project that it will grow from 410,000 to over 1,395,000, or about 2% of the total population, by 2050 (U.S. Census Bureau 2008).[1] At the time of the 2010 census, the federal government recognized 565 tribes. The total population of American Indians and Alaska Natives, including those of more than one race, was estimated to be 5.2 million people, and this estimate represents a 26.7% increase over the 2000 census count. The population now makes up roughly 1.7% of the total U.S. population. Of this total, 2.9 million identify themselves as American Indian or Alaska Native only, and 2.3 million identify themselves as American Indian or Alaska Native and one or more other races (U.S. Department of Health and Human Services 2012).

In the 2010 census, 22% of individuals who identified themselves as American Indians or Alaska Natives lived on reservations or other trust lands, and elders are considerably more likely to live on reservations than are people in other age groups (U.S. Department of Health and Human Services 2012). The Housing Assistance Council (2013) estimates that about 50% of Native elders live on reservations. Although most Native communities are rich in culture and community, many face the problems associated with financial deprivation.

James DeLaCruz Sr. (2009), chairman of the U.S. Department of Health and Human Services Eleventh Annual Tribal Budget Consultation, described Native elders as the most economically disadvantaged older-adult minority in the United States. Among American Indian and Alaska Native elders over the age of 64 years, an estimated 20% have incomes below the poverty threshold, and the rates are higher for those who live in rural and reservation areas (Housing Assistance Council 2013). Many elders who reside in such areas lack telephone service and live at great distances from other services (Jervis, Jackson, and Manson 2002). Furthermore, language and cultural barriers combine with shorter life spans to limit their use of federal entitlements such as Social Security, Medicare, and Medicaid.

Native elders live with some of the nation's highest rates of chronic health conditions (Goins and Pilkerton 2010). Compared with other groups, Native elders have less access to health care services and less insurance coverage (Zuckerman et al. 2004). In the 2010 census, about 33% of American Indians and Alaska Natives reported that they had no health insurance coverage; in contrast, 16.3% of the general population is uninsured (DeNavas-Walt, Proctor, and Smith 2011). Consequently, life expectancy is shorter for Native Americans than for the general population. This applies to both males (67 years vs. 75 years) and females (74 years vs. 80 years; Bramley et al. 2005). A study from the Center for Rural Health used 1998 Indian Health Service data to estimate geographic differences in the life expectancy of American Indians: at the time of birth, it ranges from a low of 64.3 years in the Indian Health Service's Aberdeen Area to a high of 76.3 years in California (McDonald et al. 2006). This has led some to suggest that Native peoples should be considered elders at a younger age than might apply to the majority population (Hayward and Heron 1999). If the age at which they are considered elders were adjusted by the difference in average life expectancy, 55 years might replace the more traditional age of 65 years. More than just a theoretical exercise, such an adjustment would inform policies designed to advance the financial capability of this group.

Elders occupy places of privilege and respect in Native communities. Their unique cultural and historical position allows them to serve as vital resources in the effort to improve the circumstances of their families, clans, and tribes. Elders are the living libraries of cultural knowledge, history, and tradition. They play a significant role in both family life and cultural healing within tribal groups (Barusch 2006).

There is considerable variation in language, culture, history, and resources across tribes. As we mention above, even life expectancy varies. These differences illustrate the need for nuanced policies to serve these diverse groups. Contemporary policies must also take into account the historic relationship between tribes and the federal government as well as the relationship's effects on Native elders.

■ HISTORY OF TRAUMA

Eduardo Duran (2006, 15) uses the term "soul wounding" to characterize the historical trauma experienced by Native peoples. It is a psychic and cultural trauma now recognized as a form of genocide (Legters 1998; Struthers and Lowe 2003). This history of near annihilation is manifest today in the legacy of accumulated stress, cultural bereavement, and racism that modern Native Americans must bear (Danieli 1998; Jervis et al. 2006).

The causes and effects of soul wounding differ across generations. For instance, many older Native Americans recall being forced (sometimes even kidnapped) in childhood to attend residential boarding schools. Authorized under the Civilization Fund Act of 1819, the schools were ostensibly designed to educate Native children but served instead to eradicate their values, language, customs, and religion (Struthers and Lowe 2003).[2] Native children were removed from their families of origin and forced to assimilate into white culture. By the 1930s, well over half of Native children were enrolled in boarding schools, and enrollment peaked in the early 1970s at an estimated 35,000 (Noriega 1992).

As we mention above, no single narrative captures the full diversity of elders' experiences. Each has had different experiences of the federal policies of relocation, termination, and assimilation that continued into the last half of the twentieth century. Those in their 60s will recall the Urban Relocation Program. Some may have been among the 750,000 who responded to promises by Bureau of Indian Affairs recruiters that they would receive temporary housing and help in finding a job if they left their reservations and moved to urban settings. Those in this cohort will also recall the 109 tribes and bands that lost their sovereignty (as well as their federal assistance) when their federal recognition was terminated during the 1950s and 1960s (Wilkins and Stark 2010).

Likewise, individual responses may differ. Nursing animosity toward the U.S. government, some may have turned to their Native culture and values. Others who were forcibly immersed in white culture may find themselves in a no man's land, no longer identifying as Native but not fully integrated into white culture. Contrasting the position of marginalized Native youth with the experiences of being wholly traditional or wholly bicultural, Lee Little Soldier (1985) suggested that marginalization creates psychosocial problems for youth. This may also be the case for elders. Those who remain marginalized may suffer from greater biopsychosocial difficulties (Garrett 1996).

■ POLICY HISTORY

The federal government has what is termed a "trust relationship" with the tribes (McCarthy 2004, 19), and that relationship confers an obligation to protect and support Native peoples. The relationship has been heavily influenced by Supreme Court decisions. In 1832, the court declared that Indian tribes are "domestic dependent nations" and compared their relationship to the United States to that of a "ward to his guardian" (*Cherokee Nation v. Georgia*, 30 U.S. 1, 17 [1831]). The court also affirmed the principle of tribal sovereignty, noting that tribes were "distinct independent political communities, retaining their original natural rights, as the undisputed possessors of the soil" (*Worcester*, 31 U.S. at 529). Finally, the court ruled that state governments had no authority regarding Indian affairs (Burke 1969). The court's opinions in those cases continue to influence the relationship between the U.S. government and tribal authorities.

Two federal agencies carry out most of the U.S. government's programs for Native Americans: the Bureau of Indian Affairs and the Indian Health Service. Reflecting the view that the federal government acts as guardian, the Indian Health Service provides health care and implements public health measures for Native Americans living on reservations and for those living off of them. Specific legislation arising from the mandate to provide care to Native Americans has been in force at least since the Snyder Act of 1921 (McCarthy 2004, 118).[3]

Title VI of the Older Americans Act of 1965 authorized programs for older Native Americans, including nutrition services as well as assistance for family and informal caregivers.[4] Through a grants-based program, tribal organizations apply for funds that they manage and disburse independently. The original provisions for nutritional support have expanded to include assistance with information and referral, transportation, personal care, chores, health promotion, and disease prevention. Assistance for family caregivers includes respite services, training, and individual counseling (Administration on Aging 2013).

■ FINANCIAL ASSETS AND RESOURCES

Little is known about the financial lives and capability of Native elders. This section presents a brief summary of the available literature on these subjects. Native Americans fare poorly on a variety of economic indicators. The labor force distribution shows that fewer American Indians aged 16 years or over are working in management and professional occupations (28% compared to 39.6% of whites). The median income of American Indian and Alaska Native households in the United States was $44,347 in 2010; in contrast, the median was $68,390 for non-Hispanic white households. Finally, an estimated 9.9% of non-Hispanic whites live in poverty, but 28% of American Indians and Alaska Natives report incomes below the poverty threshold (U.S. Department of Health and Human Services 2012).

Although national figures on Native elders' finances are hard to locate, a 2007–2008 study conducted in North Dakota by the National Resource Center on Native American Aging (2008) suggests that 47% had incomes below $10,000 per year and another 18% had incomes between $10,000 and $14,999 (Ruliffson et al. 2008). Native elders living in rural and frontier areas are more likely to live on extremely low incomes. In 2005, Richard Ludtke and Leander McDonald reported that 36% of those in frontier areas had annual incomes below $5,000 and 40% of rural elders had incomes between $7,000 and $14,999.

Homeownership

The owned home represents a significant asset for many older adults; however, Native elders experience cultural and economic barriers that interfere with the purchase and maintenance of a home. Several initiatives are designed to enhance the financial capacity of Native Americans by increasing homeownership. The federal Section 184 Indian Home Loan Guarantee Program, known as the "184 program," aims to increase homeownership by guaranteeing loans to Native individuals who purchase homes on tribal lands. Because of the program, the number of Section 184 loan guarantees almost tripled from 2006 to 2011 (U.S. Department of Housing and Urban Development 2014). Another facilitator of Native homeownership is a housing down payment assistance program developed by the Winnebago tribe in cooperation with the Ho-Chunk, Inc. The program provides a significant portion of a standard down payment for a new homeowner (Ho-Chunk 2014).

Land Ownership

Prior to European arrival, American Indians had access to almost all lands in the United States (Cornell and Kalt 2007; Gilbert, Wood, and Sharp 2002). Tribal people did not understand the concept of personal property until the Dawes Act of 1887, which forced them to break up tribal lands and to become landowners and farmers (Abourezk 2012).[5] When land occupied by American Indians was divided into tracts and distributed to individuals under the act, much of it was quickly lost through fraud and failure to pay taxes (Stainbrook 2009). Natives who kept their allotments had to pay property taxes on the land, and this requirement forced many to sell it (Abourezk 2012). As a result of the Dawes Act and the Indian Reorganization Act of 1934, Native individuals lost 90 million acres (Stainbrook 2009).[6] This loss was traumatic at symbolic and spiritual levels. It was also economically devastating.

Despite this difficult history, land ownership is important in contemporary Native communities. Several programs enacted since the Homestead Act have helped tribes take control of their land while improving economic conditions.[7] The Confederated Salish and Kootenai tribes of the Flathead Reservation, for example, fought for their sovereignty and gained management of their own land and natural resources in the 1960s. By the late 1960s, these tribes established a tribal realty office and offered home site leases to tribal members (Cornell and Kalt 2007). Some tribes have also begun to reclaim land lost after the Homestead Act. Ho-Chunk, Inc., has bought back $13 million of land in the past 15 years (Abourezk 2012).

In addition, the American Indian Probate Reform Act was enacted in 2004 to protect the integrity of tribal homelands.[8] The act provides the U.S. Department of the Interior with resources to assist in the consolidation of land ownership in order to restore the economic viability of Indian lands. Native Americans hold 2 million acres of privately owned land, and 46 million additional acres are on reservations. Additionally, 3 million areas of private agricultural land are held by 23,266 American Indian individuals, with an average of 146 acres per owner

(Gilbert et al. 2002). Many agricultural land owners specialize in pasture, land crops, and woodlands (Gilbert et al. 2002). The act provides tribal members with an option to maximize and diversify the use of land.

Native elders who experienced the division of their sacred land may resist efforts to accumulate private land. They may find cooperative land ventures a more palatable approach. In such ventures, tracts are held in joint ownership. Buying land in family groups might also allow for the pooling of resources. Individuals would have rights to build on the land and to use it during their lifetimes. Upon agreement, construction on the property could be authorized if it would enhance community life. Maintaining good relations among themselves and caring for the land are considered marks of good governance among American Indians (Cornell and Kalt 2007). Since 2005, the Institute for Indian Estate Planning and Probate (2014) has helped Native people make informed decisions about their property.

Savings

Traditional practices call on Native Americans to redistribute their savings to others. A potlatch, or giveaway ceremony, is an example of this. In the Coast Salish tribe, the potlatch ceremony was an expression of social stratification, and some believed that the potlatch was based on political or economic self-interest (Piddocke 1976). Vast amounts of goods and wealth were distributed, and the more one gave away, the higher one's stature within the tribe (Newman 1981). These ceremonies may have enhanced group survival, as gifts included clothing, food, blankets, and canoes. Christian missionaries objected to the practice, in part because it was an expression of aboriginal religion. But their primary opposition stemmed from the distribution of wealth, because redistribution seemed detrimental to savings (Bear and Theisz 1994; McDonald 1992). Potlatch and giveaway ceremonies are still practiced today throughout Indian country.

In part because of their unique approach to savings, American Indian households have been less likely than others to use banks. American Indians have the largest proportion of unbanked households (14.5%) of any minority group (see Figure 5.1; Federal Deposit Insurance Corporation 2012). In 2011, the Federal Deposit Insurance Corporation recommended several strategies to increase access to banks, but none of those directly addressed the unique needs of unbanked Native households.

Access to banking and money management resources is particularly important in the wake of the *Cobell* settlement.[9] Along with other settlements, such as that in the *Cheyenne River Sioux Tribe v. Salazar* case, the *Cobell* settlement should enable tribal members to accumulate and invest assets.[10] This 2010 federal court ruling called on the federal government to provide a $3.4 billion settlement to thousands of Native American plaintiffs whose land trust royalties were

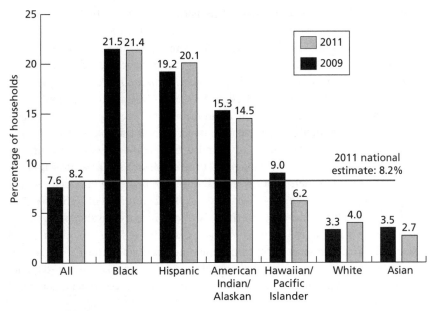

Figure 5.1 Unbanked Households by Race and Ethnicity.
Source: Federal Deposit Insurance Corporation (2012, 14).

mismanaged by the U.S. Department of the Interior. Under the terms of the agreement, the U.S. government will pay out $1.5 billion to two classes (300,000 and 500,000) of beneficiaries. Each member of the first class will be paid $1,000, and each member of the second class will be paid $800 plus a share of the balance of the settlement funds (Volz 2012). In addition, the settlement set aside $9 billion for the Interior Department to start a land consolidation program. This involves the sale of individual interests that have been split among owners over the years of complicated federal policy (Capriccioso 2012).

Small Businesses

For centuries, Native women have been at the forefront of community and national development (Nord, Wheeler, and Tovar 2011), acting as leaders in their communities, mastering skills, networking, and negotiating to ensure sustainability. A 2004 survey by the Center for Women's Business Research found 90,000 privately held companies owned by American Indian women. One out of 11 American Indian women is a business owner, and American Indian women have the highest rate of entrepreneurship among major ethnic groups. Their efforts decrease unemployment and poverty, increase personal and tribal financial assets, and foster the development of human capital (Taliman 2009).

Prior to the last recession, there were some promising trends in business ownership among Native Americans. The number of businesses owned by American

Indians and Alaska Natives increased 84% between 1992 and 1997 (U.S. Census Bureau 2001). In 2002, Mark W. Olson (then governor of the Federal Reserve Board) noted that receipts of Native-owned enterprises amounted to $22 billion in 1997, a 179% increase from 1992. Data from the 2010 census indicate further growth. In 2007, receipts for businesses owned by American Indians and Alaska Natives rose to $34.5 billion (DeNavas-Walt et al. 2011; U.S. Census Bureau 2010). Of course, it is unclear whether these gains were sustained through the recession. Also unclear is the extent to which these business trends influence assets available to elders.

Microfinancing has considerable promise for facilitating entrepreneurship, and the model has several advantages: (1) the small initial loans limit the risk faced by lenders and their reluctance to lend; (2) the loans are intended for very small start-ups, not unlike the jewelry and weaving enterprises of Native women; (3) the model emphasizes empowerment and community development, values that resonate with Native perspectives; (4) small efforts have the advantage of being easily guided by successful community members who value the Native tradition of passing knowledge from one generation to the next—a modern-day succession plan; and (5) small communities of loan recipients could act as a natural support network.

■ FINANCIAL CAPABILITY AND CULTURAL SENSITIVITY

Cultural Resilience

Despite poverty, ill health, and a history of cultural degradation, there is deep resilience among Native Americans (HeavyRunner and Morris 1997). Iris HeavyRunner and Joann Morris (1997) identify a number of factors that have been central to Native people's survival: spirituality, tribal identity, ceremonies and rituals, humor, oral traditions, extended family support networks, and the role of elders as holders of tradition and cultural identity.

Many elders retain the historical memory of assimilation and colonization, but they also retain a crucial memory of survival. That memory can help to override the collective sense of defeat and despair. Donna Grandbois and Gregory Sanders (2009) suggest that the resilience of Native elders is best understood in the context of a culturally embedded worldview. The perceived source of resilience is not just the legacy of surviving atrocities but also a more ancient legacy of survival—a legacy passed down through ancestors. Both resilience and survival emerge from the spiritual belief in "oneness with all creation" (2009, 575).

Knowledge and Skills

In Native communities, elders can safeguard traditional knowledge and skills. Thus, assets may include stories, language, and healing traditions, as well as arts and crafts. Elders mentor younger generations in vanishing languages and other tribal skills. Through these meaningful contributions, they strengthen the identities and cultural pride of younger generations. The link between elders and youth is vital for improving the well-being of both groups and for the survival of indigenous cultures.

Language Revitalization

In her discussion of the role of language in Hualapai culture, Lucille Jackson Watahomigie (1998, 6) illustrates the close connection of language with identity: "It is said that when the languages were created, language identified the people—who we are, where we came from, and where we are going." The great linguist Kenneth Hale put it in another way: "Every language lost is like dropping a bomb on the Louvre" (Ambler 2004, 9).

In 2010, UNESCO published the third edition of its *Atlas of the World's Languages in Danger* (Moseley 2010). Under the UNESCO classification scheme, most American Indian and Alaska Native languages in the United States, 70 of 139 languages, are considered endangered (Rogers, Palosaari, and Campbell 2010). The Association on American Indian Affairs (2014) places the figure at 135 out of 155. The Esther Martinez Native American Languages Preservation Act of 2006 authorizes funds for language revitalization programs in Native communities (Pub. L. 109-394, 120 Stat. 2705). Named for an Ohkay Owingeh tribal elder, the act funds immersion schools, language nests (in which multigenerational speakers work with young children), and master apprentice programs (in which an elder works with a team of learners).

Two successful programs have received worldwide recognition for the revival of Native Hawaiian and the Maori language in New Zealand (Hinton and Hale 2001). Writing about the revival of Native Hawaiian, Leanne Hinton (2003) notes that, by 1990, the only native speakers under age 50 years resided on one small, private island. A university program was established along with language nests modeled on the New Zealand experience. In these nests, elders taught the language to preschoolers and their parents. Of course, as Hinton (2003) points out, both Hawaii and New Zealand had only one indigenous language. Many U.S. states have several languages in danger, so revitalization resources are spread thin.

Education

Results from the American Community Survey indicate that growing numbers of American Indians are participating in higher education, including graduate and professional programs. Despite the improvement, educational attainment among American Indians and Alaska Natives still lags behind that of other groups. Roughly 77% of those aged 25 years or over have at least a high school diploma. In contrast, the rate is 89% among non-Hispanic whites. Similarly, about 14% of American Indian and Alaska Natives have at least a bachelor's degree, and 30% of non-Hispanic whites have at least that level of education (U.S. Census Bureau 2007). Of course, the higher education of younger generations cuts two ways. It certainly enhances the financial capability of the young; but the paucity of economic opportunities in Native communities often forces young adults to migrate, leaving their elders behind.

Economic Development on Reservations

Dating to the 1920s, economic development efforts on reservations aim to alleviate the poverty and hopelessness that have often characterized reservation life (Fitch 1974). To the extent that they are effective at creating jobs and economic activity to sustain younger generations, these efforts can indirectly benefit Native elders.

Stephen Cornell and Joseph Kalt (2007, 18) recommend a "nation-building" approach to economic development on reservations. They describe the key attributes of the approach: "(1) Native nations comprehensively assert decision-making power (practical sovereignty, or self-rule); (2) nations back up decision-making power with effective governing institutions; (3) their governing institutions match their own political cultures; (4) decision making is strategic; and (5) leaders serve as nation builders and mobilizers" (2007, 18). We see elements of this approach in the Social and Economic Development Strategies funded by the Administration for Native Americans. These typically involve microloans, technical assistance for reservation-based businesses, training, and public education campaigns (Administration for Native Americans 2007).

A different approach to economic development is evident in the opportunities offered to tribes by casinos and the extractive industries (e.g., mining and logging). In 1988, the Indian Gaming Regulatory Act legalized gaming on reservations (Pub. L. 100-497, 102 Stat. 2467). Since then, there has been an exponential increase in the number of casinos operated on tribal lands. As of 2007, there were over 350 casinos operated by nearly half of the recognized tribes (Gonzales, Lyson, and Mauer 2007). In their examination of the economic and social effects associated with casinos, William Evans and Julie Topoleski (2002) find positive effects that include increases in the number of jobs; population growth, which they attribute to the return of young adults to the reservation; declines in the number of working-poor households; and declines in mortality. Negative effects include increases in bankruptcies, violent crime, auto theft, and larceny. Another report suggested that the rise in low-wage jobs associated with casinos may lead to increased high school dropout rates (Evans and Kim 2008).

As Judith Royster (2012, 92) notes, "Energy development is the economic lifeblood of many Indian tribes." Although there is some interest in developing renewable energy on reservations, extraction industries have had a long-standing presence. On the Navajo reservation, for instance, uranium mining and coal production are associated with significant economic and health impacts. Although mineral royalties account for over half of the Navajo nation's revenue and mining and energy production provide hundreds of jobs, communities in the vicinity of these operations are exposed to contaminated water and an increased risk of disease (Jalbert 2012). Indeed, the destructive legacy of these and similar operations is often cited in controversies around expansion of mining, drilling, and logging on reservation lands (see, e.g., Fonseca 2011; McCarthy 2004; U.S. Government Accountability Office 2011).

■ IMPLICATIONS FOR POLICY AND RESEARCH

In this section, we offer some general observations about research and policy designed to improve the financial capability of Native elders. Policymaking and research must begin with the engagement of Native leadership and stakeholders. Partnerships between Natives and non-Natives must take into account the shared history of these two peoples.

It is imperative that we improve the base of evidence on which to build sound policy. The 2010 census hired Native American census workers who were culturally familiar to the respondents they interviewed, and this affected Native respondents' willingness to participate in the census (Barusch 2006). This model should be duplicated in smaller surveys and other data-gathering efforts that are conducted more regularly.

Asset-based programming that serves American Indians has not generally focused on elders but has drawn leaders from business and education to design initiatives that will help young people find careers. The focus might be shifted to the assets of older adults by beginning with cultural resources as opposed to financial ones. One innovative program gives Native elders the opportunity to convert their cultural assets (skills in traditional crafts) into much-needed cash. The Adopt-A-Native-Elder Program in Park City, Utah, collects gifts of support for Navajo elders. An online catalog and the Annual Navajo Rug Show and Sale provide markets for their traditional crafts (see http://www.anelder.org).

The unique status of American Indians and Alaska Natives as domestic nations confers significant obligations on the U.S. government. Expansion of federally funded services on tribal lands and in urban centers could directly enhance the material well-being of Native elders. In 2011, the National Indian Council on Aging recommended increased federal support of three initiatives: (1) nutrition and supportive services to Indian tribes and Native Hawaiian organizations; (2) tribal capacity building to support elder access to services; and (3) protection of vulnerable American Indian and Alaska Native elders (DeLaCruz 2009). Furthermore, Indian Health Service programs that provide health services should be considered priorities.

This chapter has implications for research questions as well as methodology. Little is known about Native elders' experiences of and attitudes toward asset accumulation. Although there have been longitudinal studies of asset accumulation over the life course, none has focused on Native peoples. Information from such work could support the development of culturally appropriate programming. Additional studies might explore the intergenerational exchange of assets and assistance between elder and younger generations. Research might also examine the cultural tension between personal and collective ownership. Finally, the involvement of elders in language revitalization programs merits further examination.

Traditional research models may not be effective in the Native context, particularly if they involve non-Native researchers. Clearly, there is a need for more Native researchers, and in the meantime, non-Native researchers must use culturally sensitive methods. Participatory models (participatory action research, community-based research partnerships) have promise for work with Native populations. Using these approaches, Native communities could control the work from conception to dissemination of findings, with non-Native researchers serving as consultants and facilitators.

▪ NOTES

1. A note on terminology is appropriate. Many reports on this population rely on census figures and so use the term *American Indian and Alaska Natives*. We adopt this term when referring to material from these sources. The more general term *Native American* is used to refer to all indigenous peoples in the United States, including Alaskan Natives and Native Hawaiians. Most of the work that we draw from focuses on individuals who are members of federally recognized tribes, but we acknowledge the presence of those who identify as Native American although their tribes have not been recognized by the government.

2. An Act Making Provision for the Civilization of the Indian Tribes Adjoining the Frontier Settlements (Civilization Fund Act), 3 Stat. 516 (1819).

3. An Act Authorizing Appropriations and Expenditures for the Administration of Indian Affairs, and for other Purposes (Snyder Act), Pub. L. 65-85, 42 Stat. 208 (1921); codified at 25 U.S.C. § 13 (2012).

4. Pub. L. 89-73, § 601, 79 Stat. 218, 225, as amended by Pub. L. 95-478, 92 Stat. 1513–1560 (1978); codified at 42 U.S.C. § 3001 (2012).

5. An Act to Provide for the Allotment of Lands in Severalty to Indians on the Various Reservations (Dawes Act; Indian General Allotment Act), 24 Stat. 388 (1887); codified as amended at 25 U.S.C. 331 (2012).

6. Indian Reorganization Act (Wheeler–Howard Act), Pub. L. 73-383, 48 Stat. 984 (1934).

7. An Act to Secure Homesteads to Actual Settlers on the Public Domain (Homestead Act of 1862), ch. 75, 12 Stat. 392 (1862), repealed 1976.

8. *The American Indian Probate Reform Act: Empowering Indian Land Owners, Before Committee on Indian Affairs*, 112th Cong. 19 (August 4, 2011) (statement of Douglas Nash,

Director, Center for Indian Law and Policy, Institute for Indian Estate Planning and Probate, Seattle University School of Law); American Indian Probate Reform Act, Pub. L. 108-374, 118 Stat. 1773 (2004).

9. *Cobell v. Salazar*, 679 F.3d 909 (D.C. Cir. 2012). See also Claims Resolution Act of 2010, Pub. L. 111-291, 124 Stat. 3064.

10. *Cheyenne River Sioux Tribe v. Salazar*, No. 06-CV-00935-JR.

■ REFERENCES

Abourezk, Kevin. 2012. "Tribe Reclaiming Land Lost after the Homestead Act." *Lincoln Journal Star*, May 20. http://journalstar.com/news/state-and-regional/nebraska/tribe-reclaiming-land-lost-after-the-homestead-act/article_08f42e25-0aee-5e08-9519-b274e7d5fc77.html.

Administration for Native Americans. 2007. *2007 Impact and Effectiveness of Administration for Native Americans Projects Report*. Washington, DC: U.S. Department of Health and Human Services. https://www.acf.hhs.gov/sites/default/files/ana/full_report_6.pdf.

Administration on Aging. 2013. "AOA Programs." Last modified April 8. http://www.aoa.gov/aoa_programs.

Ambler, Marjane. 2004. "Native Languages: A Question of Life or Death." *Tribal College Journal* 15 (3): 8–9.

Association on American Indian Affairs. 2014. "Native Language Program." Accessed January 25. http://www.indian-affairs.org/programs/language_preservation.htm.

Barusch, Amanda. 2006. "Native American Elders: Unique Histories and Special Needs." In *Handbook of Social Work in Health and Aging*, edited by Barbara Berkman, 293–300. New York: Oxford University Press.

Bear, Severt Young, and R. D. Theisz. 1994. *Standing in the Light: A Lakota Way of Seeing*. Lincoln: University of Nebraska Press.

Bramley, Dale, Paul Hebert, Leah Tuzzio, and Mark Chassin. 2005. "Disparities in Indigenous Health: A Cross-Country Comparison between New Zealand and the United States." *American Journal of Public Health* 95 (5): 844–850. doi: 10.2105/AJPH.2004.040907.

Burke, Joseph C. 1969. "The Cherokee Cases: A Study in Law, Politics, and Morality." *Stanford Law Review* 21 (3): 500–531.

Capriccioso, Rob. 2012. "Cobell Settlement to Begin Paying out by Christmas." *Indian Country Today*, November 27. http://indiancountrytodaymedianetwork.com/2012/11/27/cobell-settlement-begin-paying-out-christmas-145913.

Cornell, Stephen, and Joseph P. Kalt. 2007. "Two Approaches to the Development of Native Nations: One Works, the Other Doesn't." In *Rebuilding Native Nations: Strategies for Governance and Development*, edited by Miriam Jorgensen, 3–33. Tucson: University of Arizona Press.

Danieli, Yael. 1998. "Conclusion and Future Directions." In *International Handbook of Multigenerational Legacies of Trauma*, edited by Yael Danieli, 669–689. New York: Plenum.

DeLaCruz, James T., Sr. 2009. "FY 2011 Administration on Aging Budget Recommendation." Statement at the 11th Annual Tribal Budget Consultation,

April 29. Albuquerque, NM: National Indian Council on Aging. http://nicoa.org/wp-content/uploads/2014/05/JDeLaCruz-Testimony-on-AoA-FY-2011-Budget.pdf.

DeNavas-Walt, Carmen, Bernadette D. Proctor, and Jessica C. Smith. 2011. *Income, Poverty, and Health Insurance Coverage in the United States: 2010.* Current Population Reports: Consumer Income, P60-239, September. Washington, DC: U.S. Census Bureau. http://www.census.gov/prod/2011pubs/p60-239.pdf.

Duran, Eduardo. 2006. *Healing the Soul Wound: Counseling with American Indians and Other Native Peoples.* New York: Teachers College Press.

Evans, William N., and Julie H. Topoleski. 2002. "The Social and Economic Impact of Native American Casinos." Working Paper 9198, September. Cambridge, MA: National Bureau of Economic Research. http://www.nber.org/papers/w9198.

Evans, William N., and Wooyoung Kim. 2008. "The Impact of Local Labor Market Conditions on the Demand for Education: Evidence from Indian Casinos." Working Paper, June. Notre Dame, IN: University of Notre Dame, Department of Economics and Econometrics. http://www3.nd.edu/~wevans1/working_papers/casinos_education_update_1.pdf.

Federal Deposit Insurance Corporation. 2012. *2011 FDIC National Survey of Unbanked and Underbanked Households.* Report, September. Washington, DC: Federal Deposit Insurance Corporation. https://www.fdic.gov/householdsurvey/2012_unbankedre-port.pdf.

Fitch, James B. 1974. "Economic Development in a Minority Enclave: The Case of the Yakima Indian Nation." PhD dissertation, Stanford University.

Fonseca, Felicia. 2011. "Navajo Nation Settles Coal Mining Royalty Case." *Associated Press*, August 5.

Garrett, Michael T. 1996. "'Two People': An American Indian Narrative of Bicultural Identity." *Journal of American Indian Education* 36 (1): 1–21.

Gilbert, Jess, Spencer D. Wood, and Gwen Sharp. 2002. "Who Owns the Land? Agricultural Land Ownership by Race/Ethnicity." *Rural America* 17 (4): 55–62. http://www.ers.usda.gov/media/562463/ra174h_1_.pdf.

Goins, R. Turner, and Courtney S. Pilkerton. 2010. "Comorbidity among Older American Indians: The Native Elder Care Study." *Journal of Cross-Cultural Gerontology* 25 (4): 343–354. doi: 10.1007/s10823-010-9119-5.

Gonzales, Angela A., Thomas A. Lyson, and K. Whitney Mauer. 2007. "What Does a Casino Mean to a Tribe? Assessing the Impact of Casino Development on Indian Reservations in Arizona and New Mexico." *Social Science Journal* 44 (3): 405–419. doi: 10.1016/j.soscij.2007.07.001.

Grandbois, Donna M., and Gregory F. Sanders. 2009. "The Resilience of Native American Elders." *Issues in Mental Health Nursing* 30 (9): 569–580. doi: 10.1080/01612840902916151.

Hayward, Mark D., and Melonie Heron. 1999. "Racial Inequality in Active Life among Adult Americans." *Demography* 36 (1): 77–91. doi: 10.2307/2648135.

HeavyRunner, Iris, and Joann Sebastian Morris. 1997. "Traditional Native Culture and Resilience." *Research/Practice Newsletter* (University of Minnesota Center for Applied Research and Educational Improvement) 5 (1). http://conservancy.umn.edu/bitstream/handle/11299/145989/1/TraditionalNativeCulture-and-Resilience.pdf.

Hinton, Leanne. 2003. "Language Revitalization." *Annual Review of Applied Linguistics* 23: 44–57. doi: 10.1017/S0267190503000187.

Hinton, Leanne, and Kenneth Hale, eds. 2001. *The Green Book of Language Revitalization in Practice.* New York: Academic Press.

Ho-Chunk. 2014. "Community Support: Housing." Accessed March 5. http://www.hochunkinc.com/communitysupport/housing.html.

Housing Assistance Council. 2013. *Housing on Native American Lands.* Rural Research Report. Washington, DC: Housing Assistance Council. http://www.ruralhome.org/storage/documents/nativeamerinfosheet2.pdf.

Institute for Indian Estate Planning and Probate. 2014. "Institute for Indian Estate Planning and Probate." Accessed January 29. http://law.seattleu.edu/centers-and-institutes/center-for-indian-law-and-policy/indian-institute/.

Jalbert, Kirk. 2012. "Navajo Nation Energy Industry." Triple Helix. Last modified April 19. http://www.3helix.rpi.edu/?tag=uranium.

Jervis, Lori L., Janette Beals, Calvin D. Croy, Suzell A. Klein, Spero M. Manson, and AI-SUPERPFP Team. 2006. "Historical Consciousness among Two American Indian Tribes." *American Behavioral Scientist* 50 (4): 526–549. doi: 10.1177/0002764206294053.

Jervis, Lori L., M. Yvonne Jackson, and Spero M. Manson. 2002. "Need for, Availability of, and Barriers to the Provision of Long-Term Care Services for Older American Indians." *Journal of Cross-Cultural Gerontology* 17 (4): 295–311. doi: 10.1023/A:1023027102700.

Legters, Lyman H. 1998. "The American Genocide." *Policy Studies Journal* 16 (4): 768–777. doi: 10.1111/j.1541-0072.1988.tb00685.x.

Little Soldier, Lee. 1985. "To Soar with the Eagles: Enculturation and Acculturation of Indian Children." *Childhood Education* 61(3): 185–191. doi: 10.1080/00094056.1985.10520710.

Ludtke, Richard L., and Leander McDonald. 2005. *Policy Recommendations for Native Elders.* Report, June. Grand Forks, ND: University of North Dakota, Center for Rural Health. http://ruralhealth.und.edu/projects/nrcnaa/pdf/policy_rec61405.pdf.

McCarthy, Robert J. 2004. "The Bureau of Indian Affairs and the Federal Trust Obligation to American Indians." *BYU Journal of Public Law* 19 (1): 1–160. http://www.law2.byu.edu/jpl/Vol%2019.1/01Mccarthy.pdf.

McDonald, James. 1992. Review of *Chiefly Feasts: The Enduring Kwakiutl Potlach,* curated by Aldona Jonaitis. *American Anthropologist* 94 (3): 772–774. doi: 10.1525/aa.1992.94.3.02a00840.

McDonald, Leander R., Alan Allery, Richard L. Ludtke, Kyle Muus, and Patricia Moulton. 2006. "Using Data for Decisions, Advocacy, & Policy." Presentation to the Federal Interagency Taskforce Meeting on Older American Indians, Washington, DC, April 26. http://ruralhealth.und.edu/presentations/pdf/DCInteragencyMtg06.pdf.

Moseley, Christopher, ed. 2010. *Atlas of the World's Languages in Danger,* 3rd ed. Paris: UNESCO.

National Resource Center on Native American Aging. 2008. Untitled document. Last modified June 23. http://ruralhealth.und.edu/projects/nrcnaa/pdf /Tribal Aggregate ServicesUsage.pdf.

Newman, Judie. 1981. "Bellow's 'Indian Givers': Humboldt's Gift." *Journal of American Studies* 15 (2): 231–238. doi: 10.1017/S0021875800008343.

Nord, Jeretta Horn, Nicole Wheeler, and Molly Tovar. 2011. *A Cup of Cappuccino for the Entrepreneur's Spirit: American Indian Women Entrepreneurs' Edition*. Stillwater, OK: Entrepreneur Enterprises.

Noriega, Jorge. 1992. "American Indian Education in the United States: Indoctrination for Subordination to Colonialism." In *The State of Native America: Genocide, Colonization, and Resistance*, edited by Annette Jaimes, 371–402. New York: South End Press.

Piddocke, Stuart. 1976. "The Potlatch System of the Southern Kwakiutl: A New Perspective." In *Environment and Cultural Behavior: Ecological Studies in Cultural Anthropology*, edited by Andrew P. Vayda, 130–156. Austin: University of Texas Press.

Rogers, Christopher, Naomi Palosaari, and Lyle Campbell. 2010. "Endangered Languages of the United States." In *Atlas of the World's Languages in Danger*, 3rd ed., edited by Christopher Moseley, 108–130. Paris: UNESCO.

Royster, Judith V. 2012. "Tribal Energy Development: Renewables and the Problem of the Current Statutory Structures." *Stanford Environmental Law Journal* 31 (1): 91–137.

Ruliffson, Kim, Richard L. Ludtke, Bridget Hanson, and Leander McDonald. 2008. *Health Disparities of American Indian Elders in North Dakota*. Report, June. Grand Forks, ND: Center for Rural Health. http://ruralhealth.und.edu/projects/nrcnaa /pdf/060608_HealthDisparities.pdf.

Stainbrook, Cris. 2009. "From Removal to Recovery: Land Ownership in Indian Country." *Message Runner* (Indian Land Tenure Foundation) 4: 1. https://www.iltf.org/sites /default/files/message_runner_vol.4_fall_2009_rev.pdf.

Struthers, Roxanne, and John Lowe. 2003. "Nursing in the Native American Culture and Historical Trauma." *Issues in Mental Health Nursing* 24 (3): 257–272. doi: 10.1080/01612840305275.

Taliman, Valerie. 2009. "Taliman: Native Women Entrepreneurs: Good Business for Indian Country." Indian Country Today Media Network, September 4. http://indiancountry todaymedianetwork.com/2009/09/04/taliman-native-women-entrepreneurs -good-business-indian-country-83261.

U.S. Census Bureau. 2001. *American Indians and Alaska Natives: 1997 Economic Census*. Survey of Minority-Owned Business Enterprises, Company Statistics Series Report EC97CS-6, May 9. Washington, DC: U.S. Census Bureau. http://www.census.gov /prod/ec97/e97cs-6.pdf.

U.S. Census Bureau. 2007. *The American Community—American Indians and Alaska Natives: 2004*. American Community Survey Report ACS-07, May. Washington, DC: U.S. Census Bureau. http://www.census.gov/prod/2007pubs/acs-07.pdf.

U.S. Census Bureau. 2008. "Projections of the American Indian and Alaska Native Alone or in Combination: Population by Age and Sex for the United States: 2010 to 2050." 2008 National Population Projections, Table 23 (NP2008-T23). http://www.census .gov/population/projections/data/national/2008/summarytables.html.

U.S. Census Bureau. 2010. "Census Bureau Reports Minority Business Ownership Increasing at More than Twice the National Rate." News release, July 13. http://www .census.gov/newsroom/releases/archives/economic_census/cb10-107.html.

U.S. Department of Health and Human Services, Office of Minority Health. 2012. "American Indian/Alaska Native Profile." Last modified September 17. http://minori- tyhealth.hhs.gov/templates/browse.aspx?lvl=2&lvlID=52.

U.S. Department of Housing and Urban Development. 2014. "Homeownership." Accessed March 5. http://portal.hud.gov/hudportal/HUD?src=/program_offices /public_indian_housing/ih/homeownership.

U.S. Government Accountability Office. 2011. *Indian Issues: Observations on Some Unique Factors That May Affect Economic Activity on Tribal Lands*. Testimony of Anu K. Mittal before the Subcommittee on Technology, Information Policy, Intergovernmental Relations and Procurement Reform, Committee on Oversight and Government Reform, House of Representatives (GAO-11-543, April 7). Washington, DC: U.S. Government Accountability Office. http://www.gao.gov/assets/130/125965.pdf.

Volz, Matt. 2012. "Cobell Case: $3.4 Billion Native Land Royalty Settlement Upheld." *Missoulian*, May 22. http://missoulian.com/news/state-and-regional/cobell-case-billion-native-land-royalty-settlement-upheld/article_c15157aa-a440-11e1-98f8-001a4bcf887a.html.

Watahomigie, Lucille Jackson. 1998. "The Native Language Is a Gift: A Hualapai Language Autobiography." *International Journal of the Sociology of Language* 132: 5–7. doi: 10.1515/ijsl.1998.132.5.

Wilkins, David E., and Heidi Kiiwetinepinesiik Stark. 2010. *American Indian Politics and the American Political System*, 3rd ed. Lanham, MD: Rowman & Littlefield.

Zuckerman, Stephen, Jennifer Haley, Yvette Roubideaux, and Marsha Lillie-Blanton. 2004. "Health Service Access, Use, and Insurance Coverage among American Indians/Alaska Natives and Whites: What Role Does the Indian Health Service Play?" *American Journal of Public Health* 94 (1): 53–59. doi: 10.2105/AJPH.94.1.53.

6 Older Immigrants

Economic Security, Asset Ownership, Financial Access, and Public Policy

■ YUNJU NAM

Older immigrants face particular situations that create unusual social and economic challenges, yet relatively little research and policy have focused on this group. This chapter considers the social and economic circumstances of older immigrants, suggesting directions for policy and research.

Older immigrants are a growing population. Foreign-born adults aged 65 years or older comprised 8.6% of the older adult population in 1990, 10.8% in 2003, and 11.5% in 2007 (Borjas 2009; He et al. 2005). The proportion is projected to increase to 19% in 2050 (Passel and Cohn 2008). Older immigrants are also a diverse population. Most are naturalized citizens (69.5% in 2010; author's calculations are based on U.S. Census Bureau 2010c), but the population also includes legal permanent residents, refugees, and asylees (Congressional Budget Office 2004).[1] There is also diversity in terms of birthplace: in 2010, 35% of older immigrants came from Latin America, 29% came from Asia, 28% came from Europe, and 6% from other regions (author's calculations are based on U.S. Census Bureau 2010a). The proportions from non-European countries rose dramatically after the passage of the 1965 amendments to the Immigration and Nationality Act.[2] The act removed a quota system that restricted immigration from those countries. As a result, the proportions of Asians and Hispanics have increased respectively among immigrants (Espenshade et al. 1996/1997; Keely 1971).

Despite some diversity in their economic positions, older immigrants are economically vulnerable and generally worse off than their native counterparts. In general, immigrants face labor-market disadvantage that has lifelong impacts for their economic conditions. On average, their levels of education are lower than those of their native-born counterparts (Martin and Midgley 2010). Furthermore, their education and skills are discounted in the U.S. labor market, because foreign educational credentials differ from the credentials in the United States (De Jong and Madamba 2001; Syed 2008). Many immigrants have language issues (e.g., accents and poor English proficiency) that shape their labor prospects (Borjas 1999; Martin and Midgley 2010). Despite these disadvantages, the U.S. government provides no employment assistance (in contrast to the assistance provided by the Canadian government; Bloemraad 2006b). As a result, they earn less than do native counterparts with comparable human capital (Borjas 1994; Congressional

Budget Office 2004). In 2002, the median earnings for immigrant workers were about $27,000 and those for native workers were about $36,000 (Congressional Budget Office 2004). So too, the income of immigrant families tends to be lower than that of native families. In 2001, the median income of immigrant families was $42,980 and that of native families was $54,686 (Congressional Budget Office 2004). Although the native–immigrant earnings gap decreases as tenure in the United States increases, the gap does not completely disappear among immigrants who arrived during their adulthood (Borjas 1994).

Inferior standing in the labor market at earlier life stages results in poor economic outcomes for older immigrants. Many older immigrants have low lifetime earnings, and their Social Security benefits are therefore lower than the benefits of their native counterparts (Borjas 1994). Furthermore, rates of eligibility for Social Security benefits are lower among older immigrants because the program requires a worker to contribute to the Social Security system for 40 or more quarters (10 years or more) before receiving benefits. Some older immigrants have contributed for the required period but remain ineligible because they worked without proper immigration documentation, and Social Security Administration records do not accurately reflect their contributions (Borjas 2009; Rupp, Strand, and Davies 2003). Labor-market disadvantages also limit older immigrants' chances of receiving retirement benefits through employment. Participation rates in employment-based retirement plans (e.g., pension and 401[k] plans) are high among workers with management and professional occupations but low among those in service occupations (Bureau of Labor Statistics 2009). Because the proportion of immigrants with managerial or professional jobs is lower than that of native-born individuals in such roles, and the proportion with service jobs is higher (U.S. Census Bureau 2010b), the percentage of older immigrants with private retirement benefits is likely low. Analyses with the sample of workers at preretirement age reflect these differences in labor-market positions by immigration status: the gap between natives and immigrants in pension coverage is estimated to be 11 percentage points among men and 15 percentage points among women (Sevak and Schmidt 2007).

Accordingly, it is not surprising that income is lower among older immigrants than among native older adults. The native–immigrant difference, estimated to be 30 percentage points in 2007, is partially explained by differences in receipt of Social Security: 71.2% of older immigrants receive Social Security benefits, but 91% of native counterparts receive them. Income from other sources also partially explains the gap: other types of retirement income (e.g., pension) are received by 21.9% of older immigrants and 40% of native counterparts; 20.1% of older immigrants receive investment income (e.g., interest from savings accounts), but 34.4% of native older adults receive such income (Borjas 2009). Thus, the proportion of older adults relying on public assistance (e.g., Supplemental Security Income) is much higher among immigrants than among native counterparts (Borjas 2003; Hu 1998). Despite income from public assistance, older immigrants have a much higher poverty rate (16.8% vs. 9.8% in 2009; author's calculations based on U.S. Census Bureau 2010e).

Among older immigrants, noncitizens and recent immigrants are more economically vulnerable than are older naturalized citizens and older established immigrants. The risk of experiencing economic hardship is higher among older noncitizens than among naturalized counterparts. To acquire citizenship, immigrants must pay processing fees and pass a naturalization test. These requirements impose considerable burdens on immigrants with low income and low levels of education (Nam and Kim 2012; Yang 1994). Accordingly, the naturalization rate is higher among immigrants with economic and social advantages than among those without such advantages. This difference is reflected in poverty rates among naturalized older adults and older noncitizens: in 2009, the poverty rate was 15% among naturalized older citizens and 21% among older noncitizens (U.S. Census Bureau 2010e). Economic risk is particularly high for recent immigrants. The average income is only $6,300 among older immigrants who have lived in the United States for fewer than 10 years but $18,400 among those who have lived in the country for more than 10 years (Borjas 2009). Poverty rates are also much higher among recent immigrants than among established counterparts: 24.8% among those living in the United States for fewer than 10 years and 9.6% among those living in the country for 40 or more years (U.S. Census Bureau 2010d).

The low levels of income and high rates of poverty among older immigrants, especially among noncitizens and recent immigrants, elevate the importance of saving and assets as ways to maintain economic security. However, there is little empirical evidence on asset ownership among immigrants and even less on the assets of older immigrants (Newberger, Rhine, and Chiu 2004). Specifically, little empirical research investigates the rates at which older immigrants own homes, financial assets, or vehicles, and few studies measure the value of their total assets. Also, few previous studies have investigated whether and how the assets owned by older immigrants differ from those of native older adults. Moreover, little is known about the process of asset accumulation among immigrants, especially among older immigrants. Theoretical and empirical studies on younger immigrants suggest, however, that levels of asset ownership may be lower among older immigrants than among their native-born counterparts.

This chapter attempts to expand the knowledge in this area and to enable the development of intervention plans for economically vulnerable older immigrants. Opening with a summary of the theoretical literature on asset accumulation among immigrants, the chapter focuses on institutional barriers to financial capability. It then reviews empirical studies on assets held by younger immigrants and the limited research on older immigrants. Because asset accumulation during the working years affects the subsequent wealth levels of older adults, examining asset accumulation by working-age immigrants should provide useful information on the assets of older immigrants. The chapter concludes with recommendations for future research and policy.

■ BARRIERS TO FINANCIAL CAPABILITY AMONG IMMIGRANTS

U.S. Policies toward Immigrants

Despite growth in the number and economic vulnerability of older immigrants, American society has paid little attention to economic issues faced by this group. So too, the United States has rarely adopted policies to facilitate immigrants' settlement and incorporation into their new country. Some federal efforts have sought to address the needs of special categories of immigrants (e.g., refugees), but policy discussion has focused mainly on the number and types of immigrants to be admitted.[3]

Moreover, decisions about immigration have often involved cost–benefit calculations. The United States opens its doors to newcomers when the benefits of doing so are estimated to outweigh the costs, but the nation closes its doors when the costs seem to exceed the benefits (Bloemraad 2006b; Borjas 1999; Espenshade et al. 1996/1997; Martin and Midgley 2010).

Cost–benefit calculations also affect who is admitted. The "public charge" doctrine has been a main principle in federal immigration policy (Edwards 2001, 2). One of the first federal policies, the Immigration Act of 1882, prohibited the immigration of individuals suspected of being unable to support themselves and, thus, at risk of becoming public charges (i.e., receiving welfare assistance).[4] Indeed, concern over the fiscal burden of immigrants has been a core issue in immigration-related discussions (Borjas 1999; Edwards 2001; Espenshade et al. 1996/1997). The federal government provides two major paths to immigration: employment and family reunification. Foreign-born individuals obtain immigration visas (permanent residency, so-called green cards) if employers, prospective employers, or family members sponsor their immigration into the United States (U.S. Department of State 2014).

However, the federal government has rarely paid attention to immigrants' adjustment into the society after their entry. The government presumes that employment-based immigrants have the skills and resources necessary for adjustment to their new environments. It presumes that family-based immigrants needing financial or other assistance can rely on family members who sponsored their immigration. Thus, the U.S. government has maintained a laissez-faire approach toward immigrant settlement (Bloemraad 2006b; Espenshade et al. 1996/1997).

In recent decades, anti-immigrant policy developments have impeded the incorporation of immigrants while threatening their economic security. The most prominent of these anti-immigrant measures is the Personal Responsibility and Work Opportunity Reconciliation Act of 1996 (Pub. L. 104-193, 110 Stat. 2105). Commonly known as welfare reform, the act restricts noncitizens' eligibility for public assistance. Prior to the act's passage, citizens and legal permanent residents had the same rights to such assistance. Immigrants' access to public benefits now depends upon citizenship status, the timing of their entry into the United States, the length of their tenure in the United States, and the state of residence (Nam 2011; National Immigration Law Center 2002). For example, the 1996 law tightens eligibility for Supplemental Security Income: noncitizens are eligible only if they received benefits from the program at the time of the 1996 law's passage (August 1996) or came to the United States before that time and became disabled after welfare reform. These rules are relevant in the current discussion because older immigrants rely more on Supplemental Security Income than do their native counterparts (Hu 1998; Van Hook and Bean 1999).

Challenges in Asset Accumulation among Immigrants

Immigrants have special needs that influence their ability to achieve financial incorporation (e.g., being connected with mainstream financial services) in the United States. For example, a substantial number of immigrants have language barriers to financial services and asset accumulation. The U.S. government and the private financial sector have made little effort to address these needs. This chapter highlights four key impediments to financial incorporation and asset accumulation: labor-market disadvantage, lack of access to mainstream financial services and credit, cultural factors, and lack of financial knowledge and management skills.

First, immigrants face labor-market disadvantage. As discussed above, immigrants' earnings and family income tend to be lower than that of native counterparts (Borjas 1994; Congressional Budget Office 2004). Since economic resources and consumption level are two major determinants of asset accumulation (Beverly et al. 2008), earnings and income that are consistently low throughout the lifetime (Borjas 1994) likely hinder older immigrants' saving and asset accumulation.

Second, the lack of access to mainstream financial services and credit markets also likely hampers financial management and asset accumulation among older immigrants (Rhine and Greene 2006). The percentage of unbanked individuals (those without transaction bank accounts, such as checking or savings accounts) is much higher among immigrants (32.3%) than among native-born individuals (18.5%). The rates are especially high among those from Mexico (53.3%) and Latin America (37.2%; Rhine and Greene 2006). The native–immigrant gap can also be found in the use of other types of financial services, such as savings accounts, retirement savings, and stock ownership. The gap is particularly large in the use of sophisticated financial products; for example, the percentage of native-born adults who own stock is more than twice the percentage among immigrants (8.5% vs. 20.0%; Osili and Paulson 2005; Paulson et al. 2006). Immigrants are more likely than natives to use alternative financial products, such as check-cashing services. Such services impose higher fees than those for mainstream services and do not improve credit scores (Joassart-Marcelli and

Stephens 2010; Paulson et al. 2006). Although low education, low income, and other socioeconomic disadvantages explain a large portion of the native–immigrant gap in connection to mainstream financial services, research indicates that the gap remains if estimates account for these socioeconomic differences (Osili and Paulson 2005; Paulson et al. 2006; Rhine and Greene 2006).

Obstacles to the use of mainstream financial services are the same for immigrants and disadvantaged native-born individuals. These obstacles can include the high cost of banking services (e.g., high maintenance fees for checking accounts and minimum-balance requirements), poor or no credit history, and inconvenient locations and hours of operation (Joassart-Marcelli and Stephens 2010; Newberger et al. 2004; Osili and Paulson 2005; Rhine and Greene 2006). However, immigration status can also pose unique barriers. Documentation requirements (e.g., a Social Security number) discourage immigrants, especially undocumented immigrants, from opening bank accounts and prevent them from obtaining a mortgage through mainstream institutions. Some alternative forms of identification are accessible to immigrants. The Internal Revenue Service issues individual tax identification numbers to individuals who are ineligible for Social Security numbers, and the Mexican government issues the matricula consular to Mexican nationals living outside of Mexico. Although an increasing number of financial institutions accept alternative forms of identification, documentation requirements are not consistent across financial institutions. In addition, substantial portions of immigrants do not know that they can open a bank account with an alternative form of identification: 25% of immigrants from Latin America believe that they must present a Social Security number or driver's license to open a bank account (Paulson et al. 2006). Financial institutions are also more reluctant to accept alternative identification when approving mortgages than when opening bank accounts, because it is not easy to check an applicant's credit history without a Social Security number (Gallagher 2005; Paulson et al. 2006). Immigrants identify language barriers and unwelcoming or intimidating atmospheres at financial institutions as other barriers to financial services (Osili and Paulson 2005, 2008).

Third, cultural factors also play a role. Immigrants' experience with financial institutions in their countries of origin affects their perception of mainstream financial services in the United States. Because immigrants from countries with fragile financial infrastructure distrust banks and credit unions, they avoid services from these institutions. An analysis that controls for socioeconomic characteristics finds that a substantial proportion of the native–immigrant gap in financial market participation is explained by the quality of financial institutions in immigrants' countries of origin. In addition, the quality of those institutions has long-lasting effects on immigrants' bank account ownership—effects found to persist even 18 years after immigration (Paulson et al. 2006). Religion and cultural belief sometimes impose barriers. For example, religious tenets do not permit Muslims to pay or receive interest. Thus, many Muslim immigrants do not use savings accounts, mortgages, and other standard financial products (Paulson et al. 2006).

Fourth, lack of financial knowledge and financial management skills may hinder immigrants' asset accumulation. The inability to grasp financial issues tends to hamper prudent financial management and prevent constructive relationships with mainstream financial institutions. A qualitative study indicates that immigrants with low levels of income and education struggle to understand financial systems (e.g., the roles of credit history) and financial products (e.g., mortgage products) without financial guidance provided by community-based organizations (Pataporn, Pfeiffer, and Ong 2010).

■ **IMMIGRANTS AND ASSETS**

Asset Ownership among Immigrants

A few studies examine immigrants' asset ownership and use of financial services (e.g., Newberger et al. 2004; Paulson et al. 2006). Most of these focus on immigrants under the age of 65 years, showing that, across all types of wealth, the rates of asset ownership and values of assets are lower among immigrants than among natives. Although much of the gap in ownership is explained by differences in socioeconomic status (Borjas 2002; Cobb-Clark and Hildebrand 2006) and decreases as the time in the United States increases (Amuedo-Dorantes and Pozo 2002; Cobb-Clark and Hildebrand 2006; Hao 2004), the gap in wealth does not disappear completely even when socioeconomic characteristics and years in the United States are taken into account (Cobb-Clark and Hildebrand 2006). Studies also show that immigrants' asset ownership differs greatly by age, age at immigration, race and ethnicity, and country of origin (Borjas 2002).

Although the owned home is the most prevalent type of asset among immigrants and the native-born population, the rate of homeownership is much lower among immigrants than among the native-born (Borjas 2002; Paulson et al. 2006). As with other economic indicators, the native–immigrant gap in homeownership decreases if the analysis controls for disparities in socioeconomic factors, but a large portion of the gap remains (Borjas 2002). Variation in residency locations by immigration status explains a larger portion of the native–immigrant gap (Borjas 2002). Housing costs in areas in which immigrants live (e.g., metropolitan areas on the East and West coasts) are higher than those in areas in which the native-born population resides (Borjas 2002; Paulson et al. 2006). Studies also hypothesize that the low homeownership rates stem from the lack of immigration documents and credit history, which are essential requirements for many mortgage programs (Gallagher 2005; Paulson et al. 2006). However, no empirical study has tested this hypothesis. It is also of special interest that the native–immigrant gap in homeownership rates has been increasing: the difference was estimated to be 12 percentage points in 1980 but 20 points in 2000 (Borjas 2002).

It is noteworthy that homeownership rates are not consistent across immigrant groups. They are higher among established immigrants than among recent immigrants (Borjas 2002; McConnell and Akresh 2008) and higher among naturalized citizens than among noncitizens (Paulson et al. 2006). Immigrants fluent in English are more likely to own a house than are those with limited English (McConnell and Akresh 2008). The rate is also higher among immigrants from Europe than among those from Latin America or Asia (Borjas 2002; McConnell and Akresh 2008; Newberger et al. 2004).

Trends in levels of net worth parallel those in rates of homeownership: net worth is lower among immigrants than among native-born individuals. In analyzing data from the Survey of Income and Program Participation, Deborah Cobb-Clark and Vincent Hildebrand (2006) find that the median net worth of native couples is 2.5 times that of immigrant couples and the median net worth of single natives is three times that of single immigrants. They also estimate multivariate analyses that control for demographic and socioeconomic characteristics, finding that the native–immigrant gap in net worth is $21,000 among couples and $16,700 among singles.

The native–immigrant gap in wealth among young adults is not as large as that observed among their older counterparts. Analyzing data from the 1979 Youth Cohort of the National Longitudinal Surveys, Catalina Amuedo-Dorantes and Susan Pozo (2002) find comparable levels of wealth among immigrants and natives aged 28 to 35 years in 1993, although immigrants' levels were lower when they were younger (aged 20–27 years, or in 1985). They conduct multivariate analyses on the ratios of net worth to permanent income and financial wealth to permanent income. Estimates from the analyses, which also control for socioeconomic characteristics, show that the net worth and financial wealth ratios among immigrants are only slightly lower than those among natives: among immigrants, the average ratio of net worth to permanent income is 1.0, and the average ratio of financial wealth to permanent income is 0.27 among immigrants; among natives with the same socioeconomic characteristics, the ratios are 1.3 and 0.43 (Amuedo-Dorantes and Pozo 2002). The native–immigrant gaps are smaller than those observed in other studies (Cobb-Clark and Hildebrand 2006). Differences in native–immigrant gaps between this study and others may be explained by the age composition of the sample. Participants in the study by Amuedo-Dorantes and Pozo (2002) were first interviewed in 1979, when they were between the ages of 14 and 21 years; it is likely that they received education in the United States and acquired English language proficiency before they entered the full-time labor market. Both factors could limit the risk that they occupy a disadvantaged position in the labor market. Findings from the study suggest that the age at immigration is important in asset accumulation.

In addition, studies confirm that the number of years in the United States affects immigrants' asset accumulation. The native–immigrant gap in net worth decreases as the number of years in the United States increases (Amuedo-Dorantes and Pozo 2002; Hao 2004). The length of stay in the United States also affects investment portfolio choices among immigrants, and those choices affect the total amount of net worth: as the number of years in the United States increases, the proportion of real estate equity in immigrants' total wealth increases and that of financial equity decreases (Cobb-Clark and Hildebrand 2006).

Immigrants' assets differ by race and ethnicity and country of origin (Hao 2004). Net worth is much higher among white and Asian immigrant adults (ages 25–75 years) than among their black and Hispanic counterparts (Hao 2004). Like rates of homeownership, levels of net worth differ by country of origin. Immigrants from Europe have the highest levels, followed by those from Asia. Median net worth is much lower among immigrants from Mexico, Central and South America, and the rest of the world than among European and Asian immigrants (Cobb-Clark and Hildebrand 2006; Hao 2004).

Asset Ownership among Older Immigrants

The few studies on asset ownership among older immigrants show the financial vulnerability of this population. Analyzing data from a sample of older Mexican Americans, Jeffrey Burr, Jan Mutchler, and Kerstin Gerst (2011) find gaps in homeownership rates between natives and immigrants as well as between naturalized citizens and noncitizens. The gaps are similar to that observed in studies with a younger sample (Paulson et al. 2006). The home-ownership rate is 67.6% among Mexican older adults born in the United States and 40.9% among older Mexican immigrants. Differences in homeownership remain significant after demographic, economic, and metropolitan character-istics are considered: the likelihood of owning a home is significantly lower among older noncitizens and naturalized citizens from Mexico than among native counterparts with Mexican ancestry (Burr et al. 2011). Using data from a nationally representative sample, Purvi Sevak and Lucie Schmidt (2007) report that net worth and the homeownership rate are statistically significantly lower among older immigrants than among native older adults. Examining data col-lected from low-income older Asian immigrants in a supported employment program, Yunju Nam and colleagues (forthcoming) find that only 15% of respondents regularly save. Approximately 35% of these adults own a vehicle, and the same percentage has long-term savings. Estimates from analyses that control for demographic and family characteristics also show that the prob-abilities of owning a bank account, having long-term savings, and owning a vehicle are significantly lower among adults who immigrated at age 55 years or older than among those who came to the United States at a younger age (Nam et al., forthcoming).

■ SUMMARY AND RECOMMENDATIONS

This chapter demonstrates the economic vulnerability of older immigrants. In comparison to native older adults, older immigrants receive Social Security and private retirement benefits at lower rates. These differences are due to labor-market disadvantages imposed upon immigrants during their working years. As a result, the proportion of older adults with incomes below the federal poverty threshold is higher among immigrants than among their native counterparts. Economic vulnerability is particularly high among noncitizens, recent immigrants, older-age immigrants, and those from non-European countries (members of groups that are racial and ethnic minorities in the United States).

Little empirical research examines saving and asset accumulation among older immigrants (Burr et al. 2011; Nam et al., forthcoming; Sevak and Schmidt 2007), but this literature identifies institutional barriers to financial incorporation and suggests that the group's level of wealth is generally low. Except for initiatives to assist refugees, the U.S. government has not developed active resettlement policies for immigrants (Bloemraad 2006a; Espenshade et al. 1996/1997). The private financial sector has not been committed to removing the obstacles that prevent immigrants from using mainstream financial services, although increasing numbers of banks, credit unions, and mortgage companies have adopted innovative measures to expand their business into immigrant communities (Gallagher 2005; Paulson et al. 2006).

As a result of the barriers discussed above, the rates at which immigrants own various assets are lower than the rates of ownership among their native counterparts and lower even than those among natives with comparable socioeconomic characteristics (Borjas 2002; Cobb-Clark and Hildebrand 2006). Because savings and assets accumulated during the working years affect the resources available to older adults, immigrants who accumulate only low levels of assets before age 65 years may lack sufficient resources to sustain them during later years.

Although understanding is far from complete, the data and discussion in this chapter lead to several policy implications. First, it is urgent to remove the institutional barriers that prevent financial incorporation and asset building among immigrants. The government should develop financial policies to facilitate immigrants' settlement and incorporation into the U.S. financial system. For example, government guidelines on alternative forms of identification would reduce confusion among immigrants and financial institutions. Guidelines would also encourage immigrants to open transaction accounts, to use mainstream financial services, and to apply for mortgages. In addition, financial institutions should develop innovative, culturally sensitive financial products and services for immigrants. For example, banks could create special mortgages for Muslims and offer credit-building and credit-check programs for those without Social Security numbers. Banks might also provide translation services via telephone for nonnative speakers. These efforts would facilitate the adjustment of immigrants to the U.S. financial system.

Second, the government and other actors should develop asset-building programs for vulnerable immigrants. These programs should reach out to noncitizens, recent immigrants, those who immigrated in old age, and immigrants from non-European countries. Asset-building programs can encourage immigrants to prepare for retirement by opening and saving into products such as individual retirement accounts. The programs could also provide financial education and financial planning services to help immigrants set aside savings.

Third, those who develop asset-building programs should collaborate with community-based organizations that serve immigrants. These organizations know how to work with immigrant communities and the economically disadvantaged individuals in them. They have developed culturally sensitive programs that promote financial incorporation and financial security (Patraporn et al. 2010; Paulson et al. 2006). In addition, the organizations' trusted relationships with immigrant clients can ease the implementation of asset-building programs for older immigrants.

The paucity of empirical evidence calls for further research on the assets and financial capability of older immigrants. To expand understanding of the topic and facilitate the development of policies, this chapter proposes a research agenda. The first step should be to examine the assets and financial capability of older immigrants in order to answer four questions:

a. What types of assets do older immigrants own?
b. What percentage of older immigrants has access to mainstream financial services such as bank accounts and credit cards?
c. What is the level of financial knowledge among older immigrants?
d. What percentage of older immigrants has sufficient economic resources for retirement?

Second, we should endeavor to understand why rates of asset ownership and values of assets are lower among older immigrants than among their native counterparts. It is especially important that those efforts seek to understand the associations between ownership rates and institutional barriers to financial capability. Although demographic and socioeconomic characteristics have contributed to native–immigrant disparities in asset ownership, evidence suggests that public policies, financial sector rules, and other institutional features impede the ability of immigrants to build assets and develop financial capability in the United States. Accordingly, it is imperative to identify the unique institutional barriers that prevent older immigrants from achieving financial capability and long-term economic security. Research must also determine how these unique conditions interact with common issues that older immigrants share with native older adults. For example, we should understand how the lack of English proficiency limits the access of older immigrants to financial services and limits their ability to comprehend complex financial systems that even native older adults struggle to figure out.

Third, research should understand diversity among older immigrants. That is to say, we should identify the older immigrants at highest risk of experiencing economic insecurity and financial exclusion, and we should ascertain the unique conditions barring them from financial integration and capability. Research shows that the risk is highest among noncitizens, immigrants who come late in life, undocumented immigrants, immigrants with limited English proficiency, and immigrants from non-European countries. But we do not know how each group differs from the other high-risk groups. We also cannot distinguish the barriers that are common to these diverse groups from the barriers that are unique to the respective groups. In-depth understanding of distinct groups of older immigrants is a prerequisite for the development of effective intervention strategies.

Last but not least, research should collect information on innovative interventions (e.g., alternative forms of identification and financial education designed for immigrants) and evaluate their effectiveness. As briefly mentioned, financial institutions and community organizations have developed new programs and practice methods to meet the unique needs of immigrants. We should identify promising approaches, assess the effects of these approaches, and disseminate the findings.

■ **NOTES**

This study was supported in part by grants from the Atlantic Philanthropies and the Les Brun Research Endowment Fund, Buffalo Center for Social Research, School of Social Work, University at Buffalo. I am grateful to Ms. Sarah Nesbitt for her research assistance and Mr. Chris Leiker for his wonderful editing.

1. *Naturalized citizens* are foreign-born individuals who became citizens. *Legal permanent residents* are noncitizens who are granted permission to reside permanently in the United States and, after meeting certain requirements, to apply for naturalization. *Refugees* and *asylees* are admitted to the United States because they experienced persecution or have a well-founded fear of persecution and are unable or unwilling to return to their own countries (Congressional Budget Office 2004). In addition, older immigrants include *undocumented immigrants* (individuals who stay without legal immigration status) and *foreign-born individuals* who possess legal temporary residency (e.g., students, visiting scholars, diplomats, and those with temporary work visas). A very low proportion of older immigrants is undocumented (estimated at 2%), but older people are also unlikely to be temporary residents (Passel and Clark 1998).

2. Act to Amend the Immigration and Nationality Act, Pub. L. 89-236, 79 Stat. 911–922 (1965); codified as amended at 8 U.S.C. §§ 1151–1182 (2012).

3. The federal government provides special assistance to refugees to help their transition into American life. The Refugee Act of 1980 established a funding mechanism for

the efforts, providing federal grants to state and local governments and private voluntary agencies (e.g., coethnic community organizations; Pub. L. 96-212, 94 Stat. 102). Refugees also receive Refugee Cash Assistance, medical assistance, employment training, and English classes. However, even these policies have developed under the assumption that refugees need only temporary asylum and will return to their original countries after the emergency is over (Bloemraad 2006b; Espenshade et al. 1996/1997; Leibowitz 1983; Padilla 1997).

    4. An Act to Regulate Immigration, ch. 376, 22 Stat. 214 (1882).

■ REFERENCES

Amuedo-Dorantes, Catalina, and Susan Pozo. 2002. "Precautionary Saving by Young Immigrants and Young Natives." *Southern Economic Journal* 69 (1): 48–71. doi: 10.2307/1061556.

Beverly, Sondra G., Michael Sherraden, Reid Cramer, Trina R, Williams Shanks, Yunju Nam, and Min Zhan. 2008. "Determinants of Asset Holdings." In *Asset Building and Low-Income Families*, edited by Signe-Mary McKernan and Michael Sherraden, 89–151. Washington, DC: Urban Institute Press.

Bloemraad, Irene. 2006a. "Becoming a Citizen in the United States and Canada: Structured Mobilization and Immigrant Political Incorporation." *Social Forces* 85 (2): 667–695. doi: 10.1353/sof.2007.0002.

Bloemraad, Irene. 2006b. *Becoming a Citizen: Incorporating Immigrants and Refugees in the United States and Canada.* Berkeley: University of California Press.

Borjas, George J. 1994. "The Economics of Immigration." *Journal of Economic Literature* 32 (4): 1667–1717.

Borjas, George J. 1999. *Heaven's Door: Immigration Policy and the American Economy.* Princeton, NJ: Princeton University Press.

Borjas, George J. 2002. "Homeownership in the Immigrant Population." *Journal of Urban Economics* 52 (3): 448–476. doi: 10.1016/S0094-1190(02)00529-6.

Borjas, George J. 2003. "Welfare Reform, Labor Supply, and Health Insurance in the Immigrant Population." *Journal of Health Economics* 22 (6): 933–958. doi: 10.1016/j.jhealeco.2003.05.002.

Borjas, George J. 2009. "Economic Well-Being of the Elderly Immigrant Population." NBER Retirement Research Center Paper NB 09-02. Cambridge, MA: National Bureau of Economic Research. http://www.nber.org/aging/rrc/papers/orrc09-02.

Bureau of Labor Statistics. 2009. *Defined-Contribution Plans More Common Than Defined-Benefit Plans.* Program Perspectives on Retirement Benefits 3. Washington, DC: Bureau of Labor Statistics. http://www.bls.gov/opub/perspectives/issue3.pdf.

Burr, Jeffrey A., Jan Mutchler, and Kerstin Gerst. 2011. "Homeownership among Mexican Americans in Later Life." *Research on Aging* 33 (4): 379–402. doi: 10.1177/0164027511400432.

Cobb-Clark, Deborah A., and Vincent A. Hildebrand. 2006. "The Wealth and Asset Holdings of U.S.-Born and Foreign-Born Households: Evidence from SIPP Data." *Review of Income and Wealth* 52 (1): 17–42. doi: 10.1111/j.1475-4991.2006.00174.x.

Congressional Budget Office. 2004. *A Description of the Immigrant Population.* Report, November. Washington, DC: Congress of the United States. http://www.cbo.gov/sites/default/files/cbofiles/ftpdocs/60xx/doc6019/11-23-immigrant.pdf.

De Jong, Gordon F., and Anna B. Madamba. 2001. "A Double Disadvantage? Minority Group, Immigrant Status, and Underemployment in the United States." *Social Science Quarterly* 82 (1): 117–130. doi: 10.1111/0038-4941.00011.

Edwards, James R., Jr. 2001. *Public Charge Doctrine: A Fundamental Principle of American Immigration Policy*. Backgrounder, May. Washington, DC: Center for Immigration Studies. http://www.cis.org/sites/cis.org/files/articles/2001/back701 .pdf.

Espenshade, Thomas J., Michael E. Fix, Wendy Zimmerman, and Thomas Corbett. 1996/1997. "Immigration and Social Policy: New Interest in an Old Issue." *Focus* 18 (2): 1–10.

Gallagher, Mari. 2005. "Alternative IDs, ITIN Mortgages, and Emerging Latino Markets." *Profitwise News and Views* (Federal Reserve Bank of Chicago), March, 2–8. http://www.chicagofed.org/digital_assets/publications/profitwise_news_and _views/2005/03_2005_pnv.pdf.

Hao, Lingxin. 2004. "Wealth of Immigrant and Native-Born Americans." *International Migration Review* 38 (2): 518–546. doi: 10.1111/j.1747-7379.2004.tb00208.x.

He, Wan, Manisha Sengupta, Victoria A. Velkoff, and Kimberly A. DeBarros. 2005. *65+ in the United States: 2005*. Current Population Reports, P23-209, December. Washington, DC: U.S. Census Bureau. http://www.census.gov/prod/2006pubs/p23-209.pdf.

Hu, Wei-Yin. 1998. "Elderly Immigrants on Welfare." *Journal of Human Resources* 33 (3): 711–741. doi: 10.2307/146339.

Joassart-Marcelli, Pascale, and Philip Stephens. 2010. "Immigrant Banking and Financial Exclusion in Greater Boston." *Journal of Economic Geography* 10 (6): 883–912. doi: 10.1093/jeg/lbp052.

Keely, Charles B. 1971. "Effects of the Immigration Act of 1965 on Selected Population Characteristics of Immigrants to the United States." *Demography* 8 (2): 157–169. doi: 10.2307/2060606.

Leibowitz, Arnold. H. 1983. "The Refugee Act of 1980: Problems and Congressional Concerns." *Annals of the American Academy of Political and Social Science* 467: 163–171. doi: 10.1177/0002716283467001012.

Martin, Philip, and Elizabeth Midgley. 2010. *Immigration in America 2010*. Population Bulletin Update, June. Washington, DC: Population Reference Bureau. http://www .prb.org/pdf10/immigration-update2010.pdf.

McConnell, Eileen Diaz, and Ilana Redstone Akresh. 2008. "Through the Front Door: The Housing Outcomes of New Lawful Immigrants." *International Migration Review* 42 (1): 134–162. doi: 10.1111/j.1747-7379.2007.00116.x.

Nam, Yunju. 2011. "Welfare Reform and Immigrants: Noncitizen Eligibility Restrictions, Vulnerable Immigrants, and the Social Service Providers." *Journal of Immigrant and Refugee Studies* 9 (1): 5–19. doi: 10.1080/15562948.2010.522467.

Nam, Yunju, and Wooksoo Kim. 2012. "Welfare Reform and Elderly Immigrants' Naturalization: Access to Public Benefits as an Incentive for Naturalization in the United States." *International Migration Review* 46 (3): 656–679. doi: 10.1111/j.1747 -7379.2012.00900.x.

Nam, Yunju, Eun Jeong Lee, Jin Huang, and Junpyo Kim. Forthcoming. "Financial Capability, Asset Ownership, and Later-Age Immigration: Evidence from a Sample of Low-Income Older Asian Immigrants." *Journal of Gerontological Social Work*. doi: 10.1080/01634372.2014.923085.

National Immigration Law Center. 2002. *Guide to Immigrant Eligibility for Federal Programs*, 4th ed. Los Angeles, CA: National Immigration Law Center.

Newberger, Robin, Sherrie L. W. Rhine, and Shirley Chiu. 2004. *Immigrant Financial Market Participation: Defining the Research Questions*. Chicago Fed Letter 199, February. Chicago: Federal Reserve Bank of Chicago. http://www.chicagofed.org /digital_assets/publications/chicago_fed_letter/2004/cflfebruary2004_199.pdf.

Osili, Una Okonkwo, and Anna L. Paulson. 2005. "Individuals and Institutions: Evidence from International Migrants in the U.S." Working Paper 2004-19, September 2005 revision. Chicago: Federal Reserve Bank of Chicago. http://www.chicagofed.org /digital_assets/publications/working_papers/2004/wp2004_19.pdf.

Osili, Una Okonkwo, and Anna L. Paulson. 2008. "Institutions and Financial Development: Evidence from International Migrants in the United States." *Review of Economics and Statistics* 90 (3): 498–517. doi: 10.1162/rest.90.3.498.

Padilla, Yolanda C. 1997. "Immigrant Policy: Issues for Social Work Practice." *Social Work* 42 (6): 595–606. doi: 10.1093/sw/42.6.595.

Passel, Jeffrey S., and Rebecca L. Clark. 1998. *Immigrants in New York: Their Legal Status, Incomes, and Taxes*. Report, April. Washington, DC: Urban Institute. http://www .urban.org/publications/407432.html.

Passel, Jeffrey S., and D'Vera Cohn. 2008. *U.S. Population Projections: 2005–2050*. Report, February 11. Washington, DC: Pew Research Center. http://www.pewhispanic.org /files/reports/85.pdf.

Patraporn, R. Varisa, Deirdre Pfeiffer, and Paul Ong. 2010. "Building Bridges to the Middle Class: The Role of Community-Based Organizations in Asian American Wealth Accumulation." *Economic Development Quarterly* 24 (3): 288–303. doi: 10.1177/0891242410366441.

Paulson, Anna L., Audrey Singer, Robin Newberger, and Jeremy Smith. 2006. *Financial Access for Immigrants: Lessons from Diverse Perspectives*. Report, May. Chicago: Federal Reserve Bank of Chicago and the Brookings Institution. http://www.chicagofed .org/digital_assets/others/region/financial_access_for_immigrants/lessons_from _diverse_perspectives.pdf.

Rhine, Sherrie L. W., and William H. Greene. 2006. "The Determinants of Being Unbanked for U.S. Immigrants." *Journal of Consumer Affairs* 40 (1): 21–40. doi: 10.1111/j .1745-6606.2006.00044.x.

Rupp, Kalman, Alexander Strand, and Paul S. Davies. 2003. "Poverty among Elderly Women: Assessing SSI Options to Strengthen Social Security Reform." *Journal of Gerontology: Social Sciences* 58B (6): S359–S368. doi: 10.1093/geronb/58.6.S359.

Sevak, Purvi, and Lucie Schmidt. 2007. "How Do Immigrants Fare in Retirement?" Working Paper 2007-169, October. Ann Arbor: University of Michigan, Michigan Retirement Research Center. http://www.mrrc.isr.umich.edu/publications/papers /pdf/wp169.pdf.

Syed, Jawad. 2008. "Employment Prospects for Skilled Migrants: A Relational Perspective." *Human Resource Management Review* 18 (1): 28–45. doi: 10.1016/j.hrmr.2007.12.001.

U.S. Census Bureau. 2010a. "Foreign-Born Population by Sex, Age, and World Region of Birth: 2010." Characteristics of the Foreign-Born Population by Nativity and U.S. Citizenship Status, table 3.1, March. http://www.census.gov/population/foreign /data/cps2010.html.

U.S. Census Bureau. 2010b. "Occupation of Employed Civilian Workers 16 Years and Over by Sex, Nativity, and U.S. Citizenship Status: 2010." Characteristics of the Foreign-Born Population by Nativity and U.S. Citizenship Status, table 1.7, March. http://www.census.gov/population/foreign/data/cps2010.html.

U.S. Census Bureau. 2010c. "Population by Sex, Age, Nativity, and U.S. Citizenship Status: 2010." Characteristics of the Foreign-Born Population by Nativity and U.S. Citizenship Status, table 1.1, March. http://www.census.gov/population/foreign /data/cps2010.html.

U.S. Census Bureau. 2010d. "Poverty Status of the Foreign-Born Population by Sex, Age, and Year of Entry: 2009." Characteristics of the Foreign-Born Population by Nativity and U.S. Citizenship Status, table 2.13, March. http://www.census.gov/population /foreign/data/cps2010.html.

U.S. Census Bureau. 2010e. "Poverty Status of the Population by Sex, Age, Nativity, and U.S. Citizenship Status: 2009." Characteristics of the Foreign-Born Population by Nativity and U.S. Citizenship Status, table 1.13, March. http://www.census.gov /population/foreign/data/cps2010.html.

U.S. Department of State, Bureau of Consular Affairs. 2014. "U.S. Visas." Accessed March 7. http://travel.state.gov/content/visas/english/immigrate.html.

Van Hook, Jennifer, and Frank D. Bean. 1999. "The Growth in Noncitizen SSI Caseloads 1979–1996: Aging versus New Immigrant Effects." *Journal of Gerontology: Social Sciences* 54B (1): S16–S23. doi: 10.1093/geronb/54B.1.S16.

Yang, Philip Q. 1994. "Explaining Immigrant Naturalization." *International Migration Review* 28 (3): 449–477. doi: 10.2307/2546816.

7

The Interactions of Disability, Aging, Assets, and Financial Instability

■ MICHELLE PUTNAM

■ DISABILITY AS A CONTRIBUTOR OF FINANCIAL INSTABILITY AND BARRIER TO WEALTH CREATION

Disability in later life poses a threat to financial security. Simply put, disability is costly and financially disruptive. Income and assets can improve disabling situations by providing, among other things, access to more physical and mental health care, better care, assistive technology and supports, personal assistance, and home and environmental accommodations. Financial resources also can provide opportunities for social engagement and personal development (e.g., through educational activities).

The nature of the fiscal threat from disability can vary with the type of disease or impairment; the age of onset; the extent of disability; and the personal, environmental, social, and community context within which it is experienced. Long-term disability tends to substantially affect earnings and savings in early and midlife. Those effects have far-reaching consequences for financial security in later life.

Most federal programs that offer financial and health-related supports are linked in some way to employment records and tax contributions. Eligibility for some is also predicated on a medical disability diagnosis. Nearly all are means tested and available only to those with low incomes. Program eligibility criteria tend to funnel individuals with disabilities into negative financial pathways that often result in sustained low income, low-wealth status, and economic instability for themselves and their families. The convergence of poor financial position, disability, social isolation, and disability-related discrimination can result in economic and social marginalization at any age.

This chapter highlights policies related to employment and health care, as these have perhaps the greatest financial impact on persons with disabilities in later life. It also briefly summarizes the characteristics of the population of adults with disabilities—both those in their working years and those who have reached retirement age. It identifies key factors that contribute to financial instability, describes policy influences that affect financial security, and suggests promising ideas for addressing income and asset poverty in later life among persons with disabilities.

■ DEMOGRAPHIC PROFILE OF OLDER ADULTS EXPERIENCING DISABILITY

Estimates from the U.S. Census Bureau's American Community Survey (ACS) show that just over 14.7 million older adults (aged 65 years or older) in the United States—or 36.8%—reported having a disability in 2011 (Erickson, Lee, and Von Schrader 2013). State-based percentages ranged from a high of 47% in Mississippi to a low of 33% in Minnesota, Delaware, and Wyoming. In Puerto Rico, 52% of older adults reported experiencing disability. Estimates also suggest that rates of disability are tied to age: in 2011, 51% of adults aged 75 years and over had some kind of disability. Ambulatory, independent-living, and hearing are the most commonly reported limitations (see Tables 7.1 and 7.2 for rates and definitions). Demographers report decreasing trends in disability prevalence (the proportion of older adults with disability) related to improvements in medical treatment, the quality of assistive technology, access to that technology (e.g., hearing aids and motorized scooters), and environmental accommodations (Schoeni, Freedman, and Martin 2008). However, the incidence of disability—that is, the total number of older adults with disability—is increasing as the overall size of the older adult population grows. Additionally, there have been increases in the prevalence of multiple, co-occurring, chronic diseases: older adults are likely to have more than one health condition that affects disability status (Hung et al. 2011).

TABLE 7.1. *Prevalence of Disability by Category of Disability Identified in 2011 ACS (Percentages)*

Category of disability	Aged 65+			Aged 75+		
	Total	Women	Men	Total	Women	Men
Any disability	37	38	35	51	52	48
Self-care (difficulty dressing or bathing)	9	10	7	14	16	11
Independent living (difficulty doing routine errands alone)	16	20	12	26	31	19
Cognitive (serious difficulty concentrating, remembering, or making decisions)	10	11	8	15	16	12
Ambulatory (serious difficulty walking or climbing stairs)	24	27	19	33	37	28
Hearing (deaf or serious difficulty hearing)	15	12	19	23	20	27
Visual (blind or have serious difficulty seeing even with glasses)	7	8	6	10	11	9

Source: Erickson, Lee, and Von Schrader (2013).
Note: ACS = American Community Survey. The ACS uses a broad definition of disability. Estimates are based on self-report.

TABLE 7.2. *Prevalence of Disability by Selected Characteristics Identified in 2011 ACS (Percentages)*

Category of disability	65+			75+		
	Total	Women	Men	Total	Women	Men
Any disability	37	38	35	51	52	48
Race and ethnicity						
White	36	37	35	50	51	48
Black or African American	43	46	38	56	60	50
Asian	32	35	27	50	53	44
Native American or Alaskan Native	51	52	50	67	68	65
Hispanic (any race)	42	44	39	58	60	54
Level of education						
Less than high school	52	54	50	62	64	59
High school diploma or equivalent	38	38	37	50	51	49
Some college or associate's degree	33	32	34	47	47	47
A bachelor's degree or higher	25	26	24	40	43	38

Source: Erickson, Lee, and Von Schrader (2013).
Note: ACS = American Community Survey. The ACS uses a broad definition of disability. Estimates are based on self-report.

Experience of disability is distributed unequally across the older adult population. Recent scholarship investigating variations in the incidence and prevalence of disability attributes variations by race to socioeconomic factors. Esme Fuller-Thomson and colleagues (2009) use data from the 2003 ACS to examine black–white differences in rates of disability (as measured by functional limitations) among adults between the ages of 55 and 64 years. They find that income and education explain 90% of the difference among men and 75% of the difference among women. Subsequent research by Amani Nuru-Jeter, Roland Thorpe Jr., and Fuller-Thompson (2011) supports those findings. They evaluate 2006 ACS data to assess differences in the odds of experiencing disability at any point across the life span. Nuru-Jeter and colleagues find that the odds are consistently greater for black Americans than for their white counterparts and that the disparity persists across most age groups; the odds of experiencing disability equalize only at age 85 years. Examining three age groups of older adults in the 2005 and 2007 California Health Interview Survey, Kristin August and Dara Sorkin (2010) also find an equalizing effect: at age 75 years, the odds of experiencing a disability are no higher among Asian, Pacific Islander, and Latino Californians than among non-Hispanic white Californians. Mary Elizabeth Bowen's (2009) analysis of nationally representative data from the Health and Retirement Study suggests that the long-term effects of socioeconomic status in childhood moderate black–white differences in disability prevalence among older adults.

Findings on chronic conditions point to examples of where these disparities might start. For example, Heather Whitson and colleagues (2011) identify differences in the prevalence of diabetes and obesity, estimating that the differences account for nearly one-third of the racial disparity in disability found among older North Carolinians. The findings are also noteworthy because the models estimated by Whitson and associates (2011) control for socioeconomic status. Analyzing data from the 2006 Medical Expenditure Panel Survey of adults aged 18 years and over, Amanda Reichard, Hayley Stolzle, and Michael Fox (2011) note significant health disparities between people with and without disabilities (physical and cognitive). They link these findings to preventive services, observing that people with disabilities receive fewer of those services. Together these studies suggest that disability-related interventions for youth and working-age adults may be important in reducing differential disability outcomes in later life.

Research identifies other factors that are positively associated with disability rates among older adults. Karen Fredriksen-Goldsen and associates (2011) find that the disability rate in their study sample is 48% among gay, lesbian, bisexual, and transgendered individuals aged 50 years and older. That is higher than the rate for the general population of 18–64 year olds (10.1%) or the 65 years or older population (35.8%, as noted above; Erickson et al. 2013). Studies on immigrant status, measured as age of immigration (Choi 2012) and specific nationality within larger ethnic categories (e.g., Asian Americans; Kim et al. 2010), also point to the need for a deeper exploration of variations in disability incidence and prevalence.

Poverty can start early for persons with a disability. According to estimates from the 2010 ACS (U.S. Census Bureau 2010b), the poverty rate is 27.3% among noninstitutionalized adults aged 21–64 years who have a disability. Among individuals in that group, the 2010 employment rate was 33.4% (the rate was 72.8% for persons without disabilities; U.S. Census Bureau 2010a). In that year, median earnings for persons aged 16 years and over were $19,500 among individuals with disability and $29,997 among those without one (U.S. Census Bureau 2010c). Estimates from the 2010 Current Population Survey indicate that older adults represent over half of the 20 million adults (aged 16 years and older) who have disabilities and are not in the labor force. Approximately 13% of those older adults would like to be working (Bureau of Labor Statistics 2011). In the 2010 ACS, poverty among older adults who report a disability (13%) was nearly double that of older adults not reporting one (7%; U.S. Census Bureau 2010b).

Midlife appears to be an important financial period for adults with disabilities. Using a composite definition of disability that considers physical and mental health, functional ability, and work limitations, Richard Johnson, Melissa Favreault, and Corina Mommaerts (2010) estimate that the rate of disability doubles for adults between the ages of 55 and 64 years. Among individuals with a disability in that group, slightly less than half receive Social Security Disability Insurance (SSDI) benefits. Moreover, the onset of disability is associated with a doubling of the poverty rate among persons aged 51–64 years. The rate reaches as high as 30.5% among single adults with disabilities. This suggests that the onset of disability before age 65 years is tied to poor financial outcomes in later years. A more recent analysis of data from the Health and Retirement Study offers additional support for this hypothesis. Among people aged 51–56 years who reported the onset of a disability between 1992 and 2000, poverty increased and median income decreased (Dushi and Rupp 2013). In an attempt to broaden the discussion on how poverty is evaluated, Jin Huang, Baorong Guo, and Youngmi Kim (2010) find that both income and household assets are predictive of food insecurity among persons with disabilities. This type of analysis moves discussions beyond interpretations of financial numbers and toward an understanding of why experiencing disability at older ages can contribute to financial poverty. That understanding is important in identifying effective program and policy interventions.

■ CONTRIBUTORS TO RISK FOR POVERTY AND OTHER NEGATIVE OUTCOMES IN LATER LIFE

Although each person's experience is unique, the literature identifies well-established factors that put adults with disabilities at risk for financial poverty. I discuss four of these factors: (1) limited and uneven employment and shortened work careers; (2) out-of-pocket health and long-term care costs; (3) eligibility requirements for safety net programs; and (4) isolation and marginalization.

Limited and Uneven Employment and Shortened Work Careers

As I note, substantial evidence indicates that rates of unemployment are higher among adults who experience disability during their working-age years than among counterparts without disability. Most individuals with childhood-onset disability (including intellectual and developmental disabilities) never make it into the formal workforce (Nord et al. 2013).

Among adults who acquire a disability for the first time in midlife, spells of unemployment and limited employment are common, although employment circumstances vary substantially by diagnostic condition and disability type. For example, Kimia Honarmand and associates (2011) find that greater than two-thirds of workers with multiple sclerosis do not stay employed after diagnosis. They attribute this in large part to functional difficulty and depression. And in a systematic review, Cathryn Baldwin and Natasha Brusco (2011) find that the rate of return to work ranges from 12% to 49% among stroke survivors (aged 18–65 years) who participate in vocational rehabilitation. Early retirement is common among workers with disabilities. For example, in a microsimulation based on private insurance claims, Scott Johnson and associates (2011) find that the odds of early retirement and income loss are two times higher among adults (aged 18–64 years) newly diagnosed with Parkinson's disease than among matched counterparts without such a diagnosis. The odds are five times higher among newly diagnosed adults who use a mobility device. They estimate that the average earnings loss is just over $500,000 for a person aged 45 years and nearly $200,000 for an individual aged 55 years.

Several empirical studies demonstrate that loss of income and loss of the ability to work at younger ages reduce the postretirement income and wealth of people with disabilities, but the findings are nuanced. For example, one study (Strand 2010) analyzes 10 years of data (1996–2006) from the Survey of Income and Program Participation to identify factors that lead to low levels of retirement resources. The findings indicate that 47.2% of those with low retirement resources receive federal disability benefits before age 65 years and that nearly 62% of older adults receiving Supplemental Security Income (SSI) also receive SSI disability-related benefits prior to age 65 years. Benjamin Bridges and Sharmila Choudhury (2009) extend this line of inquiry to SSDI by matching Social Security Administration data to data from the 1990–1993 panels of the Survey of Income and Program Participation. Their analysis focuses on a subgroup of adults with disabilities who receive shared spousal benefits (at least one spouse drew a major part of his or her SSDI benefits after age 61 years), finding that the median amount of Social Security wealth (the total of all benefits, including worker, current or divorced spouse, and surviving or divorced spouse benefits received from age 62 years to death) is 28–31% lower for the subgroup than for the nondisabled comparison group. Additionally, the duration of benefit receipt (in years) is 25–29% lower for the subgroup, because the beneficiaries die at a younger age.

The income and asset accumulation patterns associated with public benefits seem to parallel the patterns associated with privately developed resources. As noted above, many workers with disabilities transition into retirement through disability-related income-support programs, and reliance on those supports curtails the financial resources available for their remaining years. In an analysis of Health and Retirement Survey data, M. Solaiman Miah and Virginia Wilcox-Gök (2007) show that private assets accumulated during work careers are lower and average retirement ages higher among persons with chronic illness than among peers without such illness. These findings suggest that adults with chronic illness possess a desire or need to continue working. Additionally, Martha Ozawa and Yeong Hun Yeo (2007) find that the proportion of older adults who hold assets of any kind is smaller among those with disabilities than among peers without disabilities. Moreover, the overall net worth is lower for older adults with disabilities, and the value of their holdings in each asset category is smaller.

Out-of-Pocket Costs of Health and Long-Term Care

Out-of-pocket health and long-term care costs affect all older adults, and adults who have a chronic condition or disability may already have high out-of-pocket expenditures when they reach age 65 years. In an analysis of data from the nationally representative Medical Expenditure Panel Survey, Sophie Mitra,

Patricia Findley, and Usha Sambamoorthi (2009) show that such expenditures are consistently and significantly higher over an 8-year period for working-age persons with disabilities than for their nondisabled counterparts. In 2004, the average out-of-pocket expenditure was $2,256 for a person without a disability and $10,508 for someone with a disability.

High out-of-pocket costs can impede access to health care. In their analysis of the 2006 Behavioral Risk Factor Surveillance System data, Jae Chul Lee, Romana Hasnain-Wynia, and Denys Lau (2011) find that such a cost is positively associated with the odds that older adults with disabilities delay seeing a doctor, and the association persists even in results from models that control for demographic, health, and financial factors. A study by Becky Briesacher and colleagues (2010) illustrates the impact of out-of-pocket health care costs on household budgets. Using a measure of medication affordability, their analysis of data from a sample of older adults in the Health and Retirement Study shows that, after meeting basic living expenses and paying for medication, poor households have on average only $16 per week for other expenditures.

Out-of-pocket costs associated with long-term support and services are perhaps the greatest financial burden for many older adults. Although both Medicare and Medicaid cover long-term care costs, each has its limits for payment and requirements for service eligibility. In general, Medicare covers 90 days of skilled nursing-facility care as well as some homecare services but importantly does not cover personal care (e.g., bathing, dressing) or homemaker services (e.g., cleaning, laundry).[1] Medicaid is the largest payer of long-term care costs nationally but requires individuals to be impoverished in order to be eligible for this insurance program.[2] Both Medicare and Medicaid have beneficiary copayments for many services and limit the types of supports and services they cover. Most private insurers cover little, if any, long-term care. Thus, out-of-pocket spending for older adults can be high.

For example, few older adults reside in nursing homes and assisted-living facilities (4% of Medicare beneficiaries; Federal Interagency Forum on Aging-Related Statistics 2010), but those who do pay high costs for skilled care: about $75,000 annually for a semiprivate nursing home room and $57,000 annually for assisted living (MetLife Mature Market Institute 2010). Recent analysis by H. Stephen Kaye, Charlene Harrington, and Mitchell LaPlante (2010) shows that 28% of older adults living in a community for long-term care services pay costs out of pocket, with a median monthly payment of $280. Median monthly out-of-pocket costs are highest for persons who reside in nursing homes ($960) and use personal assistance and professional services ($500). Courtney Coile and Kevin Milligan (2009) use Health and Retirement Study data to explore the effects of postretirement health shocks (changes in health) on private asset holdings. They find that both chronic and acute health shocks lead to significant drops in several types of holdings, including owned homes, vehicles, real estate, and businesses. Chronic health shocks are associated with significant decreases in the value of

IRAs, stocks, and bonds. Many of these drops are exacerbated in the presence of physical and mental functional limitations.

Eligibility Requirements for Safety Net Programs

Public policies offering support to persons with disabilities are generally distinguished by categorical eligibility rules related to age. In federal income-support policies, the dividing line is age 62 years: persons under that age can qualify for SSDI and SSI; those aged 62 years or older can qualify for Social Security Old-Age and Survivors Insurance and SSI. In practice, medical insurance policies are less categorical. Qualified SSDI beneficiaries and older adults are eligible for Medicare. Low-income adults of any age can qualify for Medicaid if they meet the financial eligibility criteria and, for some services, the medical eligibility criteria. Additional supports are universally available to adults aged 60 years and above through the Older Americans Act.[3] Although these supports include nutrition services, transportation assistance, health and wellness programs, and home and community-based care, budgetary restrictions tend to limit their provision to those administratively determined to be most in need.

Eligibility criteria for disability-related supports and services commonly limit the income and assets of beneficiaries. Both SSDI and SSI have monthly income caps, but only SSI has an asset cap. Eligibility is lost if a person's resources exceed these caps. To be eligible for SSDI in 2013, for example, working-age persons (aged 18–64 years) with disabilities could earn no more than $1,040 per month from gainful activity. The limit was $1,740 for blind individuals and $750 for SSDI recipients in trial work programs. In 2013, SSI's monthly resource limit (i.e., the value of income and assets except a home, one vehicle, and certain other items) was $2,000 for an individual and $3,000 for a couple (Social Security Administration 2013a). The monthly benefit levels were $710 for an individual and $1,066 for a couple. In September 2013, more than 8.9 million beneficiaries received SSDI payments, and the average monthly benefit for a disabled worker was $1,129. In the same month, just over 2.1 million older adults received SSI benefits (approximately 25% of all SSI recipients) and an average monthly payment of $423. In contrast, slightly more than 4.9 million working-age adults (aged 18–64 years) received SSI in that month, and the average monthly benefit was $544 (Social Security Administration 2013b). The combination of income caps, asset limits, and low average benefits limits recipients' wealth and prevents them from accumulating more of it.

Other than those mentioned for SSI, few federal program eligibility barriers prevent older adults from accumulating and retaining assets. Prior to health reform and the passage of the Affordable Care Act in 2010,[4] Medicaid imposed an asset test for all recipients: those with assets valued above $2,000 were ineligible. However, in January 2011, the federal government stopped requiring states to use an asset test for Medicaid. Only four states have retained the asset restriction: Missouri, South Carolina, Texas, and Utah. These states impose asset limits that vary from $2,000 to $250,000 (Kaiser Family Foundation 2011). The removal of this barrier to asset retention and accumulation in all other states is significant. However, Medicaid retains an income test that limits eligibility for people qualifying based on disability status to income at or below 133% of the federal poverty line. In 2014, that threshold was $15,521 for an individual (U.S. Department of Health and Human Services, Centers for Medicare and Medicaid Services 2014). Such thresholds have the potential to limit the development of new or additional assets.

By law, Older Americans Act programs are not allowed to impose tests on the income or assets of older adults seeking their services (42 U.S.C. § 3030c-2(a–b) [2011]). However, that act funds local area agencies on aging, and they are permitted to target programs to economically and socially disadvantaged subgroups of older adults.[5] No research documents the effects of this targeting on older adults with disabilities.

Isolation and Marginalization

Marginalization and exclusion are significant, well-established risks associated with having a disability. Detachment from social and economic networks, such as employers, volunteer agencies, adult education programs, religious institutions, friends, and family, can limit opportunities to participate, become aware of, and connect with asset-building activities. Efforts to promote social and economic inclusion for persons with disabilities have gained significant attention from national and international bodies. For example, the United Nations Convention on the Rights of Persons with Disabilities cites the absence of such inclusion as a significant problem.[6]

Older adults with disabilities may face a disproportionately high risk of social and economic marginalization because their age and condition expose them to more discrimination than is experienced by nondisabled peers (Bjelland et al. 2010; Emlet 2006). Moreover, marginalization can play out at even the most local level. Neighborhood characteristics, such as physical accessibility and personal safety, may influence whether older adults with disabilities participate in activities outside of their homes (White et al. 2010). Research finds that older adults who have disabilities and live alone are lonelier (Russell 2009) and at greater risk for depression (Meeks et al. 2010) than are nondisabled peers who live alone. These findings suggest that removing disability-related barriers to participation should be a priority.

New research supports long-standing evidence that social engagement can have positive effects on the health of older adults with disabilities. Investigators in Australia find that the presence of informal long-term care support, alone or in combination with formal support, is associated with a reduction in depression among older adults with substantial functional limitations (Chan et al. 2011). Similarly, in the United Kingdom, Vivian Isaac and colleagues (2009) find an association between higher social activity and lower late-life depression symptoms among older community residents. Moreover, emerging evidence suggests that productive activities are associated with positive health outcomes. For example, Yunkyung Jung and associates (2010) link volunteering to reduced odds of frailty among older adults, and Holly Dabelko-Schoeny, Keith Anderson, and Katie Spinks (2010) find that civic engagement among members of an adult day health center is positively associated with self-esteem and levels of purpose in life.

■ IMPLICATIONS FOR POLICY

As I note, the likelihood of financial poverty is higher for older adults with disabilities than for their nondisabled counterparts. Improving the overall financial status of older adults with disabilities should be a critical focus for public policy. Also important are programs to assist them (as well as younger adults with disabilities) in managing financial resources as they negotiate issues associated with income, health, and long-term care supports and services. A range of programs and supports is available to help older adults improve their financial literacy, planning, and advocacy efforts. These include the Consumer Financial Protection Bureau's (2012) newly formed Office of Older Americans and elder rights programs funded by the Older Americans Act. Focused on the prevention of elder abuse, neglect, and exploitation, those efforts provide pension counseling and information, retirement planning, and assistance with Medicare billing (Administration on Aging 2010a). Assistance and support for older adults with disabilities can also be found in efforts by nongovernmental organizations that often work in partnership or in coalition with federal, state, and local agencies. Examples include the AARP Foundation's (2012) Tax-Aide Program and the Economic Security Initiative of the National Council on Aging (2012). Although these and other programs are generally attuned to the financial issues associated with disability in later life, additional attention should be focused on two areas. First, it is important to pay attention to the financial needs and outcomes of older individuals who incurred disability earlier in life; that is, policy and programs should devote more attention to persons aging with disability. Second, policy and programs have identified the factors that result in asset loss among older adults with disabilities, but there is little focus on ways to enable this population to develop assets.

Accordingly, several proposals have sought to help in building the wealth of individuals aging with or into disability, and Individual Development Accounts are a key example. These proposals merit serious attention. Research from Medicaid's Cash and Counseling program identifies potential benefits of embedding Individual Development Accounts within existing programs for persons with disabilities. Margaret Lombe, Michelle Putnam, and Huang (2008) find that

Cash and Counseling participants (aged 18–90 years) in Arkansas, Florida, and New Jersey saved program funds over several months' time to purchase items that support independent living. They also note that the amount of savings accumulated by participants is greater than that accumulated by counterparts who used a program-offered financial consultant. Findings from the American Dream Demonstration, a randomized controlled trial of Individual Development Accounts, offer additional evidence that low-income people with disabilities can save through the accounts, though they save less than their nondisabled peers (Lombe et al. 2010). Age-based analysis of data from the demonstration finds that middle-aged and older adults are more successful savers than are younger adults and save more often for retirement. The findings also indicate that institutional supports, including financial education and direct deposits, are significantly related to savings outcomes (Putnam et al. 2008).

Research has studied well the "tangled web" of disability-related program supports and services for adults with a disability (Wittenburg and Favreault 2003). Some attempts have been made to coordinate eligibilities across public income-support and health insurance programs in order to test the merits of different pathways out of poverty. However, eligibility coordination merits much greater policy attention. One noteworthy example is the Social Security Administration's Ticket to Work Program, which permits beneficiaries to reenter the workforce while maintaining eligibility for SSDI and Medicare (Social Security Administration 2011). A different approach to disentanglement has been attempted by the Aging and Disability Resource Centers Program. Created as a demonstration project under the Older American's Act, the program is administered by the Administration for Community Living (U.S. Department of Health and Human Services, Center for Disability and Aging Policy 2014). The central aim of Aging and Disability Resource Centers is to help persons of all ages understand both their private and public federal, state, and local program eligibilities for long-term services and supports. They also assist individuals with disabilities in applying for and obtaining the benefits for which they are eligible. The centers do not actively coordinate federal, state, and local policy guidelines, but they are making advances in identifying where eligibility regulations are at odds and in understanding how this affects individuals with disabilities as well as public program costs.

▪ IMPLICATIONS FOR RESEARCH

As noted above, disability can have dramatic effects on financial security in later life, and those effects pose difficult policy problems. Certainly there is much need for additional research that generates a greater understanding about how to arrest the long-term poverty cycle that follows many adults as they age with disability. There is also a need to assess how to help older adults with disabilities retain assets and build new wealth in the face of social-welfare program restrictions and limited personal income and savings. Several avenues for potential research can be found in the preceding policy discussion. Research could develop and evaluate interventions that focus on financial literacy and planning. It could also consider ways to strategically embed asset-building opportunities within existing programs that permit savings. Moreover, research could test ways to decouple the financial resources of beneficiaries from the eligibility constraints imposed by public income and health insurance supports. Those constraints seem to cement recipients into a status of being financially insecure.

An approach that may be more novel and require much less policy-based research is the attempt to build this new knowledge about poverty interventions while also pursuing an agenda to reduce social isolation among older adults with disabilities. Several lines of gerontological and disability research have established some understanding of the relationship between economic marginalization and social isolation, but little empirical research has investigated the effects of interventions to address both of these outcomes (e.g., Holmes and Joseph 2011; Johnson, Douglas, et al. 2010). As work on social isolation continues to evolve, exploring these interactions may help to identify ways to improve financial stability for older adults with disabilities. Research with this aim would be consistent with the original mission and goals of the 1965 Older Americans Act and its many reauthorizations; namely, the act seeks to support positive individual, social, and economic outcomes in later life (Administration on Aging 2010b). Given demographic and economic trends as well as the policy obstacles to financial stability, such work seems a worthy course to pursue.

■ CONCLUSIONS

For many older adults with disabilities, financial stability remains elusive. Those whose disability emerged before later life usually find it difficult to gain and retain employment, pay for and access health care, and negotiate social welfare systems. Such tasks are also difficult for adults whose disability emerges in later life, although older adults are exempt from the work restrictions and requirements imposed by available supports. However, older adults with disabilities encounter other age-based limitations not discussed here (e.g., lack of eligibility for work-related services such as personal attendants). Overall, there is a significant need to bolster financial stability among older adults with disabilities, and there are important next steps to be taken. Existing knowledge should be leveraged to design programs, supports, and interventions that reduce the nearly inevitable financial hardship faced by most of these older adults.

■ NOTES

1. See Home Health Services at http://www.medicare.gov.
2. See Eligibility at http://www.medicaid.gov.

3. Codified as amended at 42 U.S.C. § 3001–3058 (2011).

4. Patient Protection and Affordable Care Act of 2010 (Affordable Care Act), Pub. L. 111-148, 124 Stat. 119; see also Kaiser Family Foundation (2011).

5. See 42 U.S.C. § 3026(a)(4)(A–B) (2011); 45 C.F.R. § 1321.61(c) (2013).

6. *Opened for signature* December 13, 2006 (*entry into force* May 3, 2008), 2515 U.N.T.S. 3.

■ REFERENCES

AARP Foundation. 2012. "About the Tax-Aide Program." Accessed October 8, 2013. http://www.aarp.org/money/taxes/aarp_taxaide.

Administration on Aging. 2010a. "Elder Rights Protection." Accessed March 22, 2014. http://www.aoa.gov/AoARoot/AoA_Programs/Elder_Rights/index.aspx.

Administration on Aging. 2010b. "Older Americans Act." Accessed March 22, 2014. http://www.aoa.gov/AoARoot/AoA_Programs/OAA/index.aspx.

August, Kristin J., and Dara H. Sorkin. 2010. "Racial and Ethnic Disparities in Indicators of Physical Health Status: Do They Still Exist throughout Later Life?" *Journal of the American Geriatrics Society* 58 (10): 2009–2015. doi: 10.1111/j.1532-5415.2010.03033.x.

Baldwin, Cathryn, and Natasha K. Brusco. 2011. "The Effect of Vocational Rehabilitation on Return-to-Work Rates post Stroke: A Systematic Review." *Topics in Stroke Rehabilitation* 18 (5): 562–572. doi: 10.1310/tsr1805-562.

Bjelland, Melissa J., Susanne M. Bruyère, Sarah von Schrader, Andrew J. Houtenville, Antonio Ruiz-Quintanilla, and Douglas A. Webber. 2010. "Age and Disability Employment Discrimination: Occupational Rehabilitation Implications." *Journal of Occupational Rehabilitation* 20 (4): 456–471. doi: 10.1007/s10926-009-9194-z.

Bowen, Mary Elizabeth. 2009. "Childhood Socioeconomic Status and Racial Differences in Disability: Evidence from the Health and Retirement Study (1998–2006)." *Social Science and Medicine* 69 (3): 433–441. doi: 10.1016/j.socscimed.2009.06.006.

Bridges, Benjamin, and Sharmila Choudhury. 2009. "Examining Social Security Benefits as a Retirement Resource for Near-Retirees, by Race and Ethnicity, Nativity, and Disability Status." *Social Security Bulletin* 69 (1): 19–44.

Briesacher, Becky, Dennis Ross-Degnan, Alyce Adams, Anita Wagner, Jerry Gurwitz, and Stephan Soumerai. 2010. "A New Measure of Medication Affordability." *Social Work in Public Health* 24 (6): 600–612. doi: 10.1080/19371910802672346.

Bureau of Labor Statistics. 2011. "Persons with a Disability: Labor Force Characteristics— 2010." News release, June 24. http://www.bls.gov/news.release/archives/disabl _06242011.pdf.

Chan, Natalie, Kaarin J. Anstey, Tim D. Windsor, and Mary A. Luszcz. 2011. "Disability and Depressive Symptoms in Later Life: The Stress-Buffering Role of Informal and Formal Support." *Gerontology* 57 (2): 180–189. doi: 10.1159/000314158.

Choi, Sunha H. 2012. "Testing Healthy Immigrant Effects among Late Life Immigrants in the United States: Using Multiple Indicators." *Journal of Aging and Health* 24 (3): 475– 506. doi: 10.1177/0898264311425596.

Coile, Courtney, and Kevin Milligan, K. 2009. "How Household Portfolios Evolve after Retirement: The Effect of Aging and Health Shocks." *Review of Income and Wealth* 55 (2): 226–248. doi: 10.1111/j.1475-4991.2009.00320.x.

Consumer Financial Protection Bureau. 2012. "Financial Protections for Older Adults." Accessed March 22, 2014. http://www.consumerfinance.gov/older-americans.

Dabelko-Schoeny, Holly, Keith A. Anderson, and Katie Spinks. 2010. "Civic Engagement for Older Adults with Functional Limitations: Piloting an Intervention for Adult Day Health Participants." *Gerontologist* 50 (5): 694–701. doi: 10.1093/geront/gnq019.

Dushi, Irena, and Kalman Rupp. 2013. "Disability Shocks Near Retirement Age and Financial Well-Being." *Social Security Bulletin* 73 (3): 23–43.

Emlet, Charles A. 2006. "'You're Awfully Old to Have This Disease': Experiences of Stigma and Ageism in Adults 50 Years and Older Living with HIV/AIDS." *Gerontologist* 46 (6): 781–790. doi: 10.1093/geront/46.6.781.

Erickson, William, Camille G. Lee, and Sarah von Schrader. 2013. *Disability Statistics from the 2011 American Community Survey (ACS).* Ithaca, NY: Cornell University Employment and Disability Institute. http://www.disabilitystatistics.org.

Federal Interagency Forum on Aging-Related Statistics. 2010. *Older Americans 2010: Key Indicators of Well-Being.* Washington, DC: Federal Interagency Forum on Aging-Related Statistics. http://www.agingstats.gov/agingstatsdotnet/Main_Site /Data/2010_Documents/Docs/OA_2010.pdf.

Fredriksen-Goldsen, Karen I., Hyun-Jun Kim, Charles A. Emlet, Anna Muraco, Elena A. Erosheva, Charles P. Hoy-Ellis, Jayn Goldsen, and Heidi Petry. 2011. *The Aging and Health Report: Disparities and Resilience among Lesbian, Gay, Bisexual, and Transgender Older Adults.* Seattle, WA: Institute for Multigenerational Health. http:// caringandaging.org/wordpress/wp-content/uploads/2011/05/Full-Report-FINAL -11-16-11.pdf.

Fuller-Thomson, Esme, A. Nuru-Jeter, Meredith Minkler, and Jack M. Guralnik. 2009. "Black-White Disparities in Disability among Older Americans: Further Untangling the Role of Race and Socioeconomic Status." *Journal of Aging and Health* 21 (5): 677– 698. doi: 10.1177/0898264309338296.

Holmes, Wendy R., and Jennifer Joseph. 2011. "Social Participation and Healthy Ageing: A Neglected, Significant Protective Factor for Chronic and Non Communicable Conditions." *Globalization and Health* 7: article 43. doi: 10.1186/1744-8603-7-43.

Honarmand, Kimia, Nadine Akbar, Nancy Kou, and Anthony Feinstein. 2011. "Predicting Employment Status in Multiple Sclerosis Patients: The Utility of the MS Functional Composite." *Journal of Neurology* 258 (2): 244–249. doi: 10.1007/s00415-010-5736-8.

Huang, Jin, Baorong Guo, and Youngmi Kim. 2010. "Food Insecurity and Disability: Do Economic Resources Matter?" *Social Science Research* 39 (1): 111–124. doi: 10.1016 /j.ssresearch.2009.07.002.

Hung, William W., Joseph S. Ross, Kenneth S. Boockvar, and Albert L. Siu. 2011. "Recent Trends in Chronic Disease, Impairment and Disability among Older Adults in the United States." *BMC Geriatrics* 11: article 47. doi: 10.1186/1471-2318-11-47.

Isaac, Vivian, Robert Stewart, Sylvaine Artero, Marie-Laure Ancelin, and Karen Ritchie. 2009. "Social Activity and Improvement in Depressive Symptoms in Older People: A Prospective Community Cohort Study." *American Journal of Geriatric Psychiatry* 17 (8): 688–696. doi: 10.1097/JGP.0b013e3181a88441.

Johnson, Scott, Matthew Davis, Anna Kaltenboeck, Howard Birnbaum, ElizaBeth Grubb, Marcy Tarrants, and Andrew Siderowf. 2011. "Early Retirement and Income Loss in Patients with Early and Advanced Parkinson's Disease." *Applied Health Economics and Health Policy* 9 (6): 367–376. doi: 10.2165/11596900-000000000-00000.

Johnson, Hilary, Jacinta Douglas, Christine Bigby, and Teresa Iacono. 2010. "The Pearl in the Middle: A Case Study of Social Interactions in an Individual with a Severe

Intellectual Disability." *Journal of Intellectual and Developmental Disability* 35 (3): 175–186. doi: 10.3109/13668250.2010.501026.

Johnson, Richard W., Melissa M. Favreault, and Corina Mommaerts. 2010. *Disability Just before Retirement Often Leads to Poverty.* Older Americans' Economic Security Brief no. 22, January. Washington, DC: Urban Institute. http://www.urban.org /UploadedPDF/412009_disability_retirement.pdf.

Jung, Yunkyung, Tara L. Gruenewald, Teresa E. Seeman, and Catherine A. Sarkisian. 2010. "Productive Activities and Development of Frailty in Older Adults." *Journal of Gerontology: Social Sciences* 65B (2): 256–261. doi: 10.1093/geronb/gbp105.

Kaiser Family Foundation. 2011. "No Asset Tests Required (or Asset Test Limit) for Children's Medicaid and CHIP." State Health Facts table. http://www.statehealthfacts .org/comparetable.jsp?cat=4&ind=228#notes-1.

Kaye, H. Stephen, Charlene Harrington, and Mitchell P. LaPlante. 2010. "Long-Term Care: Who Gets It, Who Provides It, Who Pays, and How Much?" *Health Affairs* 29 (1): 11–21. doi: 10.1377/hlthaff.2009.0535.

Kim, Giyeon, David A. Chiriboga, Yuri Jang, Seungah Lee, Chao-Hui Huang, and Patricia Parmelee. 2010. "Health Status of Older Asian Americans in California." *Journal of the American Geriatric Society* 58 (10): 2003–2008. doi: 10.1111/j.1532-5415.2010.03034.x.

Lee, Jae Chul, Romana Hasnain-Wynia, and Denys T. Lau. 2011. "Delay in Seeing a Doctor Due to Cost: Disparity between Older Adults with and without Disabilities in the United States." *Health Services Research* 47 (2): 698–720. doi: 10.1111/j.1475-6773 .2011.01346.x.

Lombe, Margaret, Jin Huang, Michelle Putnam, and Kate Cooney. 2010. "Exploring Saving Performance in an IDA Program: Findings for People with Disabilities." *Social Work Research* 34 (2): 83–93. doi: 10.1093/swr/34.2.83.

Lombe, Margaret, Michelle Putnam, and Jin Huang. 2008. "Exploring Effects of Institutional Characteristics on Saving Outcome: The Case of the Cash and Counseling Program." *Journal of Policy Practice* 7 (4): 260–279. doi: 10.1080/15588740802261676.

Meeks, Thomas W., Ipsit V. Vahia, Helen Lavretsky, Ganesh Kulkarni, and Dilip V. Jeste. 2010. "A Tune in 'A Minor' Can 'B Major': A Review of Epidemiology, Illness Course, and Public Health Implications of Subthreshold Depression in Older Adults." *Journal of Affective Disorders* 123 (1–3): 126–142. doi: 10.1016/j.jad.2010.09.015.

MetLife Mature Market Institute. 2010. *Market Survey of Long-Term Care Costs: The 2010 MetLife Market Survey of Nursing Home, Assisted Living, Adult Day Services, and Home Care Costs.* Report, October. Westport, CT: MetLife Mature Market Institute. https://www.metlife.com/assets/cao/mmi/publications/studies/2010/mmi -2010-market-survey-long-term-care-costs.pdf.

Miah, M. Solaiman, and Virginia Wilcox-Gök. 2007. "Do the Sick Retire Early? Chronic Illness, Asset Accumulation and Early Retirement." *Applied Economics* 39 (15): 1921–1936. doi: 10.1080/00036840600690165.

Mitra, Sophie, Patricia A. Findley, and Usha Sambamoorthi. 2009. "Health Care Expenditures of Living with a Disability: Total Expenditures, Out-of-Pocket Expenses, and Burden, 1996–2004." *Archives of Physical Medicine and Rehabilitation* 90 (9): 1532–1540. doi: 10.1016/j.apmr.2009.02.020.

National Council on Aging. 2012. "The Latest in the Economic Security Initiative." Accessed March 22, 2014. http://www.ncoa.org/enhance-economic-security /economic-security-Initiative/.

Nord, Derek, Richard Luecking, David Mank, William Kiernan, and Christina Wray. 2013. "The State of the Science of Employment and Economic Self-Sufficiency for People with Intellectual and Developmental Disabilities." *Intellectual and Developmental Disabilities* 51 (5): 376–384. doi: 10.1352/1934-9556-51.5.376.

Nuru-Jeter, Amani M., Roland J. Thorpe Jr., and Esme Fuller-Thomson. 2011. "Black-White Differences in Self-Reported Disability Outcomes in the U.S.: Early Childhood to Older Adulthood." *Public Health Reports* 126 (6): 834–843. http://www.jstor.org/stable/41639441.

Ozawa, Martha N., and Yeong Hun Yeo. 2007. "The Effect of Disability on the Net Worth of Elderly People." *Journal of Aging and Social Policy* 19 (4): 21–38. doi: 10.1300/J031v19n04_02.

Putnam, Michelle, Michael Sherraden, Lin Zhang, and Nancy Morrow-Howell. 2008. "Age Differences in IDA Savings Outcomes: Findings from the American Dream Demonstration." *Journal of Social Policy and Aging* 20 (1): 45–63. doi: 10.1300/J031v20n01_03.

Reichard, Amanda, Hayley Stolzle, and Michael H. Fox. 2011. "Health Disparities among Adults with Physical Disabilities or Cognitive Limitations Compared to Individuals with No Disabilities in the United States." *Journal of Disability and Health* 4 (2): 59–67. doi: 10.1016/j.dhjo.2010.05.003.

Russell, David. 2009. "Living Arrangements, Social Integration, and Loneliness in Later Life: The Case of Physical Disability." *Journal of Health and Social Behavior* 50 (4): 460–475. doi: 10.1177/002214650905000406.

Schoeni, Robert F., Vicki A. Freedman, and Linda G. Martin. 2008. "Why Is Late-Life Disability Declining?" *Milbank Quarterly* 86 (1): 47–89. doi: 10.1111/j.1468-0009.2007.00513.x.

Social Security Administration. 2011. *Your Ticket to Work.* SSA Publication 05-10061. Washington, DC: Social Security Administration. http://www.ssa.gov/pubs/10061.html.

Social Security Administration. 2013a. "2013 Social Security Changes." Accessed March 22, 2014. http://www.socialsecurity.gov/pressoffice/factsheets/colafacts2013.htm.

Social Security Administration. 2013b. "Monthly Statistical Snapshot, September 2013." Accessed March 22, 2014. http://www.socialsecurity.gov/policy/docs/quickfacts/stat_snapshot/2013-09.html.

Strand, Alexander. 2010. "Low Levels of Retirement Resources in the Near-Elderly Time Period and Future Participation in Means-Tested Programs." *Social Security Bulletin* 70 (1): 1–21. http://www.ssa.gov/policy/docs/ssb/v70n1/v70n1p1.pdf.

U.S. Census Bureau. 2010a. 2010 American Community Survey, Table B18120. American FactFinder. Accessed April 28, 2014. http://factfinder2.census.gov.

U.S. Census Bureau. 2010b. 2010 American Community Survey Table B18130. American FactFinder. Accessed April 28, 2014. http://factfinder2.census.gov.

U.S. Census Bureau. 2010c. 2010 American Community Survey, Table B18140. American FactFinder. Accessed April 28, 2014. http://factfinder2.census.gov.

U.S. Department of Health and Human Services, Center for Disability and Aging Policy, Office of Integrated Programs. 2014. "Aging & Disability Resource Centers Program/No Wrong Door System." Last modified April 16. http://www.acl.gov/Programs/CDAP/OIP/ADRC/index.aspx.

U.S. Department of Health and Human Services, Centers for Medicare and Medicaid Services. 2014. "2014 Poverty Guidelines." http://www.medicaid

.gov/Medicaid-CHIP-Program-Information/By-Topics/Eligibility/Downloads/
2014-Federal-Poverty-level-charts.pdf.

White, Daniel K., Alan M. Jette, David T. Felson, Michael P. Lavalley, Cora E. Lewis,
James C. Torner, Michael C. Nevitt, and Julie J. Keysor. 2010. "Are Features of the
Neighborhood Environment Associated with Disability in Older Adults?" *Disability
and Rehabilitation* 32 (8): 639–645. doi: 10.3109/09638280903254547.

Whitson, Heather E., S. Nicole Hastings, Lawrence R. Landerman, Gerda G. Fillenbaum,
Harvey J. Cohen, and Kimberly S. Johnson. 2011. "Black-White Disparity in
Disability: The Role of Medical Conditions." *Journal of the American Geriatrics Society*
59 (5): 844–850. doi: 10.1111/j.1532-5415.2011.03401.x.

Wittenburg, David, and Melissa Favreault. 2003. *Safety Net or Tangled Web? An Overview
of Programs and Services for Adults with Disabilities.* Assessing the New Federalism
Occasional Paper 68. Washington, DC: Urban Institute. http://www.urban.org
/uploadedpdf/310884_op68.pdf.

PART THREE

Policies and Innovations

8 Asset Development among Older Adults

A Capability Approach

■ JIN HUANG AND
JENNIFER C. GREENFIELD

Americans are living longer; life expectancy in the United States increased from 70.8 years in 1970 to 78.0 years in 2008 (U.S. Census Bureau 2011). Adults can expect to live an additional 31.5 years if they reach age 50 years, 19.2 more years if they reach age 65 years, and 6.6 more years if they reach age 85 years (Murphy, Xu, and Kochanek 2012). As life expectancy increases and fertility rates decline, the population in the United States is aging. Persons aged 65 years or above now represent 13.1% of the U.S. population and will comprise 19.3% in 2030 (Administration on Aging 2011). As people live longer, an important challenge is to determine how people can also live better. A critical and related policy concern lies in enabling seniors to be healthy, active, and economically secure.

Compared with previous generations of older adults, the current generation has higher economic status (Radner 1998). Baby boomers comprise over one-third of the population and control nearly 70% of the total net worth of American households (Feinstein and Lin 2006), but wealth is unevenly distributed among older adults: the value of assets held by households in the top decile of the wealth distribution is 2,500 times greater than that of assets held by households in the lowest decile (Smith 1997). Fundamental changes in the lives of older Americans have made it more difficult for them to maintain economic security and stability. If such stability is measured by the Senior Financial Stability Index, which considers housing and health care costs, essential expenses, home equity, and other financial assets, about 78% of senior households are in financially unstable circumstances (Meschede, Shapiro, and Wheary 2009). Estimates indicate that the current retirement income deficit—the difference between the preretirement standard of living and the standard affordable on combined income from retirement savings, pensions, and anticipated Social Security benefits—is at least $6.6 trillion, and it increases each year (Munnell, Webb, and Golub-Sass 2009).

Lifelong asset development is one strategy proposed to strengthen older adults' economic security and well-being (Meschede et al. 2009; Webb 2009). Broadly speaking, asset development refers to a wide range of asset-related activities (e.g., asset accumulation, asset management, and asset decumulation) that could be conducted by individuals, and the activity (or activities) depends on their best interest, financial knowledge and skills, and accessible services. Asset development endows older adults with economic resources, offers psychological and social benefits, encourages civic engagement and political participation, and shapes long-term opportunities for the next generation (Oliver and Shapiro 1995; Shapiro and Wolff 2001; Sherraden 1991). However, current asset-based programs are generally age regressive (i.e., the amount of benefits received declines as the age of the recipient advances). Moreover, programs for older adults focus on providing income support and services, not on asset building. Older adults have not fully realized the potential benefits of asset-based programs.

In the present study, we define asset development from the capability approach and the life course perspective. We then explore older adults' access to asset-based programs and discuss their low rates of participation in the programs. Our investigation suggests that, compared with younger counterparts, they are less likely to benefit from tax expenditures made through these programs (e.g., tax benefits on homeownership and retirement). Next, we focus on social programs and services designed specifically for older adults (e.g., income support, nutrition assistance, and transportation for older adults), evaluating opportunities to apply an asset-based approach to serve them. Finally, we discuss policy implications of asset development among older adults.

■ ASSET DEVELOPMENT FOR OLDER ADULTS

A Capability Approach

The life cycle hypothesis of saving (Ando and Modigliani 1963) holds that individuals build assets during their working lives and make use of accumulated resources during retirement to smooth consumption over the life course. Thus, older adults are expected to decumulate assets as they convert accumulated retirement assets into an income stream. Because the theory suggests that older adults have left the asset accumulation phase of their life, some may question whether older adults need asset development. However, this view overlooks the dynamics of later life and oversimplifies the idea of asset development for older adults. Evidence on the older population's saving behavior is contradictory, and these adults decumulate assets much more slowly than the life cycle hypothesis predicts. Studies find that many households continue to save well past the retirement age (Bernheim 1987; Danziger et al. 1982/1983; Hassan, Salim, and Bloch 2011; Pistaferri 2009). For many older adults, the meaning of asset development is broader than the meaning of asset accumulation; asset accumulation is only one of several asset-related activities defined by asset development.

To elaborate the concept of asset development for older adults, we employ the perspective of the capability approach (Lloyd-Sherlock 2002; Nussbaum 2000; Sen 1999; Sherraden 2010). Derived from work by Amartya Sen (1999) and

Martha Nussbaum (2000), the approach stresses the difference between two key concepts: functionings and capabilities. *Functionings* are the states and activities that a person can undertake. *Capabilities*, in contrast, are a person's real freedom to achieve functionings. For instance, the accumulation of retirement savings plans can be defined as a specific functioning. Two older persons who do not accumulate assets in their retirement savings plans have the same behavior on this functioning but may have different motivations. One may lack access to a retirement savings plan (e.g., the employer does not provide a pension) and, therefore, also may lack the *capability* to achieve this functioning; another may choose not to take advantage of the retirement savings plan offered by his or her employer. The central focus of the capability approach falls on the opportunities individuals have to pursue their functionings. People who have the capability to do or be something are in a position to choose among alternative functionings, and these choices are influenced by their particular values and preferences. For example, an older person may have the capability to decumulate assets after retirement but may choose not to do so because they wish to leave a bequest to heirs. The capability approach suggests that policy should focus on promoting capabilities and allow individual choices on functionings.

Nussbaum (2000, 84–85) further distinguishes "combined capability" from "internal capability." Internal capabilities are individual characteristics developed through environmental input across the life course (e.g., an individual's financial knowledge and skills). In contrast, combined capabilities integrate internal capabilities with structural constraints and other "suitable external conditions" (2000, 85) for achieving functionings. For instance, an older adult's financial knowledge and skills (i.e., internal capabilities) are important determinants of whether and how they use formal financial services, but an unrelated external barrier, such as lack of transportation, could prevent them from accessing such services. Although people must possess internal capabilities, certain external conditions must be met for people to be capable.

In Figure 8.1, the panel for the Later Life stage depicts the capability approach's relationship to asset development among older adults. The figure suggests that asset development consists of *financial functioning* and *financial capability*. Financial functioning includes a wide range of asset-related activities and strategies. Examples include asset accumulation, asset management, and asset decumulation. These activities and strategies represent the transformation of resources from income to assets and back; this transformation takes places over time (Schreiner 2001). *Asset accumulation* refers to the act of saving or converting income to savings, *asset management* involves the allocation of assets among different financial products, and *asset decumulation* refers to the transfer of assets into income.

An older adult's financial functioning (and the asset-related activities and strategies selected) depends on his or her combined financial capability. Financial capability has two building blocks: *financial literacy* and *financial inclusion*

Early life   Later life

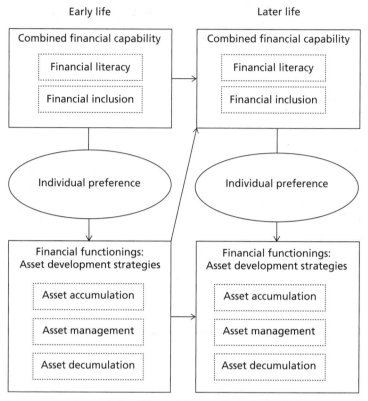

Figure 8.1 Asset Development for Older Adults: A Life-Cycle Capability Approach.

(Sherraden 2010). Financial literacy can be considered an internal capability. It includes financial knowledge, ability, skills, and confidence in the ability to make good financial decisions (Huston 2010). Financial inclusion is an external condition. It indicates whether older adults have access to financial resources, products, and services. In short, financial literacy is the ability to act, and financial inclusion is the opportunity to act. Together, ability and opportunity contribute to an older person's financial functioning in ways that lead to improved financial well-being. To be financially capable, older adults need financial knowledge and skills as well as access to financial services and resources.

This framework suggests that the concept of asset development incorporates important considerations related to older adults' economic security and financial well-being. Such considerations extend beyond the parameters of asset accumulation. If older adults have left the asset accumulation phase of their lives (as the life cycle hypothesis suggests), other financial functionings of asset development become even more important. Given increases in life expectancy and changes in retirement programs, it is critical for older adults to manage and use accumulated retirement assets effectively if they are to maintain long-term economic security.

The substitution of defined-contribution retirement plans for defined-benefit plans forces older adults to be efficient managers of their own retirement assets. Thus, the strategies of asset management and decumulation are critical for asset development among older adults.

A Life Course Perspective

The financial functionings of older adults include a diverse set of asset development strategies, and the two theoretical perspectives lend themselves to explanations for the diversity of asset outcomes. On the one hand, the capability approach suggests that heterogeneity in asset development could be caused by differences in internal capability (i.e., financial literacy) and external conditions (i.e., access to financial resources and services) in later life. On the other hand, a life course perspective suggests the importance of recognizing that financial functioning and financial capability in later life are affected in a gradual, cumulative way by asset development through the previous stages of the life course (Lloyd-Sherlock 2002). Insufficient asset development and lack of financial capability in previous life stages are likely to have substantial effects on the financial functioning and financial capability of disadvantaged older adults. For instance, lack of access to appropriate financial services and products in early life increases individuals' exposure to risk in later life. Support for the use of the life course perspective in this case can be found in the cumulative disadvantage perspective (Crystal and Shea 1990; Ferraro and Shippee 2009; O'Rand 1996), which suggests that the constrained asset development among older adults is the consequence of cumulative and current disadvantages. Inequalities in asset development and financial capability emerge over time as products of the interplay between institutional arrangements and individual life trajectories.

Figure 8.1 combines the capability and cumulative disadvantage perspectives into a dynamic framework that illustrates the process of asset development through the life course. The figure elaborates this process in two stages of life (early and later life) and shows the relationship between asset development in the two stages. It suggests that financial functioning in later life is partially determined by previous financial functioning. For example, older adults who accumulate sufficient assets in early life are able to convert those assets into income for later life. Those who do not accumulate sufficient assets in the preretirement stage cannot have such financial functioning. Similarly, financial capability in later life partly depends on financial capability and financial functioning in early life. Older persons who have high financial functioning in the early stage are also likely to have high levels of financial knowledge and skills in later life. The paths linking the two life stages in the figure reflect cumulative advantage and disadvantage accrued over the life course. The life cycle hypothesis of saving discussed above can be considered a special scenario within the life course framework. That hypothesis links one financial functioning (i.e., asset accumulation) in early life to another one (i.e., asset decumulation) in later life, but the life course perspective acknowledges that not everyone has access to these functionings at each stage in life.

Asset Development and Individual Preference

Ideally, if all older adults had sufficient financial capability to achieve financial functioning, the choice of an asset development strategy (e.g., between accumulation and decumulation) would be a matter of individual preference, which is affected by multiple factors (e.g., the purposes of asset development and individual socioeconomic characteristics). Because the capability approach suggests that policy should focus on promoting the financial capability of older adults, we review only briefly some potential factors that might influence individual strategies. We also note that an individual's reasons for asset development are likely to affect the choice of strategies. For instance, older adults who have strong bequest motives may choose asset accumulation over decumulation. About 50% of older adults in the Health and Retirement Study specify that they intend to make bequests with their estate (Fink and Redaelli 2005). Günther Fink and Silvia Redaelli (2005) also find that bequest motives largely drive the investment behavior of older adults in late old age: older adults with stronger bequest motives place a higher proportion of their assets in stock.

Employment may also be related to individual asset development preferences. Some older adults are able to accumulate assets because they still actively participate in the labor force. Among adults aged 65 years and older, approximately one-fourth of men and one-seventh of women were in the labor force in 2008 (Wacker and Roberto 2011). Earnings from employment may enable older adults to continue accumulating assets and allow those without sufficient retirement assets to prepare for retirement.

Asset development among older adults may vary with their health status as well. The utility function of consumption declines as health deteriorates (Finkelstein, Luttmer, and Notowidigdo 2013). This means that the optimal level of savings for older adults with poor health may be lower than the optimal level for counterparts with good health. Individuals in poor health face a greater risk of incurring substantial medical expenditures, and poor health may also lead to risk-averse investment behavior (Finkelstein et al. 2013).

In summary, older adults are not a homogeneous group. The period now called old age can span four decades, and adults in this stage can experience a very diverse set of circumstances. The framework proposed in Figure 8.1 focuses on financial capability and takes a broad view, acknowledging heterogeneity in the asset development among older adults.

Policy Implications of Capability-Based Asset Development among Older Adults

The framework identifies two key policy recommendations for promoting asset development among older adults. First, asset-based programs should seek to promote financial capability among older adults by improving their financial literacy and by increasing their access to financial resources and services. The literature discusses the financial literacy and financial education of older adults (Lusardi and Mitchell 2007) but pays less attention to their financial inclusion and access to asset-based programs. The institutional theory of asset development provides a way to think about improving financial inclusion and increasing access to financial services (Sherraden, Schreiner, and Beverly 2003). The theory identifies a bundle of constructs that shape the individual's opportunity to use financial services. These constructs include access, information, incentives, facilitation, expectations, restrictions, and security. They may provide a way to examine and measure how well policy promotes the financial inclusion for older adults.

Second, asset-based programs should be designed to facilitate asset development, especially among disadvantaged groups, as a way to address social inequality across the life span. This may include two approaches. One is to optimize older adults' financial capability over the life course as a whole. That is, programs would improve financial capability in later life by improving cumulative financial capability through the life course. Such improvements would be achieved via policies that enhance financial literacy and eliminate external barriers to inclusion. The other approach is static; it seeks to optimize financial capability in later life, for example, through compensatory support. In other words, the life course perspective suggests that we should think about ways to prevent later financial insecurity via programs in early life. It also suggests that we should think about intervening with older adults to increase economic stability, social justice, and advocacy.

■ ASSET-BASED PROGRAMS AND OLDER ADULTS

Access to Asset-Based Programs: Criteria

Applying the framework discussed above, this section examines the association between asset development among older adults and federal asset-based programs. It focuses particularly on older adults' access to these programs. Several federal programs promote asset development, and nearly 90% of federal dollars spent on asset development are distributed via tax expenditures (Woo and Buchholz 2006). Using a narrow definition of asset-based programs, the study focuses on four categories of asset development: savings and investment, homeownership, entrepreneurship, and retirement. To assess older adults' access to these programs, we ask seven questions:

1. *Age eligibility.* Does the program have age limits that exclude older adults from services? This question is intended to provide information on whether the program addresses cumulative inequality through the development of assets across the life span or through development of them in the specific stage of later life.
2. *Financial literacy.* Does the program intend to increase individual financial knowledge and skills (i.e., internal capability)?
3. *Financial inclusion.* Does the program intend to improve individuals' opportunity to develop assets and access to asset development? Asset-based programs generally change the external conditions faced by the target population during asset development. Therefore, the study specifically examines institutional features (e.g., access, information, incentives, and restrictions) created to promote financial inclusion in these programs.
4. *Asset development strategy.* On which asset development strategy (e.g., asset accumulation, asset management, and asset decumulation) does the program focus?
5. *Institutional support.* Does the program have institutional features that encourage asset development among older adults in particular?
6. *Institutional barriers.* Does the program have institutional barriers that impede older adults' efforts at asset development?
7. *Program data on older adults.* How many older adults participate in these programs?

Evaluation of Asset-Based Programs

The seven questions posed above form the foundation of the summary of federal asset-based programs in Table 8.1. Most of the evaluated programs have no age limits and can be used to build assets through the life course. Older adults are eligible for most of the benefits and services offered by these programs, but certain employment-based retirement savings plans (e.g., traditional IRAs) prohibit individuals from making contributions after age 70.5 years. Only three programs provide financial education or training to improve participants' financial knowledge and skills: the Assets for Independence program (i.e., Individual Development Accounts), Housing Counseling Assistance, and the Microloan Program. Although some programs apply multiple approaches to increase financial inclusion, the most common approaches pertain to access and incentives. A program may create access to new services (e.g., access to credit and loans) for the target population, and financial incentives for asset development generally are realized through tax benefits. Most programs that feature asset development strategies focus on asset accumulation.

TABLE 8.1. *Asset-Based Programs and Older Adults*

	Program overview	Financial literacy	Financial inclusion	Institutional support and barriers	Program data on older adults
Savings and investment					
Direct spending					
AFI	Helps low-income families with children save earned income in special-purpose matched-savings accounts (i.e., IDAs); *Strategy:* accum., mgmt.	Training and supportive services related to family finances and financial management	*Access:* special-purpose savings accounts; *Incentive:* matches savings in IDAs; *Information:* financial education; *Expectations:* set through maximum savings match; *Restriction:* savings in IDAs can be used only for certain types of assets	Support: none; Barriers: targeted to low-income families with dependents	9% of participants older than age 50 (1999–2004), 7% of participants older than age 50, and 2% aged 60–72 in ADD
Tax expenditure					
Tax benefits on capital gains	Tax rate on long-term capital gains reduced in 2003; capital gains on assets held at the owner's death not subject to capital gains tax; no age eligibility req.; *Strategy:* decum.	None	*Incentive:* lower tax rates for capital gains	Support: none; Barriers: none	Among taxpayers with dividend income in 2004, roughly 23% were over age 65 and nearly 36% were over age 55; among taxpayers with capital gains income, nearly 26% were over age 65 and more than 38% were over age 55
Homeownership					
Direct spending					
HOME	Provides grants to fund building, purchase, and rehabilitation of affordable housing for rental or sale to low-income families; no age eligibility req.; *Strategy:* accum.	None	*Access:* financing assistance services and credit access to low-income families for home purchase or rehabilitation	Support: guidebook on home repair and modification for older homeowners (HUD 2004); Barriers: none	Between FY1992 and FY1996, 21,457 older adult households (about 9% of units in the program) received services
Housing Counseling Assistance	Counseling to consumers on seeking, financing, maintaining, renting, or owning a home; no age eligibility req.; *Strategy:* accum., decum.	*Financial education:* pre- and postpurchase education, personal financial management, reverse-mortgage product education, and rental counseling	*Information:* information and housing counseling to eligible homeowners and tenants	Support: none; Barriers: none	Not available

TABLE 8.1. (*Continued*)

	Program overview	Financial literacy	Financial inclusion	Institutional support and barriers	Program data on older adults
USDA direct housing loans (Section 502)	Help low-income households purchase homes in rural areas; funds used to build, repair, renovate, or relocate homes, or purchase and prepare sites (e.g., providing water and sewage facilities); no age eligibility req.; *Strategy*: accum.	None	*Access*: housing loan for low-income households in rural areas	Support: none; Barriers: none	8% aged 50–61 and 6% aged 62 or older; modest participation by older households a concern because Section 502 may offer an affordable way out of substandard homes
USDA Very Low-Income Housing Repair loans and grants (Section 504)	Loans and grants to very low-income homeowners to repair or improve dwellings; no age eligibility req.; *Strategy*: accum.	None	*Access*: loans or grants to low-income families for home repair	Support: grant funds available only to very low-income homeowners aged 62 or older; Barriers: none	162,673 grants awarded (FY1950–FY2008)
Tax expenditure					
Housing tax incentives	Homeowners allowed to deduct home mortgage interest, real estate tax, and mortgage insurance from income tax; no age eligibility req.; *Strategy*: accum.	None	*Incentive*: tax deduction for homeowners	Support: none; Barriers: none	7% of mortgage interest deduction claimants are aged 65 or older, 5% of mortgage insurance deduction claimants are 65 or older, and 14% of real estate tax deduction claimants are 65 or older
Entrepreneurship					
Direct spending					
Microloan program	Small, short-term loans to small business owners for working capital, inventory, supplies, furniture, fixtures, and equipment; no age eligibility req. *Strategy*: accum.	*Financial education*: business training and technical assistance for borrowers	*Access*: loans to small business owners; *Information*: business training and technical assistance	Support: none; Barriers: none	Not available

Program	Description		Access/Incentive/Restriction	Support/Barriers	Data
Small Business Lending Program: 7(a) and 504 guaranteed loans	Financial help for businesses; no age eligibility req.; *Strategy:* accum.	None	*Access:* credit	Support: none; Barriers: none	Not available
Tax expenditure					
Amortization of start-up costs	IRS allows business owners to amortize certain business start-up costs over a period of 60 months or more; no age eligibility req.; *Strategy:* accum.	None	*Incentive:* tax deduction for certain capital costs over a fixed period	Support: none; Barriers: none	Not available
Retirement (Net exclusion of pension contributions)					
Tax expenditure					
Employer plans	Employer contributions to pension plans excluded from employee's gross income; no age eligibility req.; *Strategy:* accum.	None	*Incentive:* tax deduction for employees on employer's pension contributions; *Restriction:* asset accumulated for retirement	Support: none; Barriers: employment-based program	Among workers older than 65, 39.5% have an employer-sponsored pension and 29.6% participate; both rates are lower than those for workers aged 25–64
401(k) plans	Employees can make tax-preferred contributions to employer-provided 401(k) plans; no age eligibility req.; *Strategy:* accum.	None	*Access:* some provide automatic enrollment and automatic deposits to promote participation; *Incentive:* tax on 401(k) earnings deferred until withdrawn; some employers match workers' contributions; *Restriction:* asset accumulated for retirement; contribution deferral limits and early withdrawal penalty	Support: workers aged 50 or over can exclude $5,000 catch-up contribution; at age 70.5, workers can delay mandatory withdrawals from their current employer's 401(k) until retirement; Barriers: Employment-based program; at age 70.5, individuals are required to take minimum withdrawals	9% of employees in their 60s participated in 401(k)s in 2009
IRAs	Taxpayers can use IRAs to defer or reduce tax on returns to retirement savings; no contribution to traditional IRA after age 70.5; *Strategy:* accum.	None	*Incentive:* investment earnings tax free for qualified withdrawals; *Restriction:* asset accumulated for retirement; contribution deferral limits and early withdrawal penalty	Support: none; Barriers: must have taxable compensation during the year	20% of IRA owners are aged 65 or older

TABLE 8.1. (Continued)

	Program overview	Financial literacy	Financial inclusion	Institutional support and barriers	Program data on older adults
Saver's credit	Nonrefundable credit of up to 50% on IRA and other retirement contributions (up to $2,000) by low-income individuals; 18 or older eligible; *Strategy:* accum.	None	*Incentive:* tax credit of up to 50% on IRA and other retirement contributions of up to $2,000; *Restriction:* asset accumulated for retirement	Support: none; Barriers: none	Not available
Self-employed plans	Self-employed individuals can make deductible contributions (up to 25% of their income) to their own retirement plans; no age eligibility req.; *Strategy:* accum.	None	*Incentive:* credit of up to 25% of income; *Restriction:* asset accumulated for retirement	Support: none; Barriers: none	Less than 1% of workers aged 65 or above has a Keogh plan

Note: AFI = Assets for Independence program; IDA = Individual Development Account; ADD = American Dream Demonstration; HOME = HOME Investment Partnerships Program; FY = fiscal year; USDA = U.S. Department of Agriculture; IRS = Internal Revenue Service; req. = requirement; Accum. = asset accumulation; mgmt. = asset management; Decum. = asset decumulation.

Several programs have specific features to support asset development among older adults. For instance, the HOME Investment Partnerships Program offers a guidebook on home repair and modification for older homeowners (HUD [U.S. Department of Housing and Urban Development] 2004). By distributing such information, the program may promote service access for older adults. In addition, older homeowners are eligible for the grants provided by the U.S. Department of Agriculture (USDA) through the Very Low-Income Housing Repair Program (USDA 2013a). Other homeowners are not eligible for the grants and can apply only for the program's repair loans. Another supportive feature is the so-called catch-up provision in retirement savings plans such as the 401(k). Under this provision, individuals who are over age 50 years can set aside more in their 401(k) than the maximum contribution allowed by the plan. In 2012, for example, individuals could make a catch-up contribution of as much as $5,500. Employer-sponsored plans such as 401(k)s also support older adults by allowing individuals still working at age 70.5 years to delay mandatory withdrawals from the plan until they retire (IRS [Internal Revenue Service] 2014).

However, some asset-based programs have features that may restrain asset development among older adults. Although they have no age limits, most of these programs target working-age individuals. The Assets for Independence program, for example, targets low-income families with dependents, and the eligibility criteria exclude most older adults. Retirement savings plans are often offered through employers and require individuals to make contributions from their earnings or taxable compensation. After retirement, many older adults lack access to employer-sponsored offerings and have no earnings or taxable compensation. Furthermore, minimum withdrawal requirements in 401(k) plans can force older adults to decumulate assets held in those plans even if an individual's life circumstances do not require the liquidation of assets into income.

Data on older adults' participation in these programs could serve as a good indicator of their access to the programs. However, participation information is limited because age often is not the determining factor in a person's eligibility. Table 8.1 summarizes participation data identified by the study. The data could better indicate older adults' access to asset-based programs if it were possible to compare the proportion of older adults who participate in a program with the proportion eligible for the program; this should be addressed in future research.

Overall, the share of the older adults in these programs is smaller than that of working-age individuals. Findings from the American Dream Demonstration, a test of Individual Development Accounts, indicates that about 2% of participants are older than 60 years (Schreiner, Clancy, and Sherraden 2002). Among participants in the USDA's direct housing loans (also known as Section 502 loans), 6% are aged 62 years and older; the department has raised concerns about the low participation rate among older households (U.S. Government Accountability Office 2005). The percentage of older adults who claim housing tax benefits is also smaller than that among other age groups, and about 7% of those claiming a mortgage interest deduction are aged 65 years or older. Among workers older than 65 years, 39.5% have an employer-sponsored pension (defined-benefit or defined-contribution plan) and 29.6% participate in such a plan. Both of these figures are lower than the rates among employees between ages 25 and 64 years (Copeland 2011).

We also note that older adult participation rates are relatively high for two programs. More older adults benefit from the low tax rate on capital gains (relative to the rate on earned income) than do working-aged individuals: in 2004, nearly 26% of taxpayers with capital gains income were over age 65 years and roughly 23% of taxpayers with dividend income were over age 65 years (Dietz 2010). Administrative data also indicate that, between fiscal years 1992 and 1996, about 30% of homeowners receiving rehabilitation assistance in the HOME program were above age 62 years (U.S. Government Accountability Office 2005).

Summary of an Evaluation of Asset-Based Programs

The assessment of asset-based programs suggests ways to expand older adults' opportunities for asset development. First, most of these programs have no age limit but are grounded in the life cycle hypothesis of saving. In other words, the asset-based programs, especially those related to employment-based retirement programs, mainly target individuals in their working years and focus on asset accumulation. This may explain the low rates of participation by older adults and the paucity of program data on them. If their asset development strategy is consistent with the patterns in the life cycle hypothesis, older adults are likely to be served well by existing asset-based programs. We mentioned two examples above: home rehabilitation assistance and the tax reduction on capital gains. Nonetheless, the life cycle hypothesis allows a narrow view of asset development that seems to limit older adults' capability. The conceptual model in Figure 8.1 specifies such a view. Second, asset-based programs generally benefit older adults less than younger ones, as tax benefits are the main mechanism to deliver financial incentives for asset development. That is, tax benefits for asset development are likely to be regressive by age, since older adults are not likely at the peak of their earnings, and their taxable income after retirement is lower than it was during the working years. Only 14% of taxpayers with itemized deductions are over age 65 years, and the total adjusted gross income for itemizing taxpayers over age 65 years is 16% of that for all itemizing taxpayers, 6 percentage points lower than that of counterparts aged 55 to 65 years, 13 percentage points lower than that of itemized filers aged 45 to 55 years, and 7 percentage points lower than that of counterparts aged 35 to 45 years (Copeland 2011). In other words, older adults have less adjusted gross income eligible for tax benefits than do adults in other age groups.

■ ASSET DEVELOPMENT AND POLICIES RELATED TO OLDER ADULTS

Another way to assess the external policy conditions that influence asset development for older adults is to examine programs and services for them. The primary goal of programs grounding such development efforts is to support older adults' consumption needs (e.g., to provide support in the areas of housing, nutrition, and health care). Thus, many policies link assistance to services coordinated through governmental funding for entities such as area agencies on aging and state Medicaid programs. Cash assistance is also available through support from the Supplemental Security Income program, the Supplemental Nutrition Assistance Program, and housing subsidies. However, few federal programs for older adults take an asset-based approach in attempting to satisfy their needs. Although older adults' access to services and income support may free up resources available for asset development, programs for low-income older adults are generally means tested. Eligibility criteria that specify asset limits may create restrictions and disincentives for asset building. Table 8.2 reviews the major supportive programs for older adults and presents these programs in six categories: retirement, employment and education, housing and energy assistance, health and mental health services, community support, and family caregiving. The table also assesses each category's relationships to asset development among older adults. Our review examines (1) whether the program applies an asset-based approach to accomplish policy goals and (2) whether the program has asset limit rules.

Our examination suggests that, as expected, the asset-based approach is underused in existing programs for older adults, and the traditional income-support approach continues to predominate. Although newer and much smaller than Medicare and Medicaid, which provide vital health services for most older adults, health savings accounts are an example of an asset-based effort in programs related to health and mental health. Similarly, defined-contribution plans are the only example of a retirement income program that focuses on asset development. However, it is noteworthy that examples applying an asset-based approach can be found in almost all of the six categories. The Consumer Financial Protection Bureau, a new federal agency created to educate consumers about financial products and sources of fraud, has dedicated a web page to assisting older adults with asset protection and development. The agency's effort reflects the potential of asset development as a general strategy evident in a broad range of programs designed to promote the well-being of older adults. Asset-based programs will likely serve as important supplements to existing income-support programs and services for older adults.

The review also identifies two types of asset-limit rules in programs and services for older adults. First, the Internal Revenue Service specifies annual

TABLE 8.2. *Programs Related to Older Adults and Asset-Based Approaches*

Program	Asset-based approach	Asset limit rules
Retirement income policies		
Social Security	None	None
Private-sector pension plans	Defined-contribution plans (e.g., 401[k], 403[b], and traditional IRAs) set up individual retirement savings account for asset accumulation	Subject to IRS contribution limits
SSI	None	Individuals with no more than $2,000 (or couples with no more than $3,000) in assets may be eligible; primary home, life insurance, car, burial plot, and burial funds (up to $1,500) are not counted in asset limits
Employment and education policies		
Senior Community Service Employment Program	None	None
Hope Scholarship Credit	None	None
Lifetime Learning Credit	None	None
529 college savings plans	Offers tax-advantaged accounts to encourage saving for beneficiary's college expenses	Annual contribution limit is set by the federal gift-tax exclusion limit; each plan also has a maximum contribution limit, which varies by state but is generally set at $250,000
Housing and energy assistance policies		
Section 202 Program providing supportive housing for the elderly	None	None
Section 8 Housing Choice Voucher Program	None	None
Weatherization Assistance Program	Uses technology and testing protocols to improve the energy performance of low-income family dwellings	SSI and TANF recipients are automatically eligible
Low-Income Home Energy Assistance Program	None	Categorical eligibility for SSI, TANF, and SNAP recipients
Physical and mental health policies		
Medicare	None	None
Medicaid	None	Have countable assets less than $2,000. In Long-Term Care Partnership Program, assets are protected by private long-term care policies exempt from Medicaid asset test
Health savings accounts	Tax-advantaged savings account for individuals enrolled in a high-deductible health plan	Annual maximum deposit specified by IRS, a catch-up provision applies for participants aged 55 and above

(continued)

TABLE 8.2. *(Continued)*

Program	Asset-based approach	Asset limit rules
	Community support policies	
Food and nutrition programs	None	No SNAP eligibility if account assets exceed $3,000
Recreation and leisure	None	None
Transportation	None	None
Elder rights protection	Pension Counseling and Information Program empowers older adults to make wise decisions about pensions and savings plans The National Education and Resource Center on Women and Retirement Planning provides women with access to financial information and resources for retirement planning, health, and long-term care with Older Americans Act Programs CFPB web page for older Americans provides information on financial products and sources of fraud	None
Civic engagement	None	None
	Family caregiving policies	
Child and Dependent Care Tax Credit	None	None
Dependent care assistance programs	None	None
Family and Medical Leave Act	None	None

Note: IRA = individual retirement account; IRS = Internal Revenue Service; SSI = Supplemental Security Income; TANF = Temporary Assistance for Needy Families Program; SNAP = Supplemental Nutrition Assistance Program; CFPB = Consumer Financial Protection Bureau.

maximum-contribution limits for asset-based programs such as retirement and health savings accounts. Asset limit rules have multiple functions. They are intended to limit the amount of tax benefits received by individual taxpayers. By doing so, wealthy participants cannot enjoy additional tax benefits by contributing an amount more than the maximum. Such rules can play a role in adjusting cumulative inequality in asset development. In addition, the annual maximum contribution also establishes an annual savings goal for program participants.

The second type of asset-limit rule can be found in programs that impose some form of a means test. Means-tested assistance programs impose asset limits on older program applicants with low income, and these asset limits create disincentives to asset development. For example, the eligibility requirements for the Supplemental Nutrition Assistance Program, the largest food assistance program, state that an older recipient's net income must be lower than 100% of the federal poverty level and his or her countable assets must not exceed $3,250 (USDA 2013b). The rule excludes from the eligibility calculation the value of the primary residence and of pension and retirement plans. It also excludes at least $4,650 of a primary vehicle's value (this limit is higher in a few states). The eligibility limits are somewhat more generous than those for households without an older adult. The difference indicates that policymakers considered protecting the assets of older adults when they developed the program's features. It is particularly important that the nutrition program's rules do not require applicants to liquidate retirement assets in order to be eligible. However, the limits for nonretirement assets are still very low. Another example of this second type of asset-limit rule can be found in the Section 202 Program, which provides housing and supportive services for low-income older adults. The program has no asset test, but income from assets, including that from pensions and retirement plans, is included in income determinations; if assets total more than $5,000, a percentage of those assets may be included as income in the calculation of eligibility, even if no income is actually derived from the assets (HUD 2007).

■ IMPLICATIONS AND CONCLUSIONS

This study proposes a framework for asset development among older adults. The framework is derived from the capability and life course perspectives. An evaluation of existing federal asset-based programs shows that older adults may not be the primary target of these programs. The participation rate of older adults in asset-based programs is generally lower than that of younger groups. Because financial incentives for asset development are distributed mainly through tax expenditures, asset-based programs are likely to benefit older adults less than younger groups, and few older adult programs are designed to help older adults maintain or accumulate assets. Public assistance programs for low-income older adults are means tested, and eligibility requirements impose asset limits. Such features create disincentives for asset development.

The study has several implications for policies to promote asset development among older adults. First, the capability approach suggests that asset-based programs should focus on the financial capability of older adults, including the financial literacy and financial inclusion of this population. Despite the literature on older adults' financial literacy (Lusardi and Mitchell 2007), few of the evaluated programs are designed to improve their financial knowledge and skills (see Table 8.2). The Administration on Aging operates the Pension Counseling and Information Program and the National Education and Resource Center on Women and Retirement Planning. In addition, the Consumer Financial Protection Bureau has the potential to develop new programs to improve older adults' financial literacy; however, at present, that potential remains unfulfilled. In large part, this is due to the paucity of funding and legislative support for the new bureau's initiatives. Increasing the number of programs is important but not sufficient to meet current needs. It is also important to identify or design effective curricula for the financial education and training of older adults. Another strategy to promote financial literacy is to add a financial education component to asset-based programs; as shown in Table 8.1, most lack such a component. The research on Individual Development Accounts suggests that a combination of financial education and other financial incentives improves asset development among program participants (Schreiner et al. 2002).

Asset-based programs can incorporate different strategies to expand financial inclusion among older adults. First, programs should consider the age of participants, creating specific features to encourage program participation and asset development among older adults. Some of these features could be minor (e.g., the HOME Investment Partnerships Program's guidebook for service providers; HUD 2004). Others might be more significant. For example, the USDA offers loans and grants to enable very low-income adults to repair their homes, but the grants are available only to older adults. Second, program outreach is an important strategy for broadening financial inclusion, and asset-based programs should increase outreach to improve participation rates among older adults. Third, asset-based programs for older adults should emphasize other asset development strategies beyond asset accumulation, as asset management and decumulation may play a greater role in later life than does accumulation. Finally, asset-based programs for older adults should consider distributing financial incentives for asset development through means other than tax incentives.

It is also important that programs and services for older adults, especially those for low-income older adults, remove institutional barriers to asset development. In recent decades, the emergence of an asset-based program discussion has spurred a very important but still limited policy change in public assistance programs for older adults: policymakers have liberalized the asset limit rules that govern eligibility requirements. For example, the Food, Conservation, and Energy Act of 2008 allows the Supplemental Nutrition Assistance Program to index asset limits to inflation and excludes retirement savings from the asset test (Pub. L. 110-234, 122 Stat. 923, 1100). This is a positive step toward asset development among older adults, but the limits for nonretirement assets are still very low. Another important step for programs related to older adults is to apply the asset-based approach broadly to issues that affect those adults' well-being.

To summarize, we have offered policy recommendations built on the conceptual framework proposed in this study. Implementation of these recommendations can improve financial literacy, expand financial inclusion among older adults, and make asset development a useful strategy to maintain economic security and stability for this population.

■ NOTE

This book chapter is supported by the Center for Social Development, Washington University in St. Louis, and by the Atlantic Philanthropies. We are grateful to the two editors and Dr. Michael Sherraden for their careful review and comments, to attendees of the conference Financial Capability across the Life Course (October 2012) for insightful discussion, and to Chris Leiker for providing invaluable editorial assistance.

■ REFERENCES

Administration on Aging. 2011. *A Profile of Older Americans: 2011*. Washington, DC: U.S. Department of Health and Human Services, Administration on Aging. http://www.aoa.gov/Aging_Statistics/Profile/2011/docs/2011profile.pdf.

Ando, Albert, and Franco Modigliani. 1963. "The 'Life Cycle' Hypothesis of Saving: Aggregate Implications and Tests." *American Economic Review* 53, no. 1 (part 1): 55–84. http://www.jstor.org/stable/1817129.

Bernheim, B. Douglas. 1987. "Dissaving after Retirement: Testing the Pure Life Cycle Hypothesis." In *Issues in Pension Economics*, edited by Zvi Bodie, John B. Shoven, and David A. Wise, 237–279. Chicago: University of Chicago Press.

Copeland, Craig. 2011. *Employment-Based Retirement Plan Participation: Geographic Differences and Trends, 2010*. Issue Brief 363, October. Washington, DC: Employee Benefit Research Institute. http://www.ebri.org/pdf/briefspdf/EBRI_IB_10-2011_No363_Ret_Part.pdf.

Crystal, Stephen, and Dennis Shea. 1990. "Cumulative Advantage, Cumulative Disadvantage, and Inequality among Elderly People." *Gerontologist* 30 (4): 437–443. doi: 10.1093/geront/30.4.437.

Danziger, Sheldon, Jacques Van Der Gaag, Eugene Smolensky, and Michael K. Taussig. 1982/1983. "The Life-Cycle Hypothesis and the Consumption Behavior of the Elderly." *Journal of Post Keynesian Economics* 5 (2): 208–227.

Dietz, Robert. 2010. *Housing Tax Incentives: Most Helpful to Younger Households*. Special Studies, May 3. Washington, DC: National Association of Home Builders. http://www.nahb.org/fileUpload_details.aspx?contentTypeID=3&contentID=137280&subContentID=275336&channelID=311.

Feinstein, Jonathan S., and Ching-Yang Lin. 2006. "Elderly Asset Management." Working paper. New Haven, CT: Yale University, School of Management.

Ferraro, Keneth F., and Tetyana Pylypiv Shippee. 2009. "Aging and Cumulative Inequality: How Does Inequality Get under the Skin?" *Gerontologist* 49 (3): 333–343. doi: 10.1093/geront/gnp034.

Fink, Günther, and Silvia Redaelli. 2005. "Understanding Bequest Motives—An Empirical Analysis of Intergenerational Transfers." DNB Working Paper 42, May. Amsterdam: Netherlands Central Bank, Research Department.

Finkelstein, Amy, Erzo F. P. Luttmer, and Matthew J. Notowidigdo. 2013. "What Good Is Wealth without Health? The Effect of Health on the Marginal Utility of Consumption." *Journal of the European Economic Association* 11 (Suppl.): 221–258. doi: 10.1111/j.1542-4774.2012.01101.x.

Hassan, A. F. M., Ruhul Salim, and Harry Bloch. 2011. "Population Age Structure, Saving, Capital Flows and the Real Exchange Rate: A Survey of the Literature." *Journal of Economic Surveys* 25 (4): 708–736. doi: 10.1111/j.1467-6419.2010.00665.x.

HUD [U.S. Department of Housing and Urban Development], Community Planning and Development. 2004. *Good Habits of a Highly Effective Rehabilitation Manager*. Guidebook HUD-1408-CPB. Washington, DC: HUD. http://archives.hud.gov /offices/cpd/affordablehousing/modelguides/200317.pdf.

HUD, Office of Housing. 2007. *How Your Rent Is Determined*. Fact Sheet for HUD Assisted Residents, June. Washington, DC: HUD. http://portal.hud.gov/hudportal /documents/ huddoc?id=DOC_14955.pdf.

Huston, Sandra J. 2010. "Measuring Financial Literacy." *Journal of Consumer Affairs* 44 (2): 296–316. doi: 10.1111/j.1745-6606.2010.01170.x.

IRS [Internal Revenue Service]. 2014. "401(k) Resource Guide—Plan Sponsors—General Distribution Rules." Last modified May 6. http://www.irs.gov/ Retirement -Plans/Plan-Sponsor/401%28k%29-Resource-Guide---Plan-Sponsors---General -Distribution-Rules.

Lloyd-Sherlock, Peter. 2002. "Nussbaum, Capabilities and Older People." *Journal of International Development* 14 (8): 1163–1173. doi: 10.1002/jid.958.

Lusardi, Annamaria, and Olivia S. Mitchell. 2007. "Baby Boomer Retirement Security: The Roles of Planning, Financial Literacy, and Housing Wealth." *Journal of Monetary Economics* 54 (1): 205–224. doi: 10.1016/j.jmoneco.2006.12.001.

Meschede, Tatjana, Thomas M. Shapiro, and Jennifer Wheary. 2009. *Living Longer on Less: The New Economic (In)Security of Seniors*. By a Thread Report 4. Waltham, MA: Brandeis University Institute on Assets and Social Policy and Dēmos. http://www.demos.org/sites/default/files/publications/LivingLongerOnLess _Demos .pdf.

Munnell, Alicia H., Anthony Webb, and Francesca N. Golub-Sass. 2009. *The National Retirement Risk Index: After the Crash*. Issue in Brief 9-22, October. Chestnut Hill, MA: Boston College, Center for Retirement Research. http://crr.bc.edu/wp-content /uploads/2009/10/IB_9-22.pdf.

Murphy, Sherry L., Jiaquan Xu, and Kenneth D. Kochanek. 2012. *Deaths: Preliminary Data for 2010*. National Vital Statistics Reports 60, no. 4. Hyattsville, MD: U.S. Department of Health and Human Services, Centers for Disease Control and Prevention. http://www .cdc.gov/nchs/data/nvsr/nvsr60/nvsr60_04.pdf.

Nussbaum, Martha C. 2000. *Women and Human Development: The Capabilities Approach*. New York: Cambridge University Press.

Oliver, Melvin L., and Thomas M. Shapiro. 1995. *Black Wealth/White Wealth: A New Perspective on Racial Inequality*. New York: Routledge.

O'Rand, Angela, M. 1996. "The Precious and the Precocious: Understanding Cumulative Disadvantage and Cumulative Advantage over the Life Course." *Gerontologist* 36 (2): 230–238. doi: 10.1093/geront/36.2.230.

Pistaferri, Luigi. 2009. "The Life-Cycle Hypothesis: An Assessment of Some Recent Evidence." *Rivista di Politica Economica* 99 (2): 35–65.

Radner, Daniel. B. 1998. "The Retirement Prospects of the Baby Boom Generation." *Social Security Bulletin* 61 (1): 3–19.

Schreiner, Mark. 2001. *Measuring Savings*. Research Background Paper 01-4, September. St. Louis, MO: Washington University, Center for Social Development. http://csd.wustl.edu/Publications/Documents/73.MeasuringSavings.pdf.

Schreiner, Mark, Margaret Clancy, and Michael Sherraden. 2002. *Saving Performance in the American Dream Demonstration: A National Demonstration of individual Development Accounts*. CSD Report 02-15. St. Louis, MO: Washington University, Center for Social Development. http://csd.wustl.edu/Publications/Documents/ADDReport2002.pdf.

Sen, Amartya K. 1999. *Commodities and Capabilities*. New York: Oxford University Press.

Shapiro, Thomas M., and Edward N. Wolff, eds. 2001. *Assets for the Poor: The Benefits of Spreading Asset Ownership*. New York: Russell Sage.

Sherraden, Margaret S. 2010. "Financial Capability: What Is It, and How Can It Be Created?" CSD Working Paper 10-17. St. Louis, MO: Washington University, Center for Social Development. http://csd.wustl.edu/Publications/Documents/WP10-17.pdf.

Sherraden, Michael. 1991. *Assets and the Poor: A New American Welfare Policy*. Armonk, NY: M.E. Sharpe.

Sherraden, Michael, Mark Schreiner, and Sondra G. Beverly. 2003. "Income, Institutions, and Saving Performance in Individual Development Accounts." *Economic Development Quarterly* 17 (1): 95–112. doi: 10.1177/0891242402239200.

Smith, James P. 1997. "Wealth Inequality among Older Americans." *Journals of Gerontology Series B: Psychological Sciences and Social Sciences* 52B (special issue): 74–81. doi: 10.1093/geronb/52B.Special_Issue.74.

U.S. Census Bureau. 2011. *Statistical Abstract of the United States: 2012*. 131st ed. Washington, DC: U.S. Census Bureau.

USDA [U.S. Department of Agriculture]. 2013a. "Rural Repair and Rehabilitation Loans and Grants." Last modified January 14. http://www.rurdev.usda.gov/had-rr_loans_grants.html.

USDA. 2013b. "Supplemental Nutrition Assistance Program (SNAP): Eligibility." Last modified December 30. http://www.fns.usda.gov/snap/eligibility.

U.S. Government Accountability Office. 2005. *Elderly Housing: Federal Housing Programs That Offer Assistance for the Elderly*. Report GAO-05-174, February. Washington, DC: U.S. Government Accountability Office. http://www.gao.gov/assets/250/245318.pdf.

Wacker, Robbyn R., and Karen A. Roberto. 2011. *Aging Social Policies: An International Perspective*. Thousand Oaks, CA: Sage.

Webb, Anthony. 2009. *Providing Income for a Lifetime: Bridging the Gap between Academic Research and Practical Advice*. Research Report 2009-11, June. Washington, DC: AARP Public Policy Institute. http://assets.aarp.org/rgcenter/ppi/econ-sec/2009-11.pdf.

Woo, Lillian, and David Buchholz. 2006. "Subsidies for Assets: A New Look at the Federal Budget." Paper presented at the 2006 Assets Learning Conference, Phoenix, AZ, September 19–21.

9

Long-Term Care in the United States

Who Pays?

■ JENNIFER C. GREENFIELD

Long-term care (LTC) is a pressing—but not new—health policy issue in the United States. In 1990, the U.S. Bipartisan Commission on Comprehensive Health Care, a congressional task force also known as the Pepper Commission, concluded that the nation urgently needed LTC reform. Senator John D. Rockefeller IV, chair of the commission, stated that LTC reform would have a "clear field" for passage in Congress because most members of the American electorate "see themselves at risk of impoverishment if they or their family members need long-term care" (Rockefeller 1990, 1005). However, Rockefeller's prediction proved to be too optimistic, and significant reform has not come to fruition nearly a quarter of a century later.

Reforming LTC remains a popular topic for health policy experts and the mainstream media. In the United States, a perfect storm of factors, including the aging of the baby boomer generation and increasing life spans, has led to unsustainable growth in LTC costs. According to the National Center for Health Statistics (2013), those who reach age 65 years can now expect to live another 20 years. With this longevity comes the risk of chronic illness, and that risk increases dramatically with age (Freudenberg and Olden 2011). Forty-four percent of older adults (i.e., those aged 65 years or older) live with *multiple* chronic conditions, some of which (e.g., Alzheimer's disease) have very high treatment costs because of the length and intensity of care. Meanwhile, the price of LTC is rising much more quickly than the rate of inflation. Public programs and individual budgets are strained to the breaking point, families are becoming impoverished, and several states teeter on the brink of bankruptcy because of Medicaid spending. Although LTC most often is discussed as a health policy issue, it is clear that longevity has become an economic liability in the United States.

Recent attempts at comprehensive policy reform and innovation on the scale described in the Pepper Commission report (Rockefeller 1990), efforts that include the Community Living Assistance Services and Supports (CLASS) Act, have failed.[1] The federal government has implemented incremental changes by offering Medicaid waivers and demonstration project grants for payment-system and care-delivery reforms, but these efforts are aimed largely at reducing federal and state cost burdens. They do not address costs for individual patients and caregivers. By not offering comprehensive financing options for long-term services and supports (LTSS), the system endangers families' financial health. A large body of work documents that economic health and security are associated with increased physical and mental health, civic participation, and other measures of well-being (see Braveman, Egerter, and Williams [2011] for a review of this literature), but most public LTC programs do not protect assets and often require individuals to spend them down before services are covered. Asset development programs implemented throughout the life course will have little benefit if policies do not protect families from this type of impoverishment.

■ SCOPE OF THE LTC PROBLEM

Who Receives Care?

The National Health Policy Forum (O'Shaughnessy 2014) estimates that 11 million adults aged 18 years and older—approximately 5% of the U.S. population—use LTSS, and more that 6 million (57%) of these are aged 65 years or over. Only 1.4 million LTSS recipients live in an institutional setting (e.g., a nursing home); the rest live alone or with a family member (Centers for Medicare and Medicaid Services 2012a). Among those living in nursing homes, more than 80% are older than age 65 years, and the average age is 82 years (Kaye, Harrington, and LaPlante 2010). Only 45% of those living in the community are older than age 65 years. The average age of these adults is near 60 years. Compared with men, women have a longer life expectancy, are more likely to receive LTC, and are much more likely to live in nursing homes. Almost two-thirds of nursing home residents are female. Among LTC recipients cared for at home, 75% live with family members and half live in households with income below 200% of the federal poverty level. The median household income among in-home LTC recipients is $32,000 (Kaye et al. 2010).

Although the literature offers few data on ethnic differences among LTC recipients, some evidence suggests that the racial distribution of LTC recipients roughly mirrors that of the general population (Spector et al. 2000). However, the distribution among nursing home residents reflects significant disparities in access to nursing home beds and, increasingly, in access to assisted-living facilities (Akamigbo and Wolinsky 2007). Compared with whites, minority populations are more likely to experience chronic health problems and experience them earlier but are often excluded from access to paid LTSS because of an inability to pay the related out-of-pocket costs. There may also be cultural preferences for in-home, family-provided care among some populations, but policy barriers, including the limited number of Medicaid-financed nursing home beds and the inability to use public funds to pay for assisted-living facilities in many states, likely account for much of the discrepancy in access to formal LTSS (Akamigbo and Wolinsky 2007).

Who Provides Care?

Among LTC recipients living in the community, 92% receive at least some assistance from an unpaid helper (e.g., spouse, child, or friend) with activities of daily living and at least 62% receive help from unpaid caregivers *only* (National Alliance for Caregiving and AARP 2009). Susannah Fox, Maeve Duggan, and Kristen Purcell (2013) estimate that 36% of adults in the United States—roughly 86.5 million people—provided care for at least one adult in 2012. An earlier estimate by the National Alliance for Caregiving and AARP (2009) put the number at 62 million. These caregivers usually are not compensated for providing care; nearly half work full time, and 11% work part time. Almost half (48%) of caregivers are older than age 50 years, and 13% are older than age 65 years (National Alliance for Caregiving and AARP 2009). The average age of caregivers is approximately 49 years, which is higher than the 2004 average (46 years).

Approximately 70% of caregivers are white, and roughly 13% are African American. This distribution is consistent with the distribution of care recipients. More than 42% of caregivers report having household income of less than $50,000 per year. The median household income is approximately $57,000. Fifty-eight percent of caregivers are married, and 37% live in households with children or grandchildren. Almost one-third (31%) live with the care recipient, and most (66%) are women. Nearly one-third (31%) have provided care for longer than 5 years, and that proportion has increased in recent years (National Alliance for Caregiving and AARP 2009). All of these data show that LTC has a ripple effect across families and communities in the United States.

In addition to informal caregivers, direct-care service providers are part of a vast and growing industry that employs three million people nationwide (Paraprofessional Healthcare Institute 2011). More than half (1.7 million) work in home and community settings. Most are employed by for-profit agencies, although about 23% are self-employed or employed by private households.[2] Nursing home staff (e.g., certified nursing assistants) and homecare workers (e.g., home health and personal care aides) help clients complete activities of daily living (e.g., bathing, dressing, and eating) and instrumental activities of daily living (e.g., cooking and housekeeping). Homecare workers also provide companionship for those who are homebound or cannot be left unattended because of safety concerns.

On average, direct care workers earned an annual income of $16,800 in 2013; nursing, psychiatric, and home health aides earned more ($19,000), and personal care aides earned less ($12,300; Paraprofessional Healthcare Institute 2014). Because their salaries were below the eligibility limits for many public programs, 46% of direct care workers relied on public benefits, including the Supplemental Nutrition Assistance Program and Medicaid, to supplement their incomes in 2013. This number is expected to increase as Medicaid eligibility expands under the Affordable Care Act. Also of note is the racial distribution among direct care workers: 47% are white, 30% are African American, and 16% are Latino. The average age of these workers is 42 years, but those who are privately employed or self-employed tend to be somewhat older (the average age is 48 years), and workers employed in nursing homes tend to be slightly younger (the average age is 40 years; Paraprofessional Healthcare Institute 2014). Direct-care service providers often are members of vulnerable groups and, because of the below-average wages they earn in midlife, are more susceptible to economic insecurity in later life than is the general population.

How Much Does LTC Cost, and Who Pays?

In 2009, U.S. consumers spent $240 billion nationwide on formal LTC services provided by paid professionals. Public programs (e.g., Medicare and Medicaid) covered roughly 69% of the cost, families covered 19%, and private insurance covered 7% (Kaiser Commission on Medicaid and the Uninsured 2012). Because the average cost of a year of nursing home care in the United States was $88,000 in 2012—with costs exceeding $100,000 in 10 states—the burden on families can be quite substantial if private and public funding sources are unavailable (Ujvari 2012). Even so, less than 11% of Americans aged 55 years or older and less than 10% of the entire population have private LTC insurance (Johnson and Park 2011).

Formal LTC costs are only part of the picture. Lynn Feinberg and others (2011) estimate that the value of family-provided care, which is mostly unpaid, was roughly $450 billion in 2010. In addition to donating time, families spend substantial amounts of money on family members' care. Although the numbers vary widely, recent studies estimate that each caregiver's average annual expenditure is between $5,531 and $12,300 (Evercare and National Alliance for Caregiving 2007). With nearly 45 million people providing care for disabled adults older than age 17 years, consumers could be spending as much as $555 billion every year on formal LTC and indirect expenses, including legal services, out-of-pocket health care, and home modifications (e.g., ramps and bathroom grab bars). In other words, out-of-pocket, LTC-related household expenses may be as much as 5% of annual personal consumption expenditures in the United States.

In addition to these direct expenses, there are indirect costs of caregiving. Caregivers incur such costs, for example, by taking time off from work, forgoing promotions, reducing contributions to Social Security, and accumulating less in savings and retirement accounts than they might have saved otherwise. Using data from six waves of the National Institute on Aging's Health and Retirement Study (1998–2008), I examined how caregiving affects the income trajectories of adults who were aged 51–67 years at baseline and cared for an aging parent. Latent trajectory analysis reveals that caregiving does not have a negative impact on every caregiver's income but that it is associated with a lower income trajectory for at least 15% of respondents, and the association is marginally significant for an even larger group. Caregiving is more likely to have a negative effect on the income trajectories of those who are single, widowed, or divorced. Race and education level are also significant predictors of this negative effect. Results suggest that caregiving may exacerbate financial insecurity among already vulnerable groups by decreasing present income and future income through delayed asset accumulation and retirement planning.

A recent study found that approximately 65% of all households are at risk of being unable to maintain their preretirement standard of living in retirement. This probability increases by generation, and 72% of those in generation X (i.e., people born between 1965 and 1974) are at risk (Munnell et al. 2009). Although Social Security provides most older adults in the United States with a guarantee of some income in later life, this income alone is usually inadequate to cover significant LTC costs.

Less than 10% of Americans are covered by a private LTC insurance (LTCI) plan, and that proportion is decreasing (Andrews 2010). Because of the low uptake rate, inflated health care costs, and low interest rates, which make it difficult for insurance companies to build their existing reserves to help pay claims, many insurance companies have dropped LTCI products (Schoeff 2012; Ujvari 2012), and available plans are costly. Insurance premiums can range from $1,100 per year for a plan with minimal benefits purchased by a middle-aged adult to over $16,000 per year for a plan with more robust benefits purchased by older individuals (Brown and Finkelstein 2011). Private insurance simply may be unaffordable, or Medicaid—the payor of last resort when private funds have been depleted—may deter many families from purchasing LTCI products by providing a safety net (Brown and Finkelstein 2011). In either case, the result is an increasing dependence on public programs to pay for formal care. Therefore, taxpayers bear a large burden of LTC financing through Medicaid and (to a lesser extent) Medicare, which pay for approximately two-thirds of all LTSS (O'Shaughnessy 2014).

Total Medicaid expenditures reached $429 billion in 2011, and the 6% of Medicaid enrollees (four million people) who used Medicaid-funded LTSS accounted for roughly *half* of all Medicaid expenditures (Kaiser Commission on Medicaid and the Uninsured 2012). States' share of this spending was $156 billion, and Medicaid costs account for an average of 23.6% of state expenditures. In some states, Medicaid accounts for an even larger share: in 2010, Pennsylvania spent nearly $8 billion, or 31% of the state budget, with another $14 billion in federal matching funds (National Association of State Budget Officers 2011). Because most Medicaid LTSS are mandated by federal law, states' only alternatives are to change LTC delivery methods (i.e., prioritizing in-home care over nursing home stays) or to drop coverage of other, nonmandatory services (e.g., coverage for podiatry and mental health care).

If Current Trends Continue

The U.S. Government Accountability Office (2008) estimates that state and federal expenditures on LTC will quadruple by 2050 and that individual costs will also rise exponentially; it has concluded, therefore, that LTC financing is one of the most significant challenges the United States will face in the twenty-first century. Despite dire predictions, comprehensive policy changes have remained politically unpopular and difficult to implement.

■ **RECENT REFORM APPROACHES**

In 1990, the Pepper Commission recommended the expansion of Medicare to include a national, mandatory, public LTCI program that prioritizes home- and community-based services (HCBS), supports caregivers, and protects household assets. Since then, proponents of reform have proposed narrower efforts to address individual LTC challenges facing the United States. A few of the more important innovations are described in the following sections.

State Long-Term Care Partnership Program

The State Long-Term Care Partnership Program, which has been implemented in 44 states, uses state and federal dollars to boost the private LTCI market by allowing individuals applying for Medicaid to keep assets with a value equal to that of an LTCI plan purchased through the partnership. For example, if an individual's plan covers up to $300,000 of LTSS, the individual can keep $300,000 in assets once insurance coverage is exhausted and still qualify for Medicaid (Meiners 2009). Uptake has been very low (Tumlinson et al. 2013), but educating consumers about the program's benefits and implementing structural changes may increase participation. Government subsidies on insurance premiums may encourage participation among low- and middle-income families, which are the most vulnerable to catastrophic losses from LTC costs. The program could also include individually purchased plans to encourage people to keep the plans during lean economic times and provide additional state and federal funding to encourage insurance providers to keep and even expand their LTCI offerings.

CLASS Act

One of the less well-known components of the Patient Protection and Affordable Care Act (ACA) was an LTCI program called the Community Living Assistance Services and Supports (CLASS) Act. The program was the first major public health care effort signed into law since Medicare and Medicaid in 1965, and it was also the first public insurance plan designed specifically for HCBS. The daily cash benefit ($50 to $75) would not have been enough to pay the average daily cost of nursing home care but could have paid for a few hours of HCBS or for home modifications (Mulvey and Colello 2010). The Congressional Budget Office estimates that the voluntary program would have had only a 4% uptake in its first 10 years (Elmendorf 2009), and the U.S. Department of Health and Human Services scrapped its implementation after deciding that the program could not meet its statutory obligations (Greenlee 2011). In passing the American Taxpayer Relief Act of 2012, Congress repealed the program.

Consumer-Directed Services

The CLASS Act represents the dramatic shift underway in a number of federal LTC programs. Several policy innovations funded through the ACA are helping states move toward the goal of rebalancing Medicaid services "by expanding access to an array of home and community-based services and reducing dependence on institutional care" (Centers for Medicare and Medicaid Services 2012b, para. 1). For instance, the ACA includes a major expansion of the Cash and Counseling model of care delivery. That model allows Medicaid beneficiaries to choose their own services, medical equipment, home modifications, and other products and services using a cash benefit instead of receiving predetermined services. The ACA also includes an expansion of the Money Follows the Person program, which allows states to use Medicaid dollars to transition patients from nursing homes back into their own homes or another community-based setting. Both of these programs prioritize consumer-directed services, in which LTC recipients have the freedom to choose their care type, caregiver, and care setting. For instance, they can often use funds to pay family members or friends to provide care and to purchase home modification products that facilitate independence.

Although these programs can help keep clients in their homes and independent, a number of systemic challenges limit their effectiveness. First, family members who become caregivers need significant training and pay that offsets lost wages and other caregiving expenses. Such training is not always available. A study of Cash and Counseling programs in Arkansas, Florida, and New Jersey finds that, on average, caregivers receive compensation for fewer than half of the hours of care they provide (Dale et al. 2005). Their compensation ranged from $6 per hour in Arkansas to just over $10 per hour in Florida but usually did not include pay for travel time or fringe benefits (e.g., health insurance). Furthermore, in nearly one-third of cases, payments were sometimes late, making them unreliable as a main source of income. As the evidence suggests, cash supports do not protect caregivers from the financial consequences of intensive LTC responsibilities.

Second, covered services sometimes revert after a certain amount of time to the regular package of Medicaid LTSS provided by the state. Such changes leave informal caregivers responsible for the remaining costs. Even when increased support is available, caregiver support is not always included. For instance, 28 states have implemented the Money Follows the Person program, but as of 2012, only 22 of these state programs provided funding for caregiver supports such as respite care and caregiver training, and only 5% of participants report using the caregiver support services (Irvin et al. 2013). Over one-third (37%) of participants report receiving informal help from family or friends while living in the community (Simon and Hodges 2011). Without sustained caregiver support, this program and others that prioritize HCBS may expose families to financial, physical, and emotional strain.

Third, a recent study of the Money Follows the Person program finds that workforce shortages are a major barrier to connecting clients with HCBS (Watts 2013). Certified nursing assistants and home health aides cite poor pay, a lack of benefits, insufficient training, and the paucity of advancement opportunities as major deterrents to joining or staying in the field, which needs substantial reforms to attract enough workers to meet the demand for HCBS (Khatutsky et al. 2011).

Homecare Worker Reforms

To address these problems, the Obama administration issued a rule that extends the Fair Labor Standards Act's wage and work-condition protections to the homecare workers, including health and personal care aides. Finalized in September 2013, the rule will come into effect on July 1, 2015.[3] As part of this change, workers who perform homecare tasks for community-dwelling clients will no longer be classified as companions and, thus, will no longer be excluded from federal minimum wage and overtime pay requirements. Despite the low wages paid to these workers, the home health care industry generates more than $80 billion in revenue each year. This amount has grown by as much as 9% in each year during the past decade, making home health care one of the largest and fastest growing industries in the United States (Seavey and Marquand 2011). Regulatory changes that impose minimum wage and overtime rules on the majority of homecare workers will cost the industry approximately $4.7 million per year for each of the first 10 years (76 Fed. Reg. 81190, 81201 [2011]).

Guaranteeing a minimum wage and overtime pay for workers does not address all of the issues related to home health care. For instance, 28% of all direct care workers had no health insurance in 2013, even though they are particularly susceptible to health problems caused by physically demanding work (Paraprofessional Healthcare Institute 2014). Many also need additional training and opportunities for professional development. Without these additional reforms, the field likely will remain prone to high turnover rates, and those seeking HCBS will endure workforce shortages.

Limitations of Recent Reform Approaches

Solving the LTC crisis is difficult because of complex and interrelated problems. Various policy proposals, including those described above, have addressed one specific aspect or a set of narrowly defined issues and can be divided into four general categories:

1. Public-sector financing reforms (e.g., consumer-directed services)
2. Private financing incentives (e.g., the State Long-Term Care Partnership Program)
3. Formal care service-delivery reforms (e.g., fair wages for home health workers)
4. Informal care delivery supports (e.g., the CLASS Act).

Because comprehensive reform has been unattainable, state and federal efforts tend to focus on one area of concern at a time, though effects sometimes ripple across categories. For example, the Money Follows the Person program focuses on shifting public financing toward HCBS but also provides additional caregiver training and assistance. Economic impact is the common thread in all LTC policy proposals. Individuals' capacity to accumulate and maintain assets over time affects their ability to absorb the costs of LTC services and, therefore, determines whether they must depend on public programs and informal care. Informal caregivers' economic productivity may be affected adversely through lost work time and the long-term negative health effects of the caregiving experience. Furthermore, the burden on private funds and informal caregivers increases when public sector funding for LTSS is cut. Thus, any shift in public policy has the potential to affect household assets. Families' capacity to provide and pay for LTSS through assets may ease the burden on public programs over time.

Because of the impact of informal care on a family's financial capability, we must not think of it as free. Hours of care, whether formal or informal, are placed on a continuum separate from dollars used to pay for that care (Figure 9.1). At the theoretical extremes, we can view formal care as a complete replacement for informal care and vice versa; however, most care recipients receive a combination of both. Likewise, care recipients often use private and public sources to pay for LTSS. Although the dynamics of these care delivery and financing relationships are more complex than a simple diagram can depict, Figure 9.1 illustrates that any policy change will have ripple effects. For example, a shift away from public funding requires more private funding unless the need for care or the cost of that care is reduced.

■ WHAT'S NEXT? TOWARD A NEW APPROACH TO LTC REFORM

It is clear that the type and amount of LTSS used are tied to recipients' and caregivers' financial capability. As discussed earlier in this chapter, recent reform efforts usually aim to reduce public spending on LTC and keep people in their homes and communities for as long as possible. These reforms may undermine the economic stability of care recipients by putting additional pressure on

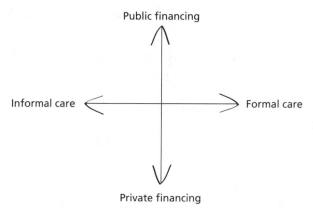

Figure 9.1 Dynamic Relationships between Sources of LTC Delivery and Funding.

caregivers. Thus, policy reforms should support the financial well-being of care recipients and their families. Reforms should include the following elements:

1. Comprehensive assessments of individual caregivers' needs
2. Dedicated programs or payment mechanisms for evidence-based caregiver supports (e.g., respite care, training, and physical and mental health care)
3. Expanded asset protections for care recipients who qualify for public programs to prevent family impoverishment
4. Comprehensive financial education for families, including education on costs of LTC and strategies for preparing to meet these needs as part of retirement planning
5. Workforce protections that enforce a living wage, health care benefits, professional development, workforce training, and access to retirement savings programs for homecare workers.

Redistribution of public spending on LTC might allow for such broad reforms, but research must verify that rebalancing efforts would result in net savings for state and federal budgets. Research also should investigate whether investments in workforce development, consumer financial education, and caregiver support programs would reduce the dependence on public programs and decrease public spending on LTC services over time. Lastly, proponents of reform need to understand how ethnic and racial minorities and other vulnerable groups access formal LTC; advocates of reform must recognize how these populations are affected by the lack of equal wages and other worker protections in the homecare field. In today's political climate, proposed public programs, including those that address the LTC crisis, must demonstrate economic expediency. Therefore, researchers must document the short- and long-term economic benefits for families and governments in order to build the political will needed to address the LTC challenge.

■ CONCLUSIONS

In 1990, the Pepper Commission concluded that the country's LTC system was headed for crisis and was in urgent need of reform. More than 20 years later, such reforms still seem out of reach. Narrower legislative efforts have sought to reduce care recipients' dependence on public programs but may have inadvertently jeopardized families' financial capability. To qualify for Medicaid, families must spend down almost all assets. This requirement results in complete impoverishment and increases burdens on informal caregivers. Policymakers must be aware that changes in LTC financing ripple across multiple domains, affecting taxpayers, formal care workers, and care recipients' families. Advocates for increasing financial capability among older adults and families should reframe LTC as an economic issue and an essential aspect of financial planning across the life course.

■ NOTES

The author acknowledges generous support for this work from the John A. Hartford Foundation, the National Association of Social Workers, and the Atlantic Philanthropies. The work was also supported by a grant from the U.S. Social Security Administration (SSA) funded as part of the Retirement Research Consortium. The opinions and conclusions expressed are solely those of the author and do not represent the opinions or policy of SSA or any agency of the federal government.

1. The CLASS Act was enacted as Title VIII of the Patient Protection and Affordable Care Act of 2010 (Pub. L. 111-148, Title VIII, § 8001, 124 Stat. 828 [2010], *repealed by* the American Taxpayer Relief Act of 2012, Pub. L. 112-240, Title VI, § 642(b)(1), 126 Stat. 2358 [2012]).

2. Application of the Fair Labor Standards Act to Domestic Service; Proposed Rule, 76 Fed. Reg. 81190, 81208 (2011) (proposed December 27).

3. Application of the Fair Labor Standards Act to Domestic Service, 29 C.F.R. § 552 (2013). For the Fair Labor Standards Act, see 29 U.S.C. §§ 201–215 (2011).

■ REFERENCES

Akamigbo, Adaeze B., and Fredric D. Wolinsky. 2007. "New Evidence of Racial Differences in Access and Their Effects on the Use of Nursing Homes among Older Adults." *Medical Care* 45 (7): 672–679. doi: 10.1097/MLR.0b013e3180455677.

Andrews, Michelle. 2010. "Few Seniors Have Long-Term Care Insurance." *Kaiser Health News*, December 14. http://www.kaiserhealthnews.org/features/insuring-your-health /michelle-andrews-on-long-term-care-policies.aspx?referrer=search.

Braveman, Paula, Susan Egerter, and David R. Williams. 2011. "The Social Determinants of Health: Coming of Age." *Annual Review of Public Health* 32: 381–398. doi: 10.1146 /annurev-publhealth-031210-101218.

Brown, Jeffrey R., and Amy Finkelstein. 2011. "Insuring Long-Term Care in the United States." *Journal of Economic Perspectives* 25 (4): 119–142. doi: 10.1257/jep.25.4.119.

Centers for Medicare and Medicaid Services. 2012a. "Balancing Long-Term Services and Supports." Accessed April 24, 2014. http://www.medicaid.gov/Medicaid -CHIP-Program-Information/By-Topics/Long-Term-Services-and-Supports /Balancing/Balancing-Long-Term-Services-and-Supports.html.

Centers for Medicare and Medicaid Services. 2012b. *Nursing Home Data Compendium 2012 Edition*. Baltimore, MD: Centers for Medicare and Medicaid Services. http://www.cms .gov/Medicare/Provider-Enrollment-and-Certification/CertificationandComplianc /downloads/nursinghomedatacompendium_508.pdf.

Dale, Stacy, Randall Brown, Barbara Phillips, and Barbara Carlson. 2005. *Experience of Workers Hired under Cash and Counseling: Findings from Arkansas, Florida, and New Jersey*. Report. Washington, DC: U.S. Department of Health and Human Services, Office of the Assistant Secretary for Planning and Evaluation. http://aspe.hhs.gov /daltcp/reports/workerexp.pdf.

Elmendorf, Douglas W. 2009. Douglas W. Elmendorf to George Miller, November 25. Congressional Budget Office. http://www.cbo.gov/sites/default/files/cbofiles /ftpdocs/107xx/doc10769/class_additional_information_miller_letter.pdf.

Evercare and National Alliance for Caregiving. 2007. *Evercare Study of Family Caregivers— What They Spend, What They Sacrifice*. Report. Minnetonka, MN: Evercare. http://www. caregiving.org/data/Evercare_NAC_CaregiverCostStudyFINAL20111907.pdf.

Feinberg, Lynn, Susan C. Reinhard, Ari Houser, and Rita Choula. 2011. *Valuing the Invaluable: 2011 Update—The Growing Contributions and Costs of Family Caregiving*. Report. Washington, DC: AARP Public Policy Institute. http://assets.aarp.org /rgcenter/ ppi/ltc/i51-caregiving.pdf.

Fox, Susannah, Maeve Duggan, and Kristen Purcell. 2013. *Family Caregivers Are Wired for Health; Part 1: Health Information Specialists*. Report, June 20. Washington, DC: Pew Research Center. http://www.pewinternet.org/2013/06/20/part-1-health -information-specialists/.

Freudenberg, Nicholas, and Kenneth Olden. 2011. "Getting Serious about the Prevention of Chronic Diseases." *Preventing Chronic Disease: Public Health Research, Practice, and Policy* 8 (4): 1–3. http://www.cdc.gov/pcd/issues/2011/jul/pdf/10_0243.pdf.

Greenlee, Kathy. 2011. *Memorandum on the CLASS Program*. Washington, DC: U.S. Department of Health and Human Services. http://aspe.hhs.gov/daltcp/reports/2011 /class/CLASSmemo.shtml.

Irvin, Carol, Noelle Denny-Brown, Matthew Kehn, Rebecca Sweetland Lester, Debra Lipson, Wilfredo Lim, Jessica Ross, et al. 2013. *Money Follows the Person 2012: Annual Evaluation Report*. Report, October 15. Cambridge, MA: Mathematica Policy Research. http://www.mathematica-mpr.com/publications/pdfs/health/MFP_2012 _Annual.pdf.

Johnson, Richard W., and Janice S. Park. 2011. *Who Purchases Long-Term Care Insurance?* Older Americans' Economic Security Report 29, March. Washington, DC: Urban Institute. http://www.urban.org/events/upload/Older-Americans-Economic -Security-27.pdf.

Kaiser Commission on Medicaid and the Uninsured. 2012. *Medicaid and Long-Term Care Services and Supports*. Medicaid Facts, June. Washington, DC: Kaiser Family Foundation. http://kaiserfamilyfoundation.files.wordpress.com/2013/01/2186-09.pdf.

Kaye, H. Stephen, Charlene Harrington, and Mitchell P. LaPlante. 2010. "Long-Term Care: Who Gets It, Who Provides It, Who Pays, and How Much?" *Health Affairs* 29 (1): 11–21. doi: 10.1377/hlthaff.2009.0535.

Khatutsky, Galina, Joshua Weiner, Wayne Anderson, Valentina Ahkmerova, E. Andrew Jessup, and Marie R. Squillace. 2011. *Understanding Direct Care Workers: A Snapshot of Two of America's Most Important Jobs.* Report. Washington, DC: U.S. Department of Health and Human Services. http://aspe.hhs.gov/daltcp/reports/2011/CNAchart .pdf.

Meiners, Mark R. 2009. *Long-Term Care Insurance Partnership: Considerations for Cost-Effectiveness.* Issue Brief. Hamilton, NJ: Center for Health Care Strategies. http://www.chcs.org/usr_doc/LTC_Partnership_Cost_Effectiveness_Brief.pdf.

Mulvey, Janemarie, and Kirsten J. Colello. 2010. *Community Living Assistance Services and Supports (CLASS) Provisions in the Patient Protection and Affordable Care Act (PPACA).* Report for Congress. Washington, DC: Congressional Research Service.

Munnell, Alicia H., Anthony Webb, Francesca Golub-Sass, and Dan Muldoon. 2009. *Long-Term Care Costs and the National Retirement Risk Index.* Issue in Brief 9-7. Boston, MA: Center for Retirement Research. http://crr.bc.edu/wp-content /uploads/2009/04/IB_9-7.pdf.

National Alliance for Caregiving and AARP. 2009. *Caregiving in the U.S. 2009: A Focused Look at Those Caring for the 50+.* Report. Bethesda, MD: National Alliance for Caregiving and AARP. http://assets.aarp.org/rgcenter/il/caregiving_09.pdf.

National Association of State Budget Officers. 2011. *State Expenditure Report: Examining Fiscal 2009–2011 State Spending.* Report. Washington, DC: National Association of State Budget Officers. http://www.nasbo.org/sites/default/files/2010%20State%20 Expenditure%20Report.pdf.

National Center for Health Statistics. 2013. "Life Expectancy at Birth, at Age 65, and at Age 75, by Sex, Race, and Hispanic Origin: United States, Selected Years 1900–2010." In *Health, United States, 2012: With Special Feature on Emergency Care*, 76–77, Table 18. Hyattsville, MD: National Center for Health Statistics. http://www.cdc.gov/nchs /data/hus/hus12.pdf.

O'Shaughnessy, Carol V. 2014. *The Basics: National Spending for Long-Term Services and Supports (LTSS), 2012.* Report, March 27. Washington, DC: National Health Policy Forum. http://www.nhpf.org/library/the-basics/Basics_LTSS_03-27-14.pdf.

Paraprofessional Healthcare Institute. 2011. *Who Are Direct-Care Workers?* Fact Sheet. New York: Paraprofessional Healthcare Institute. http://www.phinational.org/sites /phinational.org/files/clearinghouse/NCDCW%20Fact%20Sheet-1.pdf.

Paraprofessional Healthcare Institute. 2014. "Direct-Care Workers at a Glance." Accessed April 24. http://phinational.org/direct-care-workers-glance.

Rockefeller, John D., IV. 1990. "The Pepper Commission Report on Comprehensive Health Care." *New England Journal of Medicine* 323 (14): 1005–1007. doi: 10.1056 /NEJM199010043231429.

Schoeff, Mark, Jr. 2012. "LTC a Risky Business for Insurers." *Investment News*, September 16. http://www.investmentnews.com/article/20120916/REG/309169999.

Seavey, Dorie, and Abby Marquand. 2011. *Caring in America; A Comprehensive Analysis of the Nation's Fastest-Growing Jobs: Home Health and Personal Care Aides.* Report, December. Bronx, NY: Paraprofessional Healthcare Institute. http://phinational.org /sites/phinational.org/files/clearinghouse/caringinamerica-20111212.pdf.

Simon, Samuel E., and Matthew R. Hodges. 2011. *Money Follows the Person: Change in Participant Experience during the First Year of Community Living.* Reports from the Field 6, May. Princeton, NJ: Mathematica Policy Research. http://www.mathematica-mpr .com/publications/pdfs/health/mfpfieldrpt6.pdf.

Spector, William D., John A. Fleishman, Liliana E. Pezzin, and Brenda C. Spillman. 2000. *The Characteristics of Long-Term Care Users*. AHRQ Research Report 00-0049. Rockville, MD: Agency for Healthcare Research and Quality. http://www.ahrq.gov /professionals/systems/long-term-care/resources/facilities/ltcusers/index.html.

Tumlinson, Anne, Eric Hammelman, Elana Stair, and Joshua M. Wiener. 2013. *Insuring Americans for Long-Term Care: Challenges and Limitations of Voluntary Insurance*. Report, March. Washington, DC: Avalere Health. http://www.rti.org/pubs /avalere_challenges-limitations-voluntary-insurance_3-20-13.pdf.

Ujvari, Kathleen. 2012. *Long-Term Care Insurance: 2012 Update*. Fact Sheet 261, June. Washington, DC: AARP Public Policy Institute. http://www.aarp.org/content /dam/aarp/research/public_policy_institute/ltc/2012/ltc-insurance-2012-update -AARP-ppi-ltc.pdf.

U.S. Government Accountability Office. 2008. *Long-Term Care Insurance: Oversight of Rate Setting and Claims Settlement Practice*. Report. Washington, DC: U.S. Government Accountability Office. http://www.gao.gov/products/GAO-08-712.

Watts, Molly O'Malley. 2013. *Money Follows the Person: A 2012 Survey of Transitions, Services and Costs*. Issue Paper 8142-03, February. Washington, DC: Kaiser Commission on Medicaid and the Uninsured. http://kaiserfamilyfoundation.files. wordpress.com/2013/02/8142-03.pdf.

10 Workplace Policies and Practices

Opportunities for and Barriers to Accumulating Assets in Midlife and Later

■ ERNEST GONZALES

■ OVERVIEW OF THE PROBLEM

The accumulation of retirement wealth via pension plans, Social Security, and personal savings—resources collectively known as the three-legged stool—is critical for sustaining life outside of the labor force.[1] Unfortunately, workplace asset-building practices have perpetuated disparities in access, participation, contributions, and methods of distribution with pension plans. Women, racial and ethnic minorities, people with low levels of education, and individuals with poor health have historically been excluded from pension plans (Butrica and Johnson 2010; Dushi and Iams 2008). When plans have been made available to them, few have invested enough to meet their retirement needs (Orszag and Rodriguez 2005). In part, this is due to pay disparities. Many pensioners opt for a lump-sum payment over a secure, lifelong source of retirement income (Gale and Dworsky 2006; Investment Company Institute 2000; Turner 2011). Another support for retirees is the employer-sponsored health-benefit plan, which has met the needs of retirees in the past. Unfortunately, many employers have reduced the generosity of the health-benefit plan or stopped offering the plan (Fronstin 2000; Helman, Copeland, and VanDerhei 2009). These employer policies and practices contribute to the economic insecurity of certain populations in later life and heighten the risk that population members will age into poverty or financial uncertainty. Such policies may force older adults in these groups to rely heavily on Social Security or extend their working years, if they are able.

As employers have reduced contributions for retirement, few employees have saved enough on their own. Moreover, life expectancy has grown, and there are concerns about the solvency of Social Security. These issues have led several policymakers and researchers to promote efforts to extend adults' working years. Extending the duration of work can bolster the economic security of older adults immediately and provide additional financial resources for retirement, but health limitations and other workplace barriers (e.g., age discrimination, caregiving) prevent some from taking this path.

This chapter is divided into three sections. The first section focuses on access to and participation in pension plans, discussing retirement-wealth shortfalls that stem from limited access and investments. I also examine the decline of retiree health benefits. In the second section, I focus on additional barriers and challenges that vulnerable adults encounter in the labor force. The third section focuses on possible solutions to these challenges.

■ WORKPLACE ASSET-BUILDING POLICIES AND MISSED OPPORTUNITIES

Pensions

Employer-sponsored pension plans have been critical in financing retirement for millions of employees, but half of the current workforce—78 million working Americans—lacks access to such a plan (Office of Management and Budget 2012).[2] Estimates indicate that nearly six out of 10 private-sector employees had access to a qualified retirement plan in 2003. Unfortunately, only 49% participated in the plan (Bureau of Labor Statistics 2005; Joint Committee on Taxation 2005). Employer policies and practices have shifted away from defined-benefit plans and toward defined-contribution plans such as 401(k)s (Cushing-Daniels and Johnson 2008). In effect, this is a shift of fiscal responsibility for retirement savings away from employers and onto employees. Unfortunately, many workers lack the financial literacy to make critical decisions (Lusardi and Mitchell 2006).

Research indicates that access to employer-sponsored pension plans varies by demographic characteristics. Although lifetime pension access is not universal among any group (Table 10.1), it is disproportionately low among women, people of color, adults with low levels of education, individuals reporting poor or fair health, people reporting any disability, and adults in low-income households.

Sex

Pensions are critically important for women. They live longer than men do (Barford et al. 2006), the death of a spouse is associated with an increase in health care costs, and depletion of a widow's savings increases the likelihood that she will live in poverty (Burkhauser, Holden, and Feaster 1988; Hungerford 2001). As suggested in Table 10.1, the rate of access to pensions is very low among women relative to the rate among men and signals a broad, gendered disparity in retirement resources. Approximately 62 million women between the ages of 21 and 64 years earn a wage or salary, and 55% do not participate in a retirement plan (U.S. Department of Labor 2011). The absence of a pension plan across a woman's lifetime clearly suggests that

TABLE 10.1. *Lifetime Pension Access and Type of Pension among Individuals Aged 55–61 Years in 1994 and 2004, by Selected Characteristics (in Percentages)*

Characteristics	1994				2004			
	Without pension	DB only	DC only	Both	Without pension	DB only	DC only	Both
Total	35.7	27.3	12.3	24.6	28.5[a]	14.1[a]	17.9[a]	38.4[a]
Sex								
Men	22.7	33.3	11.5	32.4	23.2	15.2[a]	17.7[a]	43.2[a]
Women	47.7[b]	21.8[b]	13.0	17.4[b]	33.4[a,b]	13.1[a]	18.0[a]	34.0[a,b]
Race/ethnicity								
White	33.2	27.6	12.8	26.5	25.1[a]	14.0[a]	19.2[a]	40.5[a]
Black	39.4[b]	31.7[b]	11.1	17.1[b]	35.1[b]	18.2[a]	12.4[b]	33.5[a,b]
Other	40.1	23.8	9.4	26.3	38.3[b]	10.8[a]	16.9	34.0
Hispanic	59.9[b]	18.9[b]	9.3	12.0[b]	50.6[a,b]	11.7[a]	12.1[b]	24.7[a,b]
Education								
Less than HS	57.6	20.6	9.6	12.0	60.8	10.7[a]	12.8	15.0
HS	35.4[b]	27.6[b]	14.3[b]	22.6[b]	30.4[a,b]	13.9[a]	16.5	38.0[a,b]
Some college	28.1[b]	29.1[b]	12.2	30.7[b]	24.1[b]	15.4[a]	21.2[a,b]	38.1[a,b]
College degree	17.5[b]	33.0[b]	11.3	38.3[b]	15.8[b]	14.7[a]	18.6[a,b]	49.8[a,b]
Self-reported health								
Poor/fair	50.2	27.1	9.4	13.2	48.2	14.5[a]	12.1	23.7[a]
Good/excellent	31.8[b]	27.3	13.1[b]	27.7[b]	22.3[a,b]	14.0[a]	19.7[a,b]	43.0[a,b]
Employment status								
Full-time	21.2	27.3	15.2	36.1	14.3[a]	12.5[a]	23.8[a]	48.3[a]
Part-time	51.0[b]	21.2[b]	11.8	15.5[b]	37.9[a,b]	11.0[a]	22.4[a]	26.3[a,b]
Unemployed	47.8[b]	20.9	12.1	19.2[b]	29.7[a,b]	2.9[a, b]	28.1[a]	38.1[a]
Retired	35.4[b]	38.8[b]	9.9[b]	15.9[b]	33.0[b]	24.9[a,b]	6.9[a,b]	34.5[a,b]
Disabled or not in labor force								
Household income quintiles	81.0[b]	11.7[b]	5.3[b]	2.0[b]	79.4[b]	6.1[a,b]	4.8[b]	9.1[a,b]
Low	62.8	20.5	10.0	6.4	54.0[a]	15.1[a]	10.8	19.2[a]
2	37.2[b]	30.2[b]	12.8[b]	19.5[b]	30.1[a,b]	15.6[a]	19.5[a,b]	33.6[a,b]
3	29.4[b]	30.6[b]	13.1[b]	26.9[b]	24.2[b]	16.2[a]	17.1[a,b]	41.6[a,b]
4	24.1[b]	31.2[b]	13.3[b]	31.3[b]	16.9[a,b]	13.6[a]	18.9[a,b]	49.8[a,b]
High	24.7[b]	24.0	12.2	39.1[b]	17.1[a,b]	9.9[a,b]	23.0[a,b]	48.1[a,b]

Source: Irena Dushi and Howard M. Iams, "Cohort Differences in Wealth and Pension Participation of Near-Retirees." *Social Security Bulletin* 68 (3): 50. http://www.ssa.gov/policy/docs/ssb/v68n3.
Note: DB = defined benefit; DC = defined contribution; HS = high school diploma or equivalent. Data are drawn from the Health and Retirement Study. Lifetime measures of access to pension and pension type are determined using respondents' reports on pension participation and pension type in current or last job, or in any other job previously held for at least 5 years, as reported in current or previous waves. Respondents who report receiving pension income are considered as having at least a DB pension. To the extent that individuals misreport pension type across waves, figures on the prevalence of having had both types of plans over someone's working life may be biased. The cohort differences should not be biased, however, if the two cohorts are similar in their misreports of pension type across waves. Values may not add up to 100% because of responses: "don't know" or "refusal." Figures are weighted using survey weights for respective years.
[a]Difference between cohorts (i.e., between those without a pension in 1994 and in 2004) is statistically significant at the 5% level.
[b]Difference between subgroups (i.e., men and women without a pension in 1994) within a given cohort is statistically significant at the 5% level.

she will lack an instrumental leg of the three-legged retirement stool. It is not surprising that older women are more likely to live in poverty than are older men (Administration on Aging 2013). So too, they receive lower pension benefits (Social Security Administration 2014), and single women in particular rely almost exclusively on Social Security income (Social Security Administration 2014). Currently, women who work full time receive 77 cents for every dollar paid to men working full time (Institute for Women's Policy Research 2014). This suggests that, for every $100 a man receives, a woman will receive $77—a difference of $23. The compounded effect across the lifetime is important: substantial amounts of money are neither received nor saved for later life.

Race and Ethnicity

Several sources suggest that blacks and Hispanics accumulate fewer assets for later life than whites do, and rates of poverty are higher among older nonwhites than among their white counterparts. For example, nonwhites have fewer pension plan offerings than whites (Butrica and Johnson 2010) and lower rates of participation in pension plans when the plans are made available (Butrica and Johnson 2010; Dushi and Iams 2008). For Hispanics who participate in a pension plan, investments have been discouragingly low (Orszag and Rodriguez 2005). These results suggest a consistent pattern that is also observed in Table 10.1: lifetime rates of access to a pension plan are consistently lower among people of color. In 2004, 35% of blacks, 38% of non-Hispanic others, and 51% of Hispanics lacked lifetime access to a defined-benefit or defined-contribution plan. Other research indicates that both median and average amounts of pension savings are lower for Hispanics than for whites. The median investment is $0 for Hispanic households with an income of $50,000 or less (Orszag and Rodriguez 2005). For all households with income between $50,000 and $75,000, the average pension balance is $58,000, but the average is less than $23,000 among Hispanic households in that income range. Given the trends in employment, wages, and pension participation among nonwhites, it is not surprising that levels of economic insecurity are higher among older nonwhites than among their older white counterparts. Rates of poverty are significantly higher among older blacks and Hispanics (27.8% and 26.4%, respectively) than among whites (11.9%; Johnson, Haaga, and Simms 2011). Moreover, the poverty rate among unmarried older African American women (36% for those who are divorced or separated, 38% for those who are widowed, and 39% for those who never married) is higher than the rate among their married counterparts (14%).

Education

Some evidence suggests that education and pension access are linked. For example, estimates in Table 10.1 show that adults (aged 55–61 years) with lower levels of education have less lifetime pension access: in 1994, 18% of individuals with a college degree reported that they had no access to a pension program, but 58% of those with less than a high school education reported the same. The gap increased by 2004.

Household Income

Estimates from Irena Dushi and Howard Iams (2008) also indicate that household income is strongly associated with access to pensions (Table 10.1). For example, in 2004, 54% of low-income households (i.e., those in the lowest income quintile) reported no access to a pension plan, but 17% of households in the highest quintile reported this.

Health Benefits

Health benefits are a type of employer-sponsored asset because they offer employees a pool of financial resources for managing health care costs. Similar to pensions, employer-sponsored health benefits are eroding, and employers are expected to discontinue certain types of benefits, such as retiree health benefits, in the near future (Fronstin 2000). Paul Fronstin (2000) and others (Helman, Copeland, and VanDerhei 2009) find that most private employees in the United States will never have access to retiree health insurance. Fronstin also notes that employer subsidies will diminish and eligibility criteria will be difficult to meet if a plan is offered.

■ EXTENDING WORK INTO LATER LIFE: CHALLENGES AND OPPORTUNITIES

As noted above, a lack of assets for later life can force older adults to extend their working years by remaining in the labor force beyond the conventional point of retirement or by returning to the labor force after retirement (Choi 2000; Gonzales 2013; Ozawa and Lum 2005). The need and motivation to extend the work life may be especially high among vulnerable populations. Some research suggests that prolonging employment may have multiple positive results (including economic and health benefits) for individuals, communities, and society (Hinterlong, Morrow-Howell, and Sherraden 2001; Munnell and Sass 2008; Rowe and Kahn 1998). Unfortunately, scant research examines the outcomes of retirees who return to work (i.e., unretirement or bridge employment). Although returning to work may provide financial benefits, it is less clear how economic disparities affect decisions to continue work or return to it. The literature is mixed on paid-work and health outcomes in later life (Herzog and House 1991; Herzog et al. 1998). Few of those studies are longitudinal (Calvo 2006; Glass et al. 1999; Luoh and Herzog 2002). Thus, future research should consider the ways in which extending work affects retirement wealth, health, skills, and knowledge.

Unfortunately, not all older adults can remain in or return to the labor force. The discussion that follows focuses specifically on three potential barriers to paid work in later life: a mismatch of skills and talents with employment opportunities, age discrimination at work, and the need to provide care for a family member.

Job Demands and Older Adults

The demands of employment and particular jobs can affect workplace performance as well as the ability of older adults to extend their working years. Some research ties job demands to levels of human capital. In a 2002 survey of workers aged 55–60 years, 28% of those with less than a college education reported that their jobs require "lots of physical effort all or almost all of the time" (Johnson 2004, 53). This differs significantly from the percentages among those with some college (17%) and those with 4 or more years of college (8%). Research also suggests that job demands vary by race and ethnicity. One study indicates that people of color who are aged 50 years and older are more likely to have low-skilled and physically demanding jobs than are whites of the same age group (Johnson et al. 2011).

Many nonwhites with low education do not possess the human capital (i.e., knowledge and skills) needed to escape jobs with a high risk of injury. Additionally, older Hispanic immigrants with high levels of education may be underutilized in the labor force if they are not proficient in English; the level of language proficiency can mitigate a person's ability to secure high-status jobs (AARP 2009; Capps et al. 2003; Chiswick and Miller 2009; Pransky et al. 2002).

Technology is also relevant in the discussion of job demands faced by older workers, as research suggests that some have difficulty keeping up with job-related developments. The percentage of older Hispanic workers (46%) who report that they have difficulty keeping up with job-related technology is greater than that of whites (25%) and blacks who report the same (33%; AARP 2009). In a study of 100 low-income adults, Laura Stanley (2003) identifies perceived fear, self-concept, and relevance as psychosocial barriers to utilization of technology among blacks and Latinos aged 18 years or older. If extending the working years is to be an antidote to retirement shortfalls, then there is a great urgency to identify ways to increase the human capital of older adults with low levels of such capital.

Age Discrimination in Employment

The full range of age discrimination and all of its manifestations have yet to be documented and addressed. The Age Discrimination in Employment Act protects individuals aged 40 years or older from employment discrimination based on age.[3] It also prohibits classic forms of age-based discrimination related to hiring, firing, promotion, layoff, compensation, benefits, job assignments, and training. The number of age discrimination charges increased consistently between 1997 and 2009 (U.S. Equal Employment Opportunity Commission 2014). There was a 30% increase in the number of age discrimination claims at the start of the economic recession in 2008, and receipts from such claims exceeded those from all other types of bias claims—including those related to race and sex. The dramatic increase in cases was so distressing that the acting chair of the U.S. Equal Opportunity Employment Commission, Stuart Ishimaru, questioned whether "the public generally realizes that age discrimination is illegal" (Vogel 2009, para. 4). We can also note from the commission's data that discrimination claims relate to many forms of vulnerable social identities, including age, sex, and race. Age discrimination claims, however, are unique. Since the U.S. Supreme Court ruling in *Gross v. FBL Financial Services* in 2009 (U.S. slip op. No. 08-441, June 18, 2009), claimants must make a case that age was the primary factor for discrimination (Phipps 2012). That is certainly difficult to prove, and the requirement blunts national legislation on a growing problem, making it practically ineffective.

Although classic and perhaps blatant forms of age discrimination will be hard to prove, the law also does not cover modern forms of age discrimination in the workplace, and research in this area is nascent. Lila Cortina (2008) has proposed considering incivility a form of modern discrimination. Noting that it is subtle and covert, she asserts that incivility is more insidious and chronic than overt and blatant forms of discrimination. Examples of modern discrimination include avoidance, sneers, jokes, hostile looks, and accusations of incompetence; the intent to harm is ambiguous, and perpetrators claim to be egalitarian. A new study examines overt and covert ageism among a nationally representative sample of older adults in the Health and Retirement Study (Marchiondo, Gonzales, and Williams 2014), finding that the experience of age discrimination at work negatively affects mental health. For example, reported levels of mental health (i.e., stress, anxiety, and depression) are worse for targets of age discrimination than for those not targeted. Reported intentions of turnover are higher, levels of job satisfaction are lower, and commitment to the workforce is weaker among victims than among nonvictims. Many victims suggest that they plan to retire earlier than do nonvictims. Taken together, these findings indicate that ageism is alive and well. It negatively affects people's health and attenuates attachment to the workforce.

Caregiving

The relationship between paid work and providing care for a family member is complex. Marcie Pitt-Catsouphes and Michael Smyer (2005) suggest that older workers remain in the labor force because paid work offers financial rewards that help provide for dependent family members. It is possible that, as the caregiving demands increase, the ability to continue in the workforce decreases, and this suggests a conflict of time and resources between the two roles. The time demands of providing care to a spouse or parent, particularly to those who need help with activities of daily living, often force older women to retire (Szinovacz, DeViney, and Davey 2001). Once retired, caregivers are significantly less likely to return to work (Gonzales 2013). Workplace policies and practices can help older workers to meet their economic and family needs. Flexible work options, as well as elder- and child-care coverage, are examples of such efforts. Women and families need these policies. Single women and their relatives are perhaps more vulnerable than are their married counterparts, and single women may have a greater need.

■ POLICY AND PRACTICE INTERVENTIONS FOR THE WORKPLACE

An aging society and workforce invite policy and practice interventions to strengthen financial capacity as well as access to meaningful and rewarding work. This section reviews current practices, but there have been few evaluations, and opportunity is ripe for research in this area.

Financial Education

Financial education is a critical component to planning and saving for retirement. Results from the 2004 Health and Retirement Study show that fewer than a third of households whose head is nearing retirement have planned for the next major life stage (Lusardi and Mitchell 2006), and only 2% of workers state that they are "very knowledgeable" about investing (Gross 2005, para. 9). Providing financial education within the workplace has the potential to reach 138 million Americans (President's Advisory Council on Financial Capability 2012a). Low financial wellness is associated with stress, diminished productivity, increased absenteeism, tardiness, turnover, conflict among workers, and alcohol consumption (Kim and Garman 2003; Kim, Sorhaindo, and Garman 2006). Studies show that workplace financial education increases participation rates and contributions into pension plans (Bernheim and Garrett 1996, 2003). Such effects may in turn address the negative outcomes associated with low financial wellness.

Financial education and strategies to increase saving can be tailored to the life stage of the employee. For example, Anya Olsen and Kevin Whitman (2007) suggest a path for employers in dealing with workers who are beginning their careers. They recommend that employers encourage enrollment in a retirement plan, guide employees to increase contribution rates as they advance in their careers, and lead the workers to choose investment allocations designed to produce yields over a long time horizon. As employees age into their careers and lives, the focus of financial education and savings can shift to strengthen the "goodness-of-fit" to closely match the financial needs of the individual, investment allocations, method of distribution, and type of annuities.

Sources of information may play an important role in financial education, particularly for vulnerable populations, because they may not have reliable sources outside of the workplace (Olsen and Whitman 2007). Prohibitive fees and language barriers are also impediments to the use of formal advice (Olsen and Whitman 2007). Research suggests that these populations prefer to learn in groups, such as in a formal course or informal seminar (Burhouse, Gambrell, and Harris 2004). Pension participation is 12 percentage points higher among low-paid workers who attend seminars than among those who receive no counseling, and seminar learning is associated with a significant increase in contribution rates (Bayer, Bernheim, and Scholz 1996, 2009). This led Olsen and Whitman (2007) to suggest that providing frequent investment advice (particularly via seminars) and printed brochures may be the most successful way to increase participation and contribution rates.

The creation of the President's Advisory Council on Financial Capability in 2010 may help to expand financial education within the workplace, and efforts should be made to ensure that the council is successful, particularly in expanding financial education for vulnerable populations. In addition, the president has announced that he will create MyRA, a "simple, safe and affordable 'starter' retirement savings account that will be offered through employers and will ultimately help millions of Americans begin to save for retirement" (White House 2014, para. 1). Although this initiative is a step in the right direction, some features should be addressed. First, MyRA holds after-tax investments, which may not build assets as effectively as would pretax investments. Second, the MyRA has no matching component, and some research suggests that matching is an important inducement to continued investment (see below). Finally, investment returns are modest and may prove to be disincentives to saving (Bernard 2014). The plan and resulting evaluations warrant close attention.

Financial Capacity: Designing Savings Products to Maximize Participation, Investments, and Payouts with Vulnerable Populations in Mind

Enrollment

Scholarship on designing savings products, particularly pensions, has grown in recent years (Olsen and Whitman 2007).[4] This research has informed public and private entities on ways to increase pension participation and investment. For example, evidence suggests the benefits of switching from a program that requires participants to opt in (i.e., default is nonparticipation) to one that features automatic enrollment, and one study finds that the switch increases participation by 26 percentage points (Madrian and Shea 2001). Unfortunately, some evidence suggests that not all outcomes are positive if automatic enrollment is a default feature. Brigitte Madrian and Dennis Shea (2001) find that automatic enrollment is associated with an increased likelihood that participants will choose the default contribution rate, which does not yield an adequate postretirement income. An alternative to the choice between opt-in and automatic enrollment options is an active decision-making plan (Carroll et al. 2009). The active decision-making plan avoids the "paternalism" (2009, 17) and the low contribution rate of the automatic enrollment feature but is time consuming for potential participants, and it is unclear whether all participants are sufficiently knowledgeable to make important decisions. Given the research that women, blacks, Hispanics, and people with low levels of education are more challenged by investment concepts than are other groups (Lusardi and Mitchell 2011), the active decision-making plan may prove to be especially daunting. Research is needed to determine how the opt-in, automatic enrollment, and active decision-making plans, respectively, affect vulnerable populations when financial education is part of each plan's structure.

Investment

Once enrolled in a plan, employees must decide how to invest their money. Given the pay disparity between men and women in the same occupation (Miller 2014), investing into a pension plan poses a more serious financial challenge for women than it does for men. Income inequality exists between whites and people of color (Gordon 2012). Data from the Federal Reserve Board's triennial Survey of Consumer Finances show a consistent pattern over the past few decades: whites gain more income than do people of color. Thus, it becomes important to address these pay disparities, as they affect the resources available for women and people of color to invest in their futures. Another major concern is finding a plan that achieves the right balance of stock options (see Olsen and Whitman 2007; Sethi-Iyengar, Huberman, and Jiang 2004).

The Match

Some retirement programs combine employees' savings with matching contributions from their employer, but the prevalence of such matching arrangements varies; about half of pensioners receive a match (Hewitt Associates 2009; WorldatWork and American Benefits Institute 2013). The employer's match is capped at a certain level and is based on the amount of money contributed by the employee. Findings are mixed on whether matching increases participation and contribution rates. Some research finds a strong, positive correlation (providing a match leads employees to invest), but Gary Engelhardt and Anil Kumar (2006) find that the matching mechanism has weak associations with participation and contributions. Others, such as James Choi and associates (2001), find that employees tailor their savings rate to the match threshold.

Distributions

The method by which investments and earnings are disbursed is an important and often overlooked part of accumulating assets for later life (Turner 2011). William Gale and Michael Dworsky (2006) find that 90% of workers who are aged 60–69 years and are withdrawing from employment do not annuitize their defined-contribution balances.[5] Research suggests that many workers fail to plan for the possibility of living longer than they expect to live (Helman et al. 2006), and employers persuade employees to take retirement benefits in a lump-sum payout. Such payments ultimately reduce the administrative cost and burden for employers (Turner 2011). The relationship between household income and reinvestment rates of lump-sum distributions is clear (Investment Company Institute 2000): households with income of $250,000 or more are nearly twice as likely as people with less than $10,000 to reinvest the lump-sum distribution. John Turner (2011) suggests that defined-contribution plans with lifetime annuitization provide a guaranteed floor of retirement income, and these arrangements are worth pursuing. He suggests encouraging employers and policymakers to make annuitization partially or fully mandatory if a 401(k) is the only plan offered (Turner 2011). Research is needed to examine how partially and fully mandatory annuitization policies would respectively affect vulnerable groups.

Encourage Age-Friendly Work Environments

Research documents the graying of today's workforce (Toossi 2009). That trend places particular pressure on employers to ensure that their work environments address age-related issues. For example, employers will need to continue to train older workers, to counter age discrimination, to provide flexibility for employees—particularly women—to care for family members, to modify the work environment to reduce physical demands, and to change the overall culture of workplaces to be age neutral or age friendly. Although many agree that these efforts are important (Community Links 2012; New York Academy of Medicine 2012; United Nations Economic Commission for Europe 2011; University of Washington 2014), interventions and evaluation research are needed to measure the effectiveness of such efforts and to discern best practices.

Training

There is a need to increase the human capital of older workers with low levels of education, as their jobs are often physically strenuous (Johnson 2004). Enhancing the knowledge and skills of these workers could enable them to secure jobs with manageable physical demands. On-the-job training, employer partnerships with community colleges, and the Senior Community Service Employment Program have proven effective at retraining workers and placing them in jobs. The U.S. Department of Labor (2010a, 2010b) has released two helpful guides on how to train low-income older workers. They may help prospective trainers to understand the characteristics of the population and, thus, the implications of those characteristics for training. The guides emphasize user-friendly computer training and the importance of training logistics but also recommend softer approaches such as fostering self-confidence and offering encouragement to set goals.

Counter Age Discrimination within the Workplace

Currently, it is difficult to identify the best policies and practices for countering age discrimination. Lars-Eric Petersen and Franciska Krings (2009) suggest that ethical codes of conduct are ineffective. David Neumark (2003, 2008) offers a similar assessment of age legislation in the United States. Theoretical frameworks, measurement tools, and outcomes are needed. Interventions and evaluation research should attempt to address the wide range of prejudicial acts in the workplace. The intersection of vulnerable identities (i.e., those defined by age, sex, race, and ability) also warrants scholarly and practice attention. Interventions may ultimately change the mindsets of supervisors and coworkers toward minority populations, altering institutional cultures in ways that promote inclusiveness, belonging, and civility.

Encourage Flexible Work Options

The tension between paid work and family obligations may intensify as an aging society forces working older adults to assume responsibility for the care of spouses, parents, and others. Employers who provide flexibility in the timing and location of work have seen multiple positive results for the organization and employees. These include reduced turnover intentions, increased employer commitment, increased job satisfaction (Allen 2001; Scandura and Lankau 1997), positive lifestyle behaviors (Grzywacz, Casey, and Jones 2007), and increased physical health (Butler et al. 2009). Research is needed to determine the impact of flexibility on mental health (Artazcoz et al. 2005). Unfortunately, flexible work options have declined since 2005 (Matos and Galinsky 2012).

Expand Compliance with the Family and Medical Leave Act of 1993

The Family and Medical Leave Act of 1993 permits employees who have worked a minimum of 1,250 hours during the preceding year to take at least 12 weeks of unpaid, job-guaranteed leave for specified purposes (Matos and Galinsky 2012; 26 U.S.C. § 2601 [2012]). The law allows an eligible worker to take leave for his or her serious medical condition and for that of a child or spouse. Kenneth Matos and Ellen Galinsky (2012) find that 26% of employers appeared to be out of compliance with the law in 2012, and that statistic has not changed since 2005. Eligible employees should be made aware of their rights and know how to contact the U.S. Department of Labor's Wage and Hour Division for assistance with noncompliant employers.

Expand Paid Leave for Family and Medical Reasons

Despite the protections of the law, families cannot afford to withdraw from work with unpaid leave. Some states have enacted *paid* family-leave policies, and these efforts can serve as models for policy in other states. The administration's 2013 and 2014 budgets for the U.S. Department of Labor proposed allocating $5 million to a State Paid Leave Fund, which would "provide technical assistance and support to states that are considering paid-leave programs" (Office of Management and Budget 2012, 147; 2014). Signaling commitment to this issue, the administration has proposed this budget for several years. Evaluations are needed to identify the policy's potential impact on families, employers, communities, and state budgets.

■ CONCLUSIONS

America's workers face multiple challenges: extended longevity, financial illiteracy, barriers to the use of savings vehicles, financial insecurity, pay inequity, shortfalls of retirement wealth, discrimination, caregiving responsibilities, and mismatch of jobs with capacity. Enhancing their financial capability, eliminating pay inequity and other forms of discrimination, and achieving family–work balance are ambitious undertakings. Research suggests that women, people of color, people with low levels of education, and those with poor health are important populations for interventions. Policies endorsed by the President's Advisory Council (2012b, 2013) and the White House (2012) may have positive impacts on millions of Americans. Policies that enable work–family balance are essential and should include flexible work options as well as efforts to bolster the Family and Medical Leave Act. We must augment legislation to address discrimination, but it is equally important to methodically dismantle stereotypes and structural prejudice within the workplace. Together, these solutions may help improve the prospects for those aging in America.

■ NOTES

Funding for this project was provided by the Center for Social Development at Washington University in St. Louis through a grant from the Atlantic Philanthropies.

1. For purposes of this chapter, I use the definition of "pensions" provided by Cushing-Daniels and Johnson (2008, 1): "Pension plans are benefits offered by many employers that provide workers with cash payments in retirement."

2. Although several published studies are reported, I draw particularly upon estimates by Dushi and Iams (2008) in this section, and am very indebted to their work.

3. Age Discrimination in Employment Act, 29 U.S.C. § 621 (2011).

4. Olsen and Whitman (2007) broadly describe the latest scholarship on savings products. I note their research with vulnerable populations as the central focus here.

5. Defined-contribution plans can be paid out in five basic ways: (1) a lump sum, (2) a life annuity, (3) a phased withdrawal (based on annual recalculation of life expectancy), (4) installment (term-certain payments), and (5) ad hoc withdrawals (Turner 2011).

▪ REFERENCES

AARP. 2009. *50+ Hispanic Workers: A Growing Segment of the U.S. Workforce.* Report, June. Washington, DC: AARP. http://assets.aarp.org/rgcenter/econ/hispanic_workers_09.pdf.

Administration on Aging. 2013. "Older Women." Fact Sheet. Last modified November 4. http://www.aoa.gov/naic/may2000/factsheets/olderwomen.html.

Allen, Tammy D. 2001. "Family-Supportive Work Environments: The Role of Organizational Perceptions." *Journal of Vocational Behavior* 58 (3): 414–435. doi: 10.1006/jvbe.2000.1774.

Artazcoz, Lucía, Joan Benach, Carme Borrell, and Imma Cortès. 2005. "Social Inequalities in the Impact of Flexible Employment on Different Domains of Psychosocial Health." *Journal of Epidemiology and Community Health* 59 (9): 761–767. doi: 10.1136/jech.2004.028704.

Barford, Anna, Danny Dorling, George Davey Smith, and Mary Shaw. 2006. "Life Expectancy: Women Now on Top Everywhere." *British Medical Journal* 332 (7545): 808. doi: 10.1136/bmj.332.7545.808.

Bayer, Patrick J., B. Douglas Bernheim, and John Karl Scholz. 1996. "The Effects of Financial Education in the Workplace: Evidence from a Survey of Employers." NBER Working Paper 5655. Cambridge, MA: National Bureau of Economic Research. http://www.nber.org/papers/w5655.

Bayer, Patrick J., B. Douglas Bernheim, and John Karl Scholz. 2009. "The Effects of Financial Education in the Workplace: Evidence from a Survey of Employers." *Economic Inquiry* 47 (4): 605–624. doi: 10.1111/j.1465-7295.2008.00156.x.

Bernard, Tara Siegel. 2014. "Obama Orders Creation of 'MyRA' Savings Accounts." *New York Times*, January 29. http://www.nytimes.com/2014/01/30/your-money/obama-orders-creation-of-myRA-accounts.html?_r=0.

Bernheim, B. Douglas, and Daniel M. Garrett. 1996. "The Determinants and Consequences of Financial Education in the Workplace: Evidence from a Survey of Households." NBER Working Paper 5667. Cambridge, MA: National Bureau of Economic Research. http://www.nber.org/papers/w5667.

Bernheim, B. Douglas, and Daniel M. Garrett. 2003. "The Effects of Financial Education in the Workplace: Evidence from a Survey of Households." *Journal of Public Economics* 87 (7–8): 1487–1519. doi: 10.1016/S0047-2727(01)00184-0.

Bureau of Labor Statistics. 2005. *National Compensation Survey: Employee Benefits in Private Industry in the United States, 2002–2003.* Bulletin 2573, January. Washington, DC: U.S. Department of Labor. http://www.bls.gov/ncs/ebs/sp/ebbl0020.pdf.

Burhouse, Susan, Donna Gambrell, and Angelisa Harris. 2004. "Delivery Systems for Financial Education in Theory and Practice." *FYI: An Update on Emerging Issues in Banking* (bulletin of the Federal Deposit Insurance Corporation), September 22. http://www.fdic.gov/bank/analytical/fyi/2004/092204fyi.html.

Burkhauser, Richard V., Karen C. Holden, and Daniel Feaster. 1988. "Incidence, Timing, and Events Associated with Poverty: A Dynamic View of Poverty in Retirement." *Journal of Gerontology: Social Sciences* 43 (2): S46–S52. doi: 10.1093/geronj/43.2.S46.

Butler, Adam B., Joseph G. Grzywacz, Susan L. Ettner, and B. Liu. 2009. "Workplace Flexibility, Self-Reported Health, and Health Care Utilization." *Work and Stress: An International Journal of Work, Health and Organisations* 23 (1): 45–59.

Butrica, Barbara A., and Richard W. Johnson. 2010. "Racial, Ethnic, and Gender Differentials in Employer-Sponsored Pensions." Washington, DC: Urban Institute. http://www.urban.org/UploadedPDF/901357-racial-ethnic-gender-differentials.pdf.

Calvo, Esteban. 2006. *Does Working Longer Make People Healthier and Happier?* Work Opportunities for Older Americans Issue Brief, Series 2, February. Chestnut Hill, MA: Center for Retirement Research at Boston College. http://crr.bc.edu/briefs /does-working-longer-make-people-healthier-and-happier/.

Capps, Randy, Michael Fix, Jeffrey S. Passel, Jason Ost, and Dan Perez-Lopez. 2003. *A Profile of the Low-Wage Immigrant Workforce.* Immigrant Families and Workers: Facts and Perspectives, Brief 4. Washington, DC: Urban Institute. http://www.urban.org /UploadedPDF/310880_lowwage_immig_wkfc.pdf.

Carroll, Gabriel D., James J. Choi, David Laibson, Brigitte C. Madrian, and Andrew Metrick. 2009. "Optimal Defaults and Active Decisions." *Quarterly Journal of Economics* 124 (4): 1639–1674. doi: 10.1162/qjec.2009.124.4.1639.

Chiswick, Barry R., and Paul W. Miller. 2009. "Educational Mismatch: Are High-Skilled Immigrants Really Working at High-Skilled Jobs and the Price They Pay If They Aren't?" IZA Discussion Paper 4280, July. Bonn, Germany: Institute for the Study of Labor. http://ftp.iza.org/dp4280.pdf.

Choi, James J., David Laibson, Brigitte C. Madrian, and Andrew Metrick. 2001. "For Better or for Worse: Default Effects and 401(k) Savings Behavior." NBER Working Paper 8651. Cambridge, MA: National Bureau of Economic Research. http://www .nber.org/papers/w8651.reftx.

Choi, Namkee G. 2000. "Determinants of Engagement in Paid Work following Social Security Benefit Receipt among Older Women." *Journal of Women and Aging* 12 (3–4): 133–154. doi: 10.1300/J074v12n03_09.

Community Links. 2012. *Age Friendly Workplaces in the Nonprofit Sector: Final Report.* Report, March. Halifax, Nova Scotia: Community Links. http://www.nscommunity links.ca/publications/AFW.pdf.

Cortina, Lila M. 2008. "Unseen Injustice: Incivility as Modern Discrimination in Organizations." *Academy of Management Review* 33 (1): 55–75. doi: 10.5465 /AMR.2008.27745097.

Cushing-Daniels, Brendan, and Richard W. Johnson. 2008. *Employer-Sponsored Pensions: A Primer.* Retirement Policy Project primer, January. Washington, DC: Urban Institute. http://www.urban.org/UploadedPDF/901144_employer-sponsored_ pensions.pdf.

Dushi, Irena, and Howard M. Iams. 2008. "Cohort Differences in Wealth and Pension Participation of Near-Retirees." *Social Security Bulletin* 68 (3): 45–66.

Engelhardt, Gary V., and Anil Kumar. 2006. "Employer Matching and 401(k) Saving: Evidence from the Health and Retirement Study." *Journal of Public Economics* 91(10): 1920–1943. doi: 10.1016/j.jpubeco.2007.02.009.

Fronstin, Paul. 2000. "The Erosion of Retiree Health Benefits and Retirement Behavior: Implications for the Disability Insurance Program." *Social Security Bulletin* 63 (4): 38–46.

Gale, William G., and Michael Dworsky. 2006. "Effects of Public Policies on the Disposition of Lump-Sum Distributions: Rational and Behavioral Influences." Working Paper 2006-15. Chestnut Hill, MA: Boston College, Center for Retirement Research. http://crr.bc.edu/wp-content/uploads/2006/08/wp_2006-151.pdf.

Glass, Thomas A., Carlos Mendes de Leon, Richard A. Marottoli, and Lisa F. Berkman. 1999. "Population Based Study of Social and Productive Activities as Predictors of Survival among Elderly Americans." *British Medical Journal* 319 (7208): 478–483. doi: 10.1136/bmj.319.7208.478.

Gonzales, Guillermo Ernest. 2013. "An Examination on Un-Retirement: Retirees Returning to Work." PhD dissertation, Washington University in St. Louis. http://openscholar-ship.wustl.edu/etd/1132/.

Gordon, Colin. 2012. "Racial Inequality." Inequality.org. Accessed June 5, 2014. http://inequality.org/racial-inequality/.

Gross, Daniel. 2005. "911 for 401(k)s: Why We're So Incredibly Stupid about Retirement Investing." *Slate*, March 1. http://www.slate.com/articles/business/moneybox/2005/03/911_for_401ks.html.

Grzywacz, Joseph G., Patrick R. Casey, and Fiona A. Jones. 2007. "The Effects of Workplace Flexibility on Health Behaviors: A Cross-Sectional and Longitudinal Analysis." *Journal of Occupational and Environmental Medicine* 49 (12): 1302–1309. doi: 10.1097/JOM.0b013e31815ae9bc.

Helman, Ruth, Craig Copeland, and Jack VanDerhei. 2006. *Will More of Us Be Working Forever? The 2006 Retirement Confidence Survey.* EBRI Issue Brief 292, April. Washington, DC: Employee Benefit Research Institute. http://www.ebri.org/pdf/briefspdf/EBRI_IB_04-20061.pdf.

Helman, Ruth, Craig Copeland, and Jack VanDerhei. 2009. *The 2009 Retirement Confidence Survey: Economy Drives Confidence to Record Lows; Many Looking to Work Longer.* Issue Brief 328, April. Washington, DC: Employee Benefit Research Institute. http://www.ebri.org/pdf/briefspdf/EBRI_IB_4-2009_RCS2.pdf.

Herzog, A. Regula, and James S. House. 1991. "Productive Activities and Aging Well." *Generations* 15 (1): 49–54.

Herzog, A. Regula, Melissa M. Franks, Hazel R. Markus, and Diane Holmberg. 1998. "Activities and Well-Being in Older Age: Effects of Self-Concept and Educational Attainment." *Psychology and Aging* 13 (2): 179–185. doi: 10.1037/0882-7974.13.2.179.

Hewitt Associates. 2009. *Research Highlights: Trends and Experiences in 401(k) Plans.* Report. London: Aon Hewitt. http://www.aon.com/attachments/thought-leadership/Hewitt_Research_Trends_in_401k_Highlights.pdf.

Hinterlong, James, Nancy Morrow-Howell, and Michael Sherraden. 2001. "Productive Aging: Principles and Perspectives." In *Productive Aging: Concepts and Challenges,* edited by Nancy Morrow-Howell, James Hinterlong, and Michael Sherraden, 3–18. Baltimore, MD: Johns Hopkins University Press.

Hungerford, Thomas L. 2001. "The Economic Consequences of Widowhood on Elderly Women in the United States and Germany." *Gerontologist* 41 (1): 103–110. doi: 10.1093 /geront/41.1.103.

Institute for Women's Policy Research. 2014. "About Pay Equity and Discrimination." Accessed June 5. http://www.iwpr.org/initiatives/pay-equity-and-discrimination.

Investment Company Institute. 2000. *Defined Contribution Plan Distribution Choices at Retirement. A Survey of Employees Retiring between 1995 and 2000.* Investment Company Institute Research Series Report, Fall. Washington, DC: Investment Company Institute. http://www.ici.org/pdf/rpt_distribution_choices.pdf.

Johnson, Richard W. 2004. "Trends in Job Demands among Older Workers, 1992–2002." *Monthly Labor Review* 127 (7): 48–56. http://www.bls.gov/opub/mlr/2004/07 /art4full.pdf.

Johnson, Richard W., Owen Haaga, and Margaret Simms. 2011. *50+ African American Workers: A Status Report, Implications, and Recommendations.* Report, February. Washington, DC: AARP. http://assets.aarp.org/rgcenter/econ/aa-workers-11.pdf.

Joint Committee on Taxation. 2005. *Present Law and Background Relating to Employer-Sponsored Defined Benefit Pension Plans and the Pension Benefit Guaranty Corporation.* Brief (JCX-03-05, February 28) for the Senate Committee on Finance. Washington, DC: Joint Committee on Taxation. http://www.finance.senate.gov/imo /media/doc/x-3-052.pdf.

Kim, Jinhee, and Thomas E. Garman. 2003. "Financial Stress and Absenteeism: An Empirically, Derived Model." *Financial Counseling and Planning* 14 (1): 31–42.

Kim, Jinhee, Benoit Sorhaindo, and E. Thomas Garman. 2006. "Relationship between Financial Stress and Workplace Absenteeism of Credit Counseling Clients." *Journal of Family and Economic Issues* 27 (3): 458–478. doi: 10.1007/s10834-006-9024-9.

Luoh, Ming-Ching, and A. Regula Herzog. 2002. "Individual Consequences of Volunteer and Paid Work in Old Age: Health and Mortality." *Journal of Health and Social Behavior* 43 (4): 490–509. doi: 10.2307/3090239.

Lusardi, Annamaria, and Olivia S. Mitchell. 2006. "Financial Literacy and Planning: Implications for Retirement Wellbeing." Working paper, October. Hanover, NH: Dartmouth College. http://www.dartmouth.edu/~alusardi/Papers/Financial Literacy.pdf.

Lusardi, Annamaria, and Olivia S. Mitchell. 2011. "Financial Literacy and Planning: Implications for Retirement Well-Being." In *Financial Literacy: Implications for Retirement Security and the Financial Marketplace,* edited by Olivia S. Mitchell and Annamaria Lusardi, 17–39. New York: Oxford University Press.

Madrian, Brigitte C., and Dennis F. Shea. 2001. "The Power of Suggestion: Inertia in 401(k) Participation and Savings Behavior." *Quarterly Journal of Economics* 116 (4): 1149–1187. doi: 10.1162/003355301753265543.

Marchiondo, Lisa, Ernest Gonzales, and Larry J. Williams. 2014. "Older Age Discrimination at Work: Long-Term Relationships with Occupational and Mental Well-Being." Working paper. Detroit, MI: Wayne State University.

Matos, Kenneth, and Ellen Galinsky. 2012. *2012 National Study of Employers.* Report. New York: Families and Work Institute. http://familiesandwork.org/site/research /reports/NSE_2012_.pdf.

Miller, Claire Cain. 2014. "Pay Gap Is Because of Gender, Not Jobs." *New York Times*, April 23. http://www.nytimes.com/2014/04/24/upshot/the-pay-gap-is-because-of -gender-not-jobs.html?_r=0.

Munnell, Alicia H., and Steven A. Sass. 2008. *Working Longer: The Solution to the Retirement Income Challenge.* Washington, DC: Brookings Institution Press.

Neumark, David. 2003. "Age Discrimination Legislation in the United States." *Contemporary Economic Policy* 21 (3): 297–317. doi: 10.1093/cep/byg012.

Neumark, David. 2008. *Reassessing the Age Discrimination in Employment Act.* Research Report 2008-09, June. Washington, DC: AARP Public Policy Institute. http://www .socsci.uci.edu/~dneumark/2008_09_adea.pdf.

New York Academy of Medicine. 2012. "NYAM Gets $595K Sloan Grant for Age-Friendly Workplace." News Release, July 16. http://www.nyam.org/news/nyam-in-the-media /2012/2012-07-16.html.

Office of Management and Budget. 2012. "Department of Labor." In *Budget of the U.S. Government: Fiscal Year 2013*, 143–149. Washington, DC: U.S. Government Printing Office. http://www.whitehouse.gov/sites/default/files/omb/budget/fy2013/assets /labor.pdf.

Office of Management and Budget. 2014. *Employment and Training Administration. State Paid Leave Fund.* Fiscal Year 2014 Congressional Budget Justification. Washington, DC: Office of Management and Budget. http://www.dol.gov/dol/budget/2014/PDF /CBJ-2014-V1-14.pdf.

Olsen, Anya, and Kevin Whitman. 2007. "Effective Retirement Savings Programs: Design Features and Financial Education." *Social Security Bulletin* 67 (3): 53–72. https://www .socialsecurity.gov/policy/docs/ssb/v67n3/v67n3p53.pdf.

Orszag, Peter R., and Eric Rodriguez. 2005. *Retirement Security for Latinos: Bolstering Coverage, Savings and Adequacy.* Research Report 2005-7. Washington, DC: Retirement Security Project. http://www.nclr.org/index.php/publications/retirement _security_for_latinos_bolstering_coverage_savings_and_adequacy/.

Ozawa, Martha N., and Terry Y. Lum. 2005. "Men Who Work at Age 70 or Older." *Journal of Gerontological Social Work* 45 (4): 41–63. doi: 10.1300/J083v45n04_04.

Petersen, Lars-Eric, and Franciska Krings. 2009. "Are Ethical Codes of Conduct Toothless Tigers for Dealing with Employment Discrimination?" *Journal of Business Ethics* 85 (4): 501–514. doi: 10.1007/s10551-008-9785-1.

Phipps, Jennie L. 2012. "Age Discrimination Tough to Prove." Bankrate.com, October 9. http://www.bankrate.com/finance/jobs-careers/age-discrimination-tough-prove-1 .aspx.

Pitt-Catsouphes, Marcie, and Michael A. Smyer. 2005. *Older Workers: What Keeps Them Working?* Issue Brief 01, July 18. Chestnut Hill, MA: Boston College, Center on Aging and Work. https://www.bc.edu/content/dam/files/research_sites/agingandwork/pdf /publications/IB01_OlderWrkrs.pdf.

Pransky, Glenn, Daniel Moshenberg, Katy Benjamin, Silvia Portillo, Jeffrey Lee Thackrey, and Carolyn Hill-Fotouhi. 2002. "Occupational Risks and Injuries in Non-Agricultural Immigrant Latino Workers." *American Journal of Industrial Medicine* 42 (2): 117–123. doi: 10.1002/ajim.10092.

President's Advisory Council on Financial Capability, Partnerships Committee. 2012a. *Financial Capability at Work: A Strategic Framework for Employers.* September 4. Washington, DC: President's Advisory Council on Financial Capability. http://assets

.newamerica.net/sites/newamerica.net/files/profiles/attachments/PACFC%20
Financial%20Capability%20at%20Work_%20Framework_090412.pdf.

President's Advisory Council on Financial Capability, Partnerships Committee. 2012b.
"Workplace Financial Capability Framework—Summary of Comments." Report,
November 13. Washington, DC: U.S. Department of the Treasury. http://www
.treasury.gov/resource-center/financial-education/Documents/PACFC%20
Financial%20Capability%20at%20Work.pdf.

President's Advisory Council on Financial Capability, Partnerships Committee.
2013. *Final Report.* January 29. Washington, DC: President's Advisory Council on
Financial Capability. http://www.treasury.gov/resource-center/financial-education
/Documents/PACFC%20final%20report%20revised%2022513%20(8)_R.pdf.

Rowe, John W., and Robert L. Kahn. 1998. *Successful Aging.* New York: Pantheon.

Scandura, Terri A., and Melenie J. Lankau. 1997. "Relationships of Gender, Family
Responsibility and Flexible Work Hours to Organizational Commitment and Job
Satisfaction." *Journal of Organizational Behavior* 18 (4): 377–391. doi: 10.1002/(SICI)
1099-1379(199707)18:4%3C377::AID-JOB807%3E3.0.CO;2-1.

Sethi-Iyengar, Sheena, Gur Huberman, and Wei Jiang. 2004. "How Much Choice Is
Too Much? Contributions to 401(k) Retirement Plans." In *Pension Design and
Structure: New Lessons from Behavioral Finance,* edited by Olivia S. Mitchell and
Stephen P. Utkus, 83–95. New York: Oxford University Press.

Social Security Administration. 2014. *Social Security Is Important to Women.* Fact Sheet,
March. Baltimore, MD: Social Security Administration Press Office. http://www.ssa
.gov/pressoffice/factsheets/women-alt.pdf.

Stanley, Laura D. 2003. "Beyond Access: Psychosocial Barriers to Computer Literacy."
In "ICTs and Community Networking," edited by Murali Venkatesh, special issue.
Information Society 19 (5): 407–416. doi: 10.1080/715720560.

Szinovacz, Maximiliane E., Stanley DeViney, and Adam Davey. 2001. "Influences of
Family Obligations and Relationships on Retirement: Variations by Gender, Race,
and Marital Status." *Journal of Gerontology: Social Sciences* 56 (1): S20–S27. doi: 10.1093
/geronb/56.1.S20.

Toossi, Mitra. 2009. "Labor Force Projections to 2018: Older Workers Staying More
Active." *Monthly Labor Review* 132, no. 11 (November): 30–51. http://www.bls.gov
/opub/mlr/2009/11/mlr200911.pdf.

Turner, John A. 2011. *Longevity Policy: Facing up to Longevity Issues Affecting Social Security,
Pensions, and Older Workers.* Kalamazoo, MI: Upjohn Institute for Employment
Research.

United Nations Economic Commission for Europe. 2011. *Age-Friendly Employment:
Policies and Practices.* Policy Brief on Ageing 9, January. Geneva, Switzerland: United
Nations Economic Commission for Europe. http://www.unece.org/fileadmin/DAM
/pau/_docs/age/2011/Policy-briefs/9-Policy-Brief-Age-Friendly-Employment.pdf.

University of Washington. 2014. "Designing the Age Friendly Workplace." Accessed
January 23. http://www.agefriendlyworkplace.org/index.html.

U.S. Department of Labor, Employee Benefits Security Administration. 2011. "Women
and Retirement Savings." Accessed March 17, 2011. http://www.dol.gov/ebsa
/publications/women.html.

U.S. Department of Labor, Employment and Training Administration. 2010a. "Unique
Training Requirements of Low-Income, Older Workers. A Resource Guide for

SCSEP Practitioners." Senior Community Service Employment Program publication. Last modified January 7. http://www.doleta.gov/seniors/html_docs/docs/unique1.cfm.

U.S. Department of Labor, Employment and Training Administration. 2010b. "Different Needs, Different Strategies: A Manual for Training Low-Income, Older Workers." Senior Community Service Employment Program publication. Last modified January 7. http://www.doleta.gov/seniors/html_docs/docs/dnds.cfm.

U.S. Equal Employment Opportunity Commission. 2014. "Age Discrimination in Employment Act (Includes Concurrent Charges with Title VII, ADA and EPA) FY 1997–FY 2013." Accessed March 22. http://www.eeoc.gov/eeoc/statistics/enforcement/ adea.cfm.

Vogel, Steve. 2009. "EEOC Examines Age Discrimination as Numbers of Claims Rise." *Washington Post*, July 16. http://www.washingtonpost.com/wp-dyn/content/article/2009/07/15/AR2009071503760.html.

White House. 2012. *Every American Financially Empowered: A Guide to Increasing Financial Capability among Students, Workers, and Residents in Communities.* Report, May. Washington, DC: White House. http://www.whitehouse.gov/sites/default/files/financial_capability_toolkit_5.10.2012.pdf.

White House, Office of the Press Secretary. 2014. *Opportunity for All: Securing a Dignified Retirement for All Americans.* Fact Sheet, January 29. Washington, DC: White House. http://www.whitehouse.gov/the-press-office/2014/01/29/fact-sheet-opportunity-all-securing-dignified-retirement-all-americans.

WorldatWork and the American Benefits Institute. 2013. *Trends in 401(k) Plans and Retirement Rewards.* Report. Scottsdale, AZ: WorldatWork. http://www.worldatwork.org/waw/adimLink?id=71489.

11 Age-Friendly Banking: Policy, Products, and Services for Financial Capability

■ SEHAR N. SIDDIQI, ROBERT O. ZDENEK, AND EDWARD J. GORMAN III

▓ WHY AGE-FRIENDLY BANKING?

On January 4, 2012, President Barack Obama paid a visit to the home of William and Endia Eason to raise awareness of fraudulent lending practices victimizing older adults. In 2003, a mortgage broker came to the Easons' front door and offered them an $8,000 home loan to repair their garage and steps, which the city deemed to be in violation of the Cleveland Municipal Housing Code. Before taking on the loan, the Easons owned their home of 41 years (Galbincea 2012; Obama 2012). Over the course of a year, the broker flipped the Easons' loan three times, eventually creating a balance of almost $80,000. Their modest retirement income made it impossible to repay the debt.

Unfortunately, the Easons are not the only older adults who have fallen victim to financial abuse and predatory lending practices that take advantage of their age, finances, and diminishing capacities.[1] Moreover, changing economic circumstances, exacerbated by the Great Recession, have left too many unable to rely on traditional retirement resources, such as savings and pensions.

A growing number of older adults face these challenges. Some 35 million older adults live in the United States today, and projections indicate that there will be 79 million of them—one-fifth of the U.S. population—by 2040 (Administration on Aging 2012). Older adults are living longer, and adults over age 85 years comprise the fastest-growing segment of the older population (Dalrymple 2005). To live healthy and independent lives in the decades to come, older adults need age-friendly financial products and services and protection from financial fraud and abuse.

The National Community Reinvestment Coalition (NCRC) developed the concept of *Age-Friendly Banking* to draw attention to the importance of providing effective financial products, services, and protections for older adults. The Age-Friendly Banking approach and framework evolved through research informed by insights from a wide array of financial institution professionals, federal and state regulators, community-based practitioners, and aging experts.

195

■ METHODS

In August 2012, NCRC embarked on an exploratory study to determine the age friendliness of banking and financial institutions. Three main research questions were posed: What services, products, and protections are offered by banks and financial institutions and cater to older adults aged 55 years and up? What elements comprise Age-Friendly Banking? And how can low- and moderate-income older adults benefit from age-friendly products, services, and protections?

The NCRC conducted a survey on the campaigns, programs, and financial products offered by large financial institutions and focused on low- to moderate-income older adults (adults over the age of 55 years). The survey was designed to assess whether these institutions have a specific well-developed strategy for working with older adult customers. The participants, members of NCRC's Bankers' Community Collaborative Council, represent 14 of the largest financial institutions in the United States and 33,585 bank branches nationwide.

The survey consisted of two parts: (1) NCRC submitted a questionnaire to community investment officers at 14 of the largest financial institutions in the United States to determine the extent of their work with older adults, and (2) NCRC conducted an exploratory interview concerning the institution's focus on older adult customers. In addition, NCRC conducted a review of the most recent Community Reinvestment Act disclosure reports and financial products offered on each institution's website.

The NCRC's goal in this survey was to determine the existence of, not the benefits or problems associated with, (1) older adult–focused basic banking products, including checking accounts, savings accounts, and debit cards; (2) support for older adult–focused services and housing; (3) acknowledgment of unique older adult needs in creating physical accessibility to the financial institution, its products, and its services; (4) development of financial education specifically for older adults; and (5) reverse mortgage lending.

■ RESULTS AND ANALYSIS

Of the 14 institutions (the population) that were sent the survey and interview requests, NCRC received feedback from seven. Three financial institutions expressed interest but were unable to provide timely information. The remaining four financial institutions provided no response. From the responses collected, the NCRC determined that, despite a growing older adult population, none of the 14 surveyed institutions developed a specific, well-crafted strategy or campaign that catered to older adult customers. An analysis of Community Reinvestment Act disclosure reports indicates that 13 institutions reported lending money for community investments that specifically support senior housing. The levels of investment are substantial, with millions of dollars in financing being provided to builders of low- to moderate-income elderly housing, home modifications, and senior centers. In many cases, the financial institutions act as Low Income Housing Tax Credit investors, and at least some of the created housing is set aside for low-income older adults. All 14 banks engage in community investment lending. With respect to basic banking products, five major financial institutions offer a checking or savings account that they market as a "senior" account. Chase Bank offers a low-fee debit card that is designed to be accessible to low- to moderate-income consumers. None of the 14 financial institutions offers reverse mortgages, which enable older homeowners to withdraw equity from their home.

Questions on the physical accessibility of bank branches produced little response. Thirteen of the surveyed banks have geographically diverse branches. Some are stand-alone branches and some are integrated into other buildings or entities (such as grocery stores). Each financial institution follows the Americans with Disabilities Act requirements for each state in which it has bank branches, but not one institution has a specific set of guidelines that focus on older adult needs and are used in developing physical banking configurations.

Each institution supports the financial education of consumers. However, the public websites and our survey and analysis indicate that few financial institutions have developed a specific financial education curriculum directed toward older adults.

Although this exploratory study included limited data, the NCRC analyzed the results by identifying patterns, ideas, and concepts that framed the definition of Age-Friendly Banking. The NCRC also conducted an environmental scan of the economic issues facing older adults as well as an investigation of financial policies, strategies, products, and services that could be developed to benefit older adults. In addition, the NCRC conducted informal interviews with financial security experts in the field of aging, federal banking regulators, and financial service networks. It also conducted a roundtable exercise and follow-up interviews to assess economic security issues with 10 National Neighbors Silver community-based grantee partners, tapping their expertise in economic security through the National Neighbors Silver initiative, which focuses on older adults and economic security.

■ ECONOMIC VULNERABILITY

Economic and Demographic Context

The economic uncertainty faced by older adults has been fueled by a number of demographic and economic changes. The recession of 2007–2009 had many negative effects on this population, and the ramifications continue. Their assets have declined in value, and the housing crisis obliterated decades of home equity. Home equity is the largest asset for baby boomers (Taylor et al. 2011) and is a traditional repository of wealth for retirees, but home values have declined precisely when this burgeoning population needs that wealth most. Although the percentage of adults aged 50 years or older who own their home outright declined between 2000 and 2009, there was growth over the same period in the percentage of homeowners who spend 30% or more of their income on housing (Harrell and Guzman 2013). In recent years, 45% of older adult households spent nearly a third of their income on housing (Meschede, Shapiro, and Wheary 2009). In fact, older adults represent the fastest growing percentage of homeowners in foreclosure (Trawinski 2012).

Older adults past their prime working years are unable to recoup assets lost since the start of the Great Recession. Those seeking new work may face age discrimination and may lack the mobility to find opportunities outside of their communities (Rampell 2013). As income and asset values have declined, older adults have applied for Social Security early, and those who are ineligible look to other sources of governmental support such as disability payments (Rampell 2013).

Other threats give older adults reason to fear for their economic security (Hayutin 2012). Nearly 75% of older adult households would not be able to handle the financial repercussions of a traumatic life event such as a sudden hospitalization or home repair emergency (Meschede, Sullivan, and Shapiro 2011). As they age, some 60% of older women are unable to cover basic living expenses (Administration on Aging 2012; Wider Opportunities for Women 2012).[2]

The risk of economic insecurity is higher for older women than for older men. The population of older women is larger (by 5.5 million in 2011; Administration on Aging 2012), and they are especially reliant on income from Social Security. The benefits make up a larger portion of retirement income for older women than for older men (McGhee and Draut 2004). Moreover, the income and pension benefits of women are generally lower (Women's Institute for a Secure Retirement 2014). Women often provide care for children or another family member and therefore are more likely to have worked part time or to have interrupted work histories. Thus, their pensions and savings are generally smaller (MetLife Mature Market Institute 2011b). Women are also statistically more likely to spend their retirement years alone, subsisting only on their own retirement income (MetLife Mature Market Institute 2011b). Additionally, the poverty rate is higher among older women—almost double that among older men in 2011 (McDonnell 2010).

The risk of economic insecurity is also high for older minorities, who face differing financial obstacles and economic issues. Racial and ethnic minorities make up 20% of the older adult population, and the older minority population is growing rapidly (Administration on Aging 2012; Gerontological Society of America 1991). The two largest groups are African American and Hispanic older adults.[3] Compared with nonminorities, both groups fare poorly on a range of economic indicators. Older African Americans have had less access to education and jobs than have older nonminorities. Many of the jobs available to them have lacked the pensions and other asset-building benefits enjoyed by nonminorities (Dumez and Derbew 2011). So too, Hispanics are more likely to work in low-wage jobs, such as those in the restaurant industry or farming, that offer no retirement plan (Miranda 2010). Thus, rates of poverty are higher among older adults in both groups than among older whites: 6.7% of older whites live in poverty, but 17.3% of older African Americans and 18.7% of older Hispanics live at or below the federal poverty line (Administration on Aging 2012).

Older immigrants face the same banking and financial issues confronted by all older adults, but they also encounter problems that often affect immigrant populations. In 2010, for instance, over half of older immigrants were not proficient in English. This represents an increase from 2000, when 41% of older immigrants were not proficient (Batalova 2012). Immigrants with limited English proficiency are less likely than English-proficient counterparts to use mainstream financial institutions for their banking needs. They rely more on payday lenders and other potentially predatory financial service providers (U.S. Government Accountability Office 2010).

Comprising about 12% of the immigrant population in the United States and 12% of the nation's older adult population, the older immigrant population is projected to grow over time (Batalova 2012). Compared with native-born older adults, older immigrants are more likely to live in low-income families and are less likely to receive income from assets and savings. They have lower income and depend more on supports such as Supplemental Security Income (Batalova 2012). Undocumented immigrants generally face difficulties in opening bank accounts and accessing other basic banking services (Bellamy 2007). The intersection of age and immigration status presents issues that financial institutions cannot ignore as the immigrant older adult population increases.

Policy Context

The traditional three-legged stool, a model of retirement that includes assets, pensions, and Social Security, is increasingly dated and no longer fits the circumstances of most older adults (Mermin, Zedlewski, and Toohey 2008). Older adults' income from pensions and personal assets has dropped over time, and the changes have forced an increased reliance on Social Security.[4] In 2010, Social Security benefits accounted for 37% of the average income for older adults (Administration on Aging 2012), and the share of income from Social Security is predicted to grow over time (Butrica, Cashin, and Uccello 2005–2006).[5] Although 86% of older adults received Social Security income in 2010, much smaller percentages received income from assets, pensions, annuities, and earnings (Administration on Aging 2012). Less than a third of adults over age 60 years receive defined-benefit pension income from a former employer, and the proportion will decline as such plans give way to 401(k)s, which are favored by most employers (Porell and Oakley 2012). Many who are still working fear that they will need to postpone retirement in order to maintain a certain standard of living (Ellis 2012). Adults between the ages of

50 and 64 years have especially bleak views of their retirement futures (Cohn and Taylor 2010). They are within a few years of retirement and lost substantial retirement savings in the recent recession (Morin and Taylor 2009).

Federal and state income supports are financial lifelines for a growing number of older adults (Sherman, Greenstein, and Ruffing 2012). Roughly 8.9% of them live in poverty (Cawthorne 2010), but 45.2% would live below the federal poverty line without the income provided by Social Security (Van de Water and Sherman 2010). Nearly three million older adults receive Supplemental Nutrition Assistance Program benefits. By making food affordable, the benefits help vulnerable older adults prevent illness, manage chronic diseases, and thereby reduce health care costs (National Council on Aging 2012). Help received through the Low Income Home Energy Assistance Program often determines whether low-income older adults keep the heat on during winter months (Stouwe 2011). Benefits from Social Security Disability Insurance support older workers suffering from illness or disability, and the average age of recipients is 53 years. About 30% of them are over age 60 years (National Academy of Social Insurance 2014). The poorest older adults rely on additional support from Supplemental Security Income and the associated state supplements. State supplements enable older adults to meet long-term care expenses such as the costs of caregiver support and assisted living (Robert Wood Johnson Foundation 2011; Social Security Administration 2014).

Fraud, Abuse, and Older Adults

The research by NCRC also finds that elder financial fraud is rampant. Financial fraud poses a substantial threat to the economic security of older adults. In 2009, financial fraud cost the American public $40 billion. A growing number of those victims are over age 55 years (McCallion, Ferretti, and Park 2013), and one in five older adults has been a victim of a financial scam (Infogroup/ORC 2010). Another study finds that losses from financial fraud cost older adults $2.9 billion in 2010 (MetLife Mature Market Institute 2011a). A major issue is the worry that most elder financial fraud is never reported. A 2011 study comparing the actual and reported incidence of elder abuse in New York found that the actual incidence is 24 times greater for adults over age 60 years and that financial exploitation is the most prevalent type of mistreatment (Lifespan of Greater Rochester, Weill Cornell Medical Center of Cornell, and New York City Department for the Aging 2011). Older women, particularly those between the ages of 70 and 89 years, are at the highest risk for financial abuse (Hounsell 2009).

Scammers frequently take advantage of older adults seeking help and advice. These scams involve so-called experts and professionals trusted to handle home repairs, finances, and other major needs when the older adult lacks the requisite knowledge or ability (McCallion et al. 2013). Complaints about home improvement scams are particularly common (Consumer Federation of America and North American Consumer Protection Investigators 2012). Many perpetrators identify targets through senior centers and similar community spaces that cater to older adults (Hounsell 2009). The National Council on Aging (2014c) maintains a list of the 10 most common scams targeting older adults; health care fraud and counterfeit prescription drug sales top the list. Scams related to prepaid cards are also increasingly common. Some scammers divert directly deposited Social Security benefits, obtaining the necessary information through fake lottery and sweepstakes schemes (Associated Press 2012). This variety of scam is especially threatening because, as of March 1, 2013, most federal benefits are transferred electronically.[6] The documented types of fraud and abuse cover an incredible array of scenarios, including fake lotteries, unnecessary home repairs, and identity theft (Templeton and Kirkman 2007). Results from the research by NCRC indicate that few financial institutions train staff, including branch employees, to detect credit card fraud and abuse as well as other suspicious financial activities and patterns.

The NCRC research also shows that there is state-by-state variation in the rules that require banks to report financial fraud and abuse of older adults. Many states offer little protection for older adult customers, but legislators are becoming aware of the problem. As of 2012, nine states require banks to report possible instances of elder fraud and abuse; legislation is pending in many others (Cottle 2012; Morton 2013).

Older Adults Are Unbanked

Another major economic challenge facing older adults is that 19% of them are unbanked or underbanked (authors' calculation from Federal Deposit Insurance Corporation 2012, 15, Table 4.1). Many of these older adults engage in nontraditional financial transactions. Almost 25% of Social Security recipients have taken out a payday loan (Borné et al. 2011), and most who do so use it to cover normal monthly expenses (Pew Charitable Trusts 2012a). In the United States, $10.9 billion is spent annually on nontraditional transactions (Jacob 2006). Older adults would benefit more from this money if it were held in an interest-bearing account or other well-developed and secure financial products. Secure financial products will help older adults avoid the high fees associated with alternative financial services. Older adults often use nonbank institutions because these institutions provide quick access to cash and often require little paperwork. The institutions also offer additional services such as money transfers, electronic tax filing, photocopying, and access to fax machines (Kim 2001). These simple offerings and longer hours draw older adults away from established financial institutions, depriving both the consumers and financial institutions of a mutually beneficial relationship.

Older adults' perceptions pose additional obstacles to financial inclusion. A recent study on unbanked and underbanked older adults finds that many would prefer to borrow money from a respected financial institution, such as a bank or credit union, rather than from friends or family members; however, fears keep them from feeling comfortable with major financial institutions (Jackson et al. 2010). A common worry is that their finances are too limited to make a bank account useful. Hidden fees and charges are also major concerns. Many accounts are simply too expensive and require an excessively high minimum balance (Jackson et al. 2010). Fees on accounts with balances under $1,500 can be as high as $300 per year (Fox, Brobeck, and Naron 2012). Some unbanked older adults fear that financial institutions share information with creditors or that an account will make them ineligible for government benefits. Undocumented older adults fear that banks will reveal their immigration status (Caskey 2005). Older adults, including minorities with limited English proficiency, are less likely than other groups to have a bank account (Federal Deposit Insurance Corporation 2009). This can exacerbate the marginalization of these groups.

■ AGE-FRIENDLY BANKING PRINCIPLES

In response to its findings, NCRC proposes six principles of Age-Friendly Banking. These principles can serve as a framework for collaborations among the federal government, state governments, networks of experts on aging, community organizations, and the financial industry:

1. Protect older adults from financial abuse.
2. Customize financial products and services for older adults.
3. Improve accessibility to bank locations and services.
4. Access critical income supports.
5. Facilitate aging in the community.
6. Expand financial education and capabilities.

The principles can be implemented to improve the financial well-being of older adults without unduly burdening any stakeholder. We detail each principle below.

Protect Older Adults from Financial Abuse

The Role of Regulators in Reducing Scams

Federal regulators must articulate a clear set of national standards for financial institutions to follow in responding to fraud and abuse cases involving older adults. Some efforts represent a sound foundation that can and should be expanded. A major focus of the Consumer Financial Protection Bureau's Office on Older Americans has been identifying and preventing financial abuse and fraud targeting older adults (Humphrey 2011). The bureau pursues a two-pronged attack: it coordinates consumer protection activities with other federal agencies and state regulators, and it works in the community to educate organizations and individuals who deal with older adults on this important issue.[7] The national Do Not Call Registry allows consumers to opt out of receiving telemarketing calls; the registry may protect older adults and others from exploitive financial offers (McCallion et al. 2013). Although these are positive steps, the Consumer Financial Protection Bureau and other regulators must go further. They must require financial institutions to collect data on cases in which older adults are victims of financial fraud and abuse. They also must clearly outline the steps that financial-service employees should take if they suspect that an older adult is being financially exploited. Regulators should strongly encourage the training of tellers and customer representatives to detect fraud and empower them to correct the fraud.

The Role of Banks in Reducing Scams

Noting that staff in financial institutions have limited awareness of elder financial abuse and that not all staff have been trained in identifying and reporting it, a recent report by the U.S. Government Accountability Office (2012) indicates that these are the main challenges in responding to elder financial abuse. The report cites the observation of state and local officials that "banks are important partners in combating elder financial exploitation because they are well positioned to recognize, report, and provide evidence in these cases" (U.S. Government Accountability Office 2012, 31). An increasing number of financial institutions are reporting cases of financial exploitation, but there is still a significant need to provide training for bank tellers and to report suspicious financial activities to law enforcement. Improving education on recognizing and intervening in fraudulent situations can help financial institutions better protect at-risk older adults. Institutions should leverage available state-level resources such as those offered through state Adult Protective Services. State agencies can provide training materials on how to recognize and combat elder financial exploitation. They can also provide bank customers and employees with guidance in such matters (National Center on Elder Abuse 2014).

Some financial institutions are making strides in addressing fraud and abuse of older adults. Bank of the West, in partnership with the Elder Financial Protection Network, created the Be Aware program. A collaboration among community partners and local law enforcement officials, the network offers seminars designed to educate older adults, their families, and caregivers on how to recognize and prevent such abuse. The seminars discuss identity theft, check scams, and other relevant forms of financial fraud (Financial Services Roundtable 2014). Voluntary programs such as Be Aware demonstrate the ability of financial institutions to handle cases in which older adults are targeted, but given the prevalence of abuse in the United States, voluntary programs are not enough.

Customize Financial Products and Services for Older Adults

Banking Products and Services for Older Adults

Access to effective financial products and services can provide older adults with the basic tools to manage their lives effectively on a limited budget. Currently, financial institutions offer a limited selection of products for older adults at all income levels. The most common is the so-called senior account, which tends to involve a complex set of fees, requirements, and benefits. Some have higher monthly fees than those for basic checking accounts from the same institution (Sullivan 2012). Institutions waive monthly senior account fees only for older adults who maintain high minimum balances. These accounts are thus useful to banks because the accounts hold high balances or bring in high fees (Pew Charitable Trusts 2012b). Meanwhile, a recent study on the overall costs and fee structures of senior accounts finds that older adults would benefit from a simple, transparent, low-cost, low-fee account (Pew Charitable Trusts 2012b).

Such an account is the goal of New York's 1994 basic banking law, which requires banks in the state to offer simple, low-cost products.[8] An assessment of the law's effectiveness finds that these basic accounts can be nine times less expensive than prepaid cards and check cashing services (NYPIRG [New York Public Interest Group] 2003). Any account designed for older adults should include certain features that limit fees, which can disproportionately harm older adults on a limited income. Such accounts should have no minimum-balance requirement, no fee for limited activity, and no buried check fee (e.g., a fee for use of direct deposit). Institutions could supplement these accounts with other financial services, such as complimentary checks, discounted safe-deposit boxes, and multiple free withdrawal transactions.

Retirement Plans and Other Financial Planning Products

To further meet the financial needs of this population, financial institutions can offer retirement and financial management guidance for all older adults regardless of income and assets. Defined-benefit plans, individual retirement accounts, reduced-rate life insurance plans, and other retirement-income programs could help older adults increase their retirement wealth. Institutions could also train financial advisors to handle questions related to older adults' economic needs. Trained advisors should be available at branches or through a free, easy-to-use, customer-service phone line.

Improve Accessibility to Bank Locations and Services

Bank Branches

An NCRC study of branch banking from 2007 to 2010 finds that bank and credit union branches increased by 1,000 in middle- and upper-income neighborhoods while declining by 530 in low- and moderate-income areas (Silver and Pradhan 2012). The reduction of full-service bank branches can have a negative impact on older adults. Physical access and services from a financial institution can improve the economic security of older adults. Accessibility is an integral part of the Age-Friendly Environments Programme, an effort by the World Health Organization to help cities and communities address the social and environmental needs of older adults. The organization offers specific recommendations for adequate public seating and bathroom access as well as for features such as ramps, railings, and nonslip floors. It also suggests that ATMs should make use of large buttons and lettering (World Health Organization 2007).

Online Development

Online banking has worked for millions of Americans but not for those older adults who do not use or understand electronic technology. Seventy percent of older adults use the Internet on a daily basis, yet half of adults over the age of 65 years do not use it as part of their daily life (Zickuhr and Madden 2012). The lower rates of Internet usage among older adults can partially be attributed to lack of access and training. The RISE (Responsibility, Initiative, Solutions, Empowerment) Foundation, a National Neighbors Silver partner in Memphis, Tennessee, reports that the older adults it works with find electronic banking and mandatory electronic statements to be cost prohibitive. These older adults generally come from nonaffluent backgrounds and have limited formal education. Very few own or use computers.[9] Although some financial institutions provide financial education materials on their websites, a number of older adults do not access the sites.

In-branch computer terminals and ready-to-assist branch personnel could increase online banking among older adults, and these investments have minimal costs. In addition, websites can be designed in age-friendly ways. The National Institute on Aging (2009) has developed easy-to-follow guidelines for age-friendly websites; a simple format, large font, plain language, and the ability to hear text aloud make sites accessible. Accessibility is the first step in increasing Internet usage among older adults.

Access Critical Income Supports

One of the core goals of Age-Friendly Banking is to assist low- and moderate-income older adults in identifying new sources of income, including income supports. Banks can assist low- and moderate-income customers with benefit checkups through branch offices or by partnering with agencies that have expertise in benefit screening and enrollment. Local branches can use the National Council on Aging's BenefitsCheckUp tool and similar products to help consumers identify programs for which they are eligible.[10] Banks should help facilitate enrollment, since some low-income older adults are eligible for up to $7,000 in public and private benefits (Alwin 2013). Facilitating enrollment in benefit programs involves a minimal time commitment for financial institutions and can lead to significant returns for older adults as well as for the financial institutions, which will be managing more money.

Tax credits and deductions are also important supports for older adults. The Internal Revenue Service (2014) offers free tax preparation services through the Volunteer Income Tax Assistance program, and the AARP Foundation provides similar services through its Tax-Aide Program.[11] Financial institutions can help older adults access diverse supports. The Internal Revenue Service has also developed a split-refund product for Earned Income Tax Credit recipients. Refunds disbursed through direct deposit can be split between two accounts, with one portion going into a checking account and the other into a savings account.

Facilitate Aging in the Community

Age-Friendly Housing

Allowing older adults to age in their own communities can lead to positive economic, health, and quality-of-life outcomes. Financial institutions play a major role in developing proactive strategies for aging in the community. Many older adults want to continue living in their homes as they age, but aging housing structures require age-related modifications. Examples of such modifications include widening doorways and installing no-step entrances (Salomon 2010). Modifications can extend the duration of older adults' independence, preventing or delaying the costs associated with assisted living and other institutional options.

Furthermore, remaining at home helps to improve overall health (Unwin et al. 2009). Federal and state programs (e.g., those funded by Community Development Block Grants and the U.S. Department of Agriculture) provide important supports for aging in place. Eighty-nine percent of funding for home modifications comes from occupants; public and private sources provide the remaining 20% (Fagan 2007). Many low- and moderate-income older adults need to improve their home's accessibility features but do not meet the eligibility criteria for assistance programs and lack the funds to make the improvements themselves. Small-dollar loans can enable them to make modifications so that they can age in place. Many financial institutions, including Community Development Financial Institutions, already offer such loans. With additional funding from the Community Development Financial Institution Fund and financial institutions, it would be possible to expand the volume of small-dollar home improvement loans.

Reverse Mortgages and Other Ways to Use Home Equity

The reverse mortgage is a financing tool that allows older adults to access the equity in their homes and therefore to remain in their homes (LaBounty 2012). If used well, reverse mortgages enable homeowners to meet household expenses, cover health care needs, or even move to a new home with better accessibility features (Guttentag 2012). The U.S. Department of Housing and Urban Development requires reverse-mortgage program applicants aged 62 years or older to participate in housing counseling before receiving a Home Equity Conversion Mortgage. A 2010 survey of participants found that two-thirds of those counseled chose the reverse-mortgage option in order to reduce household debt (National Council on Aging and MetLife Mature Market Institute 2012).

Notwithstanding changes made by the Federal Housing Administration in 2012 (Galante 2012), the Home Equity Conversion Mortgage product may be viable for many older adults, but applicants should be aware of the associated risks. Following the recession and housing market crash of 2007–2008, the two largest reverse-mortgage lenders pulled out of the reverse-mortgage market, reducing the options for older adults who wish to age in place (Kawamoto 2011). These lenders determined that the time, effort, and cost of reverse-mortgage lending exceeded the potential gains (Finkle and Berry 2011; Silver-Greenberg 2012). Noting that reverse mortgages can be beneficial to certain older adults, research suggests that success depends upon well-developed housing counseling and guidance from a reverse-mortgage counselor (National Council on Aging and MetLife Mature Market Institute 2012).

Home Equity Line of Credit

A line of credit on a home equity loan is another potential tool for meeting short-term needs if the credit is structured with reasonable fees (National Council on Aging 2014a; Pond 2010). Unscrupulous lending practices involving loan flipping and hidden fees have recently raised concern with the product, and it is thus essential for older adults to be well informed about the risks and benefits of home equity lines of credit (Federal Trade Commission 2012). Equity sharing is another way to tap into home equity. A new and innovative idea, equity sharing is essentially a private reverse-mortgage arrangement in which an adult child acts as the lender. The older parent receives a stream of income from his or her child, who gains an ownership interest in the parent's home (Greene 2012). All of these devices to tap into home equity allow older homeowners to leverage their largest asset while remaining in their house. To make the best decision possible, any major financial decision involving a home should be made with guidance from certified housing counselors.

Importance of Housing Counseling

The median net worth of older adults in the United States is roughly $170,000, and the owned home represents the largest asset for many older adults. Almost 80% of older adults own their own home (Fry et al. 2011). Given the home's importance as a retirement asset, financial institutions should offer housing counseling to older adults, and the counseling should be certified by the U.S. Department of Housing and Urban Development. Financial counseling can help older adults to access home equity through the tools discussed above and can help those who wish to downsize or move into rental housing. The effectiveness of housing counseling in preventing delinquencies and foreclosures is well documented (Williams 2011).

Expand Financial Education and Capabilities

Financial education is a cornerstone of effective financial management and an important component of any effort to protect older adults from financial difficulty. Even affluent older adults express the desire for financial guidance and education in debt management. They indicate an interest in financial seminars relevant to their particular life stage, literature on making good financial decisions, and access to financial counselors for financial guidance (Bank of America 2011). Financial institutions can utilize effective financial education programs such as Money Smart for Older Adults, a curriculum created by the Federal Deposit Insurance Corporation and the Consumer Financial Protection Bureau (Federal Deposit Insurance Corporation 2014).

Many older adults are unaware of financial education programs. Financial institutions should therefore offer and market education programs geared toward the financial circumstances of these adults or partner with organizations that offer such programs. Financial institutions are ideally situated to host education seminars through their branches and online services. These training sessions can also be held at senior centers, community centers, and other locations where older adults congregate.

Several organizations have developed financial education programs specifically tailored to older adults. Through the Savvy Saving Seniors program for struggling older adults, the National Council on Aging teaches basic money management tips and connects participants to a wide variety of support and benefit programs (National Council on Aging 2014b). The Institute for Financial Literacy's (2010) Project SCREEN (Senior Citizen and Retiree Empowerment

Education Network) provided financial literacy training for practitioners in the aging field and a financial literacy program for older adults.

■ CONCLUSIONS

Older adults face stark economic challenges. Savings, pensions, and real estate investments have rapidly declined. There is no question that a coordinated, large-scale response is needed from financial institutions, government regulators, community-based advocates, and the aging network. Economically vulnerable older adults deserve quality products and services from financial institutions, which have a responsibility and a distinct opportunity to better serve the nation's growing older adult population. Keeping older adults independent and healthy in their communities benefits everyone and saves federal, state, and local governments money.

Financial institution professionals and others understand the value of protecting and supporting older adults who have strengthened their families and country and who now deserve to age in place with dignity and financial security. Financial institutions can advance their own best interests and those of their customers by expanding Age-Friendly Banking products and services.

■ NOTES

The authors would like to thank the following NCRC staff colleagues: Karen Kali for her research and editing skills and Eric Hersey and Ryan Conley for their additional editorial support in adapting the original Age-Friendly Banking white paper to the Oxford University Press publication format. Additionally, the authors would like to express their appreciation for the technical expertise from the National Neighbors Silver grantee partners and over three dozen colleagues who generously shared their time and knowledge with the authors. These individuals are listed in the NCRC white paper *A New Dawn: Age-Friendly Banking*, published in 2013.

1. In this chapter, the term *older adult* refers to adults aged 65 years or older.

2. Basic expenses are determined by the U.S. Elder Economic Security Standard Index (Wider Opportunities for Women 2012).

3. African Americans comprise 9% of older adults, and older adults of Hispanic origin represent 7% of the population aged 65 years or older. In addition, 4% of older adults identify themselves as Asian or Pacific Islander, less than 1% identify themselves as American Indian or Native Alaskan, and 0.6% identify themselves as members of two or more races (Administration on Aging 2012).

4. McDonnell (2010) notes that in 2008, 55.3% of adults aged 65 years or older received income from assets, 35.4% received income from pensions and annuities, and 20.4% received income from earnings. See also Porell and Oakley (2012).

5. In 2010, pensions accounted for 18% of income, assets for 11%, and earnings for 30% (Administration on Aging 2012).

6. Management of Federal Agency Disbursements, 75 Fed. Reg. 80315 (2010); codified at Treas. Reg. § 208.3.

7. *America's Invisible Epidemic: Preventing Elder Financial Abuse. Hearing Before the Senate Special Committee on Aging*, 112th Cong., 2nd Sess. 6–7, 42–45 (2012) (statement of Hubert H. "Skip" Humphrey III, Assistant Director, Office for Older Americans, Consumer Financial Protection Bureau). http://www.gpo.gov/fdsys/pkg/CHRG-112shrg78020/pdf /CHRG-112shrg78020.pdf.

8. Under this law and the associated regulations, every bank in the state is required to provide an account that has (1) a minimum opening deposit of $25 dollars, (2) a 1¢ minimum balance, (3) a monthly fee of no more than $3 dollars, (4) eight free withdrawal transactions per month, and (5) no charge on deposits (N.Y. Banking Law § 14-f [Consol. 2013]; N.Y. Comp. Codes R. & Regs. tit. 3 § 9.3). Banks are permitted to deviate from these standards as long as their account offering is "at least as advantageous to consumers as the basic banking account" (§14-f).

9. National Neighbors Silver Age-Friendly Roundtable, RISE Foundation, Memphis, TN.

10. See http://www.benefitscheckup.org/.

11. http://www.aarp.org/money/taxes/aarp_taxaide/.

▪ REFERENCES

Administration on Aging. 2012. *A Profile of Older Americans: 2012*. Washington, DC: U.S. Department of Health and Human Services. http://www.aoa.gov/Aging_Statistics /Profile/2012/docs/2012profile.pdf.

Alwin, Ramsey. 2013. Presentation to the National Community Reinvestment Coalition, Washington, DC, March.

Associated Press. 2012. "New Scam Pilfers Social Security Checks at Banks." October 14.

Bank of America. 2011. "Merrill Lynch Affluent Insights Quarterly Survey Finds the Vast Majority of Baby Boomers Intend to Live a More Active Retirement Lifestyle Than Their Parents." News release, January 31. http://newsroom.bankofamerica .com/press-release/global-wealth-and-investment-management/merrill-lynch -affluent-insights-quarterly-su-0.

Batalova, Jeanne. 2012. "Senior Immigrants in the United States." *Migration Information Source* (Migration Policy Institute), May 30. http://www.migrationinformation.org /usfocus/display.cfm?ID=894.

Bellamy, Calvin E. 2007. *Serving the Under-Served: Banking for Undocumented Immigrants*. Perspectives on Immigration, March 1. Washington, DC: American Immigration Council, Immigration Policy Center. http://www.immigrationpolicy.org/perspec-tives/ serving-under-served-banking-undocumented-immigrants.

Borné, Rebecca, Joshua Frank, Peter Smith, and Ellen Schloemer. 2011. *Big Bank Payday Loans: High-Interest Loans through Checking Accounts Keep Customers in Long-Term Debt*. Report, July. Durham, NC: Center for Responsible Lending. http://www.respon-siblelending.org/payday-lending/research-analysis/big-bank-payday-loans.pdf.

Butrica, Barbara A., David B. Cashin, and Cori E. Uccello. 2005–2006. "Projections of Economic Well-Being for Social Security Beneficiaries in 2022 and 2062." *Social Security Bulletin* 66 (4): 2–19. http://www.ssa.gov/policy/docs/ssb/v66n4/v66n4p1.pdf.

Caskey, John P. 2005. "Fringe Banking and the Rise of Payday Lending." In *Credit Markets for the Poor*, edited by Patrick Bolton and Howard Rosenthal, 17–45. New York: Russell Sage.

Cawthorne, Alexandra. 2010. *The Not-So-Golden Years: Continuing Elderly Poverty and Improving Seniors' Economic Security*. Memo, September 27. Washington, DC: Center for American Progress. http://www.americanprogress.org/wp-content/uploads /issues/2010/09/pdf/not_so_golden_years.pdf.

Cohn, D'Vera, and Paul Taylor. 2010. *Baby Boomers Approach 65—Glumly*. Report, December 20. Washington, DC: Pew Research Center. http://www.pewsocialtrends .org/files/2010/12/Boomer-Summary-Report-FINAL.pdf.

Consumer Federation of America and North American Consumer Protection Investigators. 2012. *2011 Consumer Complaint Survey Report*. Washington, DC: Consumer Federation of America. http://www.consumerfed.org/pdfs/Studies .Top10ConsumerComplaintsSurvey7.31.12.pdf.

Cottle, Sara. 2012. "Controlling Financial Elder Abuse: Whose Responsibility Is It?" CUInsight.com, October 9. http://www.cuinsight.com/controlling-financial-elder -abuse-whose-responsibility-is-it.html.

Dalrymple, Elli. 2005. "Livable Communities and Aging in Place: Developing an Elder-Friendly Community." Aging in Place Initiative White Paper. Washington, DC: Partners for Livable Communities and National Association of Area Agencies on Aging. http://www.nw.org/network/comstrat/aginginplace/documents/Agingin PlaceWhitePaper_000.pdf.

Dumez, Jacob, and Henoch Derbew. 2011. *The Economic Crisis Facing Seniors of Color: Background and Policy Recommendations*. Report, August. Berkeley, CA: Greenlining Institute. http://greenlining.org/wp-content/uploads/2013/02 /TheEconomicCrisisFacingSeniorsofColor.pdf.

Ellis, Blake. 2012. "More Americans Delaying Retirement until Their 80s." *CNNMoney*, October 23. http://money.cnn.com/2012/10/23/retirement/delaying -retirement/?hpt=hp_t3.

Fagan, Lisa Ann. 2007. "Funding Sources for Home Modifications." *Special Interest Section Quarterly: Home and Community Health* (American Occupational Therapy Association) 14 (3): 1–3.

Federal Deposit Insurance Corporation. 2009. *FDIC National Survey of Unbanked and Underbanked Households*. Report, December. Washington, DC: Federal Deposit Insurance Corporation. http://www.fdic.gov/householdsurvey/2009/full_report .pdf.

Federal Deposit Insurance Corporation. 2012. *2011 FDIC National Survey of Unbanked and Underbanked Households*. Report, September. Washington, DC: Federal Deposit Insurance Corporation. http://www.fdic.gov/householdsurvey/2012_unbankedreport .pdf.

Federal Deposit Insurance Corporation. 2014. "Money Smart for Older Adults." Last updated June 20. http://www.fdic.gov/consumers/consumer/moneysmart/olderadult .html.

Federal Trade Commission. 2012. "Home Equity Loans and Credit Lines." Consumer Information article, August. http://www.consumer.ftc.gov/articles/0227-home-equity -loans-and-credit-lines.

Financial Services Roundtable. 2014. *Bank of the West Financial Elder Abuse Prevention Efforts*. Accessed March 12. http://www.fsround.org/fsr/pdfs/fin-lit-corner /BOTWsCommitmenttoPreventingFinancialElderAbuse20.pdf.

Finkle, Victoria, and Kate Berry. 2011. "Big Banks Flee Reverse Mortgages, Leaving Industry Void." *American Banker*, November 18. http://www.americanbanker.com

/issues/176_225/reverse-mortgages-wells-fargo-bank-of-america-metlife-1044227-1.html.

Fox, Jean Ann, Stephen Brobeck, and Sean Naron. 2012. *Consumer Federation of America Report: Can Consumers Avoid Checking Fees?* Report, October 16. Washington, DC: Consumer Federation of America. http://www.consumerfed.org/pdfs /CanConsumersAvoidCheckingFees10.16.12.pdf.

Fry, Richard, D'Vera Cohn, Gretchen Livingston, and Paul Taylor. 2011. *The Rising Age Gap in Economic Well-Being: The Old Prosper Relative to the Young.* Pew Social and Demographic Trends Report, November 7. Washington, DC: Pew Research Center. http://www.pewsocialtrends.org/files/2011/11/WealthReportFINAL.pdf.

Galante, Carol J. 2012. Carol J. Galante, Acting Assistant Secretary for Housing— Federal Housing Commissioner, to U.S. Senator Bob Corker, December 18. http://www.corker.senate.gov/public/_cache/files/940b16a2-a401-418f -b409-5dca6e176c42/12-18-12_Letter%20from_Carol_Galante.pdf.

Galbincea, Pat. 2012. "President Obama Visits Cleveland Home of William and Endia Eason, Walks away with Sweet Potato and Peach Pies." *Cleveland Plain Dealer*, January 4. http://www.cleveland.com/open/index.ssf/2012/01/president_obama _visits_clevela.html.

Gerontological Society of America. 1991. *Minority Elders: Longevity, Economics, and Health: Building a Public Policy Base.* Washington, DC: Gerontological Society of America.

Greene, Kelly. 2012. "Before You Get a Reverse Mortgage." *TotalReturn* (blog), *Wall Street Journal*, February 29. http://blogs.wsj.com/totalreturn/2012/02/29 /before-you-get-a-reverse-mortgage/.

Guttentag, Jack. 2012. "What's Right with Reverse Mortgages." *Knowledge@ WhartonToday*, October 22. https://knowledgetoday.wharton.upenn.edu/2012/10 /whats-right- with-reverse-mortgages/.

Harrell, Rodney, and Shannon G. Guzman. 2013. *The Loss of Housing Affordability Threatens Financial Stability for Older Middle-Class Adults.* Middle Class Security Project Report. Washington, DC: AARP Public Policy Institute. http://www.aarp.org /content/dam/aarp/research/public_policy_institute/security/2013/loss-of-housing- affordability-threatens-financial-stability-for-older-middle-class-AARP-ppi-sec.pdf.

Hayutin, Adele M. 2012. "Changing Demographic Realities." In *Independent for Life: Homes and Neighborhoods for an Aging America*, edited by Henry Cisneros, Margaret Dyer-Chamberlain, and Jane Hickie, 35–44. Austin: University of Texas Press.

Hounsell, Cindy. 2009. "Protecting Your Mother from Financial Fraud and Abuse." In *Elder Abuse: A Women's Issue*, 18–22. Mother's Day Report 2009. Washington, DC: OWL. http://www.owl-national.org/Mothers_Day_Reports_files/OWL_Mothers Day_Report_09_Final_2.pdf.

Humphrey, Hubert H. (Skip), III. 2011. "Many Voices: Older American Need to Be Armed against Financial Fraud." *Portland Press Herald*, December 10. http://www.pressherald.com/opinion/older-americans-need-to-be-armed -against-financial-fraud_2011-12-10.html.

Infogroup/ORC. 2010. *Elder Investment Fraud and Financial Exploitation: A Survey Conducted for Investor Protection Trust.* Report, June 15. Papillion, NE: Infogroup/ ORG. http://www.investorprotection.org/downloads/EIFFE_Survey_Report.pdf.

Institute for Financial Literacy. 2010. "Institute for Financial Literacy Launches Financial Education Program Designed for Senior Citizens." News release, February 23. https://financiallit.org/institute- for-financial-literacy-launches- financial-education -program- designed-for-senior-citizens/.

Internal Revenue Service. 2014. "Free Tax Return Preparation for You by Volunteers." Last modified January 29. http://www.irs.gov/Individuals/Free -Tax-Return-Preparation- for-You-by-Volunteers.

Jackson, Ann McLarty, Donna V. S. Ortega, Elizabeth Costle, George Gaberlavage, Naomi Karp, Neal Walters, and Vivian Vasallo. 2010. *A Portrait of Older Underbanked and Unbanked Consumers: Findings from a National Survey*. Report. Washington, DC: AARP Foundation and AARP Public Policy Institute. http://assets.aarp.org /rgcenter/ppi/ econ-sec/underbank-economic-full-092110.pdf.

Jacob, Katy. 2006. *Highlights from the Inaugural Underbanked Financial Services Forum*. Report, July. Chicago: Center for Financial Services Innovation. http://www.cfsin-novation.com/sites/default/files/ imported/managed_documents/highlights_under-banked_forum.pdf.

Kawamoto, Dawn. 2011. "As Banks Exit the Reverse Mortgage Business, Seniors Seek Alternatives." *DailyFinance*, June 22. http://www.dailyfinance.com/2011/06/22 /reverse-mortgage-seniors-alternatives-banks-loans/.

Kim, Anne. 2001. *Taking the Poor into Account*. Report, July. Washington, DC: Progressive Policy Institute.

LaBounty, John. 2012. *True Stories of Reverse Mortgages: Meeting Monthly Medical Bills*. Report, John LaBounty presentation to National Neighbors Silver grantee part-ners, October. Washington, DC: National Community Reinvestment Coalition for National Neighbors Silver.

Lifespan of Greater Rochester, Weill Cornell Medical Center of Cornell, and New York City Department for the Aging. 2011. *Under the Radar: New York State Elder Abuse. Prevalence Study*. Report, May. Rensselaer, NY: New York State Office of Children and Family Services. http://www.ocfs.state.ny.us/main/reports/Under%20the%20 Radar%2005%2012%2011%20final%20report.pdf.

McCallion, Phillip, Lisa A. Ferretti, and Jihyun Park. 2013. "Financial Issues and an Aging Population: Responding to an Increased Potential for Financial Abuse and Exploitation." In *Financial Capability and Asset Development: Research, Education, Policy, and Practice*, edited by Julie Birkenmaier, Margaret S. Sherraden, and Jami Curley, 129–155. New York: Oxford University Press.

McDonnell, Ken. 2010. "Income of the Elderly Population Age 65 and Over, 2008." *Notes* (Employee Benefit Research Institute) 31 (6): 2–7. http://www.ebri.org/pdf/notespdf /EBRI_Notes_06-June10.Inc-Eld.pdf.

McGhee, Heather C., and Tamara Draut. 2004. *Retiring in the Red: The Growth of Debt among Older Americans*. Borrowing to Make Ends Meet Demōs Briefing Paper 1, 2nd ed. New York: Demōs. http://www.demos.org/sites/default/files/publications /Retiring_2ed.pdf.

Mermin, Gordon B. T., Sheila R. Zedlewski, and Desmond J. Toohey. 2008. *Diversity in Retirement Wealth Accumulation*. Retirement Policy Program Brief 24, December. Washington, DC: Urban Institute. http://www.urban.org/UploadedPDF/411805 _retirement_wealth_accumulation.pdf.

Meschede, Tatjana, Thomas M. Shapiro, and Jennifer Wheary. 2009. *Living Longer on Less: The New Economic (In)Security of Seniors*. By a Thread Report 4, January 28. Waltham, MA: Brandeis University Institute on Assets and Social Policy, and Dēmos. http://iasp.brandeis.edu/pdfs/LLOL%20Report.pdf.

Meschede, Tatjana, Laura Sullivan, and Thomas Shapiro. 2011. *From Bad to Worse: Senior Economic Insecurity on the Rise*. Living Longer on Less Series Research and Policy Brief, July. Waltham, MA: Brandeis University, Institute on Assets and Social Policy, and Dēmos. http://iasp.brandeis.edu/pdfs/2011/Bad_to_Worse.pdf.

MetLife Mature Market Institute. 2011a. *The MetLife Study of Elder Financial Abuse: Crimes of Occasion, Desperation, and Predation against America's Elders*. Report, June. New York: MetLife Mature Market Institute. https://www.metlife.com/assets/cao/mmi/publications/studies/2011/mmi-elder-financial-abuse.pdf.

MetLife Mature Market Institute. 2011b. *The MetLife Study of Women, Retirement, and the Extra-Long Life: Implications for Planning*. Report, September. New York: MetLife Mature Market Institute. https://www.metlife.com/assets/cao/mmi/publications/studies/2011/mmi-women-retirement-extra-long-life.pdf.

Miranda, Leticia. 2010. "Improving Retirement Security for Latinos: Overview of Racial and Ethnic Disparities and Ideas for Improvement." Statement before the U.S. Department of Labor, Employee Benefits Security Administration Advisory Council on Employee Welfare and Pension Benefit Plans, September 1. U.S. Department of Labor. http://www.dol.gov/ebsa/pdf/LaRaza090110.pdf.

Morin, Rich, and Paul Taylor. 2009. *Oldest Are Most Sheltered: Different Age Groups, Different Recessions*. Social and Demographic Trends Project Report, May 14. New York: Pew Research Center. http://www.pewsocialtrends.org/files/2010/10/recession-and-older-americans.pdf.

Morton, Heather. 2013. "Financial Crimes against the Elderly 2012 Legislation." National Conference of State Legislatures. Last modified January 15. http://www.ncsl.org/issues-research/banking/financial-crimes-against-the-elderly-2012-legis.aspx.

National Academy of Social Insurance. 2014. "What Is Social Security Disability Insurance?" Accessed February 6. http://www.nasi.org/learn/socialsecurity/disability-insurance.

National Center on Elder Abuse. 2014. "Adult Protective Services." Accessed February 6. http://www.ncea.aoa.gov/Stop_Abuse/Partners/APS/index.aspx.

National Council on Aging. 2012. "Cuts to SNAP Food Program Would Be Devastating for Struggling Older Adults." Press release, July 10. http://www.ncoa.org/press-room/press-release/cuts-to-snap-food-program.html.

National Council on Aging. 2014a. "My Solution: Take out a Home Equity Loan." Accessed February 6. http://www.homeequityadvisor.org/My-Solutions/Take-Out-a-Home-Equity-Loan.

National Council on Aging. 2014b. "Savvy Saving Seniors." Accessed February 6. http://www.ncoa.org/enhance-economic-security/economic-security-Initiative/savvy-saving-seniors/.

National Council on Aging. 2014c. "Top 10 Scams Targeting Seniors." Accessed February 6. http://www.ncoa.org/enhance-economic-security/economic-security-Initiative/savvy-saving-seniors/top-10-scams-targeting.html.

National Council on Aging and MetLife Mature Market Institute. 2012. *Changing Attitudes, Changing Motives: The MetLife Study of How Aging Homeowners Use*

Reverse Mortgages. Report, March. New York: MetLife Mature Market Institute. https://www.metlife.com/assets/cao/mmi/publications/studies/2012/studies /mmi-changing-attitudes-changing-motives.pdf.

National Institute on Aging. 2009. *Making Your Website Senior Friendly.* Tip Sheet, March. http://www.nia.nih.gov/health/publication/making-your-website-senior-friendly.

NYPIRG (New York Public Interest Research Group). 2003. "Back to Basics: A Consumer Banking Report on the Importance of Basic Banking to Low-Income New Yorkers. " New York: NYPIRG. http://www.citylimits.org/images_pdfs/pdfs/NYPIRG_bank-ing.pdf.

Obama, Barack H. 2012. *Remarks in Cleveland, Ohio.* Daily Compilation of Presidential Documents, no. DCPD201200002, January 4. Washington, DC: National Archives and Records Administration, Office of the Federal Register. http://www.gpo.gov /fdsys/pkg/DCPD-201200002/pdf/DCPD-201200002.pdf.

Pew Charitable Trusts. 2012a. *Payday Lending in America: Who Borrows, Where They Borrow, and Why.* Payday Lending in America Series Report, July. Washington, DC: Pew Charitable Trusts. http://www.pewstates.org/uploadedFiles/PCS _Assets/2012/Pew_Payday_Lending_Report.pdf.

Pew Charitable Trusts. 2012b. *Senior Checking Accounts: Are They Worth It?* Safe Checking in the Electronic Age Issue Brief, August. Washington, DC: Pew Charitable Trusts. http://www.pewstates.org/uploadedFiles/PCS_Assets/2012/000_12_CHECK%20 Seniors%20Factsheet_v5.pdf.

Pond, Jonathan. 2010. "Reverse Mortgage Alternatives: Explore All of Your Options before Resorting to a Costly Reverse Mortgage." AARP.org, September 9. http://www.aarp .org/money/credit-loans-debt/info-09-2010/pond-alternatives-to-reverse-mortgages. html.

Porell, Frank, and Diane Oakley. 2012. *The Pension Factor 2012: The Role of Defined Benefit Pensions in Reducing Elder Economic Hardships.* Report, July. Washington, DC: National Institute on Retirement Security. http://www.nirsonline.org/storage /nirs/documents/Pension%20Factor%202012/pensionfactor2012_final.pdf.

Rampell, Catherine. 2013. "In Hard Economy for All Ages, Older Isn't Better…It's Brutal." *New York Times*, February 2. http://www.nytimes.com/2013/02/03 /business/americans-closest-to-retirement-were-hardest-hit-by-recession .html?pagewanted=2&_r=0&emc=etal.

Robert Wood Johnson Foundation. 2011. *Community Partnerships for Older Adults: An RWJF National Program.* Report, December 8. Princeton, NJ: Robert Wood Johnson Foundation. http://www.rwjf.org/content/dam/farm/reports /program_results_reports/2011/rwjf71882.

Salomon, Emily. 2010. *Home Modifications to Promote Independent Living.* Fact Sheet 168, March. AARP Public Policy Institute. http://www.aarp.org/content/dam/aarp /livable-communities/learn/housing/home-modifications-to-promote-independent -living-2010-aarp.pdf.

Sherman, Arloc, Robert Greenstein, and Kathy Ruffing. 2012. *Contrary to "Entitlement Society" Rhetoric, Over Nine-Tenths of Entitlement Benefits Go to Elderly, Disabled, or Working Households.* Report, February 10. Washington, DC: Center on Budget and Policy Priorities. http://www.cbpp.org/files/2-10-12pov.pdf.

Silver, Josh, and Archana Pradhan. 2012. *Why Branch Closures Are Bad for Communities.* Issue Brief, April. Washington, DC: National Community Reinvestment Coalition.

http://www.ncrc.org/images/stories/mediaCenter_reports/issuebrief_bank%20branches_april%202012.pdf.

Silver-Greenberg, Jessica. 2012. "A Risky Lifeline for the Elderly Is Costing Some Their Homes." *New York Times*, October 14. http://www.nytimes.com/2012/10/15/business/reverse-mortgages-costing-some-seniors-their-homes.html?pagewanted=all&_r=0.

Social Security Administration. 2014. Accessed February 6. http://www.ssa.gov/policy/index.html.

Stouwe, Paul Vande. 2011. "LIHEAP Funds Available, but the Clock Is Ticking." News release, November 7. Center for Advocacy for the Rights and Interests of the Elderly. http://www.carie.org/liheap-funds-available-but-the-clock-is-ticking/.

Sullivan, Bob. 2012. "Senior Discounts? With Some Checking Accounts, It's a Senior Penalty." *NBC News*, August 14. http://www.nbcnews.com/technology/senior-discounts-some-checking-accounts-its-senior-penalty-940837.

Taylor, Paul, Richard Fry, D'Vera Cohn, Gretchen Livingston, Rakesh Kochhar, Seth Motel, and Eileen Patten. 2011. *The Old Prosper Relative to the Young: The Rising Age Gap in Economic Well-Being*. Social and Demographic Trends Report, November 7. Washington, DC: Pew Research Center. http://www.pewsocialtrends.org/files/2011/11/WealthReportFINAL.pdf.

Templeton, Virginia H., and David N. Kirkman. 2007. "Fraud, Vulnerability, and Aging: Case Studies." *Alzheimer's Care Today* 8 (3): 265–277. doi: 10.1097/01.ALCAT.0000281875.55721.0f.

Trawinski, Lori A. 2012. *Nightmare on Main Street: Older Americans and the Mortgage Market Crisis*. Research Report. Washington, DC: AARP Public Policy Institute. http://www.aarp.org/content/dam/aarp/research/public_policy_institute/cons_prot/2012/nightmare-on-main-street-AARP-ppi-cons-prot.pdf.

Unwin, Brian K., Christopher M. Andrews, Patrick M. Andrews, and Janice L. Hanson. 2009. "Therapeutic Home Adaptations for Older Adults with Disabilities." *American Family Physician* 80 (9): 963–968.

U.S. Government Accountability Office. 2010. *Consumer Finance: Factors Affecting the Financial Literacy of Individuals with Limited English Proficiency*. Report GAO-10-518, May. http://www.gao.gov/new.items/d10518.pdf.

U.S. Government Accountability Office. 2012. *Elder Justice: National Strategy Needed to Effectively Combat Elder Financial Exploitation*. Report GAO-13-110, November. Washington, DC: U.S. Government Accountability Office. http://www.gao.gov/assets/660/650074.pdf.

Van de Water, Paul N., and Arloc Sherman. 2010. *Social Security Keeps 20 Million Americans out of Poverty: A State-by-State Analysis*. Report, August 11. Washington, DC: Center on Budget and Policy Priorities. http://www.cbpp.org/files/8-11-10socsec.pdf.

Wider Opportunities for Women. 2012. *Doing without: Economic Insecurity and Older Americans*. Doing Without series, Brief 2: Gender, March. Washington, DC: Wider Opportunities for Women. http://www.wowonline.org/documents/OlderAmericansGenderbriefFINAL.pdf.

Williams, Laura. 2011. *The Role of Housing Counseling in Reducing Mortgage Delinquency and Foreclosure*. Fact Sheet. National Housing Conference, Center for Housing Policy. http://www.nhc.org/media/files/Role_of_Housing_Counseling_in_Preventing_Foreclosure.pdf.

Women's Institute for a Secure Retirement. 2014. "Top Five Retirement Challenges for Women." Accessed February 6. http://www.wiserwomen.org/index.php?id =130&page=WISER%60s_Top_Five_Retirement_Challenges_for_Women.

World Health Organization. 2007. *Checklist of Essential Features of Age-Friendly Cities.* Report WHO/FCH/ALC/2007.1. Geneva: World Health Organization. http://www .who.int/ageing/publications/Age_friendly_cities_checklist.pdf.

Zickuhr, Kathryn, and Mary Madden. 2012. *Older Adults and Internet Use.* Internet and American Life Project Report, June 6. Washington, DC: Pew Research Center. http:// pewinternet.org/Reports/2012/Older-adults-and-internet-use.aspx.

■ Conclusion

Financial Capability in Later Life: Summary and Applications

■ NANCY MORROW-HOWELL,
MICHAEL SHERRADEN, AND
MARGARET S. SHERRADEN

We set out in this book to expand on three themes related to economic security in later life: the financial vulnerability of particular older adult populations, the importance of a life course perspective in understanding late life economic circumstances, and the potential to improve economic outcomes in later life by developing financial capability across the life course. In this final chapter, we summarize key points on life course issues that may contribute to late-life economic insecurity. We also offer recommendations suggested by authors to increase financial capability across the life course and improve financial security in old age. We conclude with examples of applied research designed for innovations in policy and practice.

■ VULNERABLE POPULATIONS AND LIFE COURSE ISSUES

The Social Security Act of 1935 has greatly reduced poverty in old age.[1] The current poverty rate among people over the age of 65 years is much lower than that among children (U.S. Department of Health and Human Services 2013), but not all older Americans are financially well off, and some face extreme financial hardship. Many more are financially vulnerable and live on the edge of poverty. They are only one medical event or other crisis away from destitution.

As discussed by many authors in this book, poverty rates are high among ethnic minority and immigrant older adults, those with a disability, and those in need of long-term care. Social Security is a godsend, enabling many older adults to survive just above the poverty line, but late life challenges expose them to the risk of falling into poverty (DeNavas-Walt, Proctor, and Smith 2011). As mentioned in the introduction, there are still "two nations in old age": the advantaged and the disadvantaged (Titmuss 1958, 166). The disadvantaged nation of old age is described in these chapters.

Common themes affect ethnic minority older adults. Compared with non-Hispanic whites, African Americans, Hispanics, and Native Americans

218

enter later life in worse financial circumstances. They have less income and less savings, they rely more heavily on Social Security, and they are more likely to live near or below the poverty line. As Trina R. Williams Shanks and Wilhelmina A. Leigh detail in Chapter 3, African Americans have less retirement savings than any other racial group. For example, half of all workers in America have at least $25,000 in retirement savings, but only 30% of African American workers have this amount (Helman, VanDerhei, and Copeland 2007). Retirement income is another indicator of security. Jacqueline L. Angel and Stipica Mudrazija observe in Chapter 4 that older Hispanics have the lowest levels of such income: a mean of $17,000 per year, compared with $22,000 among African Americans and $35,000 among whites. Hispanics rely more on Social Security, with 58% of the total income of older Mexican Americans coming from Social Security. In contrast, Social Security benefits provide 37% of the total income among non-Hispanic whites and 40% of the total among non-Hispanic African Americans. As Amanda Barusch, Molly Tovar, and Tracy Golden note in Chapter 5, Native American older adults are the most economically disadvantaged. Suzanne Macartney, Alemayehu Bishaw, and Kayla Fontenot (2013) document that poverty rates among American Indians, Alaska Natives, and African Americans are 10% higher than the national average; the rate among Native Americans is higher than that among African Americans.

Factors other than ethnicity heighten the risk faced by certain groups of older adults. In Chapter 6, Yunju Nam reports that, regardless of citizenship status, older adults who immigrate to the United States have less economic security in later life than their U.S.-born counterparts. Among immigrants, the highest risk for financial insecurity is faced by noncitizens, undocumented immigrants, those who came to the United States later in life, those with limited English proficiency, and those from non-European countries. Disability also exposes older adults to increased risk for economic insecurity. As Michelle Putnam describes, disabled individuals end up poor because, "simply put, disability is costly and financially disruptive" (120). She reports that the poverty rate for older adults with disabilities is twice as high as that for nondisabled counterparts. Finally, Jennifer C. Greenfield (Chapter 9) documents that the likelihood of living in poverty is high among individuals who need long-term care and among their caregivers.

Gender cuts a distinctive channel of poverty across all vulnerable groups. The older population is disproportionately composed of women because females outlive males by an average of 5 years (Jacobsen et al. 2011), and living longer increases the likelihood of outliving available resources. In addition, women make up a disproportionate share of the caregiving workforce, and the responsibilities of these caregivers vary: they may care for partners, disabled children, or grandchildren (National Alliance for Caregiving and AARP 2009). This care is typically uncompensated and creates a double economic strain: care of the vulnerable relative imposes expenses and limits the caregiver's opportunity to earn income. For all of these reasons, older women are poorer and sicker than are older men. Older women live longer but also experience higher levels of disability (Federal Interagency Forum on Aging-Related Statistics 2012). Several chapters document the gendered nature of late-life financial vulnerability.

Life course issues may lead to economic insecurity in later years. Contributing factors include low educational attainment, low-paying jobs that lack pension coverage, and poor health and intensive medical needs in later life. Four interrelated principles find expression in a life course understanding and are illustrated throughout the book. The principle of *timing*, or when an individual experiences a life event, is illustrated by Nam (Chapter 6). She shows that financial vulnerability is greater among immigrants who come to the United States later in their lives than among those who arrive earlier. Putnam (Chapter 7) demonstrates the connection between the onset of a disability before age 50 years and adverse financial outcomes later in life.

The principle of *historical time and place* alludes to opportunities and constraints in the cultural and historical conditions through which individuals live their lives. William R. Emmons and Bryan J. Noeth (Chapter 1) present convincing evidence of cohort effects; that is, the economic times we live through shape our financial futures, sometimes creating vulnerabilities that are not fully revealed until older age. These researchers demonstrate that the later life financial outcomes of Americans born in the 1950s, 1960s, and 1970s involve being poorer than those of counterparts born in the late 1930s and 1940s. These patterns are due to trends in the national economy and to shifts in the benefits offered by employers (pensions and health benefits). Similarly, Barusch, Tovar, and Golden review the history of trauma experienced by Native Americans, discussing how current cohorts of older Native Americans have been affected by "the legacy of stress, cultural bereavement, and racism" (88).

People's lives are embedded in social relations, and these interconnections form *linked lives*, the third life course principle. Experiences in families and communities influence circumstances, outlooks, and behaviors. Greenfield (Chapter 9) shows how caregivers who step out of the workforce to care for family members pay a price in old age; she demonstrates that their work histories and savings record put them at an economic disadvantage. In reviewing patterns of participation in employer-based savings plans, Ernest Gonzales (Chapter 10) points out that the later life economic outcomes of never-married and widowed women are worse than those of married counterparts, and he attributes their poorer outcomes in part to lower lifetime participation in pension plans.

The life course perspective also includes the principle of *individual agency*, which refers to individual choices and actions, for better or worse. Too often, individual agency is less than adequate when it comes to financial decision making and saving. For example, Gonzales points out that ethnic-minority workers and workers with low levels of education have limited access to employer-based savings plans. Moreover, such workers are less likely than others to participate if they have access and are less likely to make adequate contributions to ensure income in later life. Angel and Mudrazija discuss the stigmatized nature of the Supplemental Security Income program. That stigma discourages many Hispanic older adults from taking advantage of this income source.

Jin Huang and Greenfield (Chapter 8) approach the life course from a different perspective. They document how public policies support the life cycle hypothesis of saving, which posits that individuals build assets during their working years and then spend them down during retirement (Ando and Modigliani 1963). This perspective has influenced traditional notions of later life and retirement. Such notions steer policymakers toward supporting asset accumulation for young adults as well as toward management and gradual decumulation of assets held by older adults. For example, although no age criteria limit participation in asset-building programs supported by the Assets for Independence Act (42 U.S.C. § 604 [2012]), participation is restricted to low-income families with children. This restriction effectively limits the participation of older adults. Huang and Greenfield suggest that policies targeted at older adults tend to be traditional income-support and social service programs, such as those that provide nutrition and energy assistance. Asset-building policies therefore tend to be age regressive, even in the face of extended longevity among older adults.

■ STRATEGIES FOR INCREASING FINANCIAL CAPABILITY ACROSS THE LIFE COURSE

Overall, recommendations to improve the financial situation of people in later life may be summarized in four categories: build capacity at the individual and household level, build capacity at the institutional level, develop better public policies, and advance knowledge through research. Below, we highlight key strategies in each of these categories. All of the strategies emerge from the contributions to this book.

Build Financial Capability of Individuals and Households

Along with effective and inclusive financial policies and services, it is important to help individuals and families take full advantage of available resources. Strategies identified by contributors in this book include the following:

- Maximize the use of public benefits (e.g., those from Social Security, Medicare, and Medicaid) and private resources (e.g., social supports, home equity) in poor households.
- Incorporate financial education into the school curriculum at all levels from prekindergarten through postsecondary education, and incorporate it into the workplace as well.

- Provide education and so-called portfolio management assistance, including estate planning, to poor and vulnerable individuals and families.
- Provide financial planning, practical advice, and guidance as needed throughout the life cycle but especially at key financial decision-making moments, such as when people borrow for college and plan for retirement.
- Increase the awareness of predatory lending and identity theft, especially awareness among older Americans and family members.

Build Capacity of Financial Institutions

Humans—almost all of us—have difficulty with financial matters. We do not like to pay attention, we put off what we know we should do, and we spend money today that we know we will need later. It is abundantly clear at this point that financial services should become more inclusive of the whole population and, in many respects, more paternalistic (Sunstein and Thaler 2003). They should include automatic features, restrictions, and expectations that protect humans from our worst cognitive and behavioral deficiencies. Sehar N. Siddiqi, Robert O. Zdenek, and Edward J. Gorman III (Chapter 11) propose a wide range of "age-friendly" products and services. Some of these strategies include the following:

- Offering multiple safe and progressive options for individuals to connect to financial services at a low risk, beginning this with very young children, and continuing this across the life course.
- Increasing the use of automatic (or opt-out) financial features so that people participate unless they actively decline, and employing inertia (the widespread tendency to do nothing) to peoples' advantage.
- Embedding asset-building opportunities within existing community-based programs for vulnerable populations.
- Increasing the cultural relevance and consumer-friendliness of financial services for older populations, especially for older racial and ethnic minorities and for older immigrants.

Develop and Improve Public Policies

Although many Americans do not readily recognize the public policies that affect them, each of us benefits from numerous policies throughout our lives. Social Security retirement benefits and Medicare are policy pillars that support nearly all older adults. Other policies play supporting roles. These existing policies can be tweaked for improved performance to reach vulnerable groups. Other policies should be created. Some of the policy ideas mentioned in this book include the following:

- Implementing universal Child Development Accounts (CDAs) as a means of beginning lifelong wealth accumulation for all Americans.

- Eliminating or raising asset limits for public assistance programs, especially Medicaid.
- Changing legislation and regulations that govern *defined-benefit* retirement plans to make them more attractive to employers and thereby more widely available to employees.
- Expanding the availability of *defined-contribution* accounts dedicated to retirement so that everyone has the opportunity to receive matched savings for security in old age, regardless of employment.
- Enacting a tax credit for employers that offer retirement savings accounts and providing a public match for low-income employee contributions.
- Recognizing the unpaid work of caregivers by recording this as work history for Social Security retirement benefits.
- Developing strategies to ensure that banks accept alternative identifications for immigrants and that all immigrants know they can use such identification to open a bank account.
- Increasing participation in the Earned Income Tax Credit program and in nonprofit tax-preparation services that piggy-back on other, well-established community services.
- Making long-term care more affordable, because financial security in later life cannot be achieved without advancements in long-term care policies.
- Establishing a *livable* minimum Social Security benefit, including minimum spousal payments, to reduce poverty among older adults and the disabled.

Advance Knowledge through Research

Knowledge is always fundamental for improving the world we live in, and this holds true in an applied arena such as financial capability. Good intentions and clever ideas alone do not produce innovations in financial actions, products, and services for older adults and vulnerable populations. Conditions must be documented, and ideas must be tested. Some approaches will work better than others. Only concrete results, gathered in systematic research, can identify effective options. We therefore suggest some useful and promising directions for research:

- Develop more valid and reliable ways to collect wealth and other financial information from individuals and households.
- Document intergenerational patterns observed in transfers of assets.
- Specify systematically the life course effects on economic security in later life.
- Quantify long-term financial impacts—including indirect effects such as deferred retirement savings—of providing various family supports such as unpaid care for long-term health conditions.

- Assess the strengths and weaknesses in financial capability among older adults in order to inform financial advice and counseling as well as the development of more appropriate and effective financial products and services.
- Increase research on financial capabilities in American Indian and Alaska Native communities, other minority groups, and economically disadvantaged populations.
- Increase research on financial exploitation of older adults and on the effectiveness of policies and programs designed to protect them from exploitation.

■ PROGRAMS TO INCREASE FINANCIAL CAPABILITY ACROSS THE LIFE COURSE

Most of the recommendations listed above are within reach. In fact, many are already partially or wholly in place. Thus, it may be helpful to note some examples from existing programs. Serving low-income people, including older adults, programs offered through the Financial Clinic in New York aim to build financial security by increasing consumers' abilities to use safe banking institutions, to budget, to avoid debt, and to identify threats to identity and credit.[2] At 25 sites in New York City, Financial Clinic staff members provide educational classes, individual coaching, consulting, research, and advocacy, serving over 4,500 people a year (Grote 2012). In San Francisco, EARN offers goal-based savings accounts to low-income individuals, including older adults.[3] Through research and evaluation, EARN staff members have documented that low-income savers identify emergencies and retirement as primary saving goals. Among the innovations under way to incentivize saving is a partnership with SaveUp to test gaming mechanisms that reward positive behaviors such as saving or paying down debt (Mangan 2012).[4]

The federal government has several initiatives aimed at enhancing economic security in later life. Responding to the increase in financial abuse and scams that target older adults, the Consumer Financial Protection Bureau launched an initiative in 2012 to learn more about financial exploitation of this population and to determine best practices in financial management in later life. These efforts also emerged in response to the Dodd-Frank Wall Street Reform and Consumer Protection Act of 2010, which requires the Consumer Financial Protection Bureau to facilitate financial literacy among adults over age 62 years by broadening their awareness of abusive financial practices and positive financial choices (Pub. L. No. 111-203, 124 Stat. 1376; Humphrey 2012). The Administration for Community Living, which includes the Administration on Aging, supports an economic security initiative through programs aimed at increasing access to public benefits and services, preventing financial exploitation, and facilitating employment (Washko 2012). The

Administration on Aging supports the National Resource Center on Women and Retirement Planning, which offers education and counseling. The center strives to reach underserved women, including women for whom English is a second language, women in rural areas, and women of color.

Several nongovernmental national organizations also have implemented effective strategies. The National Council on Aging, a nonprofit service and advocacy organization, offers several programs through its Economic Security Initiative. These programs include assistance in developing an economic action plan, support in using the BenefitsCheckUp service to assess eligibility for numerous financial support programs, and access to the Savvy Saving Seniors toolkit. The National Council on Aging reports that, through these programs, older adults have increased income or decreased expenses by about $250 per month (Alwin 2012). The AARP Foundation (formerly the American Association of Retired Persons) has identified four key program areas for support and advocacy: income and financial inclusion, social isolation, hunger, and housing. Focusing on low-income working adults aged 50 years or older, the organization's goals are to increase earnings and improve management of money. Local organizations across the country provide education related to goal setting, debt reduction, credit repair, asset building, and financial protection. In 2012, AARP launched a prepaid MasterCard service that customers can use for direct deposit and saving; the service provides customer service representatives who work directly with older adults (Allen 2012).

■ **CREATING AND TESTING INNOVATIONS FOR FINANCIAL CAPABILITY ACROSS THE LIFE COURSE**

Social research and demonstration can contribute to new models for increasing financial capability throughout the life course of people in financially vulnerable groups. Applied research can contribute to practice and engagement for constructive change. The three initiatives described below are testing and applying strategies to (1) build assets beginning at birth; (2) prepare professionals to inform and guide financial management across the life span; and (3) support active engagement in employment, volunteering, education, and other productive activities in later life.

Building Assets from Birth: SEED OK and CDAs

The SEED for Oklahoma Kids (SEED OK) experiment, which began in 2007, is the first experimental test of universal and progressive CDAs in the United States. A randomized, controlled, long-term experiment, SEED OK assesses the feasibility of CDAs and examines both short- and long-term impacts on several outcomes: account holding, savings deposits, asset accumulation, parents' expectations for their children's future, parenting behaviors, children's development (both socioemotional and cognitive), and eventual educational achievement.

In 2007, SEED OK randomly selected newborns from across Oklahoma and invited their primary caregivers to participate in the experiment.[5] Following a baseline interview, SEED OK randomly assigned half of the approximately 2,700 mothers to the treatment group. Each treatment mother's baby received an account through the Oklahoma 529 College Savings Plan and a $1,000 deposit.[6] The other half, mothers assigned to the control group, received no account. The experiment encouraged participants in the treatment group to open their own account and offered a savings match based on income guidelines (Sherraden and Clancy 2005).

Designed by the Center for Social Development at Washington University in St. Louis, the SEED OK research provides three types of data. First, quarterly account and savings data are collected for every SEED OK child throughout the 7-year experiment. Gathered through account monitoring, survey interviews, and in-depth interviews, these account data provide detailed financial information, including information on deposits and withdrawals. Second, SEED OK conducted a three-wave survey with treatment and control mothers to examine the treatment's impact on children's developmental outcomes as well as on family attitudes and behaviors related to higher education and saving for children (Zager et al. 2010). Third, SEED OK conducted in-depth interviews with a subsample to examine savings experiences, aspirations and expectations, participants' knowledge of and experience with savings and financial services, the meaning of savings, and for those in the treatment group, perceptions of the SEED OK account (Gray et al. 2012).

Although research continues, SEED OK has produced several key findings. The automatic account-opening feature has a substantial and positive impact. All but one member of the treatment group holds a SEED OK account 4 years after the experiment began. This indicates that a universal CDA is possible through the college savings (529) plan structure. Moreover, the treatment group saves more than the control group, though treatment members do so at modest levels (Nam et al. 2013). The SEED OK experiment also reveals that the level of depressive symptoms is lower among mothers in the treatment group than among mothers in the control group (Huang, Sherraden, and Purnell 2014). In addition, findings show that the SEED OK treatment has a positive effect on children's socioemotional development at age 4: it is better among the children of treatment mothers than among the children of counterparts in the control group (Huang, Sherraden, Kim, and Clancy 2014).

These results are having direct effects on state 529 policy. Maine announced in March 2014 that every newborn will automatically receive a 529 account and a $500 initial deposit at birth. Nevada recently announced that all kindergartners will automatically receive a 529 account with a $50 initial deposit (Clancy and

Sherraden 2014). Additional discussions about extending this policy are underway in several other states, and CDA legislation has been introduced at the federal level (see, e.g., H.R. 3740, 110th Cong. [2007]; H.R. 4682, 11th Cong. [2010]).

Prepare Professionals for Financial Guidance across the Life Span: The Financial Capability and Asset Building Initiative

Financial Capability and Asset Building (FCAB) is a research and education initiative to design and test a curriculum that will build this expertise into the training of social workers and other human service professionals who may work with low-income and financially vulnerable populations (Birkenmaier, Sherraden, and Curley 2013). The aim of FCAB is to expand professional capacity among social workers who work with individuals, families, communities, social service organizations, financial institutions, administrators, and policymakers. The initiative's larger aim is to improve financial capability and asset building among low- and moderate-income people. The first phase of FCAB, now underway, involves the creation and testing of the curriculum. The second phase, scheduled to occur from 2015 through 2018, will involve broad distribution to educators in schools of social work and human service programs.

The curriculum provides background and instructional resources to increase knowledge and skills for FCAB practice. Students learn (1) how to help families solve immediate financial problems and build financial security and mobility, (2) when to refer clients to other professionals for in-depth financial counseling and guidance, and (3) how to work in collaboration with others to generate policy and program solutions for financially capable families and communities.

The evidence-based FCAB curriculum is built upon current knowledge and understanding of financial capability and asset building. Developed through collaboration among multiple disciplines (economics, sociology, social work, and family and consumer sciences) and through insights from different population groups, the curriculum is being evaluated in colleges and universities on an ongoing basis. These evaluations employ pretests, posttests, and interviews with instructors and administrators.

Support Older Adults as a Valuable Resource: Productive Aging Research and Applied Impacts

With the challenges of population aging come opportunities. The demographic shift results in a larger number of older adults but also a healthier and better educated older population. This growth in human capital represents one part of the solution to the pressures of a growing population: one way to begin addressing them is by increasing the productive engagement of older adults.

Productive engagement refers to active participation in roles that make an economic contribution to society. Such roles include working, volunteering, and caregiving. Society may expect greater engagement of the older population in this paid and unpaid work (Morrow-Howell et al. 2001). The potential of such engagement has triggered innovations in programs and policies. It has also spurred applied research to assess and inform these developments.

For example, demonstrations and evaluations are underway to support extended working lives by increasing workplace flexibility, offering health promotion programs in the workplace, ensuring job training for older workers, and improving the age friendliness of work environments (efforts reviewed by Gonzales in Chapter 10). A specific example can be found in work by the Sloan Center for Aging and Work. The Center is assessing the business effects of workplace interventions that increase employees' options and control over where, when, and how they work (Sloan Center for Aging and Work 2013). Other emerging innovations support career planning for older adults. For example, Encore.org assists older adults in exploring and planning for second careers (Alboher 2012), and Senior Entrepreneurship Works is an educational program that assists older adults in starting their own businesses.[7] Age discrimination continues to inhibit progress in the employment arena, but new attitudes and new models for later life are emerging. Much can be gained by creating opportunities for extended working lives. Society gains experienced workers in the labor pool. Older adults gain longer access to employment income, accumulate additional savings in retirement accounts, and delay use of Social Security benefits. All of these developments are likely to yield increases in monthly retirement income.

Innovations in the civic engagement of older adults are occurring in programs and policies at the local, city, state, and federal levels. In particular, programs are emerging to engage older volunteers in social challenges. For example, Experience Corps (EC) recruits, trains, and supports older adults to provide assistance to teachers in public schools (Fried et al. 2004). Morrow-Howell and colleagues completed a national study of the effects of EC on the students as well as the older volunteers. They conducted a randomized trial with 825 students in three cities, assigning half to the EC program. Morrow-Howell and associates used standardized reading assignments to pretest first-, second-, and third-grade students before the program began in the fall; they tested the students again after the program ended at the close of the school year. Findings indicate that the EC program has significant and positive effects on reading outcomes. In addition, teachers report that the program is beneficial to them and the burden of participation is low (Lee et al. 2010). The study also documents positive effects on the older volunteers. Using a quasi-experimental design, the study compares EC participants who serve in the program for two academic terms to matched control-group members from a large, nationally representative sample of older adults. Findings indicate that participation in the EC program is associated with improvements in depression and functional ability (Hong and Morrow-Howell 2010). This research clearly supports the assertion that engaging older volunteers in socially important programs is associated with multiple positive outcomes.

Also increasingly common are national programs to increase the capacity of public and nonprofit organizations to utilize older adults. The National Association of Area Agencies on Aging's (2014) Aging Network Volunteer Collaborative is an example. In addition, there are many initiatives to support older volunteers through policy changes. For example, there is growing interest in subsidies and tax credits to encourage employers to expand community service opportunities for their employees as they approach retirement (O'Neill 2006/2007). In 2009, passage of the Edward M. Kennedy Serve America Act signaled the federal government's interest in increasing the engagement of older adults in volunteer roles (Pub. L. 111-13, 123 Stat. 1460). The act allots 10% of the AmeriCorps budget for organizations enrolling adults aged 55 years or older, and it allows older volunteers who earned educational awards to transfer those awards to their children and grandchildren (123 Stat. 1584 § 2142 [2009]). These program and policy initiatives for late life volunteering aim to increase the supply of experienced volunteers—in a sense, they seek to take advantage of the growing capability of older adults.

Increasing the financial capability and financial security of older adults can help to ensure the ongoing production of older citizens willing to contribute through volunteer service. Volunteering is also a pathway to work and other important engagements for older adults, who can build human and social capital through civic involvement (Spera et al. 2013). In sum, financial capability across the life course extends the virtuous circle of volunteering into later life.

■ GOING FORWARD

In conclusion, many older adults, especially those in vulnerable groups, face daunting financial challenges. This is not a reason for despair but rather a reason to be aware and to get busy. As this book documents, we know quite a lot about vulnerable financial circumstances. We also know quite a lot about what can be done to improve financial capability and economic security among older adults. Research and learning should always continue, but we already know enough to do better. A short list would include creating a lifelong asset-building policy for everyone; connecting all people to culturally relevant and high-quality financial services and education throughout their lifetimes; enriching the community-based fabric of social services and economic supports; and improving Social Security retirement benefits, especially for those at the bottom. These areas of work are not a mystery; significant progress has already occurred, and greater improvements are within reach.

■ NOTES

1. Social Security Act of 1935, Pub. L. No. 74-271, 49 Stat. 620, codified as amended at 42 U.S.C. §§ 1301–1397 (2011).

2. See http://thefinancialclinic.org.

3. See http://www.earn.org.

4. See also https://www.saveup.com.

5. For ease of exposition, we refer to all SEED OK caregivers as mothers.

6. Named for the relevant section of the Internal Revenue Code, 529 accounts provide a tax-favored vehicle for the accumulation of assets earmarked for postsecondary education.

7. See http://seniorentrepreneurshipworks.org/.

■ REFERENCES

Alboher, Marci. 2012. *The Encore Career Handbook: How to Make a Living and a Difference in the Second Half of Life*. New York: Workman.

Allen, Emily. 2012. "Winning Back Opportunity for Struggling Americans 50+." Presentation at the conference Financial Capability: A Life Course Perspective, St. Louis, MO, October 24–26. http://csd.wustl.edu/events/Conferences And Symposia /Pages/FCALC-Presentations.aspx.

Alwin, Ramsey. 2012. "National Council on Aging." Presentation at the conference Financial Capability: A Life Course Perspective, St. Louis, MO, October 24–26. http://csd .wustl.edu/events/ConferencesAndSymposia/Pages/FCALC-Presentations.aspx.

Ando, Albert, and Franco Modigliani. 1963. "The 'Life-Cycle' Hypothesis of Saving: Aggregate Implications and Tests." *American Economic Review* 53, no. 1 (part 1): 55–84. http://www.jstor.org/stable/1817129.

Birkenmaier, Julie, Margaret S. Sherraden, and Jami Curley, eds. 2013. *Financial Capability and Asset Development: Research, Education, Policy, and Practice*. New York: Oxford University Press.

Birkenmaier, Julie, Teri Kennedy, James Kunz, Rebecca Sander, and Shelley Horwitz. 2013. "The Role of Social Work in Financial Capability: Shaping Curricular Approaches." In *Financial Capability and Asset Development: Research, Education, Policy, and Practice*, edited by Julie Birkenmaier, Margaret S. Sherraden, and Jami Curley, 278–301. New York: Oxford University Press.

Clancy, Margaret, and Michael Sherraden. 2014. *Automatic Deposits for All at Birth: Maine's Harold Alfond College Challenge*. CSD Policy Report 14-05. St. Louis, MO: Washington University, Center for Social Development. http://csd.wustl.edu/Publications/Pages /displayresultitem.aspx?ID1=1196.

DeNavas-Walt, Carmen, Bernadette D. Proctor, and Jessica C. Smith. 2011. *Income, Poverty, and Health Insurance Coverage in the United States: 2010*. Current Population Reports: Consumer Income, P60-239, September. Washington, DC: U.S. Census Bureau. http://www.census.gov/prod/2011pubs/p60-239.pdf.

Federal Interagency Forum on Aging-Related Statistics. 2012. *Older Americans 2012: Key Indicators of Well-Being*. Washington, DC: Federal Interagency Forum on Aging-Related Statistics. http://www.agingstats.gov/agingstatsdotnet/Main_Site /Data/2012_Documents/docs/EntireChartbook.pdf.

Fried, Linda P., Michelle C. Carlson, Marc Freedman, Kevin D. Frick, Thomas A. Glass, Joel Hill, Sylvia McGill, et al. 2004. "A Social Model for Health Promotion for an Aging Population: Initial Evidence on the Experience Corps Model." *Journal of Urban Health* 81 (1): 64–78. doi: 10.1093/jurban/jth094.

Gray, Karen, Margaret Clancy, Margaret S. Sherraden, Kristen Wagner, and Julie Miller-Cribbs. 2012. *Interviews with Mothers of Young Children in the SEED for Oklahoma Kids College Savings Experiment.* CSD Research Report 12-53. St. Louis, MO: Washington University, Center for Social Development. http://csd.wustl.edu /Publications/Documents/RP12-53.pdf.

Grote, Mae Watson. 2012. "Financial Development Strategies and Opportunities for Older Adults." Presentation at the conference Financial Capability: A Life Course Perspective, St. Louis, MO, October 24–26. http://csd.wustl.edu/events /ConferencesAndSymposia/Pages/FCALC-Presentations.aspx

Helman Ruth, Jack VanDerhei, and Craig Copeland. 2007. *Minority Workers Remain Confident about Retirement, Despite Lagging Preparations and False Expectations.* Issue Brief 306, June. Washington, DC: Employee Benefit Retirement Institute. http://www.ebri.org/pdf/briefspdf/EBRI_IB_06-20079.pdf.

Hong, S. I., and Nancy Morrow-Howell. 2010. "Health Outcomes of Experience Corps: A High-Commitment Volunteer Program." *Social Science and Medicine* 71 (2): 414–420. doi: 10.1016/j.socscimed.2010.04.009.

Huang, Jin, Michael Sherraden, Youngmi Kim, and Margaret Clancy. 2014. "Effects of Child Development Accounts on Early Socio-Emotional Development: An Experimental Test." *JAMA (Journal of the American Medical Association) Pediatrics* 168 (3): 265–271. doi: 10.1001/jamapediatrics.2013.4643.

Huang, Jin, Michael Sherraden, and Jason Purnell. 2014. "Impacts of Child Development Accounts on Maternal Depressive Symptoms: Evidence from a Randomized Statewide Policy Experiment." *Social Science and Medicine* 112: 30–38. doi: 10.1016/j .socscimed.2014.04.023.

Humphrey, Skip. 2012. "Protecting Older Americans from Financial Abuse." *CFPB (Consumer Financial Protection Bureau) Blog*, June 14. http://www.consumerfinance .gov/blog/protecting-older-americans-from-financial-abuse/.

Jacobsen, Linda A., Mary Kent, Marlene Lee, and Mark Mather. 2011. "America's Aging Population." *Population Bulletin* 66 (1). http://www.prb.org/pdf11/aging-in-america .pdf.

Johnson, Elizabeth, and Margaret S. Sherraden. 2007. "From Financial Literacy to Financial Capability among Youth." *Journal of Sociology and Social Welfare* 34 (3): 119–145.

Lee, Yung Soo, Nancy Morrow-Howell, Melissa Jonson-Reid, and Stacey McCrary. 2010. "The Effect of the Experience Corps Program on Student Reading Outcomes." *Education and Urban Society* 44 (1): 97–118. doi: 10.1177/0013124510381262.

Macartney, Suzanne, Alemayehu Bishaw, and Kayla Fontenot. 2013. *Poverty Rates for Selected Detailed Race and Hispanic Groups by State and Place: 2007–2011.* American Community Survey Brief ACSBR/11-17. Washington, DC: U.S. Census Bureau. https://www.census.gov/prod/2013pubs/acsbr11-17.pdf.

Mangan, Ben. 2012. "Including Older Americans in Asset Building Efforts: Hard Truths and Promising Ideas." Presentation at the conference Financial Capability: A Life Course Perspective, St. Louis, MO, October 24–26. http://csd.wustl.edu/events /ConferencesAndSymposia/Pages/FCALC-Presentations.aspx.

Morrow-Howell, Nancy, James Hinterlong, and Michael Sherraden, eds. 2001. *Productive Aging: Concepts and Challenges*. Baltimore, MD: Johns Hopkins University Press.

Nam, Yunju, Youngmi Kim, Margaret Clancy, Robert Zager, and Michael Sherraden. 2013. "Do Child Development Accounts Promote Account Holding, Saving, and Asset Accumulation for Children's Future? Evidence from a Statewide Randomized Experiment." *Journal of Policy Analysis and Management* 32 (1): 6–33. doi: 10.1002/pam.21652.

National Alliance for Caregiving and AARP. 2009. *Caregiving in the U.S. 2009*. Report. Bethesda, MD: National Alliance for Caregiving. http://www.caregiving.org/data/Caregiving_in_the_US_2009_full_report.pdf.

National Association of Area Agencies on Aging. 2014. "The Aging Network's Volunteer Collaborative." Accessed May 30. http://www.n4a.org/programs/aging-network-volunteer-collaborative/.

O'Neill, Greg. 2006/2007. "Civic Engagement on the Agenda at the 2005 White House Conference on Aging." *Generations* 30 (4): 95–100.

Sherraden, Michael, and Margaret Clancy. 2005. *The Universal Model in SEED*. CSD Perspective. St. Louis, MO: Washington University, Center for Social Development. http://csd.wustl.edu/Publications/Documents/overview_um_seed_092005.pdf.

Sloan Center on Aging and Work. 2013. "The Time and Place Management Study." Chestnut Hill, MA: Boston College, Sloan Center on Aging and Work. http://www.bc.edu/research/agingandwork/.

Spera, Christopher, Robin Ghertner, Anthony Nerino, and Adrienne DiTommaso. 2013. *Volunteering as a Pathway to Employment: Does Volunteering Increase Odds of Finding a Job for the Out of Work?* Research Report, June. Washington, DC: Corporation for National and Community Service, Office of Research and Evaluation.

Sunstein, Cass R., and Richard H. Thaler. 2003. "Libertarian Paternalism Is Not an Oxymoron." *University of Chicago Law Review* 70 (4): 1159–1202.

Titmuss, Richard. 1958. *Essays on "The Welfare State."* London: Unwin.

U.S. Department of Health and Human Services, Office of the Assistant Secretary for Planning and Evaluation. 2013. *Information on Poverty and Income Statistics: A Summary of 2013 Current Population Survey Data*. ASPE Issue Brief, September 17. Washington, DC: U.S. Department of Health and Human Services. http://aspe.hhs.gov/hsp/13/PovertyAndIncomeEst/ib_poverty2013.pdf.

Washko, Michelle. 2012. "U.S. Administration for Community Living: Ensuring Economic Security across the Lifespan for All." Presentation at the conference Financial Capability: A Life Course Perspective, St. Louis, MO, October 24–26. http://csd.wustl.edu/events/ConferencesAndSymposia/Pages/FCALC-Presentations.aspx.

Zager, Robert, Youngmi Kim, Yunju Nam, Margaret Clancy, and Michael Sherraden. 2010. *The SEED for Oklahoma Kids Experiment: Initial Account Opening and Savings* (CSD Research Report 10-14). St. Louis, MO: Washington University, Center for Social Development. http://csd.wustl.edu/Publications/Documents/RP10-14.pdf.

■ INDEX

AARP Foundation, 129, 163, 206, 225
abbreviations, xv
abuse, of older adults, 200
ACA (Affordable Care Act), 127, 164, 166, 167
ACS (American Community Survey), 95, 121, 122, 123
Adler, Nancy, 31
Administration for Community Living, 130, 224
Administration for Native Americans, 96
Administration on Aging, 156, 224–225
Adopt-A-Native-Elder Program (Park City, Utah), 97
Adult Protective Services, 203
Affordable Care Act (ACA), 127, 164, 166, 167
African Americans
  assets, 34, 49–63
  average net worth, 28
  disposable income, 50
  effect of wealth on health of, 27
  employer-sponsored retirement plans among, 56–58
  health of across the life course, 30–32
  home equity, 52
  homeownership, 52
  labor-force participation rates compared to whites, 50
  lifetime earnings, 51
  median household income, 50
  median net worth, xxv, 52
  mental health of, 28, 31, 32
  pensions, 49, 53–54
  policy issues/implications, 55–63
  poverty rates, xviii, 30, 32, 49, 50–51, 178, 199, 201
  race and SEP, 28–32
  research issues/implications, 37
  savings, 49, 55
  social mobility, 32–34

Social Security, 54–55, 58–59
social support networks, 34–35
upward social mobility, 27, 32
age, trends in median family income/ wealth grouped by, 13–14
age discrimination, 175, 180–181, 185, 186, 198, 228
Age Discrimination in Employment Act, 180
age-friendly banking, 195–197, 202–209, 222
Age-Friendly Environments Programme, 205
age-friendly housing, 206–207
age-friendly websites, 205
age-friendly work environments, 185–187
Aging, Stress, and Health Study (2001), 31
Aging and Disability Resource Centers Program, 130
Aging Network Volunteer Collaborative, 229
alternative financial products and services, xxi, 108, 201
American Community Survey (ACS), 95, 121, 122, 123
American Dream Demonstration, 130, 151
American Indian and Alaska Natives, 98n1. See also Native Americans
American Indian Probate Reform Act, 91
Americans' Changing Lives survey, 31
Americans Saving for Personal Investment, Retirement, and Education Act (ASPIRE Act), 61
Americans with Disabilities Act, 197
American Taxpayer Relief Act of 2012, 167
AmeriCorps, 229
Amuedo-Dorantes, Catalina, 110
Anderson, Keith, 129

Angel, Jacqueline I., xi, 219, 221
Annual Navajo Rug Show and Sale, 97
anti-immigrant policy developments, 107
area agencies on aging, 128, 153, 229
Aspen Institute, 62
ASPIRE Act (Americans Saving for
    Personal Investment, Retirement,
    and Education Act), 61
asset accumulation, 70, 74, 82, 98, 106,
    108–112, 125, 139, 140, 141, 142, 144,
    146, 152, 165, 221, 225
asset-based programs
    access to, 145–146
    as age regressive, 140
    description/evaluation of, 146–152
    maximum-contribution limits for, 155
    recommended goal of, 145
    serving American Indians, 97
    as supplements, 153
asset building
    as beginning with disposable
        income, 49
    from birth, 225–227
    restrictions/disincentives for, 153
    workplace policies and missed
        opportunities, 176–179
asset-building opportunities/
    programs, 62–63, 113, 114, 128, 131,
    175, 221, 222, 225, 227
asset-building policies, xxviii, 61, 229
asset decumulation, 3, 139, 141, 144, 146
asset development
    defined, 139–140
    and individual preference, 144
    institutional theory of, 145
    for older adults: life-cycle capability
        approach, 142
    and policies related to older
        adults, 153–156
    as strategy to strengthen economic
        security/well-being, 139
asset holding among household heads
    older than age 55 years, 52
asset limit rules, 153, 154, 155, 157
asset management, 139, 141, 142, 143,
    146, 157
asset prices, 4–5
Assets for Independence Act, 221

Assets for Independence program, 146,
    151
assisted-living facilities, 126, 162
Association on American Indian
    Affairs, 95
Atlas of the World's Languages in Danger
    (UNESCO), 95
ATMs, 205
August, Kristin, 122
AutoIRAs, 62
automatic enrollment, 82, 149, 183, 184
AutoSave, 62
average net worth
    for African American families, 28
    upward trajectory of, 8
    for white families, 28

baby boomers, 5, 19, 21, 22, 23, 139,
    161, 197
baby bust, 23
balance sheet leverage, 4
Baldwin, Cathryn, 124
Bankers' Community Collaborative
    Council, 196
banking
    age-friendly, 195–197, 202–209, 222
    alternative identifications for
        immigrants, 223
    branch banking, 205
    mobile banking, xx
    online banking, xx, 205
    products/services, 204
Bank of the West, 203
Barker, David, 30
Barusch, Amanda, xi, 219, 220
Be Aware program, 203
Behavioral Risk Factor Surveillance
    System (2006), 126
benefit checkups, 206
BenefitsCheckUp, 206, 225
bias, survivorship, 17
birth year, impact of on median
    income/wealth, 3, 6, 15
birth-year cohort effects, 6, 12, 15, 17,
    18, 19, 22, 24
Bishaw, Alemayehu, 219
Bowen, Mary Elizabeth, 122
branch banking, 205

Bricker, Jesse, 6
Bridges, Benjamin, 125
Briesacher, Becky, 126
Brusco, Natasha, 124
Bullard, Kai, 36
Bureau of Indian Affairs, 89, 90
Burr, Jeffrey, 112

California Health Interview Survey
    (2007), 122
Campbell, Angelyque, xx
capabilities, defined, 141
capability approach, to asset development
    for older adults, 140–145
caregiving, 153, 155, 163–165, 167, 169,
    175, 181–182, 187, 219, 223, 228
Carlson, Elwood, 22
Carnevale, Anthony, 51
car-title and payday lenders, xxi
Cash and Counseling program
    (Medicaid), 129, 130, 167
casinos, on reservations, 96
CDAs (Child Development Accounts),
    56, 60–62, 222, 225–227
Center for Rural Health, 88
Center for Social Development
    (Washington University), 226
Center for Women's Business
    Research, 93
Central Provident Fund account
    (Singapore), 61
Chase Bank, 197
check-cashing outlets, xxi, 108
Cheyenne River Sioux Tribe v. Salazar
    case, 92
child account policies, 61
Child Development Accounts (CDAs), 56,
    60–62, 222, 225–227
child savings accounts, 55
Child Trust Fund (UK), 61
Choi, James, 184
Choudhury, Sharmila, 125
Civilization Fund Act of 1819, 89
CLASS (Community Living Assistance
    Services and Supports) Act, 161,
    166–167, 171n1
Cobb-Clark, Deborah, 110
Cobell settlement, 92

cognitive decline, xxi
cohort analysis, 14–23
Coile, Courtney, 126
Cole, Elizabeth, 34
Colen, Cynthia, 35
college savings account/plan, xxiv, 55,
    60, 154, 226
combined capability, 141
Community Development Block
    Grants, 206
Community Development Financial
    Institution Fund, 207
Community Development Financial
    Institutions, 206
Community Living Assistance Services
    and Supports (CLASS) Act, 161,
    166–167, 171n1
Community Reinvestment Act, 196
Confederated Salish and Kootenai
    Tribes, 91
Congressional Budget Office, 167
consumer-directed services, for
    LTC, 167–168
Consumer Financial Protection
    Bureau, 129, 153, 156, 202, 203,
    208, 224
contributors, xi–xiii
Cornell, Stephen, 96
Cortina, Lila, 181
cost-benefit calculations, 107
credit card balances, xx
cultural resilience, among Native
    American elders, 94
Current Population Survey (2010), 123

Dabelko-Schoeny, Holly, 129
Dawes Act of 1887, 91
debt, xix–xx, 4, 11, 52, 224, 225. *See also*
    mortgage debt
dedicated retirement accounts, 63
defined-benefit (DB) plans, xix–xx, 4,
    56, 57, 58, 81, 143, 152, 176, 178, 199,
    204, 223
defined-contribution (DC) plans, xix, xx,
    56, 57, 58, 81, 143, 153, 176, 178, 185,
    188n5, 223
DeLaCruz, James, Sr., 87
diminishing returns hypothesis, 33

disability/persons with disabilities
  contributors to risk for poverty in, 120,
    123–129
  demographic profile of older adults
    experiencing, 121–124
  employment, 123–125, 131
  financial instability and barriers to
    wealth creation, 120–121, 131
  and health care, 120, 124–129, 131
  isolation of, 128–129
  long-term care (LTC), 125–127
  marginalization of, 120, 128–129
  policy issues/implications, 120,
    129–130
  poverty rates, 123–124, 219
  research issues/implications, 123,
    130–131
  shortened work careers, 124–125
disadvantaged nation of old age, 218
distributions, of investments and
    earnings, 7, 9, 11–13, 54, 74, 139, 185
documentation requirements, 109
Dodd-Frank Wall Street Reform and
    Consumer Protection Act, 224
Do Not Call Registry, 203
Dressler, William, 33
Duggan, Maeve, 163
Duran, Eduardo, 88
Dushi, Irena, 179
Dworsky, Michael, 185
dynamic relationships between sources of
    LTC delivery and funding, 170

EARN (San Francisco), 224
Earned Income Tax Credit program, 82,
    206, 223
Eason, Endia, 195
Eason, William, 195
economic development, on
    reservations, 96
economic risk, xviii
economic security, xviii, xxvii, 60, 63,
    106–107, 114, 139, 142, 157, 175,
    197–200, 205, 218, 223–224, 229
Economic Security Initiative (National
    Council on Aging), 129, 225
economic vulnerability, 107, 113, 197–202

educational attainment
  among Hispanics, 70, 75
  among Native Americans, 95–96
  disparities, 29, 33–34, 80
  and gains in income, 33
  health and, 27, 31, 34
  influence of college savings, xxiv
  pensions and, 75, 178–179
  as predictor of income/wealth, 3,
    15, 27
  role of in amount of lifetime
    earnings, 51
  trends in median family income/wealth
    grouped by, 13–14
Edward M. Kennedy Serve America
    Act, 229
effect of family head's birth year on family
    income relative to being born in
    period 1938–1942, 17
effect of family head's birth year on family
    wealth relative to being born in
    period 1938–1942, 21
Elder, Glen, xxii, xxiii
Elder Financial Protection Network, 203
Emeka, Amon, 51
Emmons, William R., xi, 3, 14, 19, 220
employee stock-ownership plans, 57
employer-matched savings accounts, xxiii
employer-sponsored health-benefit
    plans, 175
employer-sponsored retirement
    plans, 49, 53–54, 56–58, 76. See
    also defined-benefit (DB) plans;
    defined-contribution (DC) plans
employment characteristics of employed
    population by race and Mexican
    origin, 76
employment-to-population ratios, 50, 59
Encore.org, 228
energy development, on
    reservations, 96–97
Engelhardt, Gary, 184
enrollment
  automatic enrollment, 82, 149,
    183, 184
  to increase pension participation and
    investment, 183–184

equity sharing, 207–208
Esther Martinez Native American
    Languages Preservation Act of
    2006, 95
estimated number of children under
    1 year old, 22
Experience Corps (EC), 228–229

Fair Labor Standards Act, 168
Family and Medical Leave Act, 60, 155,
    186–187
Farmer, Melissa, 32
Favreault, Melissa, 123
Fazio, Elena, 31
FCAB (Financial Capability and Asset
    Building), 227
Federal Deposit Insurance
    Corporation, 92, 208
Federal Housing Administration, 207
federal immigration policy, 107
Federal Insurance Contributions Act
    (FICA), 54
Federal Reserve, 3, 9, 184
Feinberg, Lynn, 164
Feldman, Pamela, 31
Ferraro, Kenneth, 32
financial abuse, xxi, 195, 200, 202,
    203, 224
financial capability
    as component of asset
        development, 141, 142, 143, 144, 145
    creating/testing innovations
        for, 225–229
    defined, xxiv–xxv
    development of, xxii
    programs for increasing, 224–225
    strategies for increasing, 88, 97,
        221–224
Financial Capability and Asset Building
    (FCAB), 227
financial capacity, 91, 182, 183–185, 221
Financial Clinic (New York), 224
financial counseling, 82, 208, 227
financial education, 82, 114, 115, 130, 145,
    146, 147, 148, 157, 170, 182, 183, 184,
    196, 197, 205, 208, 221
financial fraud, 195, 200–201, 203

financial functioning, xxii, 141, 142,
    143, 144
financial guidance, xxi, 110, 208, 227
financial inclusion, xx, xxiv, xxv, 141,
    142, 145, 146, 147, 148, 150, 156, 157,
    202, 225
financial institutions, building capacity
    of, 222
financial knowledge, xxiv, xxv, 108, 110,
    114, 140, 141, 142, 143, 146, 156
financial life cycle trajectory, xxii
financial literacy, xxi, 129, 131, 141, 142,
    143, 145, 146, 147–148, 150, 156–157,
    176, 208, 224
financial management, xxi, xxii, 108, 110,
    147, 202, 204, 208, 224, 225
financial products/services, ix, xvii, 108,
    114–115, 142–143, 145, 155, 195, 196,
    201, 202, 204, 224
financial profile, of older Americans
    (1989–2010), 3
financial service technologies, xx,
    108–109
financial vulnerability, xvii, xviii, xxi,
    78, 112, 218, 220
Findley, Patricia, 126
Fink, Günther, 144
529 policies/plans, 60, 61, 154,
    226–227
fixed age group framework, 15
Flathead Reservation, 91
flexible work options, 182, 186. *See also*
    job flexibility
Fontenot, Kayla, 219
Food, Conservation, and Energy Act
    of 2008, 157
food insecurity levels, 80
foreign-born individuals, 82,
    107, 115n1
401(k) plans, 56, 57, 62, 63, 82, 149, 151,
    176, 185, 199
Fox, Michael, 123
Fox, Susannah, 163
fraud, financial, 195, 200–201, 203
Fredriksen-Goldsen, Karen, 123
Freedom Savings Credit, 62
fringe benefits, 4, 167

Fronstin, Paul, 179
Fuller-Thomson, Esme, 122
functionings, 141, 142, 143, 144

Gale, William, 5, 6, 185
Galinsky, Ellen, 187
Gassoumis, Zachary, 80
generation Xers, 19, 21
Geronimus, Arline, 30
Gerst, Kerstin, 112
GI Bill, 29
Gilman, Stephen, 31
glass ceilings, 34, 36
Glover, Andrew, 5
Golden, Tracy, xii, 219, 220
Gonzales, Ernest, xii, 220
Gorman, Edward J., III, xii, 222
Grandbois, Donna, 94
Great Depression, 22
Great Recession, xix, 3, 4, 5, 58,
    195, 198
Greenfield, Jennifer C., xii, 219,
    220, 221
Gross v. FBL Financial Services, 181
Guo, Baorong, 124

Hale, Kenneth, 95
Halvorsen-Palmquist transformation, 19
Harold Alfond College Challenge
    (Maine), 61
Harrington, Charlene, 126
Hasnain-Wynia, Romana, 126
HCBS (home- and community-based
    services), 166, 167, 168, 169
health
    across the life course, 30–32
    and segregation, 29
    and socioeconomic position (SEP), 27,
        30–32, 33, 36
Health and Retirement Study, 6, 72, 73,
    74, 79, 122, 123, 126, 144, 164, 181,
    182
health benefits, 176, 179, 220
health disparities, 28, 32–33
health insurance, xxii, 11, 71, 75, 78–79,
    88, 130, 131, 167, 168, 179
health savings accounts, 153, 154, 155

HeavyRunner, Iris, 94
Heflin, Colleen, 34
Higginbotham, Elizabeth, 34
Hildebrand, Vincent, 110
Hinton, Leanne, 95
Hispanics
    economic security, 69–82
    educational attainment, 70
    employment status and retirement
        income, 74–78
    health insurance, 78–79
    intragroup differences, 80
    pensions, 77, 79, 178
    policy issues/implications, 81–82
    poverty rates, 72–73, 78, 80, 199
    research issues/implications, 80, 82
    retirement income, 71–73, 74–78
    and retirement security, 70–74
    savings, 81
    Social Security, 78
    U.S. population of, 70
    wealth accumulation, 73–74
historical time and place, xxiii,
    xxiv, 220
Hochschild, Jennifer, 34
Ho-Chunk, Inc., 91
home- and community-based services
    (HCBS), 166, 167, 168, 169
homecare worker reforms, 168
home equity
    among older African Americans, 52
    as largest asset for baby boomers, 197
    low levels of in households headed
        by non-Hispanic blacks and
        Hispanics, 74
    as most common form of wealth in
        U.S., 53
    as percentage of total wealth, 29
    as source of funds to make credit card
        payments, xx
    ways to use, 207, 208
Home Equity Conversion Mortgage, 207
home equity line of credit, 207–208
HOME Investment Partnerships
    Program, 151, 157
homeownership
    among African Americans, 52

among immigrants, 109–110, 112
among Native Americans, 90–91
recent experiences in, 6
home rehabilitation assistance, 152
Homestead Act, 91
home values, 29, 197–198
Honarmand, Kimia, 124
housing, age-friendly, 206–207
housing counseling, 147, 207, 208
Housing Counseling Assistance, 146
housing equity, xx, 73, 74
housing tax benefits, 151–152
Huang, Jin, xii, 124, 129, 221
Hudson, Darrell L., xii, 31, 36
human agency, as factor in life course
    perspective, xxiii, xxiv
human capital, 4, 15, 93, 104, 180,
    185, 227
human capital investment, 27, 28, 32–34,
    36, 38
hypothalamic–pituitary–adrenal
    cortical axis, 30

Iams, Howard, 179
IHS (inverse hyperbolic sine)
    function, 19, 21
immigrants. *See also* undocumented
    immigrants
    alternative identifications for, 223
    anti-immigrant policy
        developments, 107
    asset accumulation, 106, 108–114
    diversity among, 104, 111–115
    and financial capability, 107–110,
        113–115
    homeownership, 109, 112
    labor market and, 104–105, 108
    median household income, 105,
        106, 108
    median net worth, 111, 112
    net worth, 110, 111, 112
    pensions, 105
    population of older immigrants, 104
    poverty rates, 105–106, 113
    research issues/implications, 114–115
    savings, 112
    Social Security, 105, 113

use of financial institutions by, 108,
    113, 114, 199
    U.S. policies toward, 106–108, 113
immigration, influence of on income/
    wealth trajectories, 75
Immigration Act of 1882, 107
income/asset inadequacy, implications of
    in late life, 79–80
income deficit, xviii, 139
income/wealth trends
    by age, race/ethnicity, and educational
        attainment, 13–14
    at median of their distributions, 9–11
    at twentieth percentile of their
        distributions, 11–13
Indian Gaming Regulatory Act, 96
Indian Health Service, 88, 90, 97
Indian Reorganization Act of 1934, 91
individual agency, 220
Individual Development Accounts, 129,
    130, 146, 151, 157
individual retirement accounts
    (IRAs), 52, 53, 55, 77, 82, 114, 127,
    146, 149, 150, 154, 204. *See also*
    AutoIRAs; MyRA accounts
infant population, 22–23
inflation-adjusted family income by age
    group at twentieth percentile of
    distribution, 12
inflation-adjusted net worth by age group
    at the twentieth percentile of the
    distribution, 13
in-kind benefits, 4
Institute for Financial Literacy, 208
Institute for Indian Estate Planning and
    Probate, 92
internal capability, 141, 142, 143, 146
Internal Revenue Service, 108, 109, 206
inverse hyperbolic sine (IHS) function, 19, 21
investment, deciding strategies for, 184
IRAs (individual retirement
    accounts). *See* individual retirement
    accounts (IRAs)
Isaac, Vivian, 129
Ishimaru, Stuart, 181
isolation, of persons with
    disabilities, 128–129

job/career training/retraining, 59–60,
185–186
job demands, 180
job flexibility, 56, 60. *See also* flexible
work options
Johnson, Richard, 123
Johnson, Scott, 124
Jung, Yunkyung, 129

Kahn, Joan, 31
Kalt, Joseph, 96
Kaplan, George, 38n1
Katznelson, Ira, 29
Kaye, H. Stephen, 126
Kessler, Ronald, 35
Kim, Youngmi, 124
Kindergarten to College program
(San Francisco), 61
Kootenai tribe, 91
Krimmel, Jacob, 4
Krings, Franciska, 186
Kumar, Anil, 184

labor compensation, racial disparities in, 28
labor-force participation rates, 49–50, 59
labor market
delayed entry of young people
into, xxiii
disadvantages/disparities, xxvi, 59, 71,
79, 104, 105, 108, 111, 113
racial/ethnic differences in availability
of opportunities in, 71–72
land consolidation program, 93
land ownership, among Native American
elders, 91–92
language revitalization, among Native
American elders, 95
LaPlante, Mitchell, 126
Lareau, Annette, 35
Lau, Denys, 126
Lee, Jae Chul, 126
legal permanent residents, 104, 107,
115n1
Leigh, Wilhelmina A., xii, 219
life course perspective, xxii–xxiv, xxv,
140, 143–144, 145, 156, 218, 220, 222,
224, 225

life cycle framework, 15
life cycle hypothesis of saving, 140, 143,
152, 221
lifestyle incongruence, 33
lifetime earnings, xxiii, 17, 51, 56, 58, 59,
105
lifetime pension access and type of
pension among individuals aged
55–61 years in 1994 and 2004, by
selected characteristics, 177
limited/uneven employment, among
persons with disabilities, 124–125
linked lives, xxiii, xxiv, 220
liquid-asset holdings, 24
Little Soldier, Lee, 89
Lombe, Margaret, 129
long-term care (LTC)
affordability of, 223
among persons with
disabilities, 125–127
cost/payment of, xix, 126, 164–166
future projection, 166
overview, 161–162
providers of, 163–164
receivers of, 162
reform approaches in future, 169–170
reform approaches to date, 166–169
long-term services and supports
(LTSS), 126, 130, 162, 165, 166, 167, 169
Love, David, 6
Low Income Home Energy Assistance
Program, 154, 200
Low Income Housing Tax Credit, 197
LTC (long-term care). *See* long-term care
(LTC)
LTC insurance (LTCI), 164, 165
LTSS (long-term services and
supports), 162, 165, 166, 167, 169
Ludtke, Richard, 90
Lynch, John, 31, 38n1

Macartney, Suzanne, 219
Madrian, Brigitte, 184
marginalization, of persons with
disabilities, 120, 128–129
MasterCard service (AARP
Foundation), 225

match from employer, xxiii, 184, 223
Matos, Kenneth, 187
McDonald, Leander, 90
mean net worth, 7–8, 14
means-tested assistance programs, 155
mean wealth by age group, 7–9
median family income, trends in, 9–14
median family income by age of family
    head, 10
median household income
    American Indian and Alaska Native
        households, 90
    caregivers, 163
    in-home LTC recipients, 162
    immigrant workers, 105
    native workers, 105
    non-Hispanic white households, 90
    older African Americans, 50
median inflation-adjusted family income
    by age group, 9
median inflation-adjusted net worth by
    age group, 10
median net worth
    African Americans, xxv, 52
    by age of family head, 8
    decline in between 2007 and 2010, 14
    immigrant couples/individuals,
        111, 112
    native couples/individuals, 111
    older adults in U.S., 208
    young and middle-aged families, 10
Medicaid, xviii, xxi, 126, 127, 128, 129,
    155, 161, 163, 164, 165, 167, 223
Medical Expenditure Panel Survey
    (2006), 123, 125
Medicare, xviii, xxi, 23, 79, 126, 127, 130,
    155, 164
Medigap health insurance, 71
Mexican-origin Americans, economic
    security among, 70–82
Miah, M. Solaiman, 125
Mickelson, Kristin, 35
microfinancing, 94
Microloan Program, 146, 148
Milligan, Kevin, 126
minorities
    financial vulnerability, xviii, 69

and health insurance, 79
poverty as common experience
    among, 72
retirement savings and, xix
risk of economic insecurity as high
    for, 198
savings, 218–219
minority poverty theory, 32
Mitra, Sophie, 125
mobile banking, xx
Mommaerts, Corina, 123
Money Follows the Person program, 167,
    168, 169
Money Smart for Older Adults, 208
Morris, Joann, 94
Morrow-Howell, Nancy, xi, 228
mortgage debt, xx, 11
Mudrazija, Stipica, xii, 219, 221
multiple sclerosis, 124
Muntaner, Carles, 31
Mutchler, Jan, 112
MyRA accounts, 63, 183

Nam, Yunju, xiii, 112, 219, 220
National Alliance for Caregiving, 163
National Association of Area Agencies on
    Aging, 229
National Center for Health Statistics, 161
National Community Reinvestment
    Coalition (NCRC), 195, 196, 197,
    200, 201, 202, 205
National Comorbidity Study, 31
National Council on Aging, 129, 201, 206,
    208, 225
National Education and Resource
    Center on Women and Retirement
    Planning, 155, 156
National Health Policy Forum, 162
National Indian Council on Aging, 97
National Institute on Aging, 164, 205
National Longitudinal Surveys (1979), 111
National Neighbors Silver, 197, 205
National Resource Center on Native
    American Aging, 90
National Resource Center on Women and
    Retirement Planning, 225
National Survey of American Life, 31, 36

Native Americans
  chronic health conditions among
    elders, 88
  enhancing financial capability of, 87–98
  financial assets/resources of, 90–94
  median household income, 90
  population statistics, 87
  poverty rates, 87, 90, 201
  savings, 92–93
naturalization rate, 106
naturalized citizens, 104, 106, 111, 112,
    115n1
Navajo nation, 97
NCRC (National Community
    Reinvestment Coalition), 195, 196,
    197, 200, 201, 202, 205
Neighbors, Harold, 31
net worth. *See also* average net worth;
    mean net worth; median net worth;
    real average household net worth;
    real median household net worth
  of African Americans, 53
  by age group, 6
  of immigrants, 111, 112
  IHS as alternative transformation of, 19
  as peaking in younger-old age
    group, 13
  percent of total controlled by baby
    boomers, 139
  of persons with disabilities, 125
Neumark, David, 186
New America Foundation, 62
New Deal, 29, 38n2
Noeth, Bryan J., xiii, 3, 14, 19, 220
nursing home care, xix, 126, 164, 167
Nuru-Jeter, Amani, 122
Nussbaum, Martha, 141

Obama, Barack, 63, 195
Office of Older Americans, 129, 202
Oklahoma 529 College Savings Plan, 226
older adults, as valuable resource, 227–229
Older Americans Act of 1965, 90, 127,
    128, 129, 130, 131
older families
  compared to young families, 5–6, 24
  wealth accumulation by, 5

older-old families, defined, 3
Olsen, Anya, 182, 183
Omari, Safiya, 34
184 program (Section 184 Indian Home
    Loan Guarantee Program), 91
online banking, xx, 205
onling bill paying, xx
Orszag, Peter, 82
Ostrove, Joan, 31
Ozawa, Martha, 125

paid employment, xix, xxiii
paid leave, 187
Palumbo, Michael, 6
Parkinson's disease, 124
Patient Protection and Affordable Care
    Act (ACA), 166, 167. *See also*
    Affordable Care Act (ACA)
Pattillo, Mary, 34
pawnshops, xxi
payday loans and lenders, xxi, 199, 201
Pence, Karen, 5, 6
Pension Counseling and Information
    Program, 155, 156
Pension Protection Act of 2006, 58
pensions. *See also* defined-benefit (DB)
    plans
  among African Americans, 49,
    53–54
  among Hispanics, 71, 77, 79, 178
  among immigrants, 105
  as critically important for
    women, 176–178
  and educational attainment, 178–179
  household income as associated with
    access to, 179
  older families as relying more on, 24
  as one part of three-legged stool, 175,
    199
  opportunity for and participation rate
    in, 76, 152, 176–179
  prevalence and importance of, 76–77
  proportion of workers participating
    in, xix–xx, 57
  size of by race and Mexican origin, 71
  as strongest leg of three-legged stool,
    historically, 55

workplace financial education
  as increasing participation/
  contributions into, 182–183
Pepper Commission, 161, 166, 171
Personal Responsibility and Work
  Opportunity Reconciliation Act
  of 1996, 78, 107
Petersen, Lars-Eric, 186
Pitt-Catsouphes, Marcie, 181
policy issues/implications
  of asset development, 153–156
  of capability-based asset development
    among older adults, 145
  development and improvement of
    policies, 222–223
  for Hispanics, 81–82
  for Native Americans, 89–90, 97–98
  for older African Americans, 55–63
  for persons with disabilities, 129–130
  policy and practice interventions for the
    workplace, 182–187
Pollack, Craig, 31
pooled regression of logarithm of
    family income on demographic,
    idiosyncratic, birth-year cohort, and
    time variables, 16
pooled regression of transformed
    net worth on demographic,
    idiosyncratic, birth-year cohort, and
    time variables, 20
postretirement employment, xxii
Post-Secondary Education Account
  (Singapore), 61
potlatch (giveaway ceremony), 92
poverty
  associations with health, 32
  contributors to risk for in persons with
    disabilities, 124–129
  rates of, xviii, 30, 32, 49, 50–51, 69,
    71–73, 78, 80, 87, 90, 105–106, 123,
    177, 178, 198, 199, 200, 201, 218, 219
  relationship with exposure to stress, 30
Pozo, Susan, 110
President's Advisory Council on Financial
  Capability, 183
prevalence of disability by category of
  disability identified in 2011 ACS, 121

prevalence of disability by selected
  characteristics identified in 2011
  ACS, 122
profit-sharing plans, 57
programs related to older adults and
  asset-based approaches, 154–155
Project SCREEN (Senior Citizen and
  Retiree Empowerment Education
  Network), 208–209
public charge doctrine, 107
Purcell, Kristen, 163
Putnam, Michelle, xiii, 129, 219

race/ethnicity
  and health, 28
  pensions and, 178
  as predictor of income/wealth, 3, 15
  trends in median family income/wealth
    grouped by, 13–14
racial discrimination, 28, 35–36, 37
racial residential segregation, 29, 37
real average household income, 3
real average household net worth, 3
real median family income, 4, 14
real median household net worth, 4
recessions, 4, 37. See also Great Recession
Redaelli, Silvia, 144
redlining practices, 29, 37, 38n4
reduced-rate life insurance plans, 204
Refugee Act of 1980, 115–116n3
Reichard, Amanda, 123
rent-to-own stores, xxi
research issues/implications
  for African Americans, 37
  for asset development among older
    adults, 156–157
  for Hispanics, 80, 82
  for immigrants, 114–115
  for Native Americans, 97–98
  overview, 223–224
  for persons with disabilities, 130–131
reservations, Native American, xxvi, 87,
    89, 90, 91, 96–97
residential steering, 29, 38n5
resilience, of Native American elders, 94
Responsibility, Initiative, Solutions,
  Empower (RISE) Foundation, 205

retirement, percent of workers in 50s not
    expecting to retire, xvii
retirement income deficit, 72, 139
Retirement Investment Account Plans, 63
retirement plans of older adult households
    by race, Mexican origin, and
    nativity, 77
retirement savings, xvii, xviii, xix, xx,
    xxiii, xxiv, 55, 57, 72, 81, 108, 139,
    157, 176, 183, 200, 219, 223. See also
    retirement savings plans/programs
retirement savings plans/programs, 49,
    53, 56, 63, 69, 77, 141, 146, 151, 170
reverse mortgages, xx, 81, 147, 196,
    197, 207
RISE (Responsibility, Initiative, Solutions,
    Empower) Foundation, 205
Rockefeller, John D., IV, 161
Rodriguez, Eric, 82
Rodriguez, Eunice, 31
Roosevelt, Franklin D., 38n2
Royster, Judith, 96

Sabelhaus, John, 5
safety net, 23, 54, 72, 77, 78, 124,
    127–128, 165
Salish tribe, 91
Sambamoorthi, Usha, 126
Sanders, Gregory, 94
SaveUp, 224
savings. See also retirement savings;
    retirement savings plans/programs
    African Americans, 49, 55
    caregivers, 164
    designing products to maximize
        participation, investments, and
        payouts, 183–185
    Hispanics, 81
    immigrants, 112
    lack of among minorities, poor, and
        women, xxi
    minorities, 218–219
    Native American elders, 92–93
    as one part of three-legged stool, 53,
        175
    statistics about, xix–xx
Savings for Working Families Act, 62

Savvy Saving Seniors program, 208, 225
scams targeting older adults, 201,
    203–204
Schmidt, Lucie, 112
Section 184 Indian Home Loan Guarantee
    Program (184 program), 91
Section 202 Program, 154, 156
SEED for Oklahoma Kids (SEED
    OK), 225–226
Sellers, Sherrill, 27, 36
Sen, Amartya, 140
Senior Community Service Employment
    Program, 60, 154, 186
Senior Entrepreneurship Works, 228
Senior Financial Stability Index, 139
SEP (socioeconomic position). See
    socioeconomic position (SEP)
Sevak, Purvi, 112
Shanks, Trina R. Williams, xiii, 219
Shea, Dennis, 184
Sherraden, Margaret S., xi
Sherraden, Michael, xiii
shortened work careers, among persons
    with disabilities, 124–125
Siddiqi, Sehar N., xiii, 222
Singapore, child account policy, 61
Sloan Center for Aging and Work, 228
small business, among Native American
    elders, 93–94
Smith, Paul, 6
Smyer, Michael, 181
Snyder Act of 1921, 90
Social and Economic Development
    Strategies, 96
social mobility, 27, 28, 32–34, 35, 37
Social Security
    African Americans, 54–55
    concept of life cycle as foundational
        part of, xxiv
    concerns about solvency of, 81, 175
    early application for, 198
    Hispanics, 69, 72, 78
    immigrants, 105, 113
    impact of rules/structure on older
        African Americans, 58–59
    as inadequate to cover LTC costs, 165
    increased reliance on, 199

as key source of income in old age, xviii, 69
livable minimum benefit, 223
non-Hispanic whites, 71, 72, 78
older adults as drawing on too early, xxi
older families relying more heavily on, 24
older Mexican-origin Americans, 71, 72
original vision of, 69
projected fragility of, xviii, 81
steadily increasing generosity of, 23
women as especially reliant on, 74, 198
Social Security Act of 1935, 29, 218
Social Security Administration, 54, 105, 125
Social Security Disability Insurance (SSDI), 123, 125, 127, 130, 200
Social Security Old-Age and Survivors Insurance, 127
Social Security Trust Fund, 81
social support networks, among African Americans, 34–35
socioeconomic position (SEP)
defined, 38n1
health as associated with, 27, 30–31
impact of gains in, 34–35, 36
impact of on health, 30–32, 33, 36
intersection of with racial discrimination, 36
race and SEP, 28–30
Sorkin, Dara, 122
soul wounding, 88
sources and relative size of retirement income for older individuals by race and Mexican origin, 71
Spinks, Katie, 129
SSDI (Social Security Disability Insurance), 123, 125, 127, 130, 200
SSI (Supplemental Security Income), 78, 105, 108, 125, 127, 153, 154, 199, 200, 221
State Long-Term Care Partnership Program, 166, 169
State Paid Leave Fund, 187
status incongruence, 33

Stolzle, Hayley, 123
Strohschein, Lisa, 31
subprime mortgages, 29
Supplemental Nutrition Assistance Program, 153, 155, 157, 163, 200
Supplemental Security Income (SSI), 78, 105, 108, 125, 127, 153, 154, 199, 200, 221
Survey of Consumer Finances (Federal Reserve), 3, 4, 5, 6, 7, 15, 184
Survey of Income and Program Participation, 111, 125

Tax-Aide Program (AARP Foundation), 129, 206
tax credits/deductions, 206. See also Earned Income Tax Credit program
tax liabilities, xxii
tax reduction on capital gains, 152
Thorpe, Roland, Jr., 122
three-legged stool, 53, 175, 199
Ticket to Work Program (Social Security Administration), 130
timing, as factor in life course perspective, xxiii, xxiv, 220
Title VI of the Older Americans Act of 1965, 90
Tovar, Molly, xiii, 219, 220
training/retraining, 59–60, 185–186
trauma, history of in Native American peoples, 88–89
trends
in family income/wealth at twentieth percentile, 11–13
in median family income/wealth, 9–11
in median family income/wealth by age, race/ethnicity, and educational attainment, 13–14
Turner, John, 185

unbanked, 92, 93, 108, 201–202
unbanked households by race and ethnicity, 93
underbanked, 201–202
undocumented immigrants, 80, 109, 115, 115n1, 199, 219
unemployment, among older workers, xix

UNESCO, 95
United Kingdom, Child Trust Fund, 61
United Nations Convention on the Rights
    of Persons with Disabilities, 128
Universal 401(k)s, 62
Urban Relocation Program, 89
U.S. Bipartisan Commission on
    Comprehensive Health Care, 161
U.S. Census Bureau, 70, 121
U.S. Department of Agriculture
    (USDA), 151, 206
U.S. Department of Health and Human
    Services, 167
U.S. Department of Health and Human
    Services Eleventh Annual Tribal
    Budget Consultation, 87
U.S. Department of Housing and Urban
    Development, 207, 208
U.S. Department of Labor, 186, 187
U.S. Department of the Interior, 91, 93
U.S. Equal Opportunity Employment
    Commission, 181
U.S. Government Accountability
    Office, 166, 203

Very Low-Income Housing Repair
    Program, 151
Volunteer Income Tax Assistance
    program, 206
volunteering, xxii, 129, 225,
    228, 229
Von dem Knesebeck, Olaf, 31

Wage and Hour Division (DOL), 187
Watahomigie, Lucille Jackson, 95
wealth
    effect of on health among African
        Americans, 27
    measures, 4, 31
    native–immigrant gap in, 110, 111
    older adults as having greater wealth
        than younger counterparts, xix
    race/ethnicity and, xix, 3, 52, 70
    relationships of to mental health, 31
    trends in median, 3–23

weathering hypothesis, 30
Weber, Lynn, 34
welfare reform, 107
Whitman, Kevin, 182, 183
Whitson, Heather, 122, 123
Wilcox-Gök, Virginia, 125
Williams, David, 33, 35, 36
women
    as disproportionately represented in
        caregiving workforce, 219
    as disproportionately represented in
        older population, 219
    employment of in jobs without
        pensions, 74
    financial vulnerability and, xviii, 69
    Native women as being at forefront
        of community and national
        development, 93
    pension benefits as lower for, 198
    pensions as critically important
        for, 176–178
    poverty rates, 176, 177, 198, 219
    retirement savings and, xix
    risk of economic insecurity as higher
        for, 198
work
    age-friendly work
        environments, 185–187
    extension of into later life, 179–180, 228
    flexible work options, 186
    shortened work careers among persons
        with disabilities, 124–125
workplace policies/practices, 175–182
World Health Organization, 205
World War II, 22, 23, 76, 82

Yeo, Yeong Hun, 125
Young, Alford, 33
younger-old families, defined, 3
young families, compared to older
    families, 5–6, 24
Youth Cohort of the National
    Longitudinal Surveys (1979), 111

Zdenek, Robert O., xiii, 222